NEW AGE
MOVEMENT

Zondervan
Guide to Cults &
Religious Movements

First Series

Unmasking the Cults   *by Alan W. Gomes*
Jehovah's Witnesses   *by Robert M. Bowman, Jr.*
Masonic Lodge   *by George A. Mather and Larry A. Nichols*
Mormonism   *by Kurt Van Gorden*
New Age Movement   *by Ron Rhodes*
Satanism   *by Bob and Gretchen Passantino*
Unification Church   *by J. Isamu Yamamoto*
Mind Sciences   *by Todd Ehrenborg*

Second Series

"Jesus Only" Churches   *by E. Calvin Beisner*
Astrology and Psychic Phenomena   *by André Kole and Terry Holley*
Goddess Worship, Witchcraft and Neo-Paganism
   by Craig Hawkins
Hinduism, TM, and Hare Krishna
   by J. Isamu Yamamoto
Unitarian Universalism   *by Alan W. Gomes*
Buddhism, Taoism and Other Far Eastern Religions
   by J. Isamu Yamamoto
Truth and Error   *by Alan W. Gomes*

NEW AGE MOVEMENT

RON RHODES
Author

Alan W. Gomes
Series Editor

ZondervanPublishingHouse
Grand Rapids, Michigan

A Division of HarperCollins*Publishers*

New Age Movement
Copyright © 1995 by Ron Rhodes

Requests for information should be addressed to:
Zondervan Publishing House
Grand Rapids, Michigan 49530

Library of Congress Cataloging-in-Publication Data

Rhodes, Ron.
New Age Movement/ Ron Rhodes, author.
p. cm. — (Zondervan guide to cults & religious movements)
Includes bibliographical references.
ISBN: 0-310-70431-6 (softcover)
1. New Age movement—Controversial literature.   I. Title.
II. Series: Zondervan guide to cults and religious movements.
BP605.N48R46   1995
299'.93—dc20   94-13038
                                                                 CIP

Edited by Patti Picardi
Interior design by Art Jacobs

Printed in the United States of America

01 02 03 04 05 / ❖ DP/ 10 9 8 7 6 5 4 3

 # Contents

 # How to Use This Book

The *Zondervan Guide to Cults and Religious Movements* comprises sixteen volumes, treating many of the most important groups and belief systems confronting the Christian church today. This series distills the most important facts about each and presents a well-reasoned, cogent Christian response. The authors in this series are highly qualified, well-respected professional Christian apologists with considerable expertise on their topics.

We have designed the structure and layout to help you find the information you need as quickly as possible. All the volumes are written in outline form, which allows us to pack substantial content into a short book. With some exceptions, each book contains, first, an introduction to the cult, movement, or belief system. The introduction gives a brief history of the group, its organizational structure, and vital statistics such as membership. Second, the theology section is arranged by doctrinal topic, such as God, Christ, sin, and salvation. The movement's position is set forth objectively, primarily from its own official writings. The group's teachings are then refuted point by point, followed by an affirmative presentation of what the Bible says about the doctrine. The third section is a discussion of witnessing tips. While each witnessing encounter must be handled individually and sensitively, this section provides some helpful general guidelines, including both dos and don'ts. The fourth section contains annotated bibliographies, listing works by the groups themselves and books written by Christians in response. Fifth, each book has a parallel comparison chart, with direct quotations from the cultic literature in the left column and the biblical refutation on the right. Some of the books conclude with a glossary.

One potential problem with a detailed outline is that it is easy to lose one's place in the overall structure. Therefore, we have provided graphical "signposts" at the top of the odd numbered pages. Functioning like a "you are here" map in a shopping mall, these graphics show your place in the outline, including the sections that come before and after your current position. (Those familiar with modern computer software will note immediately the resemblance to a "drop-down" menu bar, where the second-level choices vary depending on the currently selected main menu item.) In the theology section we have also used "icons" in the margins to make clear at a glance whether the material is being presented from the cultic or Christian viewpoint. For example, in the Mormonism volume the sections presenting the Mormon position are indicated with a picture resembling the angel Moroni in the margin; the biblical view is shown by a drawing of the Bible.

We hope you will find these books useful as you seek "to give an answer to everyone who asks you to give the reason for the hope that you have" (1 Peter 3:15).

—Alan W. Gomes, Ph.D.
Series Editor

 # Part I: Introduction

I. What Is the New Age Movement?

The New Age movement has been called "the fastest growing alternative belief system in the country."[1]

A. Definition of the New Age Movement

1. The New Age movement is a loosely structured network of individuals and organizations who share a vision of a new age of enlightenment and harmony (the "Age of Aquarius") and who subscribe to a common "worldview."[2]

2. The common worldview is based on *monism* (all is one), *pantheism* (all is God), and *mysticism* (the experience of oneness with the divine).[3]

3. Because it is so broad and organizationally diffuse, the New Age movement cannot be categorized as a cult by any accepted sociological definition of "cult."[4]

   a. *Movements* are multifaceted, involving a variety of individuals and groups whose respective practices and emphases (and even some beliefs) may be distinctive and diverse.[5]

   b. To be a New Ager, there is no single organization one must join and no particular creed one must confess.

B. Diversity in Unity in the New Age Movement

1. Diversity

   a. The New Age movement is made up of many different individuals and organizations who have a wide variety of interests and are committed to different causes.

---

[1] *The Christian Herald* (February 1988), p. 51.

[2] A *worldview* may be defined as "a way of viewing or interpreting all of reality. It is an interpretive framework through which or by which one makes sense out of the data of life and the world" (Norman L. Geisler and William Watkins, *Worlds Apart: A Handbook on Worldviews* [Grand Rapids: Baker, 1989], p. 11).

[3] This definition is based on Elliot Miller, *A Crash Course on the New Age Movement* (Grand Rapids: Baker, 1989), p. 15.

[4] Miller, p. 16. Note that there are many different opinions among sociologists of religion as to what are the essential characteristics of a cult. In this context it is sufficient to note that the New Age movement is not a cult according to *any* commonly accepted sociological definition of a cult. For a more detailed treatment of defining cults, both theologically and sociologically, see *Unmasking the Cults* in this series, by Alan W. Gomes.

[5] Hank Hanegraaff made this important distinction in his book *Christianity in Crisis* (Eugene, Ore: Harvest House, 1993), p. 45.

    b. Jeremy P. Tarcher, a New Age book publisher, says: "No one speaks for the entire New Age community."[6]

    c. The New Age movement includes holistic health professionals, ecologists, political activists, educators, human potential advocates, goddess-worshipers, reincarnationists, astrologers, and much more.

  2. Unity

    a. All these diverse individuals associate comfortably under the common umbrella of "the New Age movement."

    b. Their common vision for humankind and their common worldview enable them to "network" together to accomplish their common ends, despite their distinctive interests within the movement.

C. Characteristics of the New Age Movement

One of the best ways to understand the New Age movement is to examine its primary characteristics. While not every New Ager would hold to every characteristic below, most New Agers would hold to most of them.

  1. Eclecticism

    a. New Agers draw from various sources of "truth."

    b. They feel equally at home with the Christian Bible,[7] Levi Dowling's *The Aquarian Gospel of Jesus the Christ*, the readings of the "sleeping prophet" Edgar Cayce, and advice from Ramtha (a 35,000-year-old Lemurian warrior-king as channeled through J. Z. Knight).

  2. Religious Syncretism

    a. The New Age movement is syncretistic—combining and synthesizing different and sometimes contradictory religious and philosophical teachings.

    b. The New Age movement gathers the teachings of all the world religions and syncretizes these into its mystical worldview: "We honor the truth and beauty of all the world religions, believing each to have a seed of God, a kernel of the spirit that unites us."[8]

    c. New Agers do not render exclusive devotion to any one teacher or teaching.

    d. New Agers believe that God revealed himself in Jesus, but that he also revealed himself in Buddha, Krishna, and a host of others.

    e. The Bible can therefore make no claim to be God's only revelation to humankind.

---

[6] Jeremy P. Tarcher, "New Age as Perennial Philosophy," *Los Angeles Times Book Review* (February 7, 1988), p. 15.

[7] Though, as we shall see (Part II, Section I.B.), they feel comfortable with the Bible because they interpret it through a New Age lens.

[8] Julia Spangler, "Compass Points," *Lorian Journal* 1:2, p. 3.

3. Monism

   a. Monism is a theory that sees all reality as a unified whole.

   b. The word itself comes from the Greek word *monos* ("one").

   c. Everything in the universe is viewed as composed of the same substance; all is organically one. As New Ager George Trevelyan puts it, "Life is a Divine Oneness."[9]

   d. Humanity, God, and the world of nature are likened to waves in a single cosmic ocean.

   e. Perceived differences are apparent, not real.

   f. Therefore, all of reality is *interrelated* and *interdependent*.

4. Pantheism

   a. Pantheism is the view that *God is all* and *all is God*.

   b. The word *pantheism* is based on the Greek words *pan* ("all") and *theos* ("God").

   c. Benjamin Creme explains that "everything is God. There is nothing else in fact but God."[10]

   d. The New Age pantheistic God is an impersonal, amoral "it."

   e. There is no distinction between the Creator and the creation in pantheism.

5. Deification of Humanity

   a. Humanity is God.

   b. The belief in human divinity follows from the belief in monism and pantheism (discussed above): if all is one (monism) and all is God (pantheism), then we, too, are God.

   c. Beverly Galyean states, "Once we begin to see that we are all God, that we all have the attributes of God, then I think the whole purpose of life is to reown the Godlikeness within us; the perfect love, the perfect wisdom, the perfect understanding, the perfect intelligence...."[11]

6. Transformation: There are two aspects of transformation within the New Age movement— *personal* transformation and *planetary* transformation.

   a. *Personal* transformation, a counterpart to being "born again" in Christianity, hinges on one's personal recognition of oneness with God, humanity, and the universe.

---

[9] George Trevelyan, *Operation Redemption* (Walpole, N.H.: Stillpoint Publishing, 1981), p. 29.

[10] Benjamin Creme, *The Reappearance of the Christ and the Masters of Wisdom* (Los Angeles: Tara Center, 1980), p. 103.

[11] Interview with Beverly Galyean, in Frances Adeney, "Educators Look East," *SCP Journal* (Winter 1981), p. 29.

(1) This recognition is described variously as "enlightenment," "attunement," "self-realization," "God-realization," and "self-actualization."

(2) We need such enlightenment because we have "bought the lie" (or succumbed to the illusion) of human limitation and finitude. We have forgotten our true divine identity.[12]

(3) Only by a transformation of consciousness can we escape this lie and realize our true potential.

b. *Planetary* transformation is brought about as a "critical mass" of *personally* transformed individuals takes socio-political responsibility for the world of humankind.

7. Networking

    a. Definition: The means of loosely coordinating New Agers' efforts.

        (1) Though New Agers are *diverse*—having a wide variety of interests and commitment to different causes (such as health, psychology, politics, science, and education)—they *unite* to accomplish common goals.

        (2) New Agers "all have their own turf and agendas, yet they cooperate in the network because they also have some common values and visions."[13]

    b. Media and networking

        (1) New Ager Marilyn Ferguson says networking takes place through "conferences, phone calls, air travel, books, phantom organizations, papers, pamphleteering, photocopying, lectures, workshops, parties, grapevines, mutual friends, summit meetings, coalitions, tapes, [and] newsletters."[14]

        (2) Modern telecommunications via computers is also key to the networking process.

    c. Politics and networking

        (1) New Agers believe one of the most effective ways of flexing political muscle is through networking.

        (2) As Ferguson states, networking "generates power enough to remake society. It offers the individual emotional, intellectual, spiritual, and economic support. It is ... a powerful means of altering the course of institutions, especially government."[15]

8. Ecological Orientation

    a. Since *all is one* (monism), it follows that human beings are intimately interrelated with the world of nature.

---

[12] Shirley MacLaine, *Dancing in the Light* (New York: Bantam, 1985), p. 133; cf. Douglas Groothuis, *Unmasking the New Age* (Downers Grove, Ill.: InterVarsity Press, 1986), p. 22.

[13] Jessica Lipnack and Jeffrey Stamps, *Networking* (Garden City, N.Y.: Doubleday, 1982), p. 227.

[14] Marilyn Ferguson, *The Aquarian Conspiracy* (Los Angeles: J. P. Tarcher, 1980), pp. 62–63.

[15] Ferguson, p. 213.

(1) We must care for nature.

(2) To damage nature is ultimately to damage ourselves.

b. Many New Agers view the earth as a living organism.[16] Because the earth is a living organism, it must be treated as such and cared for ecologically.[17]

c. New Age activists interested in ecology have joined together to form a powerful worldwide political movement known as "the Green movement."[18]

9. Belief in a Coming Utopia

a. New Agers believe there is a new world coming which involves one-world government, global socialism, and a New Age religion.[19]

(1) Ken Carey, author of several New Age handbooks, envisions A.D. 2000 as a kind of psychic watershed, beyond which lies "a realizable utopian society."[20]

(2) David Spangler says that the Mayan and Aztec civilizations believed that a "cycle of dark ages" would end before A.D. 2000; following this, a New Age of harmony and wholeness will emerge.[21]

10. Not a Conspiracy

a. New Agers are *not* following the lead of an individual or group in the unfolding of some sinister New Age master plan.[22]

b. Though New Agers share a common worldview and vision for the future, there is no conspiracy on a human level—even though New Agers *do* "network" to attain common goals.

c. Despite their common worldview, New Agers have *distinct* individual beliefs, interests, agendas, and strategies.

d. Still, we might say there is a conspiracy on a *spiritual* level—that is, the powers of darkness (demons) are working in the New Age movement to draw human beings away from Christ and the truth of Christianity. But in this sense of the word, *all* belief systems an-

---

[16] Fritjof Capra, *The Turning Point* (New York: Simon and Schuster, 1982), p. 284; David Spangler, *Emergence: The Rebirth of the Sacred* (New York: Dell, 1984), pp. 43–44.

[17] Spangler, *Emergence: The Rebirth of the Sacred*, pp. 5, 45.

[18] See Fritjof Capra and Charlene Spretnak, *Green Politics: The Global Promise* (New York: E. P. Dutton, 1984).

[19] Douglas Groothuis, *Confronting the New Age* (Downers Grove, Ill.: InterVarsity Press, 1988), p. 20.

[20] Bill Lawren, "Are You Ready for Millennial Fever?" *Utne Reader* (March/April 1990), p. 96.

[21] Spangler, p. 19. Note, however, that Spangler and other New Agers who cite the Mayans and Aztecs are reading their New Age ideas into the calendars of these civilizations. See Dick Roraback, "Resonating with Jose Arguelles, a New Age Scholar," *Los Angeles Times* (August 12, 1987), p. 1.

[22] Some Christian critics have wrongly interpreted the New Age movement in conspiratorial terms—including Constance Cumbey, *The Hidden Dangers of the Rainbow* (Shreveport, La.: Huntington House, 1983), and Texe Marrs, *Dark Secrets of the New Age* (Westchester, Ill.: Crossway Books, 1987).

tithetical to Christianity (including some antithetical to the New Age movement as well) are part of Satan's conspiracy.

D. New Age Spirituality

1. Multifaceted

   a. New Age spirituality is a *hybrid* spirituality, drawing from many different sources.

   b. New Age spirituality includes Eastern meditation, altered states of consciousness,[23] reincarnation, and spiritism (channeling).[24]

2. Life- and World-Affirming.

   a. New Agers value other people, worldly pleasures and amusements, culture, and the entire universe.[25]

   b. This affirmation is in contrast to classic Hinduism, which is self- and world-*denying*.

      (1) While many New Age ideas about God, humanity, salvation, and the world are rooted in Hinduism, New Age spirituality departs from Hinduism in its world-affirming emphasis.

      (2) In Hinduism the spiritual and earthly realms are viewed as being in conflict, hence earthly things must be renounced.[26]

3. Involves a Revival of Paganism (Neopaganism)

   a. Neopagans reject such allegedly Western distinctives as:

      (1) Organized religion

      (2) Male-dominated society

      (3) Patriarchal, male-exalting religion (evidenced by such phrases as "God the *Father*")

      (4) Abuse of nature

   b. Neopagans share the feminist perspective which seeks to reharmonize people with "the One," which is called "the *Goddess*."[27]

      (1) Goddess worshipers equate the Goddess with the world, which is manifest in us.[28]

      (2) Goddess worshipers often speak of kindling the "goddess within" (that is, inner divinity).

---

[23] "Conscious awareness that transcends the normal states of everyday consciousness." Altered states are induced in a variety of ways—including meditation and guided imagery. (George A. Mather and Larry A. Nichols, *Dictionary of Cults, Sects, Religions and the Occult* [Grand Rapids: Zondervan, 1993], p. 20).

[24] We shall discuss all of these in Part II, Section II.B.4.

[25] Miller, pp. 21–22.

[26] In Hinduism, "the world is *maya* (illusion), and is considered a formidable obstacle to eternal bliss" (Miller, p. 22).

[27] Miriam Starhawk, *The Spiral Dance* (San Francisco: Harper & Row, 1979), p. 9; cf. Groothuis, *Confronting the New Age*, p. 135.

[28] "The Goddess ... is the world. Manifest in each of us, she can be known by every individual, in all her magnificent diversity" (Starhawk, *The Spiral Dance*, p. 9).

(3) Humanity's inner divinity is one of the primary doctrines of New Age theology (see Part II below).

II. Pervasiveness of the New Age Movement

A. The Impact of the New Age Movement on Health Care

1. Holistic Health

   a. Marilyn Ferguson notes that "patients and professionals alike are beginning to see beyond symptoms to the context of illness: stress, society, family, diet, season, emotions."[29] This has given rise to "holistic" health care.

   b. The word *holistic*, when applied to health care, refers to an approach "that respects the interaction of mind, body, and environment."[30] Indeed, holistic health focuses on the *whole* person and his or her surroundings.

   c. New Agers typically criticize Western medicine as being *reductionistic* in its approach.

      (1) As Fritjof Capra puts it, "by concentrating on smaller and smaller fragments of the body, modern medicine often loses sight of the patient as a human being, and by reducing health to mechanical functioning, it is no longer able to deal with the phenomenon of healing."[31]

      (2) New Agers see reductionistic medicine as disease-centered, not person-centered, treating *only* the parts of the body that are ailing (the heart, for example).

   d. Holistic health is multidimensional.

      (1) A holistic approach to health is a "multidimensional phenomenon involving interdependent physical, psychological, and social aspects."[32]

      (2) The holistic approach seeks to treat the *whole* person—body, mind, and spirit—and also considers the social aspects of the patient's life as a factor to health.

      (3) Holistic health claims to be person-centered, not disease-centered.

2. The New Age Concept of Energy and Holistic Health

   a. The New Age model of holistic health is based primarily on its conception of *energy*, not matter.

---

[29] Ferguson, p. 242.

[30] Ferguson, p. 246.

[31] Capra, p. 123.

[32] Capra, p. 322.

b. The editors of the *New Age Journal* report: "All of the healing systems that can be called 'holistic' share a common belief in the universe as a unified field of energy that produces all form and substance. . . . This vital force, which supoorts and sustains life, has been given many names. The Chinese call it 'chi'i,' the Hindus call it 'prana,' the Hebrews call it 'ruach,' and the American Indians name it 'the Great Spirit.'"[33]

c. This energy is not a visible, measurable, scientifically explainable energy, but a "cosmic" or "universal" energy based on a monistic (*all is one*) and pantheistic (*all is God*) worldview.[34]

d. To enhance the flow of "healing energy" in the body, we are told that one must "attune" to it and realize one's unity with all things. Many New Age health therapies are based on this premise.

3. Examples of Popular New Age Health Therapies[35]

a. *Acupuncture* and *Acupressure* seek to unblock and redirect energy flow in the body as a means of healing.

b. *Chiropractic* seeks to correct misalignments in the spine to restore health.

  (1) Some chiropractors are New Agers and typically combine spinal adjustments with some form of "energy balancing" to treat various bodily ailments.[36]

  (2) Most chiropractors are *not* New Agers and simply use chiropractic as a therapy for neuromusculoskeletal disorders (such as backaches). In fact, there are Christian chiropractors who explicitly disavow any use of "energy balancing."[37]

c. *Iridology* seeks to diagnose bodily illness by discerning irregularities in the iris.

d. *Applied Kinesiology* tests muscles to diagnose bodily illness and problems in energy flow. (It assumes that there is a direct relationship between muscles and internal organs such that if a muscle is shown to be weak, an ailing organ is thereby indicated.)

e. *Rolfing* seeks to relieve energy blockages in the body by applying deep pressure or massage.

f. *Therapeutic Touch* is a therapy in which the therapeutic touch practitioner "channels" the universal life energy for the patient and then helps the patient to assimilate this energy.

---

[33] Rick Fields et al., eds., *Chop Wood, Carry Water* (Los Angeles: J. P. Tarcher, 1984), p. 186.

[34] Miller, p. 187.

[35] See Paul C. Reisser, Teri K. Reisser, and John Weldon, *New Age Medicine* (Chattanooga, Tenn.: Global Publishers, 1988).

[36] John Thie, *Touch for Health* (Marina del Rey, Calif.: DeVorss, 1973).

[37] See the Christian Chiropractors Association's "Policy Statement on New Age Healing" (CCA, 3200 S. Lemay Ave., Fort Collins, CO 80525–3605).

g. *Biofeedback* is a technique in which brain waves are monitored to bring normally unconscious, involuntary bodily functions under conscious, voluntary control.

   (1) Biofeedback can lead to altered states of consciousness and mystical experiences. It is a popular tool for "enlightenment" among New Agers.

   (2) Biofeedback is not *necessarily* a New Age technique. A discerning person could take part in biofeedback treatment for strictly medical purposes (controlling high blood pressure, for example) without any adverse spiritual effects.[38]

4. Scientific Validity of New Age Therapies

While some New Age therapies such as biofeedback have some scientific basis, many others do not and have been condemned accordingly by the medical profession.[39]

a. Studies have yet to establish, for example, that acupuncture is a scientifically effective treatment. An analysis published in *The Clinical Journal of Pain* (June 1991) concluded that acupuncture is at best a powerful placebo.[40]

b. Scientific studies thoroughly discredit the practice of iridology.[41]

   (1) Iridology has been thoroughly debunked in the *Journal of the American Medical Association* (Sept. 28, 1979), *Australian Journal of Optometry* (July 1982), and *Journal of the American Optometric Association* (October 1984).

   (2) Paul C. Reisser, M.D., points out that "one well-designed study at the University of California at San Diego showed that iridology was less able to identify patients with advanced kidney failure than random guessing."[42]

c. Patients must therefore be wary of new treatments that go against traditional medical practices and lack scientific basis.

B. *The Impact of the New Age Movement on Psychology*

1. The Focus on Human Potential

a. The human potential movement is a natural outgrowth of the New Age worldview—particularly as it relates to the ideas that *all is one, all is God,* and *humanity is God.*

---

[38] See Groothuis, *Confronting the New Age*, pp. 187–90.

[39] Position papers on New Age health practices are available from the National Council Against Health Fraud, Box 1276, Loma Linda, CA 92354.

[40] See also the *Journal of Clinical Epidemiology*, vol. 43 (1990), pp. 1191–99.

[41] See John Ankerberg and John Weldon, *The Facts on Holistic Health and the New Medicine* (Eugene, Ore.: Harvest House, 1992), pp. 8, 31.

[42] Paul C. Reisser, "Holistic Health: Marcus Welby Enters the New Age," in *The New Age Rage*, ed. Karen Hoyt (Old Tappan, N.J.: Revell, 1987), p. 65.

b. Human potential seminars teach attendees that "you are your own god" and "you can create your own reality."

  (1) This teaching is seen in such seminars as *Lifespring, est,* and *The Forum*.[43]

  (2) Such seminars are heavily influenced by Eastern mysticism and promise enlightenment regarding one's true potential.

  (3) These seminars typically attempt to shred attendees' former worldview and replace it with an Eastern, mystical worldview.

  (4) Sometimes these seminars seek to induce an altered state of consciousness[44] in attendees to lead them to question their *former* understanding of reality. Often such a mystical experience causes attendees to seek a *new* understanding of reality (such as the New Age worldview) that can explain their experience.

2. The Power of the Mind and Human Potential

  (1) David Gershon and Gail Straub say that "empowerment" is the key that gives people the ability to create their own reality by the power of the mind.[45]

  (2) Gershon and Straub say that empowerment can be achieved by effective use of *affirmations* (positive self-talk) and *visualizations* (mental pictures of what you want to create).

C. *The Impact of the New Age Movement on Ethics*

1. Concerning the Distinction Between Good and Evil

  a. Because "all is one," there is no distinction between good and evil.

  b. There are no absolute moral *wrongs* and *rights*. Everything is relative.

    (1) New Ager David Spangler says that New Age ethics "is not based on . . . dualistic concepts of 'good' and 'bad.'"[46]

    (2) Shirley MacLaine asserts that, "Until mankind realizes that there is, in truth, no good and there is, in truth, no evil, there will be no peace."[47]

2. Moral Implications of Humanity as God

  a. Because human beings are God, they create their own reality. That means people live in a world of their own making—a world that includes what they do as well as what is done to them.

---

[43] See Section G below for more on this.

[44] See definition in Part I, Section I.D.1.b.

[45] David Gershon and Gail Straub, *Empowerment: The Art of Creating Your Life as You Want It* (New York: Dell, 1989).

[46] David Spangler, *Revelation: The Birth of a New Age* (Middleton, Wisc.: Lorian Press, 1976), p. 13.

[47] MacLaine, p. 357, quoting what an entity named Higher Self said to her.

   b. If humans, *as God*, create their own reality, then they cannot condemn those who inflict evil upon others.

   c. For example, one must conclude that the millions of Jews who were executed under Hitler's regime created their own reality. Hence, Hitler's actions cannot be condemned as ethically wrong, since Hitler was only part of a reality that they themselves created.

   d. One cannot condemn terrorists who blow up passenger jets because the people on those jets create their own reality.

   e. When the acting teacher of Shirley MacLaine's daughter was burned beyond recognition in a head-on collision, MacLaine wondered: "Why did she choose to die that way?"[48] The other driver was not morally at fault here, since *both* drivers chose their own realities.

3. Concerning Reincarnation and Karma

   a. Many New Agers base their ethics on reincarnation and karma.

      (1) Reincarnation is the process of continual rebirths until the soul reaches a state of perfection and merges back with its source (God or the Universal Soul).

      (2) *Karma* refers to the debt a soul accumulates because of good or bad actions committed during one's life (or past lives). Good karma leads to reincarnation in a more desirable state; bad karma leads to reincarnation in a less desirable state.

   b. Many New Agers explain and cope with the *existence of evil* in the world strictly in terms of karma.

      (1) Gary Zukav says we must not presume to judge when people suffer cruelly, for "we do not know what is being healed [through karma] in these sufferings."[49]

      (2) What Zukav calls "non-judgmental justice" relieves us of having to be judge and jury regarding apparent evil; the law of karma will bring about justice in the end.

D. The Impact of the New Age Movement on Science

1. From Newtonian to Quantum Physics

   a. Newton understood the universe in terms of *predictable mechanical laws* set in the context of "absolute space and time."[50]

   b. However, when Albert Einstein set forth his *theory of relativity*, the limitations of Newton's mechanical theories became apparent. As New Age critic Douglas Groothuis explains it, "relativity ushered

---

[48] Shirley MacLaine, *It's All in the Playing* (New York: Bantam Books, 1987); for a book review of *It's All in the Playing,* see Douglas Groothuis, "A Summary Critique," *Christian Research Journal* (Fall 1987), p. 28.

[49] Gary Zukav, *The Seat of the Soul* (New York: Simon and Schuster, 1989), p. 45.

[50] Groothuis, *Unmasking the New Age*, p. 94.

Newton's view of time and space out the scientific backdoor. Space and time were no longer viewed as distinct and absolute."[51]

c. Scientists also discovered that matter behaves in a wave-like manner, and electromagnetic waves (like light) have particle-like properties. These findings directly led to quantum physics.

2. Issues in Quantum Physics

a. Quantum physics involves the idea that matter—at the atomic and subatomic levels—absorbs heat and light energy and emits light energy discontinuously in bursts called "energy packets" (quanta).[52]

b. While quantum theory has contributed to an understanding of certain atomic mysteries, it also has generated a few mysteries, including Werner Heisenberg's "Uncertainty Principle."

(1) The Uncertainty Principle says that when dealing with objects the size of subatomic particles, one deals in *probabilities* rather than *predictable certainties*. In experiments with subatomic particles there is a *spectrum* or *range* of possible results. Scientists can predict only the probabilities of those results, but they cannot predict with certainty the actual result for any given particle.

(2) Related to this principle, quantum physics has discovered that the "barrier" between the *observer* (experimental apparatus) and the *observed* (subatomic particles) is broken down; *the very act of observing* has an effect on that which is observed. For example, if one tries to determine the location of a tomato seed by touching that seed, the very act of touching shifts the seed's location—that is, the slippery seed immediately "slips" to a different position.[53]

(3) Quantum physics has broken down the imaginary barrier that was thought to exist between the instrument and the object; *to some degree the instrument and the object are always interrelated.*

3. New Agers' Use of Quantum Physics

a. New Agers appropriate quantum physics to authenticate their worldview and mystical experiences.

(1) Fritjof Capra said: "The concepts of modern physics show surprising parallels to the ideas expressed in the religious philosophies of the Far East."[54]

---

[51] Groothuis, *Unmasking the New Age*, p. 94.

[52] Fred Alan Wolf, *Taking the Quantum Leap* (San Francisco: Harper & Row, 1981), p. 63.

[53] Hanz R. Pagels, *The Cosmic Code: Quantum Physics as the Language of Nature* (New York: Simon Schuster, 1982), p. 89.

[54] Fritjof Capra, *The Tao of Physics* (Boulder, Colo.: Shambhala, 1975), pp. 17–18.

(2) Marilyn Ferguson believes: "Science is only now verifying what humankind has known intuitively since the dawn of history."[55]

b. New Agers confuse the human mind with the observing instrument.

(1) Fritjof Capra draws the following unwarranted conclusion regarding how the *observer* affects the *observed* at the subatomic level: "The electron does not have objective properties *independent of my mind* [emphasis added]."[56] In other words, Capra concludes that one's *consciousness*, not one's instruments, affects reality.

(2) Michael Talbot says: "The entire physical universe itself is nothing more than patterns of neuronal energy firing off inside our heads.... There is no physical world 'out there.' Consciousness creates all."[57]

(3) For New Agers, atomic and subatomic particles do not have an independent existence separate from the consciousness of human beings. Human consciousness and the universe are *interrelated*. There is thus a basic oneness to the universe.[58]

c. Contrary to the New Age view, human consciousness is not involved in the process at all.

(1) Dean C. Halverson explains: "New Agers are certainly correct when they say that we influence the quantum realm to some extent whenever we observe it, yet the influence is an *indirect* one. We don't influence the quantum realm by our minds, but by *our means of observation* (emphasis added).[59]

(2) Ian Barbour explains: "It is the detection apparatus, not the observer as a human being, which influences the measurement obtained."[60]

(3) The detection might be a clock, a meter stick, a photographic plate, or some other device—but *not a human mind*.[61]

d. New Agers' *worldview* governs the way they interpret reality.

(1) When people— *including scientists* —have a profound mystical experience (as is common in New Agers), this in itself has an effect on the way they view reality, and hence can *bias* their scientific outlook.

---

[55] Ferguson, p. 151.

[56] Capra, *The Turning Point*, p. 87.

[57] Michael Talbot, *Mysticism and the New Physics* (New York: Bantam Books, 1982), pp. 54, 152.

[58] Capra, *The Turning Point*, p. 80.

[59] Dean C. Halverson, "Science: Quantum Physics and Quantum Leaps," in *The New Age Rage*, p. 82.

[60] Ian Barbour, *Issues in Science and Religion* (New York: Harper and Row, 1971), p. 287.

[61] Halverson, p. 82.

(2) Fritjof Capra says, "My presentation of modern physics ... has been influenced by my personal beliefs and allegiances. I have emphasized certain concepts and theories that are not yet accepted by the majority of physicists."[62] Capra himself had a mystical experience before writing his earlier book, *The Tao of Physics*.

E. The Impact of the New Age Movement on Politics

1. Transformational Politics

   a. The New Age movement espouses transformational politics.

   b. What we need today, New Agers say, is a political paradigm shift—a political *transformation*.

   c. The old paradigm (model) is *mechanistic*, breaking down the world into small, unrelated parts.

   d. The new paradigm is *holistic*, recognizing the oneness and interdependence of all things.

2. One World Government

   a. New Agers say we must recognize the oneness of humanity as a global community, which relates closely to their emphasis on the oneness of all things. Mark Satin, author of *New Age Politics*, says we must attain a consciousness that "recognizes our oneness with all humanity and in fact with all life, everywhere, and with the planet as a whole."[63]

   b. New Agers say that the nation-state is no longer a suitable and effective unit of government.

      (1) Centralized national governments are not able to *act locally* or *think globally*.[64]

      (2) What they say we need is a government that recognizes humankind's unity and interdependence—*one-world government*.

3. The New Age Political Agenda

   a. Some items in the New Age political agenda include:

      (1) ecological conservation

      (2) nuclear disarmament

      (3) relieving overpopulation and starvation

      (4) dealing with resource depletion

      (5) transcending the masculine and feminine in society

      (6) alleviating economic distress by a redistribution of wealth on a global level

---

[62] Capra, *The Turning Point*, p. 96.

[63] Mark Satin, *New Age Politics* (New York: Delta Books, 1979), p. 148.

[64] Capra, *The Turning Point*, p. 398.

b. New Agers stress that a single *world* government would be much more effective in dealing with these kinds of issues than individual nation-state governments.

4. Networking and Politics

As mentioned earlier,[65] New Agers exercise their political muscle through networking (joining together and pooling their efforts) to influence the political process at a grassroots level.

F. The Impact of the New Age Movement on Education

New Agers recognize that if they are to succeed in bringing about a New Age of enlightenment and harmony, they must penetrate the educational institutions of the world.

1. Public School Curricula and Textbooks

a. Curriculum textbooks for public schools have removed references to Christianity but include many New Age ideas.

(1) In his book *Censorship: Evidence of Bias in Our Children's Textbooks*, Paul Vitz documents how Christianity and Christian values have been deleted from the curriculum books of children.[66]

(2) While children's textbooks are void of references to Christianity, many of them teach about Buddhism, Hinduism, Eastern meditation, magic, Indian spirituality, and yoga.[67]

b. New Age Agenda for Public School Curricula

(1) Marilyn Ferguson says that the New Age educational curriculum includes an emphasis on altered states of consciousness, centering, meditation, relaxation, yoga, and biofeedback.[68]

(2) The New Age educational curriculum also places an extreme emphasis on personal autonomy. For example: children are taught to rebel (in an "appropriate" way) against the limiting beliefs of their parents. Ferguson explains: "This is based on the belief that if our children are to be free, they must be free even from us, from our limiting beliefs and our acquired tastes and habits. At times this means teaching for healthy, appropriate rebellion, not conformity."[69]

2. Transpersonal Education (or Holistic Education)

Transpersonal education focuses on that which is *beyond* the realm of objective reality and is subjective and mystical in nature.

---

[65] See Section I.C.7.c. above

[66] Paul Vitz, *Censorship: Evidence of Bias in Our Children's Textbooks* (Ann Arbor, Mich.: Servant, 1986), pp. 18–19, 33–36, 84.

[67] Berit Kjos, *Your Child and the New Age* (Wheaton, Ill.: Victor Books, 1990), p. 26.

[68] Ferguson, p. 315.

[69] Ferguson, p. 316. See also the related discussion of values clarification in Section F.2.f.(1) below.

21

It includes—but is not limited to—right-brain learning, meditation, centering, guided imagery, confluent education, and values clarification.

a. Right-brain learning

   (1) Many educators say that the right brain governs human creative and intuitive abilities.

   (2) The right-brain/left-brain distinction is not New Age *per se*, but New Agers have appropriated the distinction to justify bringing "right-brain learning techniques" into the classroom.

   (3) Such right-brain learning techniques include yoga, meditation, chanting, and visualization. By such practices, children are led to have mystical experiences.

   (4) By including right-brain learning techniques in curricula, New Agers hope to accomplish "whole-brain" learning as opposed to strictly left-brain (objective) learning.

b. Meditation

   (1) Meditation is being taught to children in some school districts.

   (2) Deborah Rozeman's *Meditating with Children* made its way into a California school district. One visualization Rozman recommends is this: "Meditate and go into the Source within, and in that One Source feel that you are One with everyone else's Light, Intelligence, Love, and Power .... Chant 'Om' softly to fill the whole circle and the whole room with your experience of the Source within."[70]

c. Centering

   (1) Centering involves certain kinds of relaxation exercises (e.g., guided imagery and deep breathing).

   (2) Centering sounds harmless, but is in reality a form of Eastern meditation.[71]

   (3) It has been taught to children in some public school contexts.

d. Guided imagery

   (1) This is also called "visualization."

   (2) It is sometimes used to help students meet an inner "helper," "spirit guide," or "higher self."[72]

e. Confluent education

   (1) Rooted in a pantheistic worldview, confluent education seeks to enable children to recognize and act upon their inner divinity.

---

[70] Deborah Rozman, *Meditating with Children* (Boulder Creek, Calif.: Univ. of the Trees Press, 1975), p. 42.

[71] Jack Canfield and Paula Klimek, "Education in the New Age," *New Age* (February 1978), p. 36.

[72] Shirley Correll, "Quieting Reflex and Guided Imagery: Education for the New Age," *Pro-Family Forum Alert* (September 1985), p. 5.

(2) Confluent education is a system developed by Beverly Galyean that utilizes guided imagery and meditation.

(3) Galyean says that a key aspect of meditation "is the increased capacity to contact and learn from the source of wisdom, love, and intelligence within us—often called the 'higher self,' God, universal wisdom or spirit, conscience."[73]

(4) It has been used in some California public schools.

f. Values clarification

(1) Values clarification seeks to help students discover *their own* values. The idea is that values are not to be imposed from *without* (such as from Scripture or from parents) but must be discovered from *within*.

(2) The underlying assumption is that there are no absolute truths or values.[74]

3. Global Education

a. Global education refers to educating students to think of themselves as global citizens, in keeping with the New Age political agenda.

b. Global education includes such ideas as the brotherhood of man, religious syncretism, and the need for one world government.[75]

c. Global education is a prominent aspect of education among New Agers.

G. *The Impact of the New Age Movement on Business*

1. Business and the Human Potential Movement

a. The human potential movement blossomed in the 1970s.[76] Since this time, a growing stream of companies has used the services of various New Age human potential seminars.

(1) A 1989 *Wall Street Journal* article reported that "business after business is putting its managers into 'New Age seminars' ... all promise 'consciousness-raising' and nonreligious conversion resulting in a 'changed person.'"[77]

(2) "Dozens of major U.S. companies—including Ford Motor Co., Proctor & Gamble Co., TRW Inc., Polaroid Corp., and Pacific

---

[73] Beverly Galyean, "Meditating with Children: Some Things We Learned," *AHP Newsletter* (August/September 1980), p. 16.

[74] See Kjos, p. 39.

[75] Vander Velde and Hyuung-Chan, *Global Mandate*, pp. 3, 17, 25, 26; quoted in Eric Buehner, "Terminal Vision," *Education Newsline* (February/March 1987), pp. 1–3.

[76] Sources on the human potential movement include Werner Erhard and Associates, *The Forum* (1986); George Leonard, *The Transformation—A Guide to the Inevitable Changes in Humankind* (New York: Delacorte Press, 1972); and Michael Ray and Rochelle Myers, *Creativity in Business* (Garden City, N.Y.: Doubleday, 1986).

[77] Peter Drucker, *Wall Street Journal*, February 9, 1989; quoted in *SCP Journal*, 9:1, p. 8.

Telesis Group Inc.—are spending millions of dollars on so-called New Age workshops."[78]

b. One reason so many Fortune 500 companies have been eager to use New Age seminars is that they promise increased productivity, better employee relations, more creativity among workers, and—bottom line—*more sales*.

c. New Age business seminars have been a primary means of bringing new converts into the New Age movement.

2. Popular New Age Seminars

a. Popular New Age seminars include *est*, *The Forum*, and *Lifespring*.

b. These and other New Age seminars teach attendees:

(1) You are your own God

(2) You can create your own reality

(3) You have unlimited potential

3. New Age Seminar Methodology

a. Many New Age seminars encourage attendees toward an altered state of consciousness.[79]

b. Seminar leaders first attempt to dismantle or do away with the attendees' present worldview.

c. Next, an attempt is subsequently made to trigger an altered state of consciousness in hopes of inducing a mystical experience so potent that it will cause the participant to question or doubt his or her previous understanding of reality.

d. Seminar leaders then provide a New Age explanation that makes sense of the mystical experience: you are your own God and you create your own reality.

III. Factors Giving Rise to the New Age Movement [80]

A. *Nineteenth-century Transcendentalism*

1. Ralph Waldo Emerson (1803–1882)

a. Emerson and the Transcendentalists helped lay the foundation for the emergence of the New Age movement.

b. Emerson elevated intuition over the senses as the means of finding "truth."

---

[78] Peter Waldman, "Motivate or Alienate? Firms Hire Gurus to Change Their 'Cultures,'" *Wall Street Journal*, July 24, 1987, section 2.

[79] See the discussion on altered states of consciousness in Part II, Section II.B.4.

[80] Many have observed the similarities between ancient Gnosticism and the New Age movement. The treatment here begins with the more recent and direct historical antecedents. I discuss the relationship between ancient Gnosticism and the New Age movement in my book *The Counterfeit Christ of the New Age Movement* (Grand Rapids: Baker, 1990).

    c. He said that God could reveal himself through human intuition.

    d. He believed that the goal of religion was the conscious union of humanity with God.

    e. Emerson believed that God had given revelation in *all* the religions.[81]

  2. Russell Chandler notes that the Transcendentalists "eclectically borrowed from the Eastern scriptures, molding them to fit American standards of autonomy and individual determination and set the stage for New Age luminaries to take the spotlight 130 years later."[82]

B. Revival of the Occult

  1. The Theosophical Society

    a. The Theosophical Society was founded by Helena P. Blavatsky in 1875.

    b. The term *Theosophy* literally means "divine wisdom."

    c. There are many distinctive New Age ideas taught by Theosophy.[83]

      (1) The "Ascended Masters" guide humanity's spiritual evolution.

        (a) Ascended Masters are formerly historical persons who have finished their earthly evolutions through reincarnation but are continuing their evolution on a higher plane of existence.

        (b) Today, even as these Ascended Masters continue in their own evolution toward the godhead, they voluntarily help lesser-evolved human beings to reach the Masters' present level.

        (c) These Masters give revelations to spiritually attuned human beings.

      (2) Religious truth has been communicated by many other holy men besides Jesus (e.g., Buddha, Hermes, Zoroaster, and Orpheus).[84]

      (3) Jesus was just a human being who embodied the Christ spirit. Blavatsky believed that her personal revelations from the Ascended Masters marked the beginning of the Aquarian Age (a synonym for the New Age).

  2. Anthroposophy

    a. Anthroposophy, an offshoot of Theosophy, was founded by German mystic Rudolf Steiner in 1912.

---

[81] Rhodes, p. 118.

[82] Russell Chandler, *Understanding the New Age* (Dallas: Word, 1991), p. 33.

[83] Rhodes, pp. 119–21.

[84] *Hermes* was an Egyptian mythological personage after whom the "Hermetic philosophy" was named. *Zoroaster* was an Iranian prophet in the sixth century B.C. who founded Zoroastrianism. *Orpheus* was the mythical founder of a Greek mystery religion in the sixth or seventh century B.C. See H. P. Blavatsky, *The Theosophical Glossary* (Los Angeles: The Theosophical Company, 1966).

    b. The term *Anthroposophy* literally means "wisdom of man," so chosen because it teaches that people possess the truth within themselves.

    c. Steiner taught that this inner truth could be discovered by using his "occult science," which enables one to experience "supersensible perception of the spiritual worlds."[85]

    d. Modern New Agers who draw heavily from Anthroposophy include David Spangler and George Trevelyan.

  3. The Arcane School

    a. The Arcane School, an offshoot of Theosophy, was founded by Alice and Foster Bailey in 1923.

    b. Many of the Arcane school's doctrines are similar to those of Theosophy, including their teaching about Ascended Masters.[86]

    c. Alice Bailey believed she was the "mouthpiece" of a Master known as The Tibetan.

      (1) She produced nineteen books as the mouthpiece of this Master.

      (2) Two of her more significant books—both of which are very popular among New Agers—are *The Externalisation of the Hierarchy* and *The Reappearance of the Christ*.

    d. Benjamin Creme is a modern New Ager who draws heavily from the Arcane School.

  4. The I AM Movement

    a. The I AM movement, an offshoot of Theosophy, was founded by Guy and Edna Ballard in the 1930s.

    b. Like Theosophy, the I AM movement espoused belief in a stream of progressive revelations from the Ascended Masters.

      (1) The purpose of these revelations was to prepare humanity for the emergence of the Aquarian Age and a planetary rise in "Christ-consciousness."[87]

      (2) The Ballards taught that the "I AM Presence" is in each person and represents a point of contact with divine reality.

    c. A modern New Ager who draws heavily from the I AM movement is Elizabeth Clare Prophet.

  5. Spiritism

    a. Spiritism may be defined as "the practice of attempting communication with departed human or extra-human intelligences (usu-

---

[85] Rudolf Steiner, *Knowledge of the Higher Worlds and Its Attainment* (Spring Valley, N.Y.: Anthroposophic Press, 1984), pp. 1–34.

[86] See Alice Bailey, *The Externalisation of the Hierarchy* (New York: Lucis, 1957).

[87] Mrs. G. W. and Donald Ballard, *Purpose of the Ascended Masters "I am" Activity* (Chicago: Saint Germain Press, 1942), pp. 24, 35, 110.

ally nonphysical) through the agency of a human medium, with the intent of receiving paranormal information and/or having direct experience of metaphysical realities."[88]

b. The "Spiritualist movement" (involving spiritism) emerged in 1848 at the home of farmer John Fox in Hydesville, New York.[89]

c. Spiritism received a shot in the arm from spiritualist Helena Petrova Blavatsky (the founder of Theosophy) in 1875.

d. Spiritism continued to be promoted in the Arcane school in 1923 and the I AM movement in the early 1930s.

e. In the New Age movement, spiritism is renamed "channeling."

   (1) Jane Roberts (d. 1983), who channeled an entity named "Seth," had much to do with today's increased interest in channeling.

   (2) Roberts's books on Seth have attracted millions of readers.

6. Astrology

a. Astrologers believe that human evolution goes through progressive cycles which correspond to the signs of the zodiac.

b. Each of these cycles allegedly lasts between 2000 and 2400 years.

c. It is believed that humanity is now moving from the Piscean Age (the age of intellectual man) into the Aquarian Age (the age of spiritual man).

d. The New Age is often called the Aquarian Age or the Age of Aquarius.[90]

C. The Inadequacy of Secular Humanism

1. In some respects the New Age movement is a reaction against secular humanism.

2. Secular humanism focused so much on the all-sufficiency of humanity (and human reason) that God was left entirely out of the picture.

3. Human reason failed to solve all of humanity's problems. And worse, with God out of the picture, many people sensed they were all alone in a vast universe.

4. The inadequacy of secular humanism made many people crave something more—something divine, something sacred. The New Age movement rushed in to fill the void.

D. The Counterculture of the 1960s

1. The 1960s as Foundational

a. The counterculture movement of the 1960s in certain ways prepared the groundwork for the emergence of the New Age movement.

---

[88] Miller, p. 141.

[89] For a concise history of spiritism, see Jon Klimo, *Channeling* (Los Angeles: J. P. Tarcher, 1987), chapter 2.

[90] Spangler, *Emergence*, p. 18; cf. Rhodes, p. 243.

27

   b. The counterculture *countered* Western culture's traditional way of doing things.

   c. The counterculture was open to and tried new options—in religious beliefs, worldviews, and much more.

   d. The counterculture quickly became a hotbed for fringe ideas.

2. Similarities Between the New Age Movement and the 1960s Counterculture[91]

   a. Antimaterialism

   b. Utopianism

   c. Ecological outlook

   d. Rejection of traditional morality

   e. Interest in the occult

3. Differences Between the New Age Movement and the 1960s Counterculture

   a. The New Age movement spans all ages and does not just cater to youth.

   b. Rock music is not a rallying point for New Agers.

   c. New Agers cannot be distinguished from others by the way they dress.

   d. New Agers are not "anti-establishment."

   e. New Agers generally are not "druggies" like those in the counterculture movement of the 1960s.[92]

4. Conclusion: It seems fair to say that "many New Agers could be described as 'hippies come of age,' but it would be a great oversimplification to suggest that the New Age movement is little more than a new name for the hippie movement. It represents a much broader cultural trend."[93]

E. The Influx of Eastern Ideas

1. The flood of Eastern ideas into the West in the 1960s helped pave the way for the emergence of the New Age movement.

2. Hindu monism and pantheism—especially as set forth in the *Upanishads*, the *Bhagavad-Gita*, and the *Vishnu Purana* from India—all helped set aside the idea of a personal Creator-God.

3. Hindus and New Agers hold quite similar views about God, the world, humanity, and salvation.[94]

---

[91] Miller, p. 24.

[92] Miller, pp. 24–25.

[93] Miller, p. 25.

[94] Miller, p. 21. Some important differences between the Hindu and New Age worldviews are mentioned earlier (Part I, Section I.D.2.b).

IV. Vital Statistics of the New Age Movement

A. Membership Figures

1. The Difficulty of Assessing Precise Figures

   a. Because the New Age movement is so diverse and encompasses such a variety of people with distinctive interests, it is difficult to determine the precise number of New Agers.

   b. However, religious polls are highly revealing of just how thoroughly different aspects of the New Age movement have penetrated society (see below).

   c. In a 1993 article in the *Los Angeles Times*, New Ager Marilyn Ferguson said that "sociologists at UC Santa Barbara … estimate that as many as 12 million Americans could be considered active participants [in the New Age movement], and another 30 million are avidly interested. If all these people were brought together in a church-like organization, it would be the third-largest religious denomination in America."[95]

2. Statistics on New Age or New Age-related Activities[96]

   a. Psychic experiences/E.S.P.: About 67 percent of American adults claim to have had a psychic experience such as extrasensory perception.

   b. Reincarnation: Approximately 30 million Americans (one in four) believe in reincarnation.

   c. Eastern mysticism

      (1) A Gallup Poll taken in 1978 showed that 10 million Americans were involved in some form of Eastern mysticism.

      (2) The circulation of *Yoga Journal* jumped to 50,000 by 1988, representing a 40 percent increase in less than four years. This figure climbed to 66,000 by 1992.

   d. Spiritism

      (1) Some 42 percent of American adults believe they have been in contact with someone who has died.

      (2) Some 14 percent of Americans endorse the work of spirit mediums or channelers.

   e. Astrology

      (1) The Gallup organization found that between 1978 and 1984, belief in astrology among schoolchildren rose from 40 percent to 59 percent.

---

[95] Marilyn Ferguson, book review of *Heaven on Earth* by Michael D'Antonio, *Los Angeles Times* (February 16, 1993). Although Ferguson may have a vested interest in arguing for such high numbers, the statistics listed in the next section attest that a high percentage of Americans are involved in some aspect of the New Age movement.

[96] Many of the statistics in this section are based on Chandler's research, pp. 8–11.

(2) A 1987 Northern Illinois University survey found that 67 percent of American adults read astrology columns.

B. Literature Distribution

Because the New Age movement is so diverse and multifaceted, it is difficult to determine the true magnitude of the literature related to the movement. However, the available statistics are highly revealing.

1. Publishing Statistics

   a. In 1980 Marilyn Ferguson said "there are New Age publications of all kinds: radio programs and newsletters, directories of organizations, lists of resources, Yellow Pages and handbooks, and new journals about consciousness, myth, transformation, and the future. Thousands of spiritual titles roll off the presses in inexpensive editions."[97]

   b. According to Marilyn McGuire, president of the New Age Publishers and Retailers Alliance, there are some 2,500 occult bookstores in the United States and over 3,000 publishers of occult and New Age books, journals, and magazines.[98]

   c. Major publishers like Bantam and Ballantine have New Age divisions. Bantam vice-president Stuart Applebaum said that metaphysical books are "one of our strongest categories" and are "getting even stronger."[99]

   d. A 1993 article in the *San Francisco Chronicle* reported that "sales of New Age-related products [including books] 'are way over *1 billion.'*"[100] The article reports that "New Age enthusiasts are a retailer's dream.... Most New Agers are in the mid-40s. Seventy percent are female, and their household median annual incomes hover between \$40,000 and \$60,000. Eighty percent have a college degree."[101]

   e. Because New Age books are becoming so popular, it is expected that in coming years, the purely New Age bookstore will become outdated as general-interest bookstores carry New Age books on their shelves.[102]

2. Examples of Best-Selling New Age Books

   a. *A Course in Miracles* : Since its first publication in 1976, this hefty three-volume set—including the text, a workbook, and a teacher's

---

[97] Ferguson, *The Aquarian Conspiracy*, p. 151.

[98] Nina Easton, "Shirley MacLaine's Mysticism for the Masses," *Los Angeles Times Magazine* (September 6, 1987), p. 33.

[99] Stuart Applebaum; cited in Chandler, p. 116.

[100] *San Francisco Chronicle* (March 23, 1993).

[101] *San Francisco Chronicle* (March 23, 1993).

[102] "Horizon 2000," *Publisher's Weekly* (December 7, 1992), p. 42.

guide—has sold over 800,000 copies and has spawned over 1,000 study groups in the United States alone.

b. *Out on a Limb* : Shirley MacLaine's New Age book was on the *New York Times* best-seller list for fifteen straight weeks. B. Dalton booksellers reported a 95 percent increase in the sale of occult/New Age books during the week that MacLaine's miniseries *Out on a Limb* aired in January 1987.[103]

---

[103] Chandler, p. 117.

Part II:
Theology

I. Biblical Interpretation

A. *The New Age Position on Interpreting Scripture Briefly Stated*

1. The Bible contains hidden, secret, or inner meanings—especially in the sayings of Jesus.

2. The Bible supports the New Age worldview. Specifically, the Bible teaches that *all is one*, *all is God*, and *man is God*.

3. Jesus taught that there were secret meanings in Scripture that only his "initiates" could discover.

4. The Bible should be interpreted according to the truths of Esoteric Christianity. This mystical form of Christianity sees all religions as affirming the same "core truths": *all is one*, *all is God*, and *man is God*.

B. *Arguments Used by New Agers to Support Their Position on Interpreting Scripture*

1. Symbolism is found in *all* religious books.

   a. Historically, *all* religious books have been written with symbolism that can only be understood by "initiates." As Helena Petrova Blavatsky, the founder of Theosophy, states: "The greatest teachers of divinity agree that nearly all ancient books [including the Bible] were written symbolically and in a language intelligible only to the initiated."[104]

   b. David Spangler calls this symbolic language the "language of esotericism," and says it is "a new way of talking about a new way of being."[105]

   c. Since the Bible uses the language of esotericism, we must approach the Bible with a view to discovering its hidden, secret meanings.

2. Jesus established the New Age interpretive method in Matthew 13.

   a. In Matthew 13, Jesus is portrayed as being in front of a mixed multitude comprising both believers and unbelievers. He did not attempt to separate the believers from the unbelievers and then instruct only the believers.

---

[104] Cited in James Sire, *Scripture Twisting* (Downers Grove, Ill.: InterVarsity Press, 1980), p. 108.

[105] David Spangler, in *Earth's Answer*, ed. Michael Katz, William Marsh, and Gail G. Thompson (New York: Harper & Row, 1977), p. 203.

b. Rather, Jesus constructed his teaching so that believers would understand what he said but unbelievers *would not*—and he did this by using parables.

c. After hearing one such parable, a disciple asked Jesus: "Why do you speak to the people in parables?" (Matt. 13:10). Jesus answered: "The knowledge of *the secrets* of the kingdom of heaven has been given to you [believers], but not to them [unbelievers]" (v. 11, emphasis added).

d. Clearly, in view of this verse, there are secrets in the words of Jesus that only true "believers" can discern. Therefore, we are to approach the Bible with a view to finding the secret, hidden meanings in each verse.

3. Examples are cited of a secret or inner meaning of Bible verses.

a. Matthew 6:33

David Spangler says that when Jesus said to "seek first his kingdom and his righteousness" (Matt. 6:33), he was teaching his disciples to seek "the state of identification with one's true individuality, the source within, the Divine center, that I AM THAT I AM."[106] Therefore, seeking the kingdom of heaven first in one's life amounts to making one's inner divinity a top priority. After a person does this one thing, "all else will be added."

b. Matthew 11:29

Elizabeth Clare Prophet tells us that when Jesus said, "Take my yoke upon you and learn from me" (Matt. 11:29), he was teaching his disciples to "take my yoke, *yoga*, upon you and learn of me [take my consciousness of my sacred labor, my Christhood bearing the burden of world karma ... and learn of my Guru, the Ancient of Days]; for I am meek and lowly in heart, and ye shall find rest unto your souls. For my yoke, *yoga*, is easy and my burden in heaven and on earth is truly Light."[107]

C. Refutation of Arguments Used by New Agers to Support their Position on Interpreting Scripture

1. The Bible is to be interpreted literally.

a. The Bible is not a book of esoteric symbols full of hidden, secondary meanings.

(1) Jesus *never* sought a hidden or secondary meaning when interpreting the Old Testament Scriptures.

(2) Jesus consistently interpreted the Old Testament in a nonsymbolic, literal way—including the Creation account of Adam and Eve (Matt. 13:35; 25:34; Mark 10:6), Noah's Ark and

---

[106] David Spangler, *The Laws of Manifestation* (Forres, Scotland: Findhorn, 1983), pp. 23–24.

[107] Mark and Elizabeth Clare Prophet, *The Lost Teachings of Jesus 3* (Livingston, Mont.: Summit Univ. Press, 1988), pp. 273–74.

the Flood (Matt. 24:37–39; Luke 17:26–27), Jonah and the whale (Matt. 12:39–41), Sodom and Gomorrah (Matt. 10:15), and the account of Lot (Luke 17:28–29).

b. Literal interpretation allows for figures of speech.

(1) There *are* figures of speech in the Bible, but what is understood to be a figure of speech and what is taken literally should be based on the biblical text itself—such as when Jesus used obviously figurative parables to express spiritual truth.

(2) A literal approach to Scripture also recognizes that the Bible contains a variety of literary genres (i.e., different kinds of writing), each of which has certain peculiar characteristics that must be recognized to interpret the text properly.

(a) Biblical genres include the historical (e.g., Acts), the dramatic epic (e.g., Job), poetry (e.g., Psalms), wise sayings (e.g., Proverbs), epistles (e.g., Ephesians), and apocalyptic writings (e.g., Revelation).

(b) An incorrect genre judgment will lead one far astray in interpreting Scripture. For example, one would not interpret the Book of Acts in the same way as the Book of Revelation.

2. Jesus' own teaching was clear and open, not hidden or secret.

a. That Jesus taught *openly* and *with clarity* is attested by the doctrinal influence he had on his followers.

b. Several scholars have noted that if Jesus had intended to teach "Esoteric Christianity," he was a failure as a teacher, for his words led those who followed him in the precise opposite direction than he would have intended.[108] For example, instead of becoming *pantheists* (believing that *all is God*), Jesus' followers were *theists* who believed in a personal Creator God distinct from his creation.

3. The New Age view of Matthew 13 is untenable.

a. Jesus had a rationale for teaching in parables.

(1) One might legitimately ask why Jesus engineered his parabolic teaching so that *believers* could understand his teaching but *unbelievers* could not.

(2) The backdrop to this is that the disciples, having responded favorably to Jesus' teaching and having placed their faith in him, already knew much truth about the Messiah. Careful reflection on Jesus' parables would instruct them even further.

(3) Hardened unbelievers who had willfully and persistently refused Jesus' previous teachings were prevented from understanding the parables. Jesus was apparently following an injunction he

---

[108] E.g., Groothuis, *Confronting the New Age*, p. 89.

provided earlier in the Sermon on the Mount: "Do not give dogs what is sacred; do not throw your pearls to pigs" (Matt. 7:6).

(4) Yet there is grace even here. For it is possible that Jesus may have prevented unbelievers from understanding the parables because he did not want to add more responsibility to them by imparting new truth for which they would be held responsible.

b. The parables of the *sower* (Matt. 13:3–9) and the *tares* (13:24–30) show that Jesus wanted his parables to be clear to those who were receptive.

(1) Jesus himself provided the interpretation of these parables for his disciples.

(2) Jesus did this not only so there would be no uncertainty as to their meaning, but also to teach believers the proper method of interpreting the other parables.

(3) The fact that Christ did not interpret his subsequent parables shows that he fully expected believers to understand what he taught by following the methodology he illustrated for them. Clearly, then, Matthew 13 does not support but rather *argues against* esotericism.

4. The esoteric approach produces irreconcilable contradictions.

a. In the subjective approach of esotericism, the basic authority ceases to be Scripture and becomes the mind of the individual interpreter.

b. Because of this, esoteric interpreters offer us irreconcilable contradictions in their interpretations of specific Bible verses.

c. For example, New Agers come up with widely differing interpretations of biblical passages that speak of Christ's second coming.[109]

(1) Benjamin Creme believes that references in the New Testament to the second coming of Christ point to the coming of a single individual known as Maitreya.[110]

(2) Others such as David Spangler believe these same references point to an incarnation of the cosmic Christ in *all* of humanity, and are not fulfilled in a single individual.[111]

(3) A *plain* reading of Scripture shows that *Christ himself* will physically and visibly come again in cataclysmic fashion to judge the living and the dead (Matt. 24; Rev. 19).

d. It is true that orthodox Bible interpreters do not unanimously agree on all the finer points of theology. However:

(1) Their differences of opinion on relatively minor details (what might be called the *nonessentials*) must be seen in the broader

---

[109] The New Age doctrine of the second coming is treated fully in Part II, Section VII.

[110] Creme, pp. 48, 55.

[111] David Spangler, *Reflections on the Christ* (Forres, Scotland: Findhorn, 1981), p. 86.

context of their unanimous agreement on the major details (the *essentials*) of Christianity. Examples of *essential* doctrines are the deity of Christ, the bodily resurrection, salvation by grace through faith, and the literal second coming of Christ. *Nonessential* doctrines would include the mode of baptism (immersion or sprinkling), the precise nature of the millennium, and the timing of the tribulation.

(2) This widespread agreement on the essentials of Christianity (including the second coming of Christ) stems from an objective methodology that takes the words of Scripture in their ordinary, plain sense—just as God intended.

5. The esoteric approach is untestable and therefore useless.

a. Unlike objective methodology, in which interpretations can be rationally evaluated and tested by comparing Scripture with Scripture and by objectively weighing historical and grammatical considerations, there is no objective way to test esoteric interpretations of Scripture.

b. By nature, esotericism is subjective and nonverifiable; there is no way to *prove* that a given interpretation is right or wrong, since "proof" presupposes rationality and objectivity.

c. A New Ager relying on an esoteric approach cannot know for sure, then, whether Creme or Spangler is correct (or whether *either* is correct) regarding the Second Coming or *any other* doctrine.

D. Arguments Used to Prove a Proper Method of Interpreting Scripture[112]

1. Jesus, whom New Agers claim to revere as an enlightened Master, clearly demonstrated an appreciation for *context* and *grammar* in his interpretation of Old Testament Scripture.

a. Jesus affirmed the Old Testament's

(1) Divine inspiration (Matt. 22:43)

(2) Indestructibility (Matt. 5:17–18)

(3) Infallibility (John 10:34–35)

(4) Final authority (Matt. 4:4, 7, 10)

(5) Historicity (Matt. 12:40–41; 24:36–37)

(6) Factual inerrancy (Matt. 22:29–32)

(7) Spiritual clarity (Luke 24:25)

b. Jesus emphasized the importance of *each word* of Scripture (Luke 16:17).

c. Jesus emphasized the importance of interpreting Scripture in its proper historical context (Matt. 13:34–35; Mark 10:5–6; Luke 17:26–27).

---

[112]A good book on hermeneutics is Bernard Ramm's *Protestant Biblical Interpretation* (Grand Rapids: Baker, 1978).

    d. Jesus sometimes based his argumentation on a single biblical expression (Matt. 22:31–32, 43–45; John 10:34).

    e. Jesus used words according to their normal, plain meaning. In view of this:

       (1) Would New Agers say Jesus was wrong in this?

       (2) If so, then why do they call him enlightened?

       (3) If Jesus was *not* wrong, then why don't New Agers follow his enlightened example?

2. The Golden Rule of interpretation should be observed.

    a. Douglas Groothuis suggests that New Agers use the Golden Rule when interpreting the Bible: "Interpret others' texts as you would have them interpret your own."[113]

    b. If any Christians interpreted Eastern mystical texts (or New Age books) so that they came out sounding as if they support orthodox Christianity, an esoteric interpreter certainly would object.[114] The Christians would be guilty of reading something into the Eastern text that simply is not there and would be rightly reprimanded by the esotericist.

    c. The following mock conversation illustrates the point:

    Christian: So, when Shirley MacLaine—in her book *Dancing in the Light*—said, "You are unlimited. You just don't realize it," what she was really talking about was that all people are unlimited in their need for the one and only Savior, who is uniquely God in the flesh, Jesus Christ. You see, she was really saying that people are "unlimited" in their need for Christ because they are totally depraved. The sad thing is that many people are blind to their need for Christ. That's why she said, "You just don't realize it."

    New Ager: Now, wait just one minute! That's not at all what MacLaine was saying. What she was saying—if you care to look at her words *in context* and *according to her intended meaning*—is that human beings have an unlimited potential because of their divine nature. And because human beings don't "realize" their divine nature, she was saying they need enlightenment. You're reading something into MacLaine's words that is not there at all!

    d. New Agers assume the truth of objective interpretive methodology when reading *their own* books.

       (1) When David Spangler reads Rudolf Steiner's books, he does not esoterically twist Steiner's words to mean something other than what Steiner intended.

---

[113] Groothuis, *Confronting the New Age*, pp. 89–90.

[114] Groothuis, *Confronting the New Age*, pp. 89–90.

        (2) When Benjamin Creme reads the books of Alice Bailey, he does not esoterically twist Bailey's words to mean something other than what Bailey intended.

        (3) When Elizabeth Clare Prophet reads the writings of Guy and Edna Ballard, she does not esoterically twist their words to mean something other than what they intended.[115]

  e. To be fair and consistent, New Agers must not esoterically twist the words of the biblical writers to mean something other than what *they* intended.

3. Like Jesus, our interpretation must be faithful to the *context* in which a passage of Scripture is found.

  a. Every word in the Bible is part of a sentence; every sentence is part of a paragraph; every paragraph is part of a book; and every book is part of the whole counsel of Scripture.

  b. There is thus both an *immediate* and a *broad* context of a given verse, and both must be considered if we are to interpret Scripture accurately.

4. Like Jesus, our interpretation must take the *historical considerations* into account.

  a. The historical backdrop

        (1) Historical considerations are especially important *as a backdrop* in discovering the author's intended meaning.

        (2) Christianity is based on historical fact. More specifically, Christianity rests on the foundation of the historical Jesus of Nazareth whose very life represents God's full and objective self-communication to humankind (John 1:18).

        (3) In the empirical (experiential) world of sensory perceptions, Jesus was seen and heard by human beings as God's ultimate revelation (1 John 1:1–3). This is why Jesus could claim, "If you really knew me, you would know my Father as well" (John 14:7).

  b. The historicity of the resurrection as an example

        (1) The apostle Paul warned the religious men of Athens of the objective reality of the future judgment of all humanity based on the objective, historical evidence for the resurrection of Jesus (Acts 17:16–31).

        (2) The gospels record the historical evidence for us in propositional statements (i.e., affirmations of specific truths); these are documents which are based on eyewitness testimony and written very close in time to the events on which they report.

---

[115] For details on the theological connections between Spangler and Steiner, Creme and Bailey, and Prophet and Ballard, see my book *The Counterfeit Christ of the New Age Movement*, chapters 7 and 8.

(3) Based on how people respond to God's objective, historical revelation contained in Scripture, they will spend eternity in a real heaven or a real hell. Esoteric manipulation of truth will not be possible on the day of judgment.

II. The Doctrine of Revelation

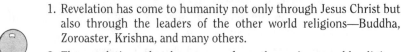

A. The New Age Position on Revelation Briefly Stated

1. Revelation has come to humanity not only through Jesus Christ but also through the leaders of the other world religions—Buddha, Zoroaster, Krishna, and many others.

2. The revelations that have come from the various world religions teach the same "core truths": *all is one* (monism), *all is God* (pantheism), and *man is God*.

3. We must therefore learn from the religious views and practices of all people.

4. Revelations continue to be received today from disembodied humans, "space brothers" (UFOs), and other entities and sources through modern channelers.[116]

B. Arguments Used by New Agers to Support Their Position on Revelation

1. Revelation has come through Jesus and through the leaders of the other world religions.

   a. If *all is one* and *all is God*, the leaders of the various world religions taught the same ultimate truth.

   b. Jesus himself taught that all the world religions worship the same God with different names. According to Levi Dowling, Jesus said: "The nations of the earth see God from different points of view, and so he does not seem the same to everyone. ... You Brahmans call him Parabrahm; in Egypt he is Thoth; and Zeus is his name in Greece; Jehovah is his Hebrew name."[117]

2. Each of the world religions teaches the same core truth.

   a. While the world religions have some *external* differences, they all teach the same "core truth." This core truth is that *all is one*, *all is God*, and *man is God*.

   b. David Spangler says that "the function of all religions and philosophical and ethical systems ... has been to reveal to man his identity ... to shepherd man in this steady unfolding of his understanding of himself as a creator, as a god."[118]

---

[116] Miller, p. 174. Note: the word *revelation* is used in a very loose sense here—as "spiritual information from the beyond," not from God.

[117] Levi Dowling, *The Aquarian Gospel of Jesus the Christ* (London: L. N. Fowler & Co., 1947), p. 56.

[118] David Spangler, *Relationship & Identity* (Forres, Scotland: Findhorn, 1978), pp. 46–47.

3. We must draw from the collective wisdom of all the world religions. For example, Matthew Fox calls for a "deep ecumenism" that will "unleash the wisdom of all world religions—Hinduism and Buddhism, Islam and Judaism, Taoism and Shintoism, Christianity in all its forms, and native religions and goddess religions throughout the world. This unleashing of wisdom holds the last hope for the survival of the planet we call home."[119]

4. Channelers continue to receive revelations today.

   a. Definition of a channeler

      (1) A channeler is a person who yields control of his or her perceptual and cognitive capacities to a spiritual entity or force with the intent of receiving paranormal information.[120]

      (2) Millions of Americans have been introduced to channeling through Shirley MacLaine's best-selling books.

      (3) Channelers can receive revelation from spirit entities or the Akashic Records.[121]

   b. Spirit channeling

      (1) Kevin Ryerson, one of today's best-known New Age channelers (he is Shirley MacLaine's channeler), wrote a book entitled *Spirit Communication* that provides an overview of what channeling is all about.

      (2) Ryerson compares channeling to a radio broadcast.

         (a) If two stations are competing for the same frequency, by slightly adjusting the dial we can tune one down and the other will come in more clearly.

         (b) "Kevin Ryerson," he tells us, is the channel that gets tuned down; this allows the other frequency (spirit entities) to come through.

         (c) Ryerson provides readers with guidelines on how to "adjust the tuning" so that they—like he—can become channels.[122]

      (3) Ryerson says that the personalities or entities that speak through him during channeling sessions are people he has known in his past lives (i.e., through reincarnation).[123]

      (4) Ryerson also believes that *he himself* has been a spirit guide who has spoken through channelers when he was in a discarnate state (between reincarnations).[124]

---

119 Matthew Fox, *The Coming of the Cosmic Christ* (San Francisco: Harper & Row, 1989), p. 288.

120 Miller, p. 142; cf. Klimo, p. 185. Klimo says channeling involves a *voluntary yielding of control* to a spirit entity.

121 The Akashic Records are discussed in point 4.c. below.

122 Kevin Ryerson and Stephanie Harolde, *Spirit Communication* (New York: Bantam Books, 1989), pp. 46–48.

123 Ryerson and Harolde, p. 16.

124 Ryerson and Harolde, p. 44.

(5) The spirit entities who speak through Ryerson bear testimony to the core "truths": you are God, you have unlimited potential, you create your own reality, and there is no death.

c. Akashic Records

(1) Some channelers receive revelations not from spirit entities but from the "Akashic Records."

(2) The physical earth is surrounded by an immense spiritual field known as *Akasha* in which is impressed—like a celestial tape recording—every impulse of human thought, will, and emotion.

(3) These records constitute a complete record of human history.

(4) Some New Age seers have the ability to "read" the Akashic Records.

(a) Levi Dowling transcribed *The Aquarian Gospel of Jesus the Christ* (1911) from the Akashic Records. This book contains a "record" of Jesus going East as a child to learn from Hindu gurus. While in the East, Jesus (the human) became "the Christ" by going through an occultic ritual involving seven degrees of initiation.[125]

(b) Edgar Cayce could also read the Akashic Records. Like Levi Dowling, Cayce said Jesus went East as a child to learn from various Eastern teachers.[126] Cayce also tells us that the person we know as Jesus had twenty-nine previous incarnations (in an earlier incarnation Jesus was the biblical Adam who sinned in the Garden of Eden). This particular soul did not become the Christ until the thirtieth incarnation—as Jesus of Nazareth.[127]

C. *Refutation of Arguments Used by New Agers to Support Their Position on Revelation*

1. The leaders of the various world religions *did not* teach the same core truth.

a. Example: the doctrine of God, the most fundamental doctrine of any religious system.

(1) *Jesus Christ* taught that there is only one personal God who is triune in nature (Mark 12:29; John 4:24; 5:18–19).

(2) *Muhammad* taught that there is only one God, but that God cannot have a son.

(3) *Confucius* was polytheistic (he believed in many gods).

(4) *Krishna* believed in a combination of polytheism (belief in many gods) and pantheism (belief that all is God).

---

[125] Dowling, p. 87.
[126] Dowling, pp. 40–41.
[127] Dowling, pp. 40–41.

(5) *Zoroaster* held to religious dualism—that is, there is both a good god and a bad god.

(6) *Buddha* taught that the concept of God was essentially irrelevant.[128]

b. Jesus made exclusive truth claims.

(1) Jesus was exclusivistic in his truth claims, indicating that what he said took precedence over all others.

(2) Jesus said he is uniquely and exclusively *humanity's only means* of coming into a relationship with God: "I am the way and the truth and the life. No one comes to the Father except through me" (John 14:6).

(3) Jesus even warned his followers to "Watch out that no one deceives you. For many will come in my name, claiming, 'I am the Christ,' and will deceive many" (Matt. 24:4–5).

c. Jesus' apostles made exclusive truth claims.

(1) Peter proclaimed that "Salvation is found in no one else [but Jesus Christ], for there is no other name under heaven given to men by which we must be saved" (Acts 4:12).

(2) Paul affirmed that "there is one God and *one mediator* between God and men, the man Christ Jesus" (1 Tim. 2:5, italics added).

2. Channeling is to be rejected by Christians.

a. God condemns channeling as a heinous sin.

(1) Deuteronomy 18:10–12 is clear: "Let no one be found among you ... who is a medium or spiritist or who consults the dead. Anyone who does these things is detestable to the LORD."

(2) Satan masquerades as an angel of light, seeking to deceive people (2 Cor. 11:14).

(a) Satan and his fallen angels are actively promoting "doctrines of demons" (doctrines purporting to be the truth but which are in fact lies) (1 Tim. 4:1 NASB).

(b) Christians are admonished to "test the spirits" (1 John 4:1).

(c) Demons are more than willing to *masquerade* as "spirit guides" if the result will be that tens of thousands of people will be deceived and drawn away from Jesus Christ in the process.

b. Departed humans are not available for contact.

(1) Departed human beings are not hovering around in the "great beyond" available for contact with human beings on earth.[129]

---

[128] For more on the beliefs of the leaders of the various world religions, see Francis J. Beckwith, *Baha'i* (Minneapolis: Bethany House, 1985), pp. 17f.

[129] This is not contradicted by the account of the witch of Endor, Saul, and Samuel in 1 Samuel 28:3–25. *See* Norman L. Geisler and Thomas Howe, *When Critics Ask* (Wheaton, Ill.: Victor Books, 1992), pp. 167–68.

    (2) Departed Christians are in the presence of Christ in heaven (Phil. 1:23).

    (3) Departed unbelievers are in a place of great suffering (Luke 16:19–31), *confined* until that future day of judgment (Rev. 20:11–15).

  c. Channeling involves an inherent contradiction. If human beings are gods and are perfect within (as New Agers hold), why is there a need for external "revelation" through channelers?[130]

D. Arguments Used to Prove the Biblical Doctrine of Revelation

1. Jude 3 indicates there are no continuing revelations of foundational, doctrinal truth occurring today: "Contend earnestly for the faith which was once for all delivered to the saints" (NASB).

  a. Meaning of "the faith"

    (1) In the Greek text, the definite article ("the") preceding "faith" points to *the one and only faith*; there is no other.

    (2) "The faith" refers to "the apostolic teaching and preaching which was regulative upon the Church."[131] (*See* Acts 6:7; Gal. 1:23; 1 Tim. 4:1.) The reference here is to foundational doctrinal truths, such as God, salvation, the person and work of Christ, etc.

    (3) Bauer, Arndt, and Gingrich tell us that "faith" in this verse refers to "that which is believed, [a] body of faith or belief, [a] doctrine."[132]

  b. Meaning of "once for all"

    (1) Jude 3 refers to this body of truth as that which was *"once for all* delivered to the saints."

    (2) The word translated "once for all" (Greek: *hapax*) refers to something that has been done for all time and *never* needs repeating.

    (3) The revelatory process was *completed* after this faith had been delivered.

    (4) Therefore there is no need of further revelation about the nature of God, the person of Christ, the way of salvation, etc.

  c. Meaning of "delivered"

    (1) "Delivered" here indicates an act that was *completed in the past* with *no continuing element*.

---

[130] Miller, p. 174.

[131] Michael Green, *The Second Epistle of Peter and the Epistle of Jude* (Grand Rapids: Eerdmans, 1968), p. 159.

[132] Walter Bauer, *A Greek-English Lexicon of the New Testament and Other Early Christian Literature,* trans. William F. Arndt and F. Wilbur Gingrich (Chicago: Univ. of Chicago Press, 1957), p. 669.

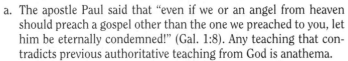
    (2) This is confirmed by the verb tense in the Greek for the verb "delivered." In this context, the verb tense (an aorist passive participle) indicates a once-for-all completed action.

    (3) There would be no new "faith" or body of truth communicated through psychics or channelers.

2. Even if one hypothetically granted that God did wish to reveal additional foundational truths today, any present-day revelation would *have* to be consistent with the previous revelation.

    a. The apostle Paul said that "even if we or an angel from heaven should preach a gospel other than the one we preached to you, let him be eternally condemned!" (Gal. 1:8). Any teaching that contradicts previous authoritative teaching from God is anathema.

    b. Paul spoke of the importance of making sure that new claims to truth be measured against what we know to be true from Scripture (Acts 17:11; 2 Tim. 3:16).

    c. Since New Age "revelations" contradict what we *know* to be a revelation from God (i.e., Scripture), they do not qualify as *true* revelations.

III. The Doctrine of God

A. *The New Age Position on God Briefly Stated*

1. God is to be viewed *pantheistically*.

2. *God is all* and *all is God*.

3. This pantheism is closely related to monism, which says that *all is one*.

4. In keeping with pantheism, God may be thought of as an impersonal Force, or Consciousness, or Energy.

B. *Arguments Used by New Agers to Support Their Position on God*

1. Revelations received from spirit entities through channeling indicate there is nothing anywhere in the universe that is not God.

    a. David Spangler (who channels an entity named "Limitless Love and Truth") says: "There is not one place, one thing, one time that does not include his presence. God is the life within all things. He contains all things."[133]

    b. Benjamin Creme (through whom Maitreya the Christ speaks) says: "God is the sum total of all that exists in the whole of the manifested and unmanifested universe—everything we know and see and hear and touch and everything we don't know or hear or see or touch, everywhere, in the totality of the cosmos. Every manifested phenomenon is part of God. And the space between these

---

[133] Spangler, *Revelation*, p. 150.

manifested phenomena is God. So, in a very real sense, there isn't anything else. You are God. I am God. This microphone is God. This table is God. All is God."[134]

2. Jesus taught both *pantheism* and *monism*.

   a. Levi Dowling's *The Aquarian Gospel of Jesus the Christ* quotes Jesus as follows: "With much delight I speak to you concerning life—the brotherhood of life. The universal God is one, yet he is more than one; *all things are God; all things are one*."[135]

   b. The New Testament portrays Jesus as teaching pantheism.

     (1) Benjamin Creme says that in the New Testament Jesus taught that God is love. What is love? Creme answers: "Love—what we call love—is a great energy, a great magnetic all-pervading energy."[136] Indeed, "there is an ancient occult axiom which says that there is nothing in the whole of the manifested universe but energy."[137] God is this all-pervading energy of the universe.

     (2) Jesus' belief in pantheism was also evident in his teaching that "the kingdom of God is within you" (Luke 17:21). Creme says this teaching indicates that "man is literally made in the likeness of God. He has to be, *because there isn't anything else*."[138]

3. The pantheistic concept of God is a core truth of all the world religions. The related ideas that *all is God*, *all is one*, and *man is God* are core truths of the world religions—such as Christianity, Hinduism, and Buddhism—despite any external differences they may have.[139]

C. *Refutation of Arguments Used by New Agers to Support Their Position on God*

   1. Pantheism contradicts common sense.

   a. The pantheistic idea that there is "nothing anywhere in the universe that is not God" goes against common sense.

   b. As Norman Geisler notes, "if all is one, then there is no difference between myself and anything else. And if there is no difference between myself and anything else, then I should not call myself 'myself.' For to call myself 'myself' is to assume that there is a difference between myself and anything else.... Common sense tells me that I am different from others."[140]

---

134 Creme, p. 115.

135 Dowling, p. 56, italics added.

136 Creme, p. 44.

137 Creme, p. 44.

138 Creme, pp. 135–36, emphasis added.

139 Spangler, *Relationship & Identity*, pp. 46–47; Trevelyan, *Operation Redemption*, pp. 16–18.

140 Norman L. Geisler and J. Yutaka Amano, *The Reincarnation Sensation* (Wheaton, Ill.: Tyndale House, 1986), p. 17.

2. Pantheism confuses the creation with the Creator.

   a. The pantheistic idea that there is "nothing anywhere in the universe that is not God" fails to distinguish between *creation* (which is finite) and the *Creator* (who is infinite).

   b. In such a system, all alleged "I-thou" relations ultimately reduce to "I."[141]

3. Jesus Christ *did not* teach a pantheistic idea of God.

   a. Though *The Aquarian Gospel of Jesus the Christ* quotes Jesus as teaching a pantheistic idea of God, this "Gospel" is clearly a human product, derived from occultism, loaded with historical errors, permeated with contradictions, and completely untrustworthy as a source of truth.[142]

   b. The biblical texts which New Agers cite to support the notion that Jesus taught pantheism are consistently misinterpreted and taken out of context.

      (1) When Jesus said "God is love" he meant that God is characterized by love: God is eternally giving, he seeks the highest good for the objects of his love, and he is benevolent, gracious, and merciful in his dealings with others.[143] He did not mean that God is an all-pervasive energy.

      (2) It is illogical for Benjamin Creme to use the *personal* attribute of love in support of an *impersonal* concept of God.

      (3) Jesus' statement, "the kingdom of God is within you," is probably better translated, "the kingdom of God is *among* you [emphasis added]."[144] This verse means that the kingdom of God had arrived and was present in some sense in the person and ministry of Jesus (the King). Regardless of which translation one adopts, this verse cannot by any stretch of the imagination mean that "all is God."

4. The world religions do not teach the same inner core truths. (See Section II.C.1 for proof of this.)

5. Pantheism cannot account for evil in the world.

   a. The pantheistic idea that there is "nothing anywhere in the universe that is not God" fails to deal adequately with the existence of *real* evil in the world.

   b. If God is the essence of *all* life forms in creation, then one must conclude that both good *and* evil stem from the same essence (God).

---

[141] Norman L. Geisler, *Christian Apologetics* (Grand Rapids: Baker, 1978), p. 187.

[142] Rhodes, pp. 45–46, 99–102; cf. Douglas Groothuis, *Revealing the New Age Jesus* (Downers Grove, Ill.: InterVarsity Press, 1990).

[143] Millard J. Erickson, *Christian Theology* (Grand Rapids: Baker, 1985), pp. 292–98.

[144] See *The Expositor's Bible Commentary*, ed. Frank E. Gaebelein, vol. 8 (Grand Rapids: Zondervan, 1984), pp. 996–97.

   c. The Bible teaches that God is good and not evil (1 John 1:5; cf. Hab. 1:13; Matt. 5:48).

   d. In their book *The Infiltration of the New Age*, Yutaka Amano and Norman Geisler provide an excellent example of how evil is problematic for the New Age worldview:

> When Francis Schaeffer spoke to a group of students at Cambridge University, there was a Hindu who began criticizing Christianity. Schaeffer said, "Am I not correct in saying that on the basis of your system, cruelty and noncruelty are ultimately equal, that there is no intrinsic difference between them?" The Hindu agreed. One of the students immediately caught on to what Schaeffer was driving at. He picked up a kettle of boiling water that he was going to use to make tea and held the steaming pot over the Indian's head. This young Hindu looked up and asked the student what he was doing. The student said with a cold yet gentle finality, "There is no difference between cruelty and noncruelty." Thereupon the Hindu walked out into the night.[145]

D. Arguments Used to Prove the Biblical Doctrine of God

  1. The biblical God is personal.

    a. Whereas the God of pantheism is an *impersonal force*, the God of the Bible is a personal Being with whom one can establish a relationship.

    b. The biblical idea of God involves a loving personal Father unto whom believers may cry, *"Abba"* (Mark 14:36; Rom. 8:15; Gal. 4:6).[146]

    c. There is biblical evidence of God's personal nature.

      (1) God *hears* (Ex. 2:24)

      (2) God *sees* (Gen. 1:4)

      (3) God *knows* (2 Tim. 2:19; Jer. 29:11)

      (4) God has a *will* (1 John 2:17; Matt. 6:10, 26:39; Rev. 4:11)

      (5) God *communicates* (Ex. 3:13–14)

      (6) God *plans* (Eph. 1:11)

      (7) God demonstrates *emotion* (Gen. 6:6)

      (8) God demonstrates *character* (2 Peter 3:9)

    d. The God who bestowed personal characteristics on humankind is himself personal.

      (1) As Psalm 94 puts it, "Does he who implanted the ear not hear? Does he who formed the eye not see?" (vs. 9).

      (2) *Impersonal forces do not see and hear.*

---

[145] Geisler and Amano (Wheaton, Ill.: Tyndale House, 1989), p. 20.

[146] *Abba* is an Aramaic word for "father," conveying a warm sense of intimacy.

e. Jesus repeatedly affirmed the personal nature of God.

(1) This is most vividly expressed in his many references to God as "my Father" (e.g., John 14:2, 7).

(2) Jesus' ministry at the Jordan began with a *verbal testimony of love* from the Father: "You are my Son, whom I love; with you I am well pleased" (Mark 1:11).

(3) Throughout his earthly sojourn, Jesus' *fellowship* with the Father was uninterrupted. He said to some of his disciples: "You will leave me all alone. Yet I am not alone, for my Father is with me" (John 16:32).

(4) Near the end of Jesus' three-year ministry, we again hear the Father speaking of *his love* for the Son, this time to the disciples during the Transfiguration: "This is my Son, whom I love. ... Listen to him" (Matt. 17:5).

(5) Clearly, Jesus perceived God not as an "it" or a "cosmic force," but as a person with whom personal relations can be entered. A cosmic, impersonal force does not speak and it surely cannot love.

2. The creation and the Creator are distinct.

a. God is eternally distinct from what he created.

b. God, who is infinite and eternal, created all things out of absolute nothingness (Heb. 11:3; see also Gen. 1:1; Neh. 9:6; Ps. 33:8–9; 148:5). Having existed in sovereign self-sufficiency for all eternity past, the triune God sovereignly and eternally decided to create that which was not himself and yet which was utterly dependent on him for its continuing existence (Col. 1:17).

c. God is not "one" with the universe (Heb. 11:3).

d. God is distinct from humankind.

(1) Ecclesiastes 5:2 affirms, "God is in heaven and you are on earth." In other words, God and humanity are distinct.

(2) Numbers 23:19 affirms, "God is not a man, that he should lie, nor a son of man, that he should change his mind."

3. The biblical God is both transcendent *and* immanent.

a. The theological phrase "transcendence of God" refers to God's otherness or separateness from the created universe and from humanity (e.g., 1 Kings 8:27; Ps. 113:5–6).

b. The phrase "immanence of God" refers to God's active presence within the creation and in human history, though all the while remaining *distinct* from the Creation (e.g., Ex. 29:45–46; Deut 4:7).

c. In some verses, the transcendence and immanence of God are linked together (e.g., Deut. 4:39; Isa. 57:15; Jer. 23:23–24).

d. Conclusion: God is *above and beyond* the creation, yet is simultaneously *active in the midst of* the creation.

IV. The Person of Jesus Christ

A. The New Age Position on the Person of Jesus Christ Briefly Stated

1. The mere human vessel *Jesus* is to be distinguished from *the Christ* (variously defined, but always divine).

2. While New Agers do not always agree on *how* the human Jesus became the Christ, they are unanimous *that* he became the Christ.

3. Christ went East as a child to learn from Hindu gurus and holy men.

4. Jesus is an enlightened "way-shower," and is on a par with other holy men such as Buddha, Krishna, and Zoroaster.

B. Arguments Used by New Agers to Support Their Position on the Person of Jesus Christ

1. Revelations received via channeling indicate that *Jesus* and *the Christ* are to be distinguished.[147]

   a. *Jesus* refers to the mere human vessel, while *the Christ*, variously defined, is divine.[148]

   b. Some New Agers see the Christ as a cosmic, divine entity that dwelt for a time in Jesus' body.

   (1) Heline Corinne says that "the vehicle of the Master Jesus, the fairest and most perfect this earth could produce, now became the abode of the Lord Christ for the three years of His earthly ministry."[149] In other words, the human Jesus embodied the cosmic Christ for the three years from his baptism to his crucifixion.

   (2) George Trevelyan says, "Esoteric Christianity sees Jesus as the human vehicle for the Cosmic Being of the Christ."[150]

   c. Not all New Agers see the "Christ" as a cosmic spirit that embodied the Christ. Some interpret the word "Christ" as being more of an office or a functional role (see the following examples).

2. Revelations received through various channelers point to different ways the human Jesus became the Christ.

   a. While not all New Agers give the same explanation for *how* the human Jesus became the Christ, they are unanimous *that* he became the Christ.

---

147 E.g., Spangler, *Reflections on the Christ*, p. 8.

148 See, for example, Annie Besant, *Esoteric Christianity* (Wheaton, Ill.: Theosophical Publishing House, 1970), pp. 90–91.

149 Heline Corinne, *New Age Bible Interpretation* (Santa Monica, CA: New Age Bible & Philosophy Center, 1961), p. 251.

150 Trevelyan, *Operation Redemption*, p. 37.

b. David Spangler says that the human Jesus merely "attuned" to the cosmic Christ and that the Christ descended upon the human Jesus at his baptism.[151]

c. Edgar Cayce believes that Jesus became the Christ in his thirtieth reincarnation, after shedding his bad karma.[152]

d. Levi Dowling said that Jesus underwent seven degrees of initiation (an occultic ceremony) in Egypt, the seventh degree being THE CHRIST.[153]

e. Elizabeth Clare Prophet says Jesus traveled to India as a child and underwent a learning process under Hindu gurus that led to his eventual Christhood.[154]

3. Jesus received spiritual training in the East.

a. Many New Agers say Jesus went East as a child (during the so-called lost years) to study and learn from Hindu gurus.

b. The idea that Jesus went East as a child received wide publicity in Shirley MacLaine's book, *Out on a Limb*: "A lot of people think that those eighteen missing years were spent traveling in and around India.... There are all kinds of legends and stories about a man who sounds just like Christ.... They say he became an adept yogi and mastered complete control over his body and the physical world around him."[155]

c. A manuscript discovered by Nicolas Notovitch documents Jesus' sojourn in India.

(1) The "legends and stories" to which Ryerson refers are rooted in a manuscript discovered in 1887 by Nicolas Notovitch (a Russian war correspondent) in a Buddhist monastery near the city of Leh, the capital of Ladakh in Northern India, along the Tibetan border.

(2) Notovitch, while at the monastery, had a monk read the manuscript to him, had it translated by an interpreter (since he did not understand Tibetan), and edited it into publishable form.[156] Notovitch's book, *The Life of Saint Issa*, was published in 1894.

---

[151]Spangler, *Reflections on the Christ*, p. 8; David Spangler, *Towards a Planetary Vision* (Forres, Scotland: Findhorn, 1977), p. 30.

[152]Philip J. Swihart, *Reincarnation, Edgar Cayce, and the Bible* (Downers Grove, Ill.: InterVarsity Press, 1978), p. 18.

[153]Dowling, p. 87.

[154]Elizabeth Clare Prophet, *The Lost Years of Jesus* (Livingston, Mont.: Summit Univ. Press, 1987), pp. 218–46.

[155]Shirley MacLaine, *Out on a Limb* (New York: Bantam Books, 1983), pp. 233–34, quoting Kevin Ryerson, her channeler.

[156] See Joseph Gaer, *The Lore of the New Testament* (Boston: Little, Brown, 1952), p. 118.

51

(a) *The Life of Saint Issa* chronicles the life of a monk named Issa (the Tibetan form of "Jesus"). Issa preached the same doctrines in India as he later did in Israel.

(b) Notovitch's book, based on the manuscript, says that when Issa was thirteen years old, he left his parents' home and studied for six years among the Brahmins in Indian holy cities. The priests of Brahma "taught him to read and understand the Vedas [India's most sacred scriptures], to cure by aid of prayer, to teach, to explain the holy scriptures to the people, and to drive out evil spirits from the bodies of men, restoring unto them their sanity."[157]

4. Jesus came as one of many enlightened "way-showers" for humanity.

  a. *The Aquarian Gospel of Jesus the Christ* quotes Jesus as saying: "I am your brother man just come to show the way to God."[158]

  b. David Spangler said "Jesus was one of a line of spiritual teachers, a line that continues today."[159]

C. *Refutation of Arguments Used by New Agers to Support Their Position on the Person of Jesus Christ*

  1. "Jesus" and "the Christ" are not two distinct persons or entities.

    a. Jesus and the Christ refer to one and the same person.

    b. Jesus did not "become" a Christ as an adult, but was *the one and only* Christ from the very beginning.

      (1) When the angel announced the birth of Jesus to the shepherds, he identified Jesus this way: "Today in the town of David a Savior has been born to you; *he is Christ* the Lord" (Luke 2:11, emphasis added).

      (2) Simeon, filled with the Holy Spirit, recognized the babe Jesus as Christ, in fulfillment of God's promise to him that "he would not die before he had seen *the Lord's Christ*" (Luke 2:26, emphasis added).

    c. The Greek word for Christ (*Christos*) means "anointed one," and is a direct parallel to the Hebrew word for Messiah; "Messiah" and "Christ" refer to the same person. John 1:41 says that Andrew went to his brother Simon and said to him: "'We have found *the Messiah*' (that is, *the Christ*)."

    d. Jesus made his identity *as* the Christ the primary issue of faith.

      (1) This is seen on two different occasions in the New Testament (Matt. 16:13–20; John 11:25–27).

157 Nicolas Notovitch; cited in Elizabeth Clare Prophet, *The Lost Years of Jesus*, p. 219.

158 Dowling, p. 54.

159 Spangler, *Reflections on the Christ*, p. 28.

(2) When Jesus was acknowledged as the Christ, he did not say to people, "You, too, have the Christ within." Instead, he warned them that others would come *falsely* claiming to be the Christ (Matt. 24:4–5, 23–25).[160]

2. Jesus did not go East.

a. Scholars have found Notovitch's theory to be completely fictitious.

(1) F. Max Müller: Müller was an orientalist at Oxford University who debunked Notovitch's claims. He was himself an advocate of Eastern philosophy and therefore could not be accused of having a Christian bias. Among the many problems he found with Notovitch's account, Müller cites a woman who visited the Buddhist monastery that contained the alleged manuscript, and according to her testimony (which Müller considered reliable): "There is not a single word of truth in the whole story! There has been no Russian here.... There is no life of Christ there at all!"[161]

(2) J. Archibald Douglas: Douglas was a professor at Government College in Agra, India. In 1895 he retraced Notovitch's steps at the Buddhist monastery. When the chief monk was asked if he was aware of a scroll on the life of Issa, he stated absolutely: "There is no such book in the monastery."[162] There is virtually no historical evidence that the single manuscript on which Notovitch claims to have based his entire book, *The Life of Saint Issa*, ever existed.

(3) Edgar J. Goodspeed: Goodspeed was a professor at the University of Chicago. In 1926 he examined Notovitch's *Life of Saint Issa* and, among other things, pointed out factual and historical errors as well as literary dependence on the New Testament Gospels.[163]

b. If Jesus learned how to do sensational miracles (like healing, controlling the weather, casting out demons, and raising the dead) from various teachers in the East, then why didn't these alleged teachers become well known like Jesus for having such Godlike powers? Why didn't throngs of people follow and worship them like they did Jesus of Nazareth?

c. The New Testament Gospels contradict the Jesus-goes-East theory.

(1) The New Testament Gospels not only show that Jesus did not go East but that he remained in and around Nazareth as he grew up.

---

160 Dean Halverson, *Crystal Clear* (Colorado Springs: NavPress, 1990), pp. 55–56.

161 F. Max Müller, "The Alleged Sojourn of Christ in India," *The Nineteenth Century* 36 (April 1894), pp. 515ff.

162 J. Archibald Douglas, "The Chief Lama of Himis on the Alleged 'Unknown Life of Christ,'" *Nineteenth Century* 38 (April 1896), pp. 667–77.

163 Edgar J. Goodspeed, *Modern Apocrypha* (Boston: Beacon Press, 1956), pp. 5–14.

(a) Luke 4:16 specifically says Jesus was "brought up" in Nazareth.

(b) Jesus was well known in his community. Mark 6:3 and Matthew 13:55 show how Jesus was known as "the carpenter's son." How could Jesus have been known in this way if he had been away in India for the thirteen years before his public ministry? Also, in the Gospels, the people in and around Nazareth display obvious familiarity with Jesus, as if they have had regular contact with him for a prolonged time. After Jesus spoke in a synagogue, the people said: "Isn't this Joseph's son?" (Luke 4:22), implying that those in the synagogue recognized Jesus as a local resident.

(2) Jesus' Jewish opponents never accused him of Eastern teaching.

(a) The Jewish leaders, among those who became angriest at Jesus, accused him of many offenses, but they never accused him of teaching or practicing anything learned in the East.

(b) The Jews considered Eastern teachings and practices to be idolatry and sorcery. Had Jesus actually gone to India to study under "the great Brahmins," this would have been excellent grounds for discrediting and disqualifying him regarding his claim to be the promised Jewish Messiah.

(c) If the Jewish leaders *could* have accused Jesus of this, they certainly would have.

3. Jesus was not "one of many" enlightened masters.

a. Jesus clearly considered himself uniquely and exclusively *humanity's only means* of coming into a relationship with God.

b. Jesus asserted: "I am the way and the truth, and the life. No one comes to the Father except through me" (John 14:6).

c. Peter boldly proclaimed that "salvation is found in no one else, for there is no other name under heaven given to men by which we must be saved" (Acts 4:12).

d. Jesus' exclusivity caused him to warn: "Watch out that no one deceives you. For many will come in my name, claiming, 'I am the Christ,' and will deceive many" (Matt. 24:4–5; cf. vv. 23–25).

D. Arguments Used to Prove the Biblical Doctrine of the Person of Jesus Christ

1. Jesus Christ is uniquely and eternally God.

a. Jesus' deity is proved by the names ascribed to him in Scripture.[164]

(1) Jesus is *Yahweh*.

---

[164] See Ron Rhodes, *Christ Before the Manger: The Life and Times of the Preincarnate Christ* (Grand Rapids: Baker, 1992), pp. 159–74.

(a) *Yahweh* is the Old Testament Hebrew term for Lord.

(b) Many scholars believe this name carries the idea of eternal self-existence (Ex. 3:14–15).[165] The use of this name with Jesus (John 8:58 [cf. Ex. 3:14]; Mark 1:2–4 [cf. Isa. 40:3]; Rom. 10:13 [cf. Joel 2:32]) shows that Jesus is eternally self-existent, and is *uniquely* God in the same sense the Father is.

(2) Jesus is *Kurios*.

(a) *Kurios* is the New Testament Greek word for "Lord."

(b) When used of Christ (Rom. 10:9; 1 Cor. 12:3; Phil. 2:11), it is intended to be taken as a parallel of the name *Yahweh* in the Old Testament.

(c) The name conveys Christ's absolute authority over humanity.

(3) Jesus is *Elohim*.

(a) *Elohim* is the Old Testament word translated "God."

(b) The term is used of Christ in Isaiah 9:6 and 40:3.

(c) It literally means "strong one."

(d) It pictures Christ as the powerful and sovereign Governor of the universe.

(4) Jesus is *Theos*.[166]

(a) *Theos* is the New Testament name for God.

(b) Every verse pointing to Christ as *Theos* (John 20:28; Acts 16:31, 34; Titus 2:13; Heb. 1:8; 2 Peter 1:1) in turn points to his identity as *Elohim* (i.e., God).

b. Jesus' deity is proved in that he has all the unique attributes of God (no mere human possesses such attributes).

(1) Self-existence: As the Creator of all things (John 1:3; Col. 1:16; Heb. 1:2), Christ himself must be *un*-created. Indeed, he is the uncaused First Cause.

(2) Immutability: Christ as God is unchangeable, and thus unchanging (Heb 1:10–12; 13:8).

(3) Omnipresence: Christ is *everywhere-present* (Matt. 18:19–20; 28:19–20; John 1:47–49). (Note: saying that Christ, as God, is everywhere-present is different from the pantheistic notion that God *is* all and all *is* God. Pantheism binds God to the universe; the attribute of omnipresence does not. In other words, while God is everywhere-present, he is nevertheless *distinct* from the universe.)

---

[165] E.g., John J. Davis, *Moses and the Gods of Egypt: Studies in Exodus* (Grand Rapids: Baker, 1986), pp. 72–73; Robert P. Lightner, *The God of the Bible* (Grand Rapids: Baker, 1978), p. 117.

[166] See Murray J. Harris, *Jesus as God* (Grand Rapids: Baker, 1993).

(4) Omniscience: Christ is *all-knowing*. Christ's omniscience is evident in John 13:19 where he claims deity based on his knowledge of Judas's future betrayal (cf. John 1:47–48; 2:23–25; 4:16–19; 6:64; 16:30; 21:17).

(5) Omnipotence: Christ is *all-powerful*. This attribute is proved in that Christ created the universe (see point c. below), exercised power over nature (Luke 8:22–25), over physical diseases (Mark 1:29–31), over demonic spirits (Mark 1:32–34), and over death by raising people from the dead (John 11:1–44).

(6) Sovereignty: Christ possesses sovereignty that can only belong to God. Peter speaks of the "angels, authorities, and powers in submission to him" (1 Peter 3:21–22).

c. Jesus' deity is proved in that he does things that only God can do (mere humans cannot do these things).

(1) Christ created the universe (John 1:3; Col. 1:16; Heb. 1:2; cf. Isa. 44:24).

(2) Christ also *sustains* the universe (Col. 1:17; Heb. 1:3): everything in the universe owes its continuing existence to his sustaining power and will.

(3) Christ forgives sins. Christ continually exercised the authority to forgive peoples' sins—something only God can do (Mark 2:1–12; Luke 7:48).

d. Conclusion: Since Christ has all the *names* of deity, possesses all the *attributes* of deity, and performs the *works* of deity, it is undeniable that Jesus Christ is God Almighty.

2. The incarnation of Jesus Christ is both personal and permanent.

a. The Incarnation is that glorious event in which the preexistent, eternal Son of God took upon himself a human nature, born of the Virgin Mary.

b. Contrary to the typical New Age scenario (a three-year incarnation of an *impersonal* Christ in a *human* adult Jesus), Scripture asserts that Christ—*personal* and *eternal* God—became incarnate through the Virgin Birth (Luke 1:35), and *this* incarnation lasts forever.

c. After Christ was resurrected, he made many appearances to people, proving beyond any doubt the continuance of his human-divine union.

(1) Jesus ascended *bodily* (in a glorified *human* body) into heaven after the resurrection (Luke 24; John 20:24–28; Acts 1:1–11).

(2) When Christ returns in glory, he will sit on the throne as the *Son of Man* (Matt. 26:63–64; Acts 7:56). Therefore, Jesus' human-divine union lasts forever (see 1 Tim. 2:5).

3. Jesus Christ did not come to earth to be a mere "way-shower," but rather as *Prophet*, *Priest*, and *King*.

   a. Jesus' role as Prophet

      (1) Jesus called himself a prophet (Matt. 13:53–57).

      (2) Jesus communicated God's message to humankind, thus fulfilling the role of a prophet.

      (3) Jesus was the greatest of all prophets, for he not only communicated God's message to humankind, he also revealed God in his life and person (John 1:14–18).

   b. Jesus' role as Priest

      (1) Christ's priestly office relates to his work as Savior and Mediator.

      (2) Christ as Priest offered a sacrifice for humankind's sin through the shedding of his own blood (Matt. 26:26–28).

      (3) Christ as Priest represents his people before the Father (Heb. 5:1–10).

      (4) Christ as Priest *continues today* to intercede for us before the Father (Heb. 7:23–25).

   c. Jesus' role as King

      (1) Christ as King is the Supreme Ruler to whom all of Scripture points (e.g., 2 Sam. 7:1–16; Dan. 7:13–14; Matt. 2:1–2; Luke 1:29–33).

      (2) During his three-year ministry, Jesus proclaimed the good news of the kingdom of God to thousands of people (Matt. 9:35). The kingdom of God was one of his central teachings.

      (3) Christ's role as King will come to full fruition at the Second Coming when he comes as KING OF KINGS AND LORD OF LORDS (Rev. 19:16).

4. Jesus Christ rose bodily from the dead.

   a. The biblical evidence for Christ's bodily resurrection is abundant.

      (1) The tomb was empty (Luke 24:2–3).

      (2) Jesus showed his disciples "his hands and side" (e.g., John 20:19–20).

      (3) On three different occasions Jesus is recorded eating (Luke 24:40–43).

      (4) "He [bodily] appeared to more than five hundred of the brothers at the same time" (1 Cor. 15:6).

   b. The resurrection of Jesus Christ is the heart of historic Christianity.

      (1) Jesus "was declared with power to be the Son of God by his resurrection from the dead" (Rom. 1:4).

(2) The resurrection confirmed the truth of all that Jesus said while he was on earth (Matt. 28:6).

    (3) Christ's resurrection guarantees the future resurrection of all humanity, as well as the approaching judgment of all who reject him (1 Cor. 15:20–22; Acts 17:31).

  c. No other religious leader ever rose from the dead.

    (1) No other leader of any world religion—Muhammad, Buddha, Zoroaster, Krishna, or anyone else—was ever resurrected from the dead.

    (2) This in itself shows that Jesus was not "one of many" holy men.

V. The Doctrine of Man

A. *The New Age Position on Man Briefly Stated*

1. Man is God.
2. This is based on *pantheism* (all is God) and *monism* (all is one).
3. Because man is God, he has unlimited potential.
4. Man, as God, can create his own reality.

B. *Arguments Used by New Agers to Support Their Position on Man*

1. The idea that man is God follows from the *monistic* (all is one) and *pantheistic* (all is God) view of reality.

  a. Since *all is one* and *all is God*, man must logically be God.

  b. Of course, not all people *realize* they are God, but that is a problem of ignorance, not a reflection of reality.

  c. Shirley MacLaine said: "I am God, because all energy is plugged in to *the same source*. We are each aspects of that source. We are all part of God."[167]

  d. Theodore Roszak said that a goal of the New Age movement is "to awaken to the god who sleeps at the root of the human being."[168]

2. Revelations received through channelers indicate that man is God.

  a. Ramtha (a 35,000-year-old Lemurian knight), as channeled through J. Z. Knight, said: "You be unequivocally God! You say you are tired of hearing the word? Never tire of hearing the word; you cannot say it nearly enough.... Do not reckon yourself less, for if you do you will become the lessness of your reckoning."[169]

---

[167] MacLaine, *Dancing in the Light*, p. 354, italics added.

[168] Theodore Roszak, *Unfinished Animal* (New York: Harper & Row, 1977), p. 225.

[169] "Ramtha" with Douglas James Mahr, *Voyage to the New World* (Friday Harbor, Wash.: Masterworks, 1985), p. 24.

b. Channeler Kevin Ryerson says: "We are one with God.... We are co-creators with God. Everything comes from God and everything returns to God."[170]

3. Jesus himself taught that human beings are God.

a. John 10:34

(1) In John 10:34, Jesus said to some of his Jewish critics: "Is it not written in your Law, 'I have said you are gods'?"

(2) David Spangler exults that "we can be the God that Jesus proclaimed us to be: 'Ye are Gods.'"[171]

(3) Spangler explains that such godhood is *the* revelation for the New Age: "And that [the divinity of man] ultimately is *the* revelation, the eternal revelation, the only revelation. Everything else leads to that, contributes to it in some fashion."[172]

b. John 8:58

(1) In John 8:58 Jesus said to some of his Jewish critics: "I tell you the truth ... before Abraham was born, I am!" (John 8:58).

(2) When Jesus said this, Mark and Elizabeth Clare Prophet assert he did so "in the full awareness that the 'I AM' of him had always been the Christ. And he also knew that the permanent part of each one of you was and is that same Christ."[173]

(3) Mark and Elizabeth Clare Prophet tell us that "Jesus' I AM Presence looks just like yours. This is the common denominator. This is the coequality of the sons and daughters of God. He created you equal in the sense that he gave you an I AM Presence—he gave you a Divine Self."[174]

4. Because human beings are God, they have unlimited potential.

a. Shirley MacLaine said, "You are unlimited. You just don't realize it."[175]

b. George Trevelyan said that each human being is "an eternal droplet of the Divine Ocean, and that potentially it can evolve into a being who can be a *co-creator* with God."[176]

c. Jesus himself taught that human beings have unlimited potential.

(1) Levi Dowling's *Aquarian Gospel of Jesus the Christ* quotes Jesus as saying: "Because I have the power to do these things

---

[170] Ryerson and Harolde, pp. 73–74.

[171] Spangler, *Reflections on the Christ*, p. 73.

[172] Spangler, *Reflections on the Christ*, p. 73.

[173] Mark and Elizabeth Clare Prophet, *The Lost Teachings of Jesus 2* (Livingston, Mont.: Summit Univ. Press, 1988), p. 254.

[174] Prophet and Prophet, *The Lost Teachings of Jesus 2*, p. 62.

[175] MacLaine, *Dancing in the Light*, p. 133.

[176] Trevelyan, *Operation Redemption*, p. 83.

is nothing strange. All men may gain the power to do these things.... So man is God on earth, and he who honors God must honor man."[177]

    (2) Dowling also cites Jesus as saying: "I came to show the possibilities of man; what I have done all men may do, and what I am all men shall be."[178] And again, "What I can do all men can do. Go preach the gospel of the omnipotence of Man."[179]

5. Because man is God, he can create his own reality.

    a. David Gershon and Gail Straub, authors of the best-selling book *Empowerment: The Art of Creating Your Life as You Want It*, are representative: "Your thoughts are always creating your reality—it's up to you to take charge of your thoughts and consciously create a reality that is fulfilling."[180]

    b. Devotees to Seth (an entity that speaks through channelers) said, "We literally create our reality through the beliefs we hold, so by changing those beliefs, we can change reality."[181]

C. Refutation of Arguments Used by New Agers to Support Their Position on Man

1. Man's ignorance of alleged divinity proves that humans are *not* God.

    a. "The fact that a man 'comes to realize' he is God proves that he is not God. If he were God he would never have passed from a state of unenlightenment to a state of enlightenment as to who he is."[182]

    b. To put it another way, "God cannot bud. He cannot blossom. God has always been in full bloom. That is, God is and always has been God."[183]

2. Human beings do *not* display divine qualities.

    a. If it were true that all people possess divinity and are unlimited beings who can create their own reality, then one would expect them to display qualities similar to those *known* to be true of God. This is not the case.

    b. Consider these obvious differences between God and man:

        (1) God is *all-knowing* (Matt. 19:26), but man is limited in knowledge (Job 38:1–4). If man were all-knowing there would be no need for New Agers to buy or read New Age books.

---

[177] Dowling, p. 126.

[178] Dowling, p. 15.

[179] Dowling, p. 263.

[180] Gershon and Straub, pp. 21; see all pp. 22, 25, 36.

[181] Jennifer Donovan, "Seth Followers Spoon Up Fun in Their Goal to Enjoy Living," *Dallas Morning News*, July 1, 1986.

[182] Norman L. Geisler and Ronald M. Brooks, *Christianity Under Attack* (Dallas: Quest Publications, 1985), p. 43.

[183] Geisler and Amano, p. 18.

(2) God is *all-powerful* (Rev. 19:6), but man is weak (Heb. 4:15).

(3) God is *everywhere-present* (Ps. 139:7–12), but man is confined to a single space at a time (e.g., John 1:50).

(4) God is *holy* (Rev. 4:8), but (fallen) man's "righteous" deeds are as filthy garments before God (Isa. 64:6).

(5) God is *eternal* (Ps. 90:2), but man was created at a point in time (Gen. 1:1, 21, 26–27).

(6) God is *truth* (John 14:6), but (fallen) man's heart is deceitful above all else (Jer. 17:9).

(7) God is characterized by *justice* (Acts 17:31), but (fallen) man is lawless (1 John 3:4; cf. Rom. 3:23).

(8) God is *love* (1 John 4:16), but (fallen) man is plagued with many vices like jealousy and strife (1 Cor. 3:3).

c. Conclusion: Human beings show that they are not unlimited gods by their attributes.

3. Jesus *did not* teach that human beings are gods.

a. When Jesus said, "Is it not written in your Law, 'I have said you are gods'?" (John 10:34), he was alluding to Psalm 82.

(1) In Psalm 82 we find God's judgment against the evil Israelite judges.

(2) In Psalm 82:6, Asaph, speaking of these unjust human judges, says: "I said, 'You are "gods"; you are all sons of the Most High.' But you will die like mere men; you will fall like every other ruler."

(3) The Hebrew word for "god" (*Elohim*) can sometimes be used of human beings. The judges were called "gods" because they pronounced life and death judgments against people.

(4) Clearly, though, Asaph is using *irony* in this verse. He is saying in effect: "I have called you 'gods,' but in fact you will die like the men that you really are."

(5) Conclusion: When Jesus alluded to this psalm in John 10, he was saying that what the Israelite judges were called in irony and in judgment, *he is in reality*.

b. When Jesus said, "Before Abraham was born, I am" (John 8:58), he was implicitly and uniquely ascribing the divine name *Yahweh* to himself.

(1) The backdrop of this is that "I AM" and "Yahweh" are equated in Exodus 3:14–15.

(a) The phrase "I am" is not the word *Yahweh*. However, I AM (in v. 14) and *Yahweh* (v. 15) are both derivatives of the same Hebrew verb "to be."

(b) The name "I AM WHO I AM" which God revealed to Moses in verse 14 is intended as a full expression of his eternal nature, and is then shortened to *Yahweh* in verse 15.

(2) The Jews wanted to stone Jesus to death because they recognized that he was uniquely identifying himself as *Yahweh* (death by stoning was the prescribed penalty for blasphemy in Old Testament Law—Lev. 24:13–16). Note that the Jews did not understand Jesus to be teaching that *they too* were identified as "I AM."

(3) Many scholars believe the name *Yahweh* conveys the idea of eternal self-existence.[184]

(4) In John 8:58 Jesus deliberately contrasted the created origin of Abraham with his own eternal, uncreated nature. This adds significance to Jesus' encounter with the Jews, given their veneration of Abraham. Notice that in contrasting himself with Abraham, Jesus was clearly revealing that Abraham *was not* "I AM" as he was.

(5) Conclusion: Jesus' claim to be "I AM" distinguished him from all humanity.

4. *No human being* comes even remotely close to God's greatness and majesty.

   a. The teaching of Scripture flatly contradicts the idea that man is God.

   b. The encounter with Pharaoh illustrates well God's sovereignty over man.

      (1) God instructed Moses to tell Pharaoh: "I will send the full force of all my plagues against you and against your officials and your people, *so you may know that there is no one like me in all the earth*" (Ex. 9:14, italics added).

      (2) Note that these words were spoken to a man who was himself considered a god. The Pharaoh was thought to be the incarnation of the Egyptian sun god, Re, and was therefore considered a god in his own right.[185]

   c. Herod's folly in Acts 12:21–23 shows that man is not God.

      (1) After Herod gave a public address, the people shouted, "'This is the voice of a god, not of a man.' Immediately, because Herod did not give praise to God, an angel of the Lord struck him down, and he was eaten by worms and died."

      (2) Clearly, God does not look lightly on humans who pretend to be divine.

---

[184] E.g., Davis, pp. 72–73; Lightner, p. 117.
[185] Davis, p. 81.

(3) Herod's behavior stands in stark contrast to Paul and Barnabas's example in Acts 14. When the people prepared to worship Paul and Barnabas for having healed a man, "they tore their clothes and rushed out into the crowd, shouting: 'Men, why are you doing this? We too are *only men, human like you.* We are bringing you good news, telling you to turn from these worthless things to the living God, who made heaven and earth and sea and everything in them" (vv. 14–15, italics added). Paul and Barnabas not only denied that they were gods, they also pointed to the true God who created the universe, thereby drawing a clear distinction between the Creator and the creation. Pantheism and monism are thus refuted in this passage.

D. Arguments Used to Prove the Biblical Doctrine of Man

1. Human beings are creatures, created in the "image of God" (Gen. 1:26–27).

   a. Though human beings are created in God's image, this does not mean that they are divine or can become gods.

   b. Genesis 1:26–27 teaches that people are created in God's image in the sense that they are a finite reflection of God in his rational nature (Col. 3:10), in his moral nature (Eph. 4:20–24), and in his dominion over creation (Gen. 1:27–28). In the same way that the moon reflects the brilliant light of the sun, so finite human beings (as created in God's image) reflect God *in these aspects.*

2. Human beings are intrinsically weak, helpless, and dependent upon God.

   a. The apostle Paul affirms: "Not that we are competent *in ourselves* to claim anything for ourselves, but our competence *comes from God*" (2 Cor. 3:5).

   b. Jesus says, "I am the vine; you are the branches. If a man remains in me and I in him, he will bear much fruit; *apart from me you can do nothing*" (John 15:5).

3. Human beings—since the Fall (Gen. 3)—have a radical propensity for evil.

   a. Romans 3:23—"All have sinned and fall short of the glory of God."

   b. Jeremiah 17:9—The human heart is "deceitful above all things and *beyond cure.*"

   c. Romans 7:18—"I [Paul] know that *nothing good lives in me*, that is, in my sinful nature. For I have the desire to do what is good, but *I cannot carry it out.*"

   d. Romans 5:6—Thanks be to God, though, for "at just the right time, *when we were still powerless*, Christ died for the ungodly."

4. God wants people to recognize that they are finite creatures.

a. People must recognize that they are *creatures* who are responsible to their *Creator*. As the psalmist says, "Know that the LORD is God. It is he who made us, and we are his; we are his people, the sheep of his pasture" (Ps. 100:3).

b. The recognition of creaturehood should also lead to humility and a worshipful attitude toward God. "Come, let us bow down in worship; let us kneel before the LORD our Maker; for *he* is our God" (Ps. 95:6–7, italics added).

c. Humility is the mark of one who is properly related to God.

(1) Micah 6:8—"What does the LORD require of you? To act justly and to love mercy and to walk humbly with your God."

(2) James 4:6—"God opposes the proud but gives grace to the humble."

(3) 1 Peter 5:6—"Humble yourselves, therefore, under God's mighty hand."

VI. The Doctrines of Sin and Salvation

A. *The New Age Position on Sin and Salvation Briefly Stated*

1. Human beings do not have a sin problem.

2. Men and women's primary problem is that they are ignorant or unaware of their divinity.

3. Since human beings do not have a sin problem, they are *not* in need of salvation from sin.

4. Consequently, Jesus did not die on the cross to provide salvation from sin.

5. The only thing people need is enlightenment regarding their divinity.

6. Through reincarnation a person is eventually "reunited" with God.

B. *Arguments Used by New Agers to Support Their Position on Sin and Salvation*

1. The New Age worldview denies the reality of sin.

a. Since all is one *(monism)*, the distinction between good and evil disappears.

b. Since *pantheism* (all is God) is true, then human beings—since they are divine—are a law unto themselves and cannot be held guilty of "sin."[186]

2. Revelations from the "other side" indicate there is no sin. In a conversation Shirley MacLaine had with an entity called "Higher Self," she was told: "Until mankind realizes there is, in truth, no good and there is, in truth, no evil—there will be no peace."[187]

---

[186] Spangler, *Revelation*, p. 13.
[187] MacLaine, *Dancing in the Light*, p. 357.

3. Human beings are not in need of *salvation* from sin.

a. Since there is no sin, any talk of the need for salvation is meaningless.

b. Annie Besant said we should "surrender all the fallacious ideas of forgiveness, vicarious atonement, divine mercy, and the rest of the opiates which superstition offers to the sinner."[188]

4. Jesus did not die on the cross to provide salvation from sin.

a. Benjamin Creme states: "To my way of thinking, the Christian churches have released into the world a view of the Christ which is impossible for modern people to accept: as the one and only Son of God, sacrificed by a loving Father to save us from the results of our sins—a blood sacrifice, straight out of the old Jewish dispensation."[189]

b. Mark and Elizabeth Clare Prophet also dismiss the idea that Jesus died on the cross to atone for the sins of man.

(1) They say: "The erroneous doctrine concerning the blood sacrifice of Jesus—which he himself never taught—has been perpetuated to the present hour. God the Father did not require the sacrifice of His son Christ Jesus ... as an atonement for the sins of the world; nor is it possible according to cosmic law for any man's sacrifice to balance either the original sin or the subsequent sins of the one or the many."[190]

(2) The crucifixion of Jesus must be completely reinterpreted.

(a) Since there was so much bad karma on the earth at the time Jesus lived, the planet was in danger of self-destruction.

(b) Jesus therefore needed to be crucified to help balance the planetary karma.[191]

5. The problem is that people are simply ignorant of their divinity.

a. Shirley MacLaine said: "The tragedy of the human race was that we had forgotten we were each Divine."[192]

b. Joseph Campbell, in his best-selling book *The Power of Myth*, said: "We are all manifestations of Buddha consciousness, of Christ consciousness, only we don't know it."[193]

---

188 Annie Besant, *Karma* (London: Theosophical Publishing Society, 1904), p. 23.

189 Creme, p. 47.

190 Mark and Elizabeth Clare Prophet, *Climb the Highest Mountain* (Los Angeles: Summit Univ. Press, 1974), pp. 279–80.

191 Prophet and Prophet, *Climb the Highest Mountain*, p. 443. It seems odd and inconsistent to say "it is not possible" for one man's sacrifice to "balance" man's sin problem, but that one man's sacrifice *can* "balance" planetary karma.

192 MacLaine, *Out on a Limb*, p. 347.

193 Joseph Campbell, *The Power of Myth* (Garden City, N.Y.: Doubleday, 1988), p. 57.

6. The only thing that human beings need is *enlightenment* regarding their divinity.

    a. This enlightenment or change of consciousness is called various things, such as *attunement, personal transformation, new consciousness, self-realization, God-realization*, and *at-one-ment*.

    b. Various consciousness-altering techniques are used to cause this change in consciousness:

        (1) Meditation techniques

        (2) Centering (see Part I, Section II.F.2.c. for definition)

        (3) Guided imagery/visualization

        (4) Yoga

        (5) Hypnosis

        (6) Chanting

        (7) Ecstatic dancing

        (8) Conversations with disembodied entities through channelers

    c. These means of altering one's consciousness are sometimes called "psychotechnologies." Marilyn Ferguson says, "All of these approaches might be called *psychotechnologies*—systems for a deliberate change in consciousness."[194]

7. Reincarnation eventually can lead to one's reuniting with God.

    a. The word *reincarnation* literally means to "come again in the flesh." The process of reincarnation (continual rebirths in human bodies) continues until the soul has reached a state of perfection and merges back with its source (God or the Universal Soul).

    b. When bad things happen in one's life, it is the outworking of karma.

        (1) As noted earlier,[195] karma refers to the debt a soul accumulates because of good or bad actions committed during one's life (or past lives).

        (2) If one accumulates bad karma, he or she will be reincarnated in a less desirable state. If one accumulates good karma, he or she will be reincarnated in a more desirable state.

    c. Shirley MacLaine says, "Reincarnation is like show business. You just keep doing it until you get it right."[196]

    d. Jesus himself taught reincarnation or "cyclical rebirth."

        (1) Matthew 11:14—Jesus said that "if you are willing to accept it, he [John the Baptist] is the Elijah who was to come."

---

194 Ferguson, p. 87.

195 See Part I, Section II.C.3.

196 MacLaine, *Out on a Limb*, p. 233.

(2) John 3:3—Jesus said, "I tell you the truth, no one can see the kingdom of God unless he is born again."

C. Refutation of Arguments Used by New Agers to Support Their Position on Sin and Salvation

1. Because the monistic/pantheistic worldview is false (see arguments in Section III.C.), the ethical conclusions flowing from it are erroneous also.

   a. Christianity begins with the distinction between the Creator and the creation.

      (1) Contrary to the monistic/pantheistic worldview, there is an eternal distinction between the [holy] Creator and the creation (Isa. 45:18).

      (2) Because man has in fact sinned against God (Rom. 3:23), man is very much in need of salvation (Rom. 5:18; 6:23).

   b. Christian morality begins with God *as a personal being*.

      (1) Because the God of Scripture *is* a personal being, moral terms *do* apply in regard to how we relate to him. Because the person of God is holy and we *are not* holy, alienation is real and we are morally culpable.

      (2) This is directly contrary to the monistic/pantheistic worldview, which does away with God's personality: Moral terms such as right and wrong simply do not apply to an impersonal force, any more than we hold a hurricane morally responsible for its actions. Moral issues are not involved when relating to an impersonal force. Lying and stealing are irrelevant for relating to electrical energy, and the same is true of the New Age god.[197]

2. New Agers have misrepresented Christ's teaching about sin and salvation. (See Section D below.)

   a. The biblical Jesus did not teach that human beings have merely an *ignorance* problem but a grave *sin* problem that is altogether beyond their means to solve (Matt. 12:33–34; Luke 11:13).

   b. The biblical Jesus also taught that his mission was to provide atonement for the sins of humanity by his sacrificial death on the cross (Matt. 26:26–28).

   c. The biblical Jesus further taught that salvation is found only by placing one's faith in him (John 3:16) (*not* by enlightenment).

3. There are many problems with reincarnation's salvation-by-works doctrine.

   a. Practical problems

      (1) Why does one get punished for something he or she cannot remember having done in a previous life?

---

[197] Halverson, *Crystal Clear*, p. 38.

(2) If the purpose of karma is to rid humanity of its selfish desires, then why has there not been a noticeable improvement in human nature after all the millennia of reincarnations?

(3) If reincarnation and the law of karma are so beneficial on a practical level, as New Agers claim, how do they explain the immense and *ever-worsening* social and economic problems in India (including widespread poverty, starvation, disease, and horrible suffering), where reincarnation has been systematically taught throughout its history?

b. Biblical problems

(1) The apostle Paul states, "We are confident, I say, and would prefer to be away from the body and at home with the Lord" (2 Cor. 5:8). At death, then, the Christian goes into the presence of the Lord.

(2) Unbelievers at death go to a place of suffering (Luke 16:19–31).

(3) Hebrews 9:27 says, "Man is destined to die once, and after that to face judgment." Each human being *lives once* as a mortal on earth, *dies once*, and then *faces judgment*. He or she does not have a second chance by reincarnating into another body.

(4) Contrary to the New Age teaching of reincarnation, the biblical Jesus predicted his resurrection from his earliest ministry. In John 2:19 Jesus said to some Jews: "Destroy this temple [my body], and I will raise it again in three days."

(5) When Jesus said, "if you are willing to accept it, he [John the Baptist] is the Elijah who was to come" (Matt. 11:14), he was not teaching reincarnation. Luke 1:17 points out that the ministry of John the Baptist was carried out "in the *spirit and power* of Elijah" (italics added). New Agers conveniently forget that John the Baptist, when asked if he was Elijah, flatly answered, "No." (John 1:21).

(6) Regarding being "born again" (John 3:3), the context clearly shows that Jesus was referring to a *spiritual* rebirth or regeneration. In fact, the phrase *born again* carries the idea of "born from above," and can even be translated that way. Jesus clarified his meaning by affirming that "flesh gives birth to flesh, but the Spirit gives birth to spirit" (v. 6).

D. Arguments Used to Prove the Biblical Doctrines of Sin and Salvation

1. Jesus taught that people are sinful.

a. The biblical Jesus taught that human beings have a grave sin problem that is altogether beyond their means to solve (see below).

b. Jesus taught that human beings, since the Fall, are evil (John 3:19–20) and that man is capable of great wickedness (Mark 7:20–23).

　(1) People are utterly lost (Luke 19:10).

　(2) People are sinners (Luke 15:10).

　(3) People are in need of repentance before a holy God (Mark 1:15).

　(4) People need to be born again (John 3:3, 5, 7).

c. Jesus often spoke of sin in metaphors that illustrate the havoc sin can wreak in one's life.

　(1) Blindness (Matt. 23:16–26)

　(2) Sickness (Matt. 9:12–13)

　(3) Slavery (John 8:34)

　(4) Darkness (John 8:12; 12:35–46)

d. Jesus taught that sin is a *universal condition* and that all people are guilty before God (Luke 7:37–48).

e. Jesus also taught that both inner thoughts and external acts render a person guilty (Matt. 5:27–28).

　(1) Jesus said that from within the human heart comes evil thoughts, sexual immorality, theft, murder, adultery, greed, malice, deceit, envy, slander, arrogance, and folly (Mark 7:21–23).

　(2) Jesus affirmed that God is fully aware of every person's sin, in both external acts and inner thoughts; nothing escapes his notice (Matt. 22:18; Luke 6:8; John 4:17–19).

2. Jesus taught that he died for our sins.

a. He said that his mission was to provide atonement for human sin by his sacrificial death (Mark 10:45; John 12:23–27; Luke 19:10).

　(1) Jesus perceived his death as a sacrificial offering for the sins of humanity; his blood was "poured out for many for the forgiveness of sins" (Matt. 26:26–28).

　(2) Jesus took his sacrificial mission with utmost seriousness, for he knew that without him, humanity would certainly perish (Matt. 16:24–25) and spend eternity apart from God in a place of great suffering (Matt. 10:28; 23:33; 25:41).

b. *Others* also perceived his mission as one of sacrificial atonement.

　(1) When John saw Jesus walking toward him to be baptized in the Jordan River, John said, "Look, the Lamb of God, who takes away the sin of the world!" (John 1:29).

　(2) Mary, the mother of Jesus, even perceived her son as the Savior (Luke 1:47).

　(3) The Samaritans recognized that Jesus was "the Savior of the world" (John 4:42).

3. Jesus taught that salvation comes by placing faith in him, not by enlightenment.

   a. By his sacrificial death on the cross, Jesus took the sins of the entire world on himself and made salvation available to everyone (1 John 2:2).

   b. This salvation is not automatic.

      (1) Only those who choose to believe in Christ are saved: "For God so loved the world that he gave his one and only Son, that *whoever believes in him* shall not perish but have eternal life" (John 3:16, italics added), and "everyone who looks to the Son and *believes in him* shall have eternal life, and I will raise him up at the last day" (John 6:40, italics added).

      (2) Choosing *not* to believe in Jesus leads to eternal condemnation: "Whoever believes in [the Son] is not condemned, but whoever does not believe stands condemned already because he has not believed in the name of God's one and only Son" (John 3:18).

VII. The Doctrine of the Second Coming of Christ

A. *The New Age Position on the Second Coming of Christ Briefly Stated*

1. The Second Coming will not involve the reappearing of the person of Jesus Christ.

2. Some New Agers believe in a *singular* "Second Coming" involving an individual known as Maitreya, who will take the primary leadership role in the New Age.

3. Other New Agers believe in a *mass* "Second Coming," by which they mean a mass incarnation of the cosmic Christ in all of humanity.

B. *Arguments Used by New Agers to Support Their Position on the Second Coming of Christ*

1. View #1: Maitreya is the Christ, who is coming again.

   a. Some New Agers, such as Benjamin Creme, believe in a singular "Second Coming" involving an individual known as Maitreya, who will take the primary leadership role in the New Age.

   b. From 1977 to the present Creme has traveled around the world proclaiming that the coming of Maitreya (the Christ) is imminent.

      (1) Maitreya, says Creme, is the leader of the "Planetary Hierarchy"—a group of exalted Ascended Masters (see definition at Part I, Section III.B.1.c.[1]) who guide mankind's spiritual evolution.

      (2) Maitreya has been living incognito among human beings since 1977 when his consciousness entered a specially created human-like body called the "Mayavirupa."

   c. Creme announced the Christ in newspapers worldwide.

      (1) In April of 1982, a full-page ad appeared in fourteen major newspapers around the world—from Rome to Jerusalem, from Kuwait to Karachi, from New York to Los Angeles—announcing that "The Christ is Now Here."

      (2) The ad, sponsored by Creme's Tara Center in Los Angeles, California, predicted that "within the next two months [the Christ] will speak to humanity through a worldwide television and radio broadcast. His message will be heard inwardly, telepathically, by all people in their own language."[198]

   d. Maitreya was to declare his message on a specific day.

      (1) Maitreya was to deliver his message on the "Day of Declaration," after which time a new era of peace and happiness would begin.

      (2) This Christ would come not as a religious, political, economic, or social leader, but as an "educationalist" who would solve all the world's problems in these areas and usher in a New Age of love, peace, and shared wealth.

   e. Human apathy prevented Maitreya's scheduled appearance.

      (1) Obviously 1982 has come and gone and the Christ has yet to appear.

      (2) The reason the Christ did not appear is that the *media* prevented it by refusing to report the event.

      (3) Since the media represents humanity, the media's apathy shows the *broader* apathy of humanity.

      (4) Creme says that since the Christ's manifestation cannot occur against man's wishes, his coming has been delayed.

   f. The Christ will soon reveal himself.

      (1) From 1982 to 1990, Creme continued to maintain that the Christ would soon reveal himself to humanity.

      (2) In April 1990, the Tara Center distributed a press release saying that Maitreya presented his credentials as the Messiah before 200 media representatives and world leaders at an April 21–22 conference in London.

      (3) Creme says that the April 1990 conference is a prelude to the Christ's Day of Declaration, though the date has not been revealed.

  2. View #2: The Second Coming is a mass "incarnation" of the cosmic Christ in all of humanity.

---

[198] Elliot Miller, "Benjamin Creme and the Reappearance of the Christ," *Forward*, 6:1, p. 3.

a. This is the view of New Agers such as David Spangler and George Trevelyan.

b. Spangler says "the Second Coming is occurring now in the hearts and minds of millions of individuals of all faiths as they come to realize this spiritual presence within themselves and each other."[199]

c. Spangler refers to this Second Coming as a "mass" coming.

(1) "The second coming of the Christ in our age will be fundamentally, most importantly, a mass coming. It will be the manifestation of a consciousness within the multitudes."[200]

(2) The Second Coming has nothing to do with a *physical* event, for it is something that happens on the level of *consciousness*.

(3) Spangler writes, "Within each of us is the Second Coming, revealing itself more powerfully as time goes on."[201] He says, "the Second Coming is a universal experience, not confined to any one person or group of people."[202]

d. The second coming of Christ relates to an *impersonal*, cosmic Christ.

(1) Spangler says that the Christ "is not a person; *it* is a life which quickens a comparable Christ life within each of us, revealing *itself* through group activity and a greater love flow within individuals."[203]

(2) Spangler says "the Christ and the Second Coming do not refer to specific people but to *universal events and principles manifesting within all life*" (italics added).[204]

e. Spangler sometimes refers to the Christ's habitation in humanity as a "mass *incarnation*."

(1) "This incarnation will not take the form of a specific individual; rather many individuals will manifest the energy of this presence to varying degrees. The work of the Christ principle is planetary."[205]

(2) Such an incarnation is not unlike that which occurred in Jesus. Spangler says Jesus "was the prototype or the expression of the reality of the Christ consciousness which is inherent in us all."[206]

[199] David Spangler, *Cooperation with the Spirit* (Middleton, Wisc.: Lorian Press, 1982), p. 4.

[200] Spangler, *Towards a Planetary Vision*, p. 108.

[201] Spangler, *Revelation*, p. 141.

[202] Spangler, *Revelation*, p. 141.

[203] Spangler, *Revelation*, p. 141.

[204] Spangler, *Revelation*, p. 176.

[205] David Spangler, *Conversations with John* (Middleton, Wisc.: Lorian Press, 1983), p. 4.

[206] Spangler, *Reflections on the Christ*, pp. 14–15.

(3) As such, human beings can actually become "the Word made flesh." Spangler says that the Word will eventually be made *all flesh.*[207]

C. Refutation of Arguments Used by New Agers to Support Their Position on the Second Coming of Christ

1. Creme's claim that Maitreya has appeared is unsubstantiated.

   a. Although the Tara Center claimed that Maitreya presented his credentials as the Messiah before 200 media representatives and world leaders at a conference in London in April 1990,[208] Creme never revealed precisely where the meeting took place or who the 200 participants were.

   b. Not one article has appeared in any publication alluding to the event, even though fifty of the participants allegedly were reporters. Apparently, the media's apathy toward Creme's Christ has not diminished!

2. New Agers present contradictory views of the Second Coming.

   a. New Agers present contradictory, irreconcilable scenarios and interpretations of the Second Coming based on their alleged "revelations" from the other side.

      (1) Rudolf Steiner claimed in the 1920s (based on "revelations" from the other side) that the Christ would not come again as an individual but would come again *spiritually* in all humanity.

      (2) Responding to Steiner's scenario, Benjamin Creme said that the Christ *later* decided (by 1945, some twenty years after Steiner's death) that he would come again, *not* in all humanity, but in his own "body of manifestation."[209] Creme learned of this change of plans through "revelations" from the Christ.

      (3) Ironically, David Spangler—a modern-day disciple of Steiner—is also receiving current "revelations" that the Christ is not coming again in one body, but—like Steiner said—in *all of humanity.*

      (4) Whose "revelation" would New Agers say is correct?

   b. New Agers could try to counter that Christians also disagree about the end times.

      (1) For example, they could point out that Christians differ as to whether the Rapture will take place *before, during,* or *after* the Tribulation period (1 Thess. 4:13–17).

      (2) However, regardless of *secondary* issues such as the timing of the Rapture, Christians of all persuasions have *always* agreed

---

[207] Spangler, *Reflections on the Christ*, p. 86.

[208] See B.1.f.(2) above.

[209] Creme, *The Reappearance of the Christ*, pp. 54–55.

on the *essential* issues of the end times. That is, they agree that Christ is physically coming again, that there will be a judgment, and that there will be an eternal state.

3. Scripture teaches that *the same Jesus* who ascended into heaven will come again at the Second Coming (Acts 1:11). (See Section D below for a detailed discussion of the Second Coming.)

4. The Second Coming of Christ will not be a coming of an invisible, cosmic Christ in all of humanity but rather will be a *visible, physical* coming of the glorified Jesus.

5. The Second Coming will be a glorious event that is accompanied by magnificent signs in the heavens.

6. The timing of the Second Coming (according to Scripture) is entirely in God's hands, not in the hands of human beings whose "apathy" can prevent the Christ from "emerging."

7. The Second Coming *will not* be a universal experience in the sense that all people will incarnate the cosmic Christ but it *will* be a universal experience in the sense that "every eye" will see Christ coming in the clouds of heaven.

D. Arguments Used to Prove the Biblical Doctrine of the Second Coming of Christ

1. The same Jesus who ascended into heaven will come again at the Second Coming. In Acts 1:11 some angels appeared (in the form of men) to Christ's disciples after he ascended and said to them: "Men of Galilee . . . why do you stand here looking into the sky? *This same Jesus*, who has been taken from you into heaven, will come back in the same way you have seen him go into heaven" (italics added).

2. The Second Coming of Christ will be a *visible, physical, bodily* coming of the glorified Jesus.

   a. Words used to describe the Second Coming show that it is visible, physical, and bodily.

      (1) *Parousia*

         (a) One of the common Greek words used to describe the Second Coming is *parousia.*

         (b) This word has several nuances of meaning, including "present," "presence," "being physically present," "coming to a place," and "arriving."[210] *Vine's Expository Dictionary of Biblical Words* says that *parousia* "denotes both an 'arrival' and a consequent 'presence with.'"[211]

         (c) The word *parousia* is typically used in the New Testament of a visible, physical coming (1 Cor. 16:17; 2 Cor. 7:6–7).

---

[210] Bauer, p. 635.

[211] *Vine's Expository Dictionary of Biblical Words*, ed. W. E. Vine, Merrill F. Unger, and William White (Nashville: Nelson, 1985), p. 111.

    (d) Greek scholar Joseph Thayer defines *parousia*: "In the [New Testament the word is used] especially of the advent, [that is] the future, *visible, return from heaven of Jesus*, the Messiah, to raise the dead, hold the last judgment, and set up formally and gloriously the kingdom of God."[212]

(2) *Apokalupsis*

    (a) This word carries the basic meaning of "revelation," "visible disclosure," "unveiling," and "removing the cover" from something that is hidden.

    (b) The word is used of Christ's second coming in 1 Peter 4:13: "But to the degree that you share the sufferings of Christ, keep on rejoicing; so that also at the *revelation* of his glory, you may rejoice with exultation" (NASB).

(3) *Epiphaneia*

    (a) In the New Testament, *epiphaneia* carries the basic meaning of "to appear."

    (b) *Vine's Expository Dictionary of Biblical Words* says *epiphaneia* literally means "a shining forth." The dictionary provides several examples from ancient literature of how the word points to a *physical, visible appearance* of someone.[213]

    (c) The word *epiphaneia* is used several times by the apostle Paul concerning Christ's visible second coming. In Titus 2:13, Paul speaks of "looking for the blessed hope and the *appearing* of the glory of our great God and Savior, Christ Jesus" (NASB), and in 1 Timothy 6:14, Paul urges Timothy to "keep the commandment without stain or reproach until the *appearing* of our Lord Jesus Christ (NASB)."

    (d) Significantly, Christ's *first* coming—which was both *bodily* and *visible* ("the Word become flesh")—was called an *epiphaneia* (2 Tim. 1:10). In the same way, Christ's second coming will be both *bodily* and *visible*.

(4) Conclusion: The consistent testimony of Scripture—whether the word *parousia*, *apokalupsis*, or *epiphaneia* is used—is that Christ's second coming will be visible to all humankind (see Dan. 7:13; Zech. 9:14; 12:10; Matt. 16:27–28; 24:30; John 1:51; 2 Tim. 4:1).

b. Christ will be seen by all at his Second Coming. The Second Coming will not be a universal experience in the sense that all people will incarnate the Christ but it will be a universal experience in the sense that "every eye" will witness it. "Look, he is coming

---

[212] J. H. Thayer, *A Greek-English Lexicon of the New Testament* (Grand Rapids: Zondervan, 1963), p. 490.

[213] *Vine's Expository Dictionary of Biblical Words*, p. 32.

with the clouds, and every eye will see him, even those who pierced him; and all the peoples of the earth will mourn because of him" (Rev. 1:7).

   c. The Second Coming will be a glorious event, accompanied by magnificent signs in the heavens. Matthew 24:29–30: "Immediately after the distress of those days 'the sun will be darkened, and the moon will not give its light; the stars will fall from the sky, and the heavenly bodies will be shaken.' At that time the sign of the Son of Man will appear in the sky, and all the nations of the earth will mourn. They will see the Son of Man coming on the clouds of the sky, with power and great glory."

3. The timing of the Second Coming is entirely in God's sovereign hands.

   a. Before he ascended into heaven, Jesus said to the disciples: "It is not for you to know the times or dates the Father has set by his own authority" (Acts 1:7).

   b. Jesus said, "No one knows about that day or hour, not even the angels in heaven, nor the Son, but only the Father" (Matt. 24:36).

   c. Scripture clearly states that the Second Coming is not in the hands of human beings whose "apathy" can prevent the Christ from "emerging."[214]

4. The biblical Second Coming is the antithesis of the new age Second Coming.

   a. One is Christ-exalting; the other is human-exalting.

   b. One is glorious and majestic; the other is nebulous and mystical.

   c. One involves a sovereign King of kings who shall reign forever; the other lacks any distinctive identity and makes no claim to have authority to reign over humanity.

   d. One will be seen by every eye; the other involves a mystical (invisible) incarnation of the cosmic Christ into all humanity (or, according to other New Agers, involves Maitreya, who apparently cannot convince the media to report on his coming).

   e. One will come in judgment against those who have rejected him; the other never speaks of judgment and welcomes people of all religions and creeds.

   f. One will establish a glorious, eternal, God-centered Kingdom; the other seeks to bring about a temporal, human-centered New Age.

   g. One will come according to God's sovereign timing; the other cannot come until mankind sufficiently prepares for his coming.

---

[214] Some Christians have taught that Christ cannot come again until Christians communicate the Gospel to the whole world. Though it is clear that the Gospel *will* be communicated to all nations prior to the Second Coming (Matt. 24:14; Mark 13:10), Scripture is nevertheless clear that the timing of the Second Coming is *entirely* in God's sovereign hands (Acts 1:7).

5. Conclusion: In view of the above, Jesus' warning about false Christs takes on increased significance (Matt. 24:4–5). His words to his followers were succinct and spoken with utmost seriousness: "Watch out that no one deceives you" (v. 4). He knew that many would attempt such a deception (Matt. 24:23–25).

Part III:
Witnessing Tips

I. Suggested Approaches to Witnessing to New Agers

A. Common Ground

1. Begin your discussion on a topic on which you likely have compatible views. By doing this, the door may be opened for you to then move on to evangelistic ground (see Paul's approach with the Athenians in Acts 17).

2. Possible common ground discussions to focus on could include ecology, rejection of humanism, patriotism, human rights, or social justice.

B. Problems with Mysticism and Mystical "Revelations"

1. Mystical revelations are too uncertain.

   a. R. D. Clements says that subjective human experience is insufficient as a ground upon which to build our knowledge of God: "It is too uncertain in every way. The Christian points instead to history, and in particular to Jesus Christ, as the arena of God's personal, objective self-revelation and the proper ground for man's knowledge of God."[215]

   b. The Bible, on the other hand, stresses the importance of objective, certain, historical revelation.

2. Spiritual deception is possible through mysticism.

   a. Those who place their faith in mysticism seem blind to the possibility of spiritual deception.

   b. The question we must ask New Agers is: What if that which you assume to be genuine "god-consciousness" is in fact less than God, or at worst Satan, the great impersonator of God and the father of lies?

   c. 2 Corinthians 4:4 tells us that "the god of this age [Satan] has blinded the minds of unbelievers, so that they cannot see the light of the gospel of the glory of Christ, who is the image of God."

   d. The fact that revelations obtained through New Age mysticism consistently contradict the biblical account supports the idea that Satan is behind them.

---

[215] R. D. Clements, *God & the Gurus* (Downers Grove, Ill.: InterVarsity Press, 1975), pp. 38–39.

e. R. D. Clements warns, "Satan is quite capable of providing spiritual experiences for the undiscerning. And there is evidence that some, if not all, of the mystic experiences obtained by using Eastern meditative techniques are being exploited by Satan in this way."[216]

C. New Age Pantheism and the Problem of Evil

1. If all is one and all is God, then good and evil are one. Such a view, however, fails the test of real life. For example, how can it be said that Hitler's extermination of six millions Jews was a part of God (pantheism)?

2. Rabi Maharaj speaks of the ethical dissatisfaction he felt regarding his monistic, pantheistic worldview: "My growing awareness of God as the Creator, separate and distinct from the universe he had made, contradicted the Hindu concept that God was everything, that the Creator and the Creation were one and the same. If there was only One Reality, then [God] was evil as well as good, death as well as life, hatred as well as love. That made everything meaningless, life an absurdity. It was not easy to maintain both one's sanity *and* the view that good and evil, love and hate, life and death were One Reality."[217]

Rabi eventually became a Christian after hearing the Good News of the gospel.

D. Weakness of New Age Relativity[218]

1. New Agers say they do not believe in absolute truth [i.e., all truth is relative].

   a. They believe that "*anything* can be true for the individual, but *nothing* can be true for everyone."[219]

   b. As Elliot Miller puts it, New Agers believe "it is the height of presumption to think that one knows the key truth for all people. On the other hand, it is the apex of love to 'allow' others to have their own 'truth.' 'Thou shalt not interfere with another's reality' might be called the First Commandment of New Age revelation."[220]

2. Point out that the "all truth is relative" position is not logical. (See Section II below for how to break the "relativity barrier.")

   a. The statement "all truth is relative" could mean that *it is an absolute truth that all truth is relative*. Such a statement is self-defeating (since there supposedly are no absolute truths) and therefore is false.

---

216 Clements, p. 42.

217 Rabi Maharaj, "Death of a Guru," *Christian Research Newsletter* 3:3, p. 2.

218 See also Part I, Section II.C. on New Age ethics.

219 Elliot Miller, "Breaking Through the 'Relativity Barrier,'" *Christian Research Journal* (Winter/Spring 1988), p. 7.

220 Miller, "Breaking Through the 'Relativity Barrier,'" p. 7.

b. Second, one could understand this as saying that *it is a relative truth that all truth is relative*. Such a statement is ultimately meaningless. If all truth is relative, then it must be relative to some other truth. But if *all* truth is relative, then this second truth (to which the first is relative) must in turn be relative to yet another truth, which is itself relative to another truth, and so on. One thus falls into a bottomless pit of relative truths from which one can never emerge: one cannot affirm anything at all.

3. Point out to the New Ager that absolute morals are grounded in the absolutely moral God of the Bible.

   a. Scripture tells us: "Be holy as the Father in heaven is holy" (Matt. 5:48 paraphrase).

   b. Moral law flows from the moral Law-giver of the universe—God.

   c. God stands against the moral relativist whose behavior is based on "whatever is right in his own eyes" (Deut. 12:8 NASB; Judg. 17:6; 21:25; Prov. 21:2).

E. **The Personal God of Christianity and the Impersonal "It" of the New Age Movement**

   1. Gordon Lewis says, "an impersonal energy does not provide as adequate an explanation of either the fact or value of personal human existence. Only against a personal God can your friends understand their sin. Only a personal God can pronounce a verdict of guilt and judgment. Only a personal God can create personal agents responsible for their thoughts, desires, and actions."[221]

   2. Emphasize to the New Ager that the idea of an impersonal God is utterly unsatisfying because one cannot have a personal relationship with a force.

   3. You might share your own testimony of what your personal relationship with God means to you.

F. **Problems with Reincarnation**

   1. Explain that belief in reincarnation is inconsistent with a monistic (all is one) worldview.

   As Douglas Groothuis notes, "if all is one, and individuality is ultimately illusory (monism), how can individual souls be reincarnated from one body to another? The 'oneness' teaching contradicts the concept of the individual; yet individual souls are required for a coherent doctrine of karma and personal responsibility."[222]

   2. Point out the scriptural teaching that each human being *lives once, dies once*, and then *faces judgment* (Heb. 9:27).

---

[221] Gordon Lewis, "The New Age," in *Evangelizing the Cults*, ed. Ron Enroth (Ann Arbor, Mich.: Servant, 1990), p. 62.

[222] Douglas Groothuis, "Evangelizing New Agers," *Christian Research Journal* (Winter/Spring 1987), p. 7.

3. Explain that Jesus taught that people decide their eternal destiny *in a single lifetime* (Matt. 25:31–46). This is precisely why the apostle Paul emphasized that "now is the day of salvation" (2 Cor. 6:2).

4. After noting the problems of believing in reincarnation, point the New Ager to the biblical teaching of resurrection.

   a. Read key portions of Luke 24 aloud to the New Ager.

   b. Ask the person what he or she thinks it means when the risen Christ said to the disciples: "Look at my hands and my feet. It is I myself! Touch me and see; a ghost does not have flesh and bones, as you see I have" (v. 39).

G. The Uniqueness of Jesus Christ

1. Christians worship Jesus as God.

   Point out that while New Agers typically revere Jesus as a mere human being who sought godhood (or Christhood), Christians worship Jesus as the eternal God (John 1:1) who became human (John 1:14), and then atoned for our sins at the cross, rose from the grave, and ascended back to heaven, far above all other beings.

2. Jesus was not a mere enlightened master.

   Jesus was and continues to be the *"Light of the world "* (John 8:12). True "enlightenment" involves believing in and following the one who is the Light of the world.

3. Jesus taught absolute truth.

   Jesus clearly did not believe that each person could have his own truth. Jesus taught that there is *only one truth* that truly saves (John 14:6; cf. Acts 4:12; 1 Tim. 2:5). The absolute truth is that *Jesus* is the only way to eternal salvation.

H. Sin is the Real Problem

1. Show that man's problem is *sin* and not just an ignorance of divinity.

2. New Agers stand morally condemned before a holy and righteous God (Rom. 3:23), like all human beings apart from Christ.

3. New Agers are especially guilty of blurring the distinction between the Creator and the creation, resulting in sinful idolatry (Rom. 1:25).

4. Because of the sin problem, New Agers—like all other human beings who refuse to trust in the true Christ of Scripture—face a future day of judgment (Acts 17:31).

5. Just as the apostle Paul called the pantheists at Athens to repent,[223] so we must call New Age pantheists to repent and turn to the true God of Scripture (Acts 17).

---

[223]According to Acts 17:18, Paul addressed Stoic philosophers in Athens, who held to a form of pantheism. See F. F. Bruce, *The Book of the Acts* (Grand Rapids: Eerdmans, 1986), p. 350.

I. Befriend New Agers

1. As Gordon Lewis puts it: "the most effective ministry comes out of personal relationships. When you have taken time to build a relationship with a New Ager, your witness is more likely to be well received. . . . Friendship evangelism has been found to be one of the most effective ways of gaining permanent converts to Jesus Christ."[224]

2. 2 Timothy 2:24–26 tells us: "The Lord's servant *must not quarrel*; instead, he must be *kind to everyone*, able to teach, *not resentful*. Those who oppose him he must *gently instruct*, in the hope that God will grant them repentance leading them to a knowledge of the truth, and that they will come to their senses and escape from the trap of the devil, who has taken them captive to do his will" (italics added).

II. Breaking the Relativity Barrier: A Sample Dialogue

In a "witnessing tips" article in the *Christian Research Journal*, Elliot Miller suggested the following approach:

Christian: Do you mean that there are no moral principles that are absolutely true and right for everyone?

New Ager: We each create our own reality and have our own truth.

Christian: OK, let's pretend I'm a "pedophile"—it's a part of my reality to "love" children in every way possible, including sexually. So, while you're at work I'm going to invite your children into my home to play a "game" that I've made up. Is that all right with you?

New Ager: It most certainly is not! It would be part of my reality to report you to the police.

Christian: Why? After all, it's the reality I've sovereignly chosen to create for myself. What gives you the right to interfere in the reality of another god?

New Ager: Simple. Your reality is infringing on my children's reality.

Christian: But according to your belief, before they incarnated *they* chose *you* as their parent and they also chose whatever happens to them, including my act, and you've no right to interfere.

New Ager: I do too, in *this* case.

Christian: Can you see my point now? Something within you *knows* that such an act is wrong in and of itself.

New Ager: You're right.

Christian: But that can *only* be so if there are absolute rights and wrongs *independent* of our personal realities. Yet, try as you may, you will not find a ground for such moral absolutes in your worldview. Your God

---

[224]Lewis, p. 59.

is impersonal, "beyond good and evil." And, since in your view we are all *equally* gods, my truth about any subject is as good as your truth. So, New Age beliefs fail the test of human experience.[225]

III. Common Mistakes Christians Make in Speaking with New Agers

A. False Assumptions

1. Do not assume that just because New Agers use words that sound Christian—such as "Jesus," "Christ," "atonement," "ascension," and so forth—that they are using these words in the same way you are. Ask New Agers to define these words. Then point out how their definitions fall short of the biblical definitions.

2. Do not assume all New Agers believe exactly the same things. As Gordon Lewis notes, "your friends and relatives may be involved in the New Age movement to very different degrees and may, or may not, be involved in some of its practices. So it is important not to assume that you know what every New Ager believes or does. Talk with each person you seek to reach individually."[226]

B. Unhelpful Behaviors

1. Do not approach a New Ager with a spiritual chip on your shoulder.

   a. A "spiritual chip" is the communication of the feeling that you are looking down on the New Ager because you have something he or she does not have. Such an attitude will turn off the New Ager as fast as anything you could imagine.

   b. Especially for Christians who have thoroughly prepared themselves by learning scriptural answers to New Age errors, the temptation may be to intellectually *talk down* at the New Ager instead of *conversing with* the New Ager. Do not let this happen.

   c. Be on your guard against pride and make every effort to *remain humble* during your witnessing encounter.

2. Do not lose your patience, regardless of how uncomprehending you may think the New Ager is. Dr. Walter Martin advises: "Remember how dense you and I were—until the Lord managed to break through. Because [New Agers] are bound in the chains of slavery to sin, you need to be patient. And being patient means being willing to go over something ten times if necessary, believing that the Lord will bless your efforts."[227]

---

[225] Lewis, p. 59.

[226] Lewis, p. 56.

[227] Lewis, p. 56.

Part IV:
Selected Bibliography

I. Books Written by New Agers

Bailey, Alice A. *The Reappearance of the Christ*. New York: Lucis, 1948.

Argues that mankind's destiny is being guided by Ascended Masters. Jesus himself is believed to be one such Master.

Besant, Annie. *Esoteric Christianity*. Wheaton, Ill.: Theosophical Publishing House, 1970.

Offers a mystical interpretation of Christianity that sees the human Jesus as distinct from the Cosmic Christ.

Blavatsky, H. P. *The Key to Theosophy*. Pasadena, Calif.: Theosophical University Press, 1972.

Focuses on the three goals of the Theosophical Society: (1) form a universal brotherhood, (2) do comparative study of world religions, science, and philosophy, and (3) explore the psychic and spiritual powers latent in man.

Capra, Fritjof. *The Turning Point: Science, Society, and the Rising Culture*. New York: Simon & Schuster, 1982.

Shows the alleged parallels between modern physics and Eastern mysticism.

Creme, Benjamin. *The Reappearance of the Christ and the Masters of Wisdom*. Los Angeles: Tara Center, 1980.

Argues that the second coming of Christ has already occurred in the person of Lord Maitreya.

Dowling, Levi. *The Aquarian Gospel of Jesus the Christ*. Santa Monica, Calif.: DeVorss, 1907.

Argues that Jesus came, not to free people from their sins, but to display and prove the possibilities of man. Promotes the New Age doctrines of pantheism (all is God) and monism (all is one).

Ferguson, Marilyn. *The Aquarian Conspiracy*. Los Angeles: J. P. Tarcher, 1980.

Explores New Age activities and inroads into Western culture and suggests that these changes signal a transformation so radical that it may lead to an entirely new phase in human evolution.

Fox, Matthew. *The Coming of the Cosmic Christ*. San Francisco: Harper & Row, 1988.

Espouses "Creation Spirituality"—a system of thought characterized by mysticism, feminism, pantheism (God is in all), and environmentalism.

Gershon, David, and Gail Straub. *Empowerment: The Art of Creating Your Life as You Want It*. New York: Dell, 1989.

Suggests that the secret of getting what you want in life may be found in "empowerment," based on the effective use of guided imagery and positive affirmations (positive self-talk).

Keys, Donald. *Earth at Omega: Passage to Planetization*. Boston: Branden Press, 1982.

Suggests that humanity is on the verge of a giant evolutionary leap that will lead to a global civilization.

Lipnack, Jessica, and Jeffrey Stamps. *Networking*. Garden City, N.Y.: Doubleday, 1982.

Catalogs some 1,500 diverse New Age networks. Stresses the benefits of networking in accomplishing common goals.

Prophet, Elizabeth Clare. *The Lost Years of Jesus*. Livingston, Mont.: Summit Univ. Press, 1987.

Argues that Jesus went to India as a child to learn from Eastern gurus how to perform miracles.

Ryerson, Kevin, and Stephanie Harolde. *Spirit Communication: The Soul's Path*. New York: Bantam Books, 1989.

Teaches readers how to become New Age channelers (or mediums).

Satin, Mark. *New Age Politics*. New York: Dell, 1978.

Suggests that the "new politics" (*holistic* politics) will arise out of diverse movements (including environmental, feminist, and human potential groups) that can unite to work toward a common goal.

Spangler, David. *Emergence: The Rebirth of the Sacred*. New York: Dell, 1984.

Traces the historical emergence of the New Age worldview in Western society.

Steiner, Rudolf. *Knowledge of the Higher Worlds and Its Attainment*. Spring Valley, N.Y.: Anthroposophic Press, 1947.

Teaches that people possess "the truth" within themselves. By cultivating one's occult powers through spiritual exercises, anyone can allegedly become a "master of clear vision," thereby gaining extraordinary spiritual insight.

Thompson, William Irwin. *Passages About Earth: An Exploration of the New Planetary Culture*. New York: Harper Colophon, 1981.

Traces the emergence of the New Age worldview in Western society. Suggests that our worldview is presently moving from "civilization" to "planetization."

Trevelyan, George. *A Vision of the Aquarian Age*. Walpole, N.H.: Stillpoint, 1984.

Focuses on the "emerging spiritual worldview." Promotes pantheism (all is God) and monism (all is one).

Wilbur, Ken. *Up from Eden*. Boulder, Colo.: Shambhala, 1983.

Provides insights on the New Age worldview and belief system.

Zukav, Gary. *The Dancing Wu Li Masters*. New York: Morrow, 1979.

Focuses on New Age quantum physics.

II. Books Written About the New Age by Others

Chandler, Russell. *Understanding the New Age*. Dallas: Word, 1991.

One of the best overall treatments of the different aspects of the New Age movement. Includes a helpful glossary of New Age terms. Very readable.

Groothuis, Douglas. *Confronting the New Age*. Downers Grove, Ill.: InterVarsity Press, 1988.

A comprehensive treatment on how to reach a New Ager for Christ and how to counteract the influences of the New Age movement in our society.

———. *Unmasking the New Age*. Downers Grove, Ill.: InterVarsity Press, 1986.

The best overall treatment of the different aspects of the New Age movement. Must reading for those interested in studying the movement in more detail.

Halverson, Dean C. *Crystal Clear*. Colorado Springs: Navpress, 1990.

A study guide that focuses on the "big picture" of the New Age movement. Ideal for use in small groups. Includes scriptural responses to different aspects of the New Age worldview.

Hoyt, Karen, and the Spiritual Counterfeits Project. *The New Age Rage*. Old Tappan, N.J.: Fleming H. Revell, 1987.

A general treatment of the New Age movement by the staff of the Spiritual Counterfeits Project.

Kjos, Berit. *Under the Spell of Mother Earth*. Wheaton, Ill.: Victor, 1992.

A thorough treatment on the revival of paganism and goddess-worship in our culture.

Miller, Elliot. *A Crash Course on the New Age Movement*. Grand Rapids: Baker, 1989.

A former New Ager discusses major aspects of the New Age movement. Scholarly and thoroughly documented.

Rhodes, Ron. *The Counterfeit Christ of the New Age Movement*. Grand Rapids: Baker, 1990.

Thoroughly examines various aspects of the New Age view of Christ, including the popular ""Jesus Goes East" theory.

Part V:
Parallel Comparison Chart

New Age	The Word of God

Continuing Revelation

"Never has there been a time, cycle, or world period when there was not the giving out of the teaching and spiritual help which human need demanded."[1]

"Dear friends . . . I felt I had to write and urge you to contend for *the faith* that was *once for all* entrusted to the saints" (Jude 3, italics added).

Esoteric Interpretation of Scripture

"The greatest teachers of divinity agree that nearly all ancient books [including the Bible] were written symbolically and in a language intelligible only to the initiated."[2]

"We do not use deception, *nor do we distort the word of God*. On the contrary, by *setting forth the truth plainly* we commend ourselves to every man's conscience in the sight of God" (2 Cor. 4:2).

God

"God is the sum total of all that exists in the whole of the manifested and unmanifested universe."[3]

"It is I who *made* the earth and *created* mankind upon it. My own hands *stretched out* the heavens; I *marshaled* their starry hosts" [God is distinct from the creation] (Isa. 45:12, italics added).

1. Bailey, p. 147.
2. Cited in Sire, p. 108.
3. Creme, p. 115.

89

God (continued)

"The nations of the earth see God from different points of view, and so he does not seem the same to everyone. ... You Brahmans call him Parabrahm; in Egypt he is Thoth; and Zeus is his name in Greece; Jehovah is his Hebrew name."[4]

"There is not one place, one thing, one time that does not include his presence. God is the life within all things. He contains all things."[5]

"Who among the gods is like you, O LORD[Jehovah]? Who is like you—majestic in holiness, awesome in glory, working wonders?" (Ex. 15:11).

"Who is like the LORD our God [Jehovah], the One who sits enthroned on high, who stoops down to look on the heavens and the earth?" (Ps. 113:5–6).

"God is *in heaven* and you are *on earth* " (Eccl. 5:2, italics added).

"They exchanged the truth of God for a lie, and worshiped and served created things rather than the Creator—who is forever praised. Amen" (Rom. 1:25).

Humanity Is God

"I think the whole purpose of life is to reown the Godlikeness within us; the perfect love, the perfect wisdom, the perfect understanding."[6]

[Yahweh speaking] "See now that I myself am He! *There is no god besides me*. I put to death and I bring to life, I have wounded and I will heal, and no one can deliver out of my hand" (Deut. 32:39, italics added).

"You shall have no other gods before me" (Ex. 20:3).

---

4. Dowling, p. 56.
5. D. Spangler, *Revelation*, p. 150.
6. Galyean, "Educators Look East," *SCP Journal*, p. 29.

Humanity Is God (continued)

"You are God. You know you are Divine. But you must continually remember your Divinity and, most important, act accordingly."[7]

"On the appointed day Herod, wearing his royal robes, sat on his throne and delivered a public address to the people. They shouted, 'This is the voice of a god, not of a man.' Immediately, because Herod did not give praise to God, an angel of the Lord struck him down, and he was eaten by worms and died" (Acts 12:21–23).

"We are all part of God. We are all individualized reflections of the God source. God is us and we are God."[8]

[Yahweh speaking] "I will send the full force of my plagues against you and against your officials and your people, so you may know that *there is no one like me in all the earth*" (Ex. 9:14, italics added).

Sin

"The tragedy of the human race was that we had forgotten we were each Divine" [i.e., there is no *sin*, just *ignorance*].[9]

"If we claim to be without sin, we deceive ourselves and the truth is not in us" (1 John 1:8).

"There is no evil—only the lack of knowledge."[10]

"Until mankind realizes that there is, in truth, no good and there is, in truth, no evil, there will be no peace."[11]

"Dear friend, do not imitate *what is evil* but *what is good*. Anyone who does *what is good* is from God. Anyone who does *what is evil* has not seen God" (3 John 11, italics added).

---

7. MacLaine, *Out on a Limb*, p. 209.
8. MacLaine, *Dancing in the Light*, p. 354.
9. MacLaine, *Dancing in the Light*, p. 347.
10. MacLaine, *Dancing in the Light*, p. 259.
11. MacLaine, *Dancing in the Light*, p. 357.

Salvation

"Your thoughts are always creating your reality—it's up to you to take charge of your thoughts and consciously create a reality that is fulfilling" [self-salvation].[12]

"You are unlimited. You just don't realize it" [no need of salvation from sin].[13]

"For it is by grace you have been saved, through faith—and this *not from yourselves*, it is the gift of God— *not by works*, so that no one can boast" (Eph. 2:8–9).

"All of us have become like one who is unclean, and all our righteous acts are like filthy rags; we all shrivel up like a leaf, and like the wind our sins sweep us away" (Isa. 64:6).

Reincarnation

"Reincarnation is like show business. You just keep doing it until you get it right."[14]

"Man is destined to die once, and after that to face judgment" (Heb. 9:27).

Jesus

"Jesus was one of a line of spiritual teachers, a line that continues today."[15]

"Jesus, Buddha, Zoroaster, Lao Tse, Muhammad and many others known and unknown to history are representatives of divinely anointed individuals representing part of the goal for the human race."[16]

Jesus answered, "I am the way and the truth and the life. *No one comes to the Father except through me*" (John 14:6, italics added).

"Salvation is found in *no one else*, for there is *no other name* under heaven given to men by which we must be saved" (Acts 4:12, italics added).

"For there is one God and *one mediator* between God and men, the man Christ Jesus" (1 Tim. 2:5, italics added).

---

12. Gershon and Straub, pp. 21– 36.
13. MacLaine, *Dancing the the Light*, p. 133.
14. MacLaine, *Out on a Limb*, p. 233.
15. Spangler, *Reflections on the Christ*, p. 28.
16. J. Spangler, "Compass Points," p. 4.

Jesus (continued)

"To my way of thinking, the Christian Churches have released into the world a view of the Christ which is impossible for modern people to accept: as the one and only Son of God, sacrificed by a loving Father to save us from the results of our sins—a blood sacrifice, straight out of the old Jewish dispensation."[17]

"This is my *blood* of the covenant, which is *poured out for many for the forgiveness of sins*" (Matt. 26:28, italics added).

"For you know that it was not with perishable things such as silver or gold that you were *redeemed* from the empty way of life handed down to you from your forefathers, but with the *precious blood of Christ, a lamb without blemish or defect*" (1 Peter 1:18–19, italics added).

The Second Coming

"To the Christians he will be the second coming of Christ, to the Jews the Messiah, the Imam Mahdi to the Muslims, Krishna to the Hindus, and to the Buddhists he will be the fifth Buddha."[18]

[Angels speaking to disciples] "Men of Galilee," they said, "why do you stand here looking into the sky? *This same Jesus*, who has been taken from you into heaven, *will come back in the same way you have seen him go into heaven*" (Acts 1:11, italics added).

"The Second Coming is occurring now in the hearts and minds of millions of individuals of all faiths as they come to realize this spiritual presence within themselves and each other."[19]

"Immediately after the distress of those days 'the sun will be darkened, and the moon will not give its light; the stars will fall from the sky, and the heavenly bodies will be shaken.' At that time the sign of the Son of Man will appear in the sky, and all the nations of the earth will mourn. They will see the Son of Man coming on the clouds of the sky, with power and great glory" (Matt. 24:29–30).

---

17. Creme, p. 47.
18. Miller, "Benjamin Creme and the Reappearance of the Christ," pp. 3, 7.
19. D. Spangler, *Cooperation*, p. 4.

The Second Coming (continued)

"The second coming of the Christ in our age will be fundamentally, most importantly, a mass coming. It will be the manifestation of a consciousness within the multitudes."[20]

"Look, he is coming with the clouds, and every eye will see him, even those who pierced him; and all the peoples of the earth will mourn because of him. So shall it be! Amen" (Rev. 1:7).

"On his robe and on his thigh he has this name written: KING OF KINGS AND LORD OF LORDS" (Rev. 19:16).

---

20. D. Spangler, *Planetary Vision*, p. 108.

A FALCON GUIDE®

Camping
Utah

Donna Lynn Ikenberry

FALCONGUIDE®

GUILFORD, CONNECTICUT
HELENA, MONTANA

AN IMPRINT OF THE GLOBE PEQUOT PRESS

*A*FALCONGUIDE®

Cover photo of Canyonlands National Park by Cheyenne Rouse
All other photographs by Donna Lynn Ikenberry

Library of Congress Cataloging-in-Publication Data
Ikenberry, Donna Lynn.
    Camping Utah / Donna Lynn Ikenberry.—1st ed.
      p. cm.—(A Falcon guide)
    ISBN-13: 978-0-7627-1080-5
    ISBN-10: 0-7627-1080-2
      1. Camping—Utah—Guidebooks. 2. Camp sites, facilities, etc.—Utah—Directories. 3. Utah—Guidebooks. I. Title. II. Series.

GV191.42.U8 I54 2001
647.9792'09'025—dc21

                                                                2001040721

Manufactured in the United States of America
First Edition/Third Printing

Text pages printed on recycled paper.

The author and The Globe Pequot Press assume no liability for accidents happening to, or injuries sustained by, readers who engage in the activities described in this book.

For my dad

Acknowledgments

As with every project I undertake, I must first give thanks to God for keeping me safe, and for allowing the undertaking to happen in the first place. How very fortunate I was to spend the spring and summer in Utah, exploring its every corner while checking out more than 300 public campgrounds.

Second, I must acknowledge my husband, Mike Vining. This kind, wonderful, loving man, not only checked out campgrounds with me but also chauffered me from one campground to the next, driving about 6,000 miles while I took notes, planned our routes, and so on.

Though our families weren't able to join us in Utah, they were always in our hearts. I want to thank my parents, Donald and Beverly Ikenberry, for their never-ending love and endless support. While I traveled full time for sixteen years, my parents forwarded my mail, relayed messages, and did most of my banking for me. On a special note, this book is dedicated to my dad. I've dedicated several books to my mom—this time the honor goes to him. Thanks Dad. I love you both.

My brother Don Ikenberry has always been there for me, too. A big thank-you goes to him, and to his wife, Yolie Gutierrez. My youngest brother, David Ikenberry, and his wife, Laura, and children, Andrew and Sarah, must also be remembered.

My family has gotten bigger since I met and married Mike. Thanks Mom and Dad, Roger and Arlene Vining, daughters Teri Woodman and Lori Sturdavant, son-in-laws Blaine Woodman and Gary Sturdavant, and grandsons Mitchell Vining, Dillon Sturdavant, Kyle Alan Sturdavant, and Victor Woodman for coming into my life.

Additional thanks go to the folks at the U.S. Forest Service, the Bureau of Land Management, the Bureau of Reclamation, the Utah State Parks Department, and the National Park Service, who so patiently answered my questions and mailed me information when I requested it. I also want to thank the state of Utah for granting us free day-use passes to all of its state parks.

And of course, I am also indebted to the folks at Falcon and The Globe Pequot Press for their continued help and support. Thanks everyone!

Contents

Christmas Meadow in Wasatch-Cache National Forest.

Introduction

When I said yes to writing a guide to Utah's public campgrounds, both disappointment and elation welled up inside me at the same time. Why? I was disappointed because I had told myself I'd take a break from writing books. I had spent every summer since 1986 working on either a new book or a book revision, and I felt as though I needed a break.

At the same time I was thrilled at the prospect of spending time in Utah, because it was a state I'd left pretty much unexplored. For years I had wanted to see the region, to get to know it intimately. I wanted to say I'd actually lived in the state for a few months.

I signed the contract knowing I would be driving thousands of miles over the period of a few months, but I also knew I'd spend time exploring the region both on foot and by bicycle. Utah is an outdoor enthusiast's paradise, and I knew I'd have to get off the beaten path on a regular basis. What I didn't know was that I would enter the state with my very own chauffeur and personal rock climbing guide.

A couple of months before arriving in Utah, Mike Vining and I got married on top of Mauna Kea, the highest point in Hawaii. We like to say we are on a fifty-year honeymoon, so I suppose you could say we spent the first part of that honeymoon in Utah, climbing magnificent rock, hiking many a trail, riding our bicycles both off and on the road, and observing wildlife. We checked out all of Utah's campgrounds together, with Mike doing more than just the driving—he checked out many a toilet for me, too.

Am I glad I made the decision to go ahead and write this book? I am. In fact, I wouldn't have missed it for anything.

Utah was all I had imagined and a whole lot more. A potpourri of landscapes, the Beehive State affords everything from world-famous redrock canyons to heaven-bound mountains, elaborate river systems, lonely desert, fertile valleys, and a maze of rock spires and pinnacles just waiting to be explored.

Several thousand years ago the place we today know as Utah was inhabited by nomadic desert peoples. About A.D. 1300 the Ancestral Puebloan Culture reached its peak; later Native American tribes, including the Ute, Paiute, and Gosiute, lived here when early Spanish explorers happened upon the region. Once claimed by Mexico, in 1847 it was chosen by the members of the Church of Jesus Christ of Latter-day Saints, or Mormons, as a refuge from persecution. The Mormons lived in isolation until Utah became part of the United States in 1848 via the Treaty of Guadalupe Hidalgo, which ended the Mexican War.

The state is comprised of portions of three major natural regions, or physiographic provinces: the Basin and Range Province (also known as the Great Basin), the Middle Rocky Mountains or Rocky Mountain Province, and the Colorado Plateau.

The Basin and Range Province covers about one-third of Utah. A region of shimmering white salt flats, gray plains, and high mountains, here rivers terminate not at the sea but in the Great Salt Lake Desert or the Great Salt Lake.

Utah's northeastern mountain ranges consist of the Uinta and the Wasatch Ranges. The Wasatch is known for its majestic granite peaks, its glacier-carved valleys, and its endless glacial lakes. The Uintas are older and one of the few major ranges in the Rocky Mountains that stretch in an east-to-west direction. The highest point, Kings Peak, is also, at 13,528 feet, the highest point in the state. The highest points in the Wasatch Range are Mount Timpanogos (11,750 feet) and Mount Nebo (11,877 feet). Given these facts, it's easy to see how Utah got its name. The state's moniker comes from a Native American word meaning "those who dwell high up" or "mountain dwellers."

The Colorado Plateau is a rainbow of colors and unique physical characteristics. Here, uplifted plateaus rise to more than 11,000 feet. Carved by rivers and eroded by wind and water, there are hundreds of canyons garnished in yellows, purples, reds, and pinks. The Colorado River snakes through these colorful canyons, as do the Green River and some of its other tributaries.

The Great Salt Lake is the largest and most famous lake in Utah. With several times more saline than the oceans, it is the largest inland body of salt water in North America. It is also the largest remnant of Lake Bonneville, which in prehistoric times blanketed much of Utah and Nevada.

Utah is a land of extremes—even the climate varies dramatically. The valleys and plateaus are hot and dry in summer, and in winter they are usually dry as well. The climate is pretty mild in the south and cold in the north. As you might expect, the mountains are cooler and receive more precipitation. Most of Utah claims an annual precipitation of from 8 to 16 inches, though the Great Salt Lake Desert boasts of 5 inches annually. The mountains average about 40 inches of precipitation a year, with most of it falling in the form of heavy winter snow. Snow in the Wasatch Mountains can be particularly heavy, with single storms dumping several feet. Annual snowfall can reach 30 feet. In summer local thunderstorms often drop enormous quantities of rain, creating flash floods.

Forests cover about one-fifth of Utah. The southwestern corner of the state is blanketed with desert plants such as the Joshua tree, mesquite, a variety of cacti, and creosote bush. Sagebrush, greasewood, and bluegrass are the most common plants in the canyon section of the Colorado Plateau. Adding color to the scene are prickly pear and Indian paintbrush.

Open woodlands cover the foothills and lower slopes up to about 7,000 feet. A potpourri of Rocky Mountain and Utah junipers, as well as pinyon trees and quaking aspens, is also found in scattered groves at about the same elevation. Mountain mahogany and Gambel oak are common, too. Along streams, look for willows, mountain alder, dogwood, and box elder.

Conifer forests consist of lodgepole pines and ponderosa pines, along with aspen, Douglas fir, and limber pine. Higher up, you'll find Engelmann spruce, subalpine fir, and white fir. Ironically, the Colorado or blue spruce, which happens to be the state tree, is not a Utah native.

Hosting an abundance of colorful wildflowers in spring and summer, Utah is home year-round to a number of large mammals. These include mule deer, elk, moose, pronghorn, bison, black bears, Rocky Mountain bighorns, Rocky Mountain goats, and cougars. Smaller mammals include lynx, both Canada and bay, foxes—gray, red, and kit—coyotes, badgers, beavers, otters, raccoons, mink, ringtails, weasels, and martens, as well as prairie dogs, rabbits, squirrels, skunks, and porcupines.

Reptiles are plentiful in the plateau areas of the state. In addition to two poisonous snakes, the western rattlesnake and the sidewinder, there are garter snakes, coachwhip snakes, and yellow-belly racers. The only poisonous lizard in the United States, the Gila monster, is found in southwestern Utah. Other reptiles include the horned and collared lizards, and the desert tortoise.

Utah's bird life is stunning, especially in spring and fall when migratory birds pass through. Then, bird observers may see the tundra swan, both the Canada and snow goose, and a variety of ducks, such as the redhead, canvasback, mallard, pintail, and shoveler. A number of waterbirds breed on Great Salt Lake islands, including the white pelican, the snowy egret, the double-crested cormorant, the green heron, and the white-faced ibis.

Game birds are sought after by hunters and bird-watchers alike. While you're out and about, look for ring-necked pheasant, both California and Gambel quail, mourning doves, chukars, and both sage and ruffed grouse. Protected by law, there are both golden and bald eagles in the mountainous areas. Fifty-five species of fish are found in Utah's lakes and streams. The most popular game fish are brook, rainbow, brown, and cutthroat trout, as well as smallmouth and largemouth bass.

Obviously, Utah has an abundance of natural gifts to offer both visitors and those who live here. Fortunately, there are 307 public campgrounds from which to enjoy the wide variety of flora, fauna, wonderful vistas, and multitude of outdoor activities. Happy camping!

How to Use This Book

This book was written with you, the camping enthusiast, in mind. Though my husband and I didn't physically view all of the public campgrounds found in Utah, we did drive to and check out about 303 of the 307 public campgrounds here.

To keep this book as up to date as possible, I invite you to tell me about those campgrounds that we may have missed. I'd also appreciate knowing about any new campgrounds, and about those that may have been improved or have deteriorated. If any have closed, I'd like to know that, too. Please send your comments and suggestions to Donna Ikenberry, c/o The Globe Pequot Press, P.O. Box 480, Guilford, CT 06437.

Choosing a Campground

Utah is a big place, with 307 public campgrounds to help you explore it. The campgrounds are managed by a number of agencies. Of the 307 campgrounds, 188 are managed by the National Forest Service and 40 are Utah state park campgrounds; the Bureau of Land Management cares for another 29. In addition, there are forty-four national park, national monument, and national recreation area campgrounds, as well as five county and city campgrounds. And one area is being temporarily cared for by the Bureau of Reclamation.

The Utah Department of Tourism has divided the state into nine travel regions. It's a good format, one that works, thus I've used the same travel regions to help you locate and select a campground in the area of your choice. These nine areas are known as Bridgerland, the Golden Spike Empire, Great Salt Lake Country, Mountainland, Dinosaurland, Panoramaland, Castle Country, Color Country, and Canyonlands.

MAP LEGEND

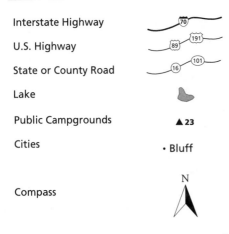

Interstate Highway	70
U.S. Highway	89 191
State or County Road	16 101
Lake	
Public Campgrounds	▲ 23
Cities	• Bluff
Compass	N

4

UTAH TOUR REGIONS

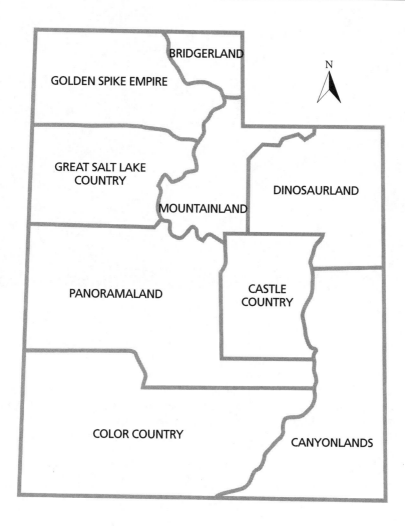

For each chapter or area, I've included a map of the travel region, as well as a summary introducing you to the area. And of course, all of the public campgrounds found there are described as well.

Each campground description includes information on location, detailed instructions as to how to get there, number of sites, whether or not they can be reserved, cost, contact information, activities, and more. Read on for a better understanding of the information provided within some of these categories.

Location. The location lets you quickly find the approximate site of the campground.

Glen Canyon National Recreation Area's Hite campground at sunset.

Facilities. This includes everything from fire grates and water to toilets, showers, boat ramps, horseshoe pits, and any other amenities worthy of notice.

Sites. Sites are listed as the total number of sites found in each area and include group areas, hookups (if available), and those sites that will accommodate both tents and RVs. These are all lumped together, but a quick look at the "At-a-Glance" section will tell you if there are group sites or RV sites, as well as the maximum length RV allowed.

Fee. Because fees change from year to year, I have opted to use the following price-range code, based on 2001 prices:

$ = for campsites costing from $1.00 to $9.00 per night

$$ = for campsites costing $10.00 to $15.00

$$$ = for campsites costing $16.00 to $19.00

$$$$ = for campsites costing $20.00 or more

Many public campgrounds offer a reduced rate for folks with either a Golden Access or a Golden Age Passport. (Please note that none of Utah's state parks offers such a reduction.) A Golden Access Passport is a free lifetime entrance pass available to citizens or permanent residents of the United States, regardless of age, who have been determined to be blind or permanently disabled. A Golden Age Passport is a lifetime entrance pass for those age sixty-two or older. It has a one-time processing charge of $10. Both passes also provide a 50 percent discount on federal use fees charged for facilities and services such as camping, swimming, parking, boat launching, or cave tours. They do not cover or reduce special recreation permit fees or fees charged by concessionaires.

Reservations. If reservations are accepted, you'll find a number listed for you to call. Making reservations is a good idea, especially during the peak summer months, weekends, and holidays. Additional fees are required for reservations so it makes a campground stay more costly, but it assures you of a place to camp, too.

Activities. I've listed popular activities to be enjoyed at each campground. Some offer nothing more than a nice place to relax and picnic, while others abound with opportunities for rock climbing, hiking, backpacking, mountain biking, fishing, off-highway driving, and much more.

Season. A season is listed when there is one, though you should know that most of the campgrounds open when conditions allow it. If a campground that usually opens by Memorial Day is buried under 4 feet of snow one year, it will open at a later date than usual. On the other hand, if early snow falls in a region that is normally open until the end of October, you may find it closed earlier than usual.

Information Included in the "At-a-Glance" Sections

Use the "At-a-Glance" charts to quickly find the campground that is right for you. Categories denote the availability of group sites, RV sites, hookups, showers, drinking water, dump stations, and whether or not pets are allowed. You'll also learn the total number of sites at each campground, the maximum length RV allowed, the kinds of toilets found there, and whether or not there are wheelchair-accessible sites. In addition, campers can quickly find out what kinds of recreation are enjoyed in each area, fee information, stay limit, season, and whether or not a site can be reserved. A description of some of these categories follows.

Maximum RV length. This is usually the total length of the RV itself. If it is listed as "30 feet," that means a 30-foot motor home, a 30-foot travel trailer, or a 30-foot fifth-wheel trailer would fit in the space. In one case—Natural Bridges National Monument—the maximum length allowed is the total length of both the tow vehicle and the trailer.

Hookups. When available, these are listed using the following code: W = Water, E = Electric, and S = Sewer.

Toilets. These are also listed by code: F = Flush, V = Vault, P = Pit, and C = Chemical.

Drinking water. Water is always listed where available, but you should know that if water is available one week it may not be the next. Why? Because it may pass water-quality tests on one occasion, only to fail the next time around. Also, water is turned off in many areas in winter, so early- or late-season visitors may find it unavailable. Streams or creeks often flow through Utah's campgrounds: Be sure to treat such water before using it.

Pets. Traveling with pets can be fun and rewarding, but pets can also cause problems for other campers if they are not well behaved. Keep your pet quiet, make sure that you clean up after it, and keep it on a leash, for best results. Also, please note that pets are not allowed in the Big Cottonwood Canyon and Little Cottonwood Canyon areas near Salt Lake City.

Recreation. Outdoor activities are listed by code: H = Hiking, C = Rock Climbing, M = Mountain Biking, S = Swimming, F = Fishing, B = Boating, L = Boat Launch, O = Off-highway Driving, and R = Horseback Riding.

On a Special Note

- Fireworks (firecrackers, rockets, or other explosives) are not allowed on national forest system land due to fire hazard. It is illegal to possess or ignite any type of firework on national forest system land. This includes sparklers.

- Though I didn't list each specifically, many campgrounds do sell firewood. Firewood collecting is prohibited in many areas; besides, it's really best to leave the natural resources alone. Please plan on bringing your own firewood or buying some.

- In most campgrounds vehicles must be parked on roads or designated parking spurs only.

- Occupancy limits vary from campground to campground. Some may have a limit of one family or a total of ten people per single unit, and two families or twenty people per double unit. Please stick to the regulations for each individual campground.

- In some areas of Utah, particularly the Colorado Plateau, you'll find cryptobiotic crust covering the soil. A thin, dark organism, it blankets the arid landscape in preparation for future plant communities. Its crusty, lumpy top is born from a unification of mosses, algae, lichens, and fungi. The crusts can take a century to develop and mere seconds to destroy. Step on a crust and it'll be pulverized into dust. Please do not step on the crust— stay on trails or rocks instead.

Getting to the Campground

Reach the campground of your choosing by using the individual campground description in conjunction with a detailed state map or the appropriate forest service or Bureau of Land Management map. *The Utah Atlas & Gazetteer* by DeLorme was especially useful to us as we toured around the state.

Playing in the Outdoors

A great outdoor experience can be had by just about anyone, but those who respect and appreciate the out-of-doors seem to gain a whole lot more from the encounter. Please do not leave garbage at your campsite (or on the trail), do not destroy the toilets that are there for our use, and remember: When you are out and about, take only pictures, leave only footprints. Do this, and you'll leave a treasure for future generations to enjoy.

Preparation

Some of the campgrounds in this guide are located off well-maintained, well-traveled paved roads. A cell phone is probably all you need in an emergency. But you should know that there are also campgrounds in more remote areas—places out of cell-phone range, where another car may pass by only rarely. For this reason, you should make sure that your tires and engine are in good shape. You'll want to top off the gas tank when leaving civilization for long, and you'll want to carry emergency vehicle gear. A jack and all the necessities for changing a flat tire are essential; you'll also want jumper cables, spare belts, and, when you're in snow country, tire chains (a must).

If you have your camping gear and food with you, you'll have fewer things to worry about should you break down in the boondocks. When traveling in remote areas, always carry food, water, a sleeping bag or blankets, matches, a flashlight, and a first-aid kit. Most important, if you'll be away for a while, notify friends or family of your intended destination and time of return.

Camping

Low-impact camping is a necessity, whether you are camping in the wilderness or at a developed campground, like the ones found in this guide. If trash pickup isn't available—and it's not at many campgrounds—then always pack out what you brought in. If you build a campfire, conserve on wood, and keep it small. Of course, you should heed all regulations regarding wood gathering, fires, and smoking.

Once you choose a campsite, keep it neat and tidy. If you find trash around the site, pick it up and pack it out. If you have a pet, keep it on a leash and keep it quiet. Do not let it roam around, bothering others. It's important to respect those who are in the surrounding sites. If you need to hear music, keep it low. If you want to walk around, stay on main pathways—do not cut across your neighbor's site.

All food should be stored in closed containers, inside your vehicle. Bears are smart critters, and in some places they can recognize an ice chest. If there are smart bears around your area, cover the coolers so they are not visible.

Although some campgrounds offer showers, many do not. If you need to wash off, do so away from natural bodies of water, such as lakes or streams.

A view of Flaming Gorge Recreation Area from Canyon Rim.

You should also bathe away from the drinking-water spigots in the campground. A plastic bucket or a black shower bag is good for bathing.

Most public campgrounds have stay limits that range from a few days to a month or so, with the average stay being around fourteen days. Please adhere to the limit and plan your stay accordingly.

Getting Ready to Enjoy the Great Outdoors

When I'm out hiking a trail or rock climbing or mountain biking, I often see folks who've forgotten a few of the basics—things like food and water and maybe even a jacket or some other piece of warm clothing. Certainly by the end of their recreational pursuit, they must be thinking that being outdoors isn't any fun at all.

To best enjoy and savor the day, always bring water on a hike; a few snacks or a lunch will be handy, too. Also, it is best to dress in layers of clothing. Don't don a T-shirt and then throw on a big parka. Instead dress in layers, wearing a breathable fabric next to your skin. Fleece is a nice second layer, with a breathable, rainproof jacket and pants for outer wear. Footwear depends on the activities you enjoy. Walking shoes are fine for short trails, but if you are going to be taking long hikes, hiking boots will offer more protection. They are also more comfortable.

If you're doing any hiking, mountain biking, or rock climbing, and you'll be away from your vehicle for any length of time, a small day pack should be room enough for a few necessities such as money, keys, sunglasses, a map, water, snacks, a camera, binoculars, and a lightweight jacket. Longer trips will require more gear and a bigger pack.

Safety

Nature is unpredictable, thus you always need to use common sense and good judgment when spending time in the outdoors. If you leave your campsite to spend time in the backcountry, you are taking some risks, but you will reap riches beyond measure. Besides, the drive from your home to the campground was probably even more of a risk!

Hypothermia. Hypothermia occurs when you lose body heat faster than you can generate it, resulting in a decline in core body temperature. Common causes are exposure to cold, physical exhaustion, and too little food intake. Contributing factors may include exposure to wind, rain, or snow; dehydration; wearing damp or wet clothing; prolonged inactivity.

The best treatment for hypothermia is prevention. Wear layers of clothing, stripping them off before you break a sweat and adding them to keep out the cold. Snack throughout the day on high-energy foods such as fruit, granola, trail mix, soup, and sandwiches. Drink plenty of fluids to prevent dehydration.

If someone in your hiking party is suffering from hypothermia, stop and get that person dry and warm. Hot fluids can help restore body heat. If the patient is unconscious, try zipping two sleeping bags together and have two helpers lie with the patient, one on either side. Do not give liquids to a person who is unconscious.

Heat exhaustion. Exposure to hot ambient air temperatures, when combined with too much sun or strenuous exercise, will lead to an elevated body temperature. Protect yourself from overheating by wearing a hat or draping a wet bandanna over your head and the back of your neck. Water intake is the most important factor in preventing heat-related illnesses. The human body doesn't signal that it's thirsty until it's too late. An adult may need a gallon and a half of water a day when exercising in hot weather. Drink plenty of water before you get thirsty, and drink frequently. Plain water is best, though electrolyte-replacement drinks are effective in extremely hot weather or during strenuous activity. *Do not* take salt tablets.

Lightning. Take extra precautions when dealing with stormy skies. According to the National Oceanic and Atmospheric Association (NOAA), about 300 people in the United States die each year from lightning strikes. Many more are injured, some permanently. To avoid being struck by a lightning bolt, watch the weather. Spring and summer are the busiest seasons for lightning, though discharges can occur any time of year, even during snowstorms. Most lightning storms occur in mid- to late afternoon. Storms are usually preceded by wind and the approach of dark, towering clouds. Lightning may travel far ahead of the storm.

If you're out hiking, seek shelter away from open ground or exposed ridges. Dropping even a few yards off a ridgetop will reduce your risk. In the forest, stay away from single, tall trees. On open ground, find a low spot free of standing water. Stay out of shallow caves, crevasses, or overhangs. During a lightning storm, assume a low crouch with only your feet touching the ground. Put a sleeping pad or pack (be sure it has no frame or other metal in it) beneath your feet for added insulation against shock. Do not huddle together; members of a group should stay at least 30 feet apart. This way, if someone is hit, the others can give CPR and first aid for burns and shock.

In a tent, get in the crouch position. Stay in your sleeping bag and keep your feet on a sleeping pad. Signs of an imminent lightning strike include hair standing on end; an itchy feeling—one hiker described it as "bugs crawling all over"—on your skin; an acrid, "hot metal" smell; and buzzing or crackling noises in the air. Tuck into a crouch immediately if any of these signs are present.

Bears. What should you do if you meet a black bear on the trail? Most bears will detect you before you ever detect them, and will leave the area. If you do meet a bear before it has had time to leave, stay calm. Talk aloud to let the bear know that you are present, and back away slowly. Stay facing the animal all the while. Avoid direct eye contact, which bears may perceive as a threat. Give the bear plenty of room to escape; if you're on a trail, step off the path on the downhill side. Then *slowly* leave the area. Don't run—this will prompt the bear to chase you. Besides, you can't outrun a bear. There's no sense in trying.

Water. By now most backcountry visitors have heard about the protozoan *Giardia lamblia.* It won't kill you, but in some cases you may wish it had. Symptoms include severe abdominal cramps, gas and bloating, loss of appetite, and acute diarrhea. Fortunately, not all water is contaminated, but you can't tell by looking. No matter how pure the water looks, never drink from any spring, stream, river, or lake without treating the water first. It's better to be safe than sick.

There are several methods for treating water. First, you can boil all water—a good method if you want hot drinks or a boiled dinner, but a lousy idea if you need a cool drink right away. Boiling for a minimum of one minute at altitudes below 4,000 feet should suffice. Add several minutes of boiling time for higher altitudes; experts recommend a minimum of five minutes anywhere in Utah, due to high elevation. Increase time for very high elevations or whenever the water is cloudy or muddy. Some hikers find a water purifier more convenient. This is the method I use: Run water through the purifier and it's ready to drink. In emergencies, commercial water purification chemicals will do.

Altitude or mountain sickness. Altitude or mountain sickness can be a problem for some campers. It usually takes about two or three days to acclimatize to high altitude. If you or someone in your party feels a bit nauseated or dizzy, or experiences a headache or loss of appetite, you'll all need to stop and rest. Drink water, and make sure to get plenty of sodium and high-energy foods. If symptoms don't go away, your only option is to descend to a lower elevation where there's more oxygen. Never ascend if you are suffering from mountain sickness.

Biting insects. Ticks themselves are harmless, but the diseases they carry can be deadly—including Lyme disease, Colorado tick fever, and Rocky Mountain spotted fever. After traveling in tick country, watch for symptoms of tick-borne disease, including a high fever, arthritislike pain in the bones and joints, or a rash. During tick season (spring and summer), stay out of tall grass or brushy areas, and inspect yourself and clothing after each outing. Look for ticks nightly before going to bed. Carefully inspect legs, groin, armpits, ears, and scalp.

To remove a loose tick, flick it off with a fingernail. If the tick is firmly embedded in your skin, use tweezers to pinch a small area around its mouth and pull it out. (You may have to remove a tiny chunk of skin to get all of the tick.) Try not to squeeze the tick's body, since this increases the risk of infection. Clean the wound with an antiseptic.

Mosquitoes are more of a nuisance than a danger. Most North American mosquitoes can transmit a form of encephalitis, however, which is potentially fatal. The best way to avoid mosquito-borne diseases is to avoid being bitten. Bug sprays with N, N-diethyl-3-methylbenzamide (Deet) seem to work best. Wear long pants, a long-sleeved shirt, ankle-high shoes, and a cap that covers your ears. Try not to camp near stagnant water or fields of damp or dewy grass.

The Campgrounds

Bridgerland

Located in Utah's Rocky Mountain Province, Bridgerland is situated smack dab in the north-central part of the state. Bordered on the north and east by the neighboring states of Idaho and Wyoming, respectively, it is also flanked on the west by the Golden Spike Empire travel region and on the south by the travel region known as Mountainland.

A photographer's delight, Bridgerland is a place of unparalleled beauty, a place where anglers fly fish "blue-ribbon" streams and folks come to canoe along the Bear River. In addition, rock climbers come to scale various routes in Logan Canyon, while mountain bikers and hikers hit some of the area trails and bird-watchers and scuba divers explore the lovely domain of Bear Lake.

Bridgerland is the smallest of Utah's nine travel regions—a mere 2,205 square miles. Even so, the place is packed with campgrounds, offering a total of nineteen sites for visitors to call upon and enjoy. Encompassing both Rich and Cache Counties, a potpourri of sites exist in the likes of the Wasatch-Cache National Forest, both Hyrum and Bear Lake State Parks, and Birch Creek, a Bureau of Land Management site.

At Bear Lake State Park, campgrounds on the west, south, and east sides of the natural lake make sailing, swimming, and scuba diving easily accessible. And in winter, ice fishing for the unique Bonneville cisco is popular. The lake is known as the Caribbean of the Rockies for its lovely turquoise blue water; you may be tempted to ask the locals if they put blue dye in Bear Lake. Of course, residents will tell you that the unique color isn't caused by a dye. Instead, light rays reflect off limestone particles suspended in the water, changing the lake to random shades of blue.

The lake boasts year-round fun. Typical spring weather offers up migrating birds, while summer brings boaters and scuba divers. The raspberry harvest occurs in August, with a rodeo, a parade, and fireworks to celebrate the annual event. Bear Lake Raspberry Days are usually held the first week of August. In fall you can enjoy foliage colors at their best, while winter offers snowmobiling and skiing through miles of famous Utah powder snow.

Hyrum Lake State Park is a popular place, too. The Little Bear River supplies the 450-acre reservoir, where water sports and fishing are big attractions. Visitors can also enjoy a few sandy beaches, though there are no lifeguards. During freeze-up, from about the middle of December through late March, some visitors fish through the ice, while others ice skate or sail their iceboats across the lake.

Several campgrounds are situated near the community of Logan, known for its music festivals and high-quality arts. In July and August the Utah Festival Opera Company performs in the beautifully restored Ellen Eccles Theatre, while the Utah Music Festival brings chamber music to the area from late June through August. In addition, summer visitors find a bevy of musicals, comedies, and dramas in the historic Old Lyric Repertory Theatre in downtown Logan.

Logan Canyon is an unparalled delight, a place that could take days to explore. In fact, my husband and I spent three days driving what for many is less

BRIDGERLAND

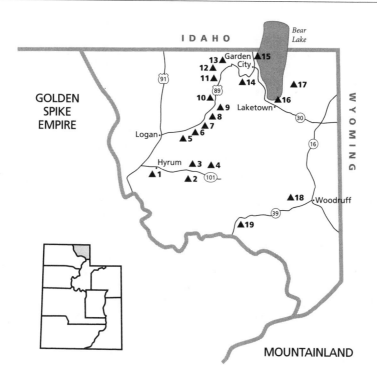

than a one-hour drive. U.S. Highway 89 meanders more than 20 miles into the Bear River Range, a northern branch of the Wasatch Mountains. The route is particularly beautiful in fall, when the colors are vibrant and photogenic. A mile-by-mile guide is available from the Bridgerland Travel Region in Logan. For more information contact the office at 160 North Main, Logan, UT 84321; (801) 752–2161 or (800) 882–4433, fax (801) 753–5825; btr@sunrem.com.

1 Hyrum Lake State Park

Location: Just south of downtown Hyrum
Facilities: Fire grates, picnic tables, flush toilets, showers, drinking water, boat ramps and docks, and volleyball and horseshoes for the group sites
Sites: 46
Fee: $$ for single sites; call for group sites
Elevation: 4,700 feet
Road conditions: Paved at Cottonwood; gravel at Lakeview
Management: Hyrum State Park, 405 West 300 South, Hyrum, UT 84319-1547; (435) 245–6866.
Reservations: In the Salt Lake area, call (801) 322–3770; elsewhere, (800) 322–3770; fee

	Group sites	RV sites	Total sites	Max. RV length	Hookups	Toilets	Showers	Drinking water	Dump station	Pets	Wheelchair	Recreation	Fee($)	Season	Can reserve	Stay limit
1 Hyrum Lake S.P.	•	•	46			VF	•	•		•	•	FSBL	$$		•	14
2 Pioneer		•	18	20		P		•	•			F	$	May–Oct.		7
3 Friendship	•		6			C			•			F	$	May–Oct.		7
4 Spring			3			P			•			F	$	May–Oct.		7
5 Bridger		•	10	20		F		•	•			CMFH	$	May–Oct.		7
6 Spring Hollow	•	•	12	20		V		•	•			CMFH	$	May–Oct.	•	7
7 Guinavah-Malibu	•	•	43	25		F		•	•			CMFH	$$	May–Oct.	•	7
8 Preston Valley		•	8	20		F		•	•			MFC	$	May–Oct.		7
9 Lodge		•	10	20		V		•	•			FOCM	$	May–Oct.		7
10 Wood Camp		•	6	20		V		•	•			FMHC	$	May–Oct.		7
11 Lewis M. Turner		•	10	20		F		•	•			M	$	June–Oct.		7
12 Tony Grove Lake		•	37	20		V		•	•			FHR	$$–$$$	July–Sept.	•	7
13 Red Banks		•	12	20		P		•	•			HFM	$	June–Oct.		7
14 Sunrise		•	27	25		V		•	•				$$	June–Sept.	•	7
15 Bear Lake Marina		•	13			F	•	•	•	•	•	SBFL	$$		•	14
16 Rendezvous Beach	•	•	136		WES	F	•	•	•	•	•	FBS	$$–$$$		•	14
17 Eastside	•	•	25,*			V		•	•			SBFL	$		•	14
18 Birch Creek			4			V			•			F				14
19 Monte Cristo	•	•	49	25		P		•	•			OHM	$$	June–Sept.		5

* Dispersed Camping—no designated sites **Hookups:** W = Water E = Electric S = Sewer **Toilets:** F = Flush V = Vault P = Pit C= Chemical **Recreation:** H = Hiking S = Swimming F = Fishing B = Boating L = Boat Launch O = Off-highway driving R = Horseback Riding C = Rock Climbing M = Mountain Biking **Maximum Trailer/RV length** given in feet. **Stay Limit** given in days. **Fee** given in dollars. If no entry under **Season,** campgound is open all year. If no entry under **Fee,** camping is free.

Activities: Fishing, swimming, boating, waterskiing, ice skating and fishing, and picnicking

Season: Year-round

Finding the campground: From the junction of Utah Highways 101 and 165 at the east end of Hyrum, drive west on UT 101 for 1.7 miles, then turn left (south) onto 400 West; you'll reach the entrance station in another 0.4 mile.

About the campground: Nestled in Cache Valley, a scenic mountain valley, and located on the south shore of Hyrum Lake, this year-round park offers the usual summer activities plus ice fishing for trout and yellow perch in winter. There are two campgrounds, both along the south shore. Maple trees, willows, and pines shade the wide, graveled sites of the Lakeview Campground, while those who opt for the Cottonwood or East Campground will sit parking-lot-style on asphalt.

The 400-plus-acre reservoir provides an abundance of recreational opportunities. In addition to boating and swimming, visitors will enjoy the many bird species found here, including grebes, egrets, herons, pelicans, and an assortment of songbirds.

2 Pioneer

Location: In the Wasatch-Cache National Forest, about 8 miles east of Hyrum
Facilities: Fire grates, picnic tables, drinking water, and pit toilets
Sites: 18
Fee: $
Elevation: 5,200 feet
Road conditions: Paved to the campground, then gravel
Management: Logan Ranger District, 1500 East Highway 89, Logan, UT 84321-4373; (435) 755–3620.
Reservations: None
Activities: Fishing and picnicking
Season: May through October
Finding the campground: From the junction of Utah Highways 165 and 101 on the east edge of Hyrum, drive paved UT 101, also called Blacksmith Fork Canyon Road, east for 8 miles.

About the campground: An assortment of miniature roses, box elders, willows, and maple trees serves to decorate this lush campground. Located along the Blacksmith Fork, it's a good place for trout fishing or a picnic. Although 20-foot RVs are allowed, please note that the only turnaround is located to the left (south), where you'll find sites 6 through 15.

3 Friendship

Location: In the Wasatch-Cache National Forest, about 11 miles east of Hyrum
Facilities: Fire grates, picnic tables, and chemical toilets
Sites: 6
Fee: $ for single sites; call for group site
Elevation: 5,600 feet
Road conditions: Gravel
Management: Logan Ranger District, 1500 East Highway 89, Logan, UT 84321-4373; (435) 755–3620
Reservations: For the group site, call (435) 755–3620
Activities: Fishing and picnicking
Season: May through October
Finding the campground: From the junction of Utah Highways 165 and 101 on the east edge of Hyrum, head east on paved UT 101, also called Blacksmith Fork Canyon Road. Travel 7.2 miles to a gravel road heading north and then east up the Left Fork Blacksmith Fork Canyon. There are signs for both the Friendship and Spring Campgrounds along the way. You'll reach the campground after 3.6 miles.

About the campground: Six tiny, shaded sites rest along the Left Fork Blacksmith Fork, offering a place to enjoy some trout fishing and have a picnic under the maple trees. Sites are small, so tents and vans are best. A group site is available for one to twenty-five users.

4 Spring

Location: In the Wasatch-Cache National Forest, approximately 12 miles east of Hyrum
Facilities: Fire grates, picnic tables, and pit toilets
Sites: 3
Fee: $
Elevation: 6,000 feet
Road conditions: Gravel
Management: Logan Ranger District, 1500 East Highway 89, Logan, UT 84321-4373; (435) 755-3620
Reservations: None
Activities: Fishing and picnicking
Season: May through October
Finding the campground: From the junction of Utah Highways 165 and 101 on the east edge of Hyrum, head east on paved UT 101, also called Blacksmith Fork Canyon Road. Travel 7.2 miles to a gravel road heading north and then east up the Left Fork Blacksmith Fork Canyon. There are signs for both the Spring and Friendship Campgrounds along the way. You'll reach the campground after 4.5 miles.

About the campground: Three small sites are shaded with maple and box elder, while the Left Fork Blacksmith Fork offers a place to enjoy some trout fishing and have a picnic. Sites are small, so tents and vans are best.

5 Bridger

Location: In the Wasatch-Cache National Forest, approximately 6 miles east of Logan
Facilities: Fire grates, picnic tables, drinking water, and flush toilets
Sites: 10
Fee: $
Elevation: 5,000 feet
Road conditions: Paved
Management: Logan Ranger District, 1500 East Highway 89, Logan, UT 84321-4373; (435) 755-3620
Reservations: None
Activities: Climbing, hiking, mountain biking, fishing, and picnicking
Season: May through October
Finding the campground: From the junction of U.S. Highways 89 and 91 in Logan, travel east on paved US 89 for 5.5 miles to the campground, which is on the south side of the road.

About the campground: Located in beautiful Logan Canyon, a place with an abundance of campgrounds, this is a wonderful place from which to climb, hike, bike, fish for trout, or just sit and enjoy a picnic. Box elders, maples, and miniature roses shade the campsites and add to the lovely scene, with the Logan River roaring nearby.

Logan Canyon is a climber's paradise, with its sheer-walled limestone and quartzite cliffs offering up more than 300 mostly bolted routes, ranging from 5.5 to 5.14. See *Rock Climbing Utah*, a Falcon guide by Stewart Green, for more information.

6 Spring Hollow

Location: In the Wasatch-Cache National Forest, about 7 miles east of Logan
Facilities: Fire grates, picnic tables, drinking water, and vault toilets
Sites: 12
Fee: $ for single sites; call for group sites
Elevation: 5,100 feet
Road conditions: Paved
Management: Logan Ranger District, 1500 East Highway 89, Logan, UT 84321-4373; (435) 755–3620
Reservations: For single sites, call (877) 444–6777 or TDD (877) 833–6777; fee. For group sites, call (435) 755–3620
Activities: Climbing, hiking, mountain biking, fishing, photography, and picnicking
Season: May through October
Finding the campground: From the junction of U.S. Highways 89 and 91 in Logan, travel east on paved US 89 for 6.5 miles to the campground, which is on the south side of the road.

About the campground: Located in the stunning realms of Logan Canyon, where campgrounds are plentiful, this is a great place from which to climb, hike, bike, and fish. The Logan River borders the north side of the shady campground, while Spring Hollow Creek rushes through it. Two trails begin here; the Riverside Nature Trail is for hikers and travels east to the Guinavah-Malibu Campground. Head back down the river and you'll enjoy 4 miles along the River Trail, which is open to both bicyclists and hikers.

Group-site costs vary; the sites can handle from 1 to 135 users.

7 Guinavah-Malibu

Location: In the Wasatch-Cache National Forest, approximately 7 miles east of Logan
Facilities: Fire grates, picnic tables, drinking water, and flush toilets
Sites: 43
Fee: $$
Elevation: 5,200 feet
Road conditions: Paved

Management: Logan Ranger District, 1500 East Highway 89, Logan, UT 84321-4373; (435) 755-3620
Reservations: For single sites, call (877) 444-6777 or TDD (877) 833-6777; fee. For group sites, call (435) 755-3620
Activities: Climbing, hiking, mountain biking, fishing, photography, and picnicking
Season: May through October
Finding the campground: From the junction of U.S. Highways 89 and 91 in Logan, travel east on paved US 89 for 7.4 miles to the campground, which is on the south side of the road.

About the campground: Here in the kingdom of Logan Canyon, where the scenery is stunning, campgrounds are numerous, and outdoor activities plentiful, you'll find more than enough to do in the way of climbing, hiking, biking, and fishing. The Logan River cuts through the campground, while cottonwood, box elder, and maple trees serve to shade it. One trail begins in the campground, and another starts just across the street. The Riverside Nature Trail is for hikers and travels west to the Spring Hollow Campground. Across the road you'll find the Wind Caves Trailhead. It leads 1.3 miles to a triple arch and natural limestone cave.

Group sites can handle from 1 to 150 users; prices vary, so you should call for more information.

8 Preston Valley

Location: In the Wasatch-Cache National Forest, approximately 10 miles east of Logan
Facilities: Fire grates, picnic tables, drinking water, and flush toilets
Sites: 8
Fee: $
Elevation: 5,500 feet
Road conditions: Paved
Management: Logan Ranger District, 1500 East Highway 89, Logan, UT 84321-4373; (435) 755-3620
Reservations: None
Activities: Climbing, mountain biking, fishing, and picnicking
Season: May through October
Finding the campground: From the junction of U.S. Highways 89 and 91 in Logan, travel east on paved US 89 for 10.4 miles to the campground, which is on the south side of the road.

About the campground: This small campground is located about midway through glorious Logan Canyon, with easy access to rock climbing and fishing. Deciduous trees shade the sites, while the Logan River flows nearby. Please note that RVers should stay away from sites 1 and 2, because there is no place for trailers to turn around.

Climbers should note that Logan Canyon is a paradise of sheer-walled limestone and quartzite cliffs offering up more than 300 mostly bolted routes.

Routes range from 5.5 to 5.14; see Stewart Green's book *Rock Climbing Utah* for more information.

9 Lodge

Location: In the Wasatch-Cache National Forest, approximately 13 miles east of Logan
Facilities: Fire grates, picnic tables, drinking water, and vault toilets
Sites: 10
Fee: $
Elevation: 5,600 feet
Road conditions: Paved
Management: Logan Ranger District, 1500 East Highway 89, Logan, UT 84321-4373; (435) 755–3620
Reservations: None
Activities: Climbing, mountain biking, fishing, off-highway driving, and picnicking
Season: May through October
Finding the campground: From the junction of U.S. Highways 89 and 91 in Logan, drive east on paved US 89 for 11.5 miles; then turn right (south) onto a narrow paved road for 1.3 miles to the campground. A sign points the way.

About the campground: Popular with ATVers, this shaded campground offers box elder and other deciduous trees as well as the waters of the Right Hand Fork. It's a good place from which to base activities such as rock climbing, fishing, and exploring off the main highway. There are many places to mountain bike, including a ride to Ephraim's Grave—the site at which the largest grizzly bear in America was killed—and a trip to the top of Logan Peak. For more information, see the Falcon book *Mountain Biking Utah,* by Gregg Bromka.

10 Wood Camp

Location: In the Wasatch-Cache National Forest, about 13 miles east of Logan
Facilities: Fire grates, picnic tables, and vault toilets
Sites: 6
Fee: $
Elevation: 5,600 feet
Road conditions: Paved
Management: Logan Ranger District, 1500 East Highway 89, Logan, UT 84321-4373; (435) 755–3620.
Reservations: None
Activities: Climbing, mountain biking, hiking, fishing, photography, and picnicking
Season: May through October
Finding the campground: From the junction of U.S. Highways 89 and 91 in Logan, drive east on paved US 89 for 12.5 miles. The campground is on the north side of the road.

About the campground: You won't find drinking water here, but you will find the Logan River and shady sites for fishing. Best of all, the Jardine Juniper Trailhead is just 100 yards away. A sign points the way.

The Jardine Trail leads to a gnarled, 3,200-year-old juniper. The trail is about 4 or 5 miles long and accessible to hikers, mountain bikers, and horseback riders. It's a great hike, climbing approximately 1,800 feet while gaining the ridge then descending a short distance to the tree.

11 Lewis M. Turner

Location: In the Wasatch-Cache National Forest, about 22 miles northeast of Logan
Facilities: Fire grates, picnic tables, drinking water, and flush toilets
Sites: 10
Fee: $
Elevation: 5,600 feet
Road conditions: Paved
Management: Logan Ranger District, 1500 East Highway 89, Logan, UT 84321-4373; (435) 755–3620
Reservations: None
Activities: Photography, mountain biking, and picnicking
Season: June through October
Finding the campground: From the junction of U.S. Highways 89 and 91 in Logan, head east on paved US 89 for 21.7 miles. At this point, make a left (southwest) at the sign for Tony Grove. The road forks immediately; keep straight (northwest) to reach the campground in 0.2 mile.

About the campground: Set among aspens, this partially open campground makes a great base camp for exploring the nearby area. It's also a fine place from which to watch for wildlife and have a picnic. If you want to do some mountain biking, check out Gregg Bromka's Falcon book *Mountain Biking Utah.*

12 Tony Grove Lake

Location: In the Wasatch-Cache National Forest, approximately 28 miles northeast of Logan
Facilities: Fire grates, picnic tables, drinking water, and vault toilets
Sites: 37
Fee: $$ for single sites; $$$ for double sites
Elevation: 8,050 feet
Road conditions: Paved
Management: Logan Ranger District, 1500 East Highway 89, Logan, UT 84321-4373; (435) 755–3620
Reservations: Call (877) 444–6777 or TDD (877) 833–6777; fee

Wildflowers and lichen-covered rocks in the Mount Naomi Wilderness.

Activities: Hiking, fishing, horseback riding, photography, and picnicking
Season: July through September
Finding the campground: From the junction of U.S. Highways 89 and 91 in Logan, head east on paved US 89 for 21.7 miles, then make a left (southwest) at the sign for Tony Grove. Keep left at the fork (which you'll reach almost immediately) and continue another 6.6 miles, mostly heading west on the paved road. You'll reach the campground just before the road ends at Tony Grove Lake.

About the campground: Grouse, moose, and a whole lot more might await those who decide to camp at Tony Grove. Set among aspens, spruce, and other conifers, with some sites overlooking scenic Tony Grove Lake, this campground offers access into the Mount Naomi Wilderness.

Trails lead into the 45,000-acre preserve, which encompasses some of the most rugged and spectacular country in the Bear River Range. A trail leads about 2,000 feet up and nearly 3 miles to the top of 9,979-foot Mount Naomi, the highest in the northern part of the Wasatch Range. Climb in the summer months and you're sure to indulge in fields of wildflowers—you might even see some wildlife, too.

13 Red Banks

Location: In the Wasatch-Cache National Forest, approximately 23 miles northeast of Logan
Facilities: Fire grates, picnic tables, drinking water, and pit toilets
Sites: 12
Fee: $
Elevation: 6,500 feet
Road conditions: Paved to the campground, then gravel
Management: Logan Ranger District, 1500 East Highway 89, Logan, UT 84321-4373; (435) 755-3620
Reservations: None
Activities: Hiking, fishing, mountain biking, and picnicking
Season: June through October
Finding the campground: From the junction of U.S. Highways 89 and 91 in Logan, travel east on paved US 89 for 22.7 miles to the campground, which is on the north side of the road.

About the campground: Aspens, cottonwoods, and willows grace this spot, with the Logan River flowing nearby. The campground is right next to the road and probably not the most quiet place come summer, but the river should drown out some of the noise. The site was named for the steep red bank of sandstone and conglomerate visible from the campground.

14 Sunrise

Location: In the Wasatch-Cache National Forest, about 6 miles west of Garden City
Facilities: Fire grates, picnic tables, drinking water, and vault toilets
Sites: 27
Fee: $$
Elevation: 7,800 feet
Road conditions: Paved
Management: Logan Ranger District, 1500 East Highway 89, Logan, UT 84321-4373; (435) 755-3620.
Reservations: Call (877) 444-6777 or TDD (877) 833-6777; fee
Activities: Picnicking
Season: June through September
Finding the campground: From the junction of Utah Highway 30 and U.S. Highway 89 in Garden City, drive west on paved US 89 for about 6 miles to the campground, which is on the south side of the road.

About the campground: Shady sites are the norm in this beautiful—and popular—camping area set among aspens and conifers. Some of these sites offer views of Bear Lake. Ranging from azure to turquoise to sky blue, the lake is more than 20 miles long and 8 miles wide. Once a hunting and gathering grounds for Native Americans, it was later a meeting place for almost every mountain man who trapped in the Rocky Mountains. Today it's a popular destination for campers.

15 Bear Lake Marina: Bear Lake State Park

Location: 1 mile north of Garden City
Facilities: Fire grates, picnic tables, flush toilets, sewage disposal station, showers, drinking water, and boat ramps and docks
Sites: 13
Fee: $ $
Elevation: 5,900 feet
Road conditions: Paved
Management: Bear Lake State Park, P.O. Box 184, Garden City, UT 84028-0184; (435) 946-3343
Reservations: In the Salt Lake area, call (801) 322-3770; elsewhere, (800) 322-3770; fee
Activities: Fishing, swimming, boating, waterskiing, and picnicking
Season: Year-round
Finding the campground: From the junction of Utah Highway 30 and U.S. Highway 89 in Garden City, head north on US 89 for 1.3 miles to the campground, which is on the east side of the road.

About the campground: Located along the west shore of Bear Lake, called the Caribbean of the Rockies for its incredible turquoise blue water, campsites sit parking-lot-style on pavement, one next to the other. The marina offers a sheltered harbor, an 80-foot-wide concrete launching ramp, 283 seasonal boat slips, 22 transient boat slips, and a visitor center. A concessionaire offers food, souvenirs, gas, and boating and fishing items.

Water-related sports activities are popular here, as is fishing for Bonneville cisco, trout, and whitefish.

16 Rendezvous Beach: Bear Lake State Park

Location: About 8 miles south of Garden City
Facilities: Fire grates, picnic tables, flush toilets, showers, drinking water, sewage disposal station, public telephone, boat rentals, snack bar, and boat ramps and docks
Sites: 136
Fee: $ $ to $ $ $
Elevation: 5,900 feet
Road conditions: Paved
Management: Bear Lake State Park, P.O. Box 184, Garden City, UT 84028-0184; (435) 946-3343
Reservations: In the Salt Lake area, call (801) 322-3770; elsewhere, (800) 322-3770; fee
Activities: Fishing, swimming, boating, waterskiing, and picnicking
Season: Year-round
Finding the campground: From the junction of Utah Highway 30 and U.S. Highway 89 in Garden City, drive south on UT 30 for 8.1 miles to the campground, which is on the east side of the road.

About the campground: Enter the park at Rendezvous Beach, along the south shore of Bear Lake where there's a wide sandy beach, and you'll find three campgrounds—Willow, Cottonwood, and Big Creek—for your enjoyment. Family reunions and other big group meetings are popular here, with people renting two or more sites to accommodate their large groups.

The Willow Campground offers thirty sites. You'll sit parking-lot-style, which means right next to your neighbor, but those with tents will be able to pitch them under the trees that line the beach. A concessionaire offers boat and Jet Ski rentals and a snack shop.

At Cottonwood you'll find sixty sites scattered throughout an immense grove of cottonwoods. Once again, vehicles line up in parking-lot fashion. There won't be much space between you and your neighbor in the parking lot, but you can spread out under the trees.

The Big Creek Campground is the best place for RVers and others wanting a space of their own with room to spare. Forty-four sites among cottonwoods and wild roses offer full hookups, electricity, water, and sewer connections.

17 Eastside: Bear Lake State Park

Location: About 10 miles north of Laketown
Facilities: Fire grates, picnic tables, vault toilets, drinking water (at South Eden only), and two boat-launching areas, one at Rainbow Cove and the other at First Point
Sites: 25, plus dispersed camping

RVs at Rendezvous Beach Campground in Bear Lake State Park.

Fee: $

Elevation: 5,900 feet

Road conditions: Paved to the camground, then gravel

Management: Bear Lake State Park, P.O. Box 184, Garden City, UT 84028-0184; (435) 946–3343

Reservations: In the Salt Lake area, call (801) 322–3770; elsewhere, (800) 322–3770; fee

Activities: Fishing, boating, swimming, waterskiing, scuba diving, and picnicking

Season: Year-round

Finding the campground: From the junction of Utah Highway 30 and a paved road leading to the east shore of Bear Lake (a sign points the way), go north on the paved county road. You'll pass the First Point, Second Point, South Eden, Cisco Beach, Rainbow Cove, and North Eden Campgrounds as you head north.

About the campground: Six primitive campgrounds along the east shore of Bear Lake offer dispersed camping in an open setting. Recent improvements to the campground at South Eden include twenty-five sites with picnic tables and fire pits. There are also two group sites with pavilions. Sites here are available by reservation or on a first-come, first-served basis.

South Eden is the only site with drinking water. Boat ramps are found at First Point and Rainbow Cove. Cisco Beach is famous among scuba divers, who enjoy the steep underwater drop-offs. Bear Lake is also popular with boaters, while anglers look forward to trout, Bonneville cisco, and whitefish.

---

18 Birch Creek

Location: About 9 miles west of Woodruff

Facilities: Fire grates, picnic tables, and vault toilets

Sites: 4

Fee: None

Elevation: 6,850 feet

Road conditions: Dirt

Management: Bureau of Land Management, Salt Lake Field Office, 2370 South 2300 West, Salt Lake City, UT 84119; (801) 977–4300; UT-SALT-LAKE@blm.gov

Reservations: None

Activities: Fishing and picnicking

Season: Year-round

Finding the campground: From the junction of Utah Highways 16 and 39 in Woodruff, drive west on UT 39 for 7.8 miles. A sign points the way north to Birch Creek Reservoir. Follow the maintained dirt road for 1.1 miles.

About the campground: Tucked away in the willows, you'll find four sites at the west end of one reservoir, with another reservoir above and to the west. An unmaintained path leads to both areas, which are popular for rainbow and cutthroat trout fishing.

This nonfee area is best for tents and vans—there is absolutely no place for trailers to turn around, let alone park.

19 Monte Cristo

Location: In the Wasatch-Cache National Forest, about 20 miles west of Woodruff
Facilities: Fire grates, picnic tables, drinking water, and pit toilets
Sites: 49
Fee: $$
Elevation: 9,000 feet
Road conditions: Paved
Management: Ogden Ranger District, 507 25th Street, Ogden, UT 84401; (801) 625-5112
Reservations: None; for group sites only, call (800) 280-2267; fee
Activities: Hiking, off-highway driving, mountain biking, and picnicking
Season: June through September
Finding the campground: From the junction of Utah Highways 16 and 39 in Woodruff, drive west on UT 39 for 20.2 miles to the campground, which is on the south side of the road.

About the campground: Aspen, spruce, and fir add to the already lovely high-elevation setting of this campground. Two group sites, available by reservation only, make this a nice spot for groups and others who just want a base camp from which to explore, or a place for relaxing and picnicking.

There's a 16-mile loop that will be of interest to those with mountain bikes or ATVs. Ranging from 8,400 feet to 8,800 feet, the loop receives moderate use, while its series of ridge roads provides views of the Wasatch, Uinta, and Wellsville Mountains.

Golden Spike Empire

The Golden Spike Empire is a vast and varied place located in the northwest corner of Utah. One of nine state travel regions, it is comprised of 7,129 square miles and includes part of the Utah geologic regions known as the Great Basin, Wasatch Front Cities, and Rocky Mountain Province. Bordered by Nevada on the west, the Golden Spike Empire abuts Idaho on the north, while Utah travel regions Great Salt Lake Country, Mountainland, and Bridgerland snuggle up to it on the south and east sides. Four counties—Box Elder, Weber, Morgan, and Davis—call the place home.

In addition to grand desert and mountain scenes, there is an abundance of animal life. Visitors may see big-game species such as moose, elk, and mule deer, while the more fortunate may even see bighorn sheep and mountain goats. Smaller but no less significant mammals include marmots, snowshoe hares, porcupines, beavers, and several kinds of chipmunks and ground squirrels. Many bird species can be found here, too.

An extreme diversity in plant communities results from rapid changes in topography. As a result, there's a wide array of plants to appreciate: everything from sagebrush and rabbitbrush in the desert, to oak woodlands on the western slopes of the Wasatch Mountains. Higher still, aspen woodlands lead to forests of Douglas fir, lodgepole pine, and spruce. Stunning canyons offer an array of maples, red-barked dogwood, cottonwoods, and many species of wildflowers.

Twenty-four campgrounds make exploring the Golden Spike Empire both fun and easy. These sites allow you to enjoy a mix of wildlife watching, history, and recreation at places such as Antelope Island State Park, or to thrill to a drive up the Ogden Canyon Scenic Byway, which leads to a multitude of pretty places including Pineview Reservoir. In addition, bird-watchers will find hundreds of species of song- , wading, and shorebirds at both the Farmington Bay Waterfowl Management Area and farther north at the Bear River Migratory Bird Refuge west of Brigham City.

A number of different agencies manage the campgrounds found here. Lost Creek Reservoir is temporarily managed by the Bureau of Reclamation, while Weber County Parks and Recreation manages the campgrounds at both Weber County Memorial Park and North Fork Park. The primitive campground at Clear Creek is the only Utah site managed by the Sawtooth National Forest, though there are thirteen campgrounds cared for by the Wasatch-Cache National Forest. Several state parks take care of the remaining campgrounds.

Fort Buenaventura State Park is the only park where camping is restricted to one group site. It's also the only place where you can go to participate in Mountain Men Rendezvous. The remaining state parks offer much in the way of water-related activities. Two campgrounds are located along Willard Bay, where water sports and bird-watching are the main activities. The same is true for Antelope Island State Park, where folks also come to hike, mountain bike, and so on. Three campgrounds at East Canyon State Park offer fishing opportunities for anglers and waterskiing for those who enjoy the sport.

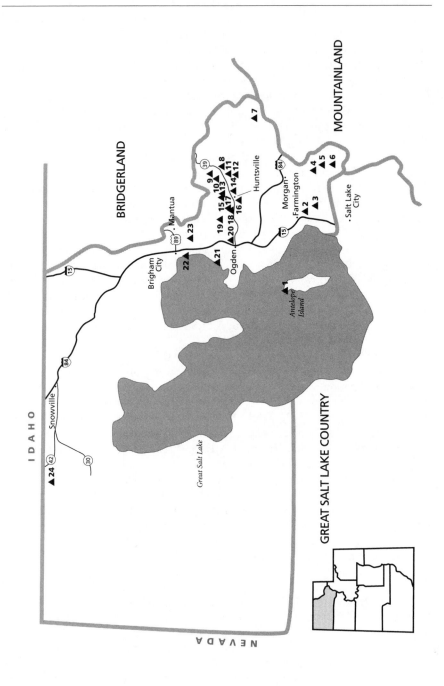

	Group sites	RV sites	Total sites	Max. RV length	Hookups	Toilets	Showers	Drinking water	Dump station	Pets	Wheelchair	Recreation	Fee($)	Season	Can reserve	Stay limit
1 Antelope Island S.P.	•	•	31			CVF	•	•	•	•		SBHMR	$		•	14
2 Sunset			11			P		•		•		MH	$	June–Sept.		14
3 Bountiful Peak			32			P		•		•		OMHR	$	June–Sept.		7
4 East Canyon S.P.		•	31	35		F	•	•	•	•		SBLF	$$		•	14
5 Big Rock		•	26			V				•		FBS	$			14
6 River Edge		•	5			P				•		FBS	$			14
7 Lost Creek Reservoir		•	*			V				•		BF		Mem. Day–Labor Day		14
8 Weber County Memorial Park	•	•	49	35		P		•		•		FH	$–$$	May–Oct.		7
9 Willows		•	17	30		V		•		•	•	F	$$–$$$	May–Oct.		7
10 Upper Meadows		•	24	35		V		•		•	•	F	$$–$$$	May–Oct.		7
11 Lower Meadows			8			P		•		•		F	$	May–Oct.		7
12 Perception Park	•	•	27	35		V		•		•	•	FH	$$	May–Oct.		7
13 South Fork		•	43	35		V		•		•	•	F	$$–$$$	May–Oct.		7
14 Botts			7			V		•		•		F	$$–$$$$	May–Oct.		7
15 Hobble			4			V				•		F	$	May–Oct.		7
16 Magpie		•	9	35		P		•		•		F	$$–$$$$	May–Oct.		7
17 Jefferson Hunt		•	27	40		VP		•		•	•	SBF	$	June–Sept.		7
18 Anderson Cove	•	•	70	40		V	•	•	•	•		SMBF	$$–$$$$	May–Sept.	•	7
19 North Fork Park	•	•	181			F		•		•	•	FHMR	$–$$	May–Oct.		7
20 Ft. Buenaventura S.P.	•		1			C				•		FB	$$$$	Apr.–Nov.	•	14
21 South Marina	•	•	*			F	•	•		•		SLFB	$$	Apr.–Oct.		14
22 Willow Creek	•	•	62	30		F	•	•	•	•	•	SLFB	$$		•	14
23 Box Elder	•	•	28	30		F		•		•		F	$	5/15–Sept.	•	7
24 Clear Creek		•	14			P		•		•		HO		May–Oct.		14

* Dispersed Camping—no designated sites **Hookups:** W = Water E = Electric S = Sewer **Toilets:** F = Flush V = Vault P = Pit C= Chemical **Recreation:** H = Hiking S = Swimming F = Fishing B = Boating L = Boat Launch O = Off-highway driving R = Horseback Riding C = Rock Climbing M = Mountain Biking **Maximum Trailer/RV length** given in feet. **Stay Limit** given in days. **Fee** given in dollars. If no entry under **Season,** campgound is open all year. If no entry under **Fee,** camping is free.

Campgrounds in the Wasatch Mountain Range are numerous, especially along the South Fork Ogden River, where you can engage in hiking, biking, fishing, boating—or just relaxing and enjoying your surroundings.

While most of the campgrounds in the region are closed during winter, some remain open year-round. For additional information, contact the Golden Spike Empire at 2501 Wall Avenue, Ogden, UT 84401; (801) 627–8288 or (800) 255–8824; Fax (801) 399–0783, TDD at (801) 627–8290; info@ogdencvb.org.

---

1 Antelope Island State Park

Location: About 10 miles south of the fee station

Facilities: Fire grates, picnic tables, drinking water, and both chemical and vault toilets in the campgrounds. Nearby there are showers, flush toilets, a sewage disposal station, public telephone, ice machine, and soda pop machines. When you first reach the island, there's a marina and boat ramp

Sites: 31

Fee: $

Elevation: 4,200 feet

Road conditions: Paved at Bridger Bay; dirt at White Rock Bay

Management: Antelope Island State Park, 4528 West 1700 South, Syracuse, UT 84075-6868; (801) 773–2941

Reservations: In the Salt Lake area, call (801) 322–3770; elsewhere 800-322-3770; fee

Activities: Mountain biking, hiking, horseback riding, swimming, boating, and picnicking

Restrictions: No campfires

Season: Year-round

Finding the campground: Leave Interstate 15 at exit 335 (Utah Highway 108), which leads to Syracuse. A sign points the way to the state park. Head west on UT 108 for 3.9 miles until you reach its junction with Utah Highway 127; stay straight, now traveling UT 127 for another 3 miles to the fee station. Drive the 7.2-mile causeway to the island, where you'll find a marina, a boat ramp, and a memorial. Make a right and drive an additional 2.7 miles to the Bridger Bay Campground. The group campground at White Rock Bay is located to the east.

About the campground: Huge, open camp spaces make this a delight for RVers with monster rigs. There are nice western views from all twenty-six sites, and there's access to the Lakeside Trail, which spans 3 miles from this campground to the group campground at White Rock Bay—it consists of five group sites. Though the amenities are primitive at both campgrounds, you will find full services (showers, water, flush toilets, telephone, ice and soda pop machines) at the day-use area, which is less than 1 mile away.

A 7.2-mile causeway leads from the mainland to the largest of the ten islands found in the Great Salt Lake. There are opportunities to view wildlife such as pronghorn antelope, bison, and jackrabbits, as well as the chance to do some saltwater bathing, bird-watching, hiking, biking, and horseback riding, or to explore historical sites. For those who like to hike to high points, there's a 4.5-mile trail leading to the top of Frary Peak—at 6,597 feet the highest point on the island. The trail is closed from May 15 to June 15, the antelope fawning season.

2 Sunset

Location: In the Wasatch-Cache National Forest, about 6 miles east of Farmington
Facilities: Fire grates, picnic tables, drinking water, and pit toilets
Sites: 11
Fee: $
Elevation: 6,400 feet
Road conditions: Gravel
Management: Salt Lake Ranger District, 6944 South 3000 East, Salt Lake City, UT 84121; (801) 943–1794
Reservations: None
Activities: Mountain biking, hiking, and picnicking
Season: June through September
Finding the campground: From Interstate 15, go east at exit 327 (Lagoon Drive, Utah Highway 225) in Farmington, and continue east on UT 225 for 0.4 mile to Main Street. Now make a right (south) onto Main and travel another 0.3 mile; go left (east) onto 600 North for 0.2 mile. There's a sign reading SCENIC BYWAY. At the T junction, go left (north, then east) onto 100 East and continue up the paved road. Though unsigned as such, the road later becomes Forest Road 007 and is quite steep, narrow, and winding. It turns to gravel after 1.6 miles. Continue an additional 3.6 miles on the gravel road to the campground, which is on your right. The campground sign is tucked away in the trees, so look closely or you'll miss the turnoff.

About the campground: Small sites are tucked away in the oak and maple forest found here, so car or tent camping is best; the place just isn't suited for trailers. Mountain biking and hiking are popular in this canyon.

3 Bountiful Peak

Location: In the Wasatch-Cache National Forest, about 10 miles southeast of Farmington
Facilities: Fire grates, picnic tables, drinking water, and pit toilets
Sites: 32
Fee: $
Elevation: 7,500 feet
Road conditions: Gravel
Management: Salt Lake Ranger District, 6944 South 3000 East, Salt Lake City, UT 84121; (801) 943–1794
Reservations: None
Activities: Mountain biking, hiking, horseback riding, off-highway driving, and picnicking
Season: June through September

Finding the campground: From Interstate 15, go east at exit 327 (Lagoon Drive, Utah Highway 225) in Farmington, and continue east on UT 225 for 0.4 mile to Main Street. Now make a right (south) onto Main and travel another 0.3 mile; go left (east) onto 600 North for 0.2 mile. There's a sign reading SCENIC BYWAY. At the T junction, go left (north, then east) onto 100 East and continue up the paved road. Though unsigned as such, the road later becomes Forest Road 007 and is quite steep, narrow, and winding. It turns to gravel after 1.6 miles. Continue an additional 6.3 miles on the gravel road to a fork; keep right (south) and drive another 0.8 mile to the campground.

About the campground: Conifers, aspens, and some nice views of Bountiful Peak and the surrounding area are yours for the asking at this pleasant campground. ATVs are popular here, with nearby Skyline Drive being a frequent destination. There's also a trail to the top of Bountiful Peak, a favorite for hikers and horseback riders, and Farmington Flats is a popular mountain bike ride. Check into *Mountain Biking Utah,* by Gregg Bromka, for more information.

4 East Canyon State Park

Location: About 12 miles southeast of Morgan
Facilities: Fire grates, covered picnic tables, flush toilets, showers, sewage disposal station, drinking water, volleyball court, boat ramp, dry boat storage, fish cleaning station, and public telephone. A concessionaire offers a gas dock, snack bar, boat rentals, and a convenience store
Sites: 31

The campground at East Canyon Reservoir in East Canyon State Park.

Fee: $$
Elevation: 5,700 feet
Road conditions: Paved
Management: East Canyon State Park, 5535 South Highway 66, Morgan, UT 84050-9694; (801) 829-6866
Reservations: In the Salt Lake area, call (801) 322-3770; elsewhere, (800) 322-3770; fee
Activities: Fishing, swimming, boating, waterskiing, bird-watching, and picnicking
Restrictions: ATVs are not permitted
Season: Year-round
Finding the campground: From the junction of Interstate 84 and Utah Highway 66 in Morgan, go southeast on UT 66 for 12 miles to the park entrance.

About the campground: Set on a sunny, open slope overlooking 680-acre East Canyon Reservoir, this campground is a popular spot for those interested in water-related activities. It's also a delight for anglers, who vie for rainbow trout and kokanee salmon. Crawfishing and ice fishing are popular as well.

Look for wildlife while visiting the park. If you're lucky, you might see a mule deer, a badger, a fox, a great horned owl, or even a loon. Migrating birds often stop here on their journeys so keep your binoculars ready.

5 Big Rock: East Canyon State Park

Location: About 17 miles southeast of Morgan
Facilities: Fire grates, picnic tables, and vault toilets
Sites: 26
Fee: $
Elevation: 5,700 feet
Road conditions: Paved to the campground, then gravel
Management: East Canyon State Park, 5535 South Highway 66, Morgan, UT 84050-9694; (801) 829-6866
Reservations: None
Activities: Fishing, swimming, boating, waterskiing, bird-watching, and picnicking
Restrictions: ATVs are not permitted
Season: Year-round
Finding the campground: From the junction of Interstate 84 and Utah Highway 66 in Morgan, go southeast on UT 66 until it ends at Utah Highway 65 in 13.5 miles. Now go right (west, then south) on UT 65 for another 3.9 miles.

About the campground: Located on the south end of 680-acre East Canyon Reservoir, these large sites are divided by big rocks—thus the name. This place is a good spot for those who want primitive access to a pretty reservoir. It's a popular spot for all sorts of water-related activities as well as fishing. Anglers often pursue trout and kokanee salmon.

6 River Edge: East Canyon State Park

Location: About 17 miles southeast of Morgan
Facilities: Picnic tables and pit toilets
Sites: 5
Fee: $
Elevation: 5,700 feet
Road conditions: Gravel
Management: East Canyon State Park, 5535 South Highway 66, Morgan, UT 84050-9694; (801) 829–6866
Reservations: None
Activities: Fishing and picnicking, with swimming, boating, and waterskiing at the nearby reservoir
Season: Year-round
Restrictions: ATVs are not permitted
Finding the campground: From the junction of Interstate 84 and Utah Highway 66 in Morgan, go southeast on UT 66 until it ends at Utah Highway 65 in 13.5 miles. Now go right (west, then south) on UT 65 for another 4.1 miles.

About the campground: Located along the river a short distance from East Canyon Reservoir, this primitive campground consists of dispersed sites, with five picnic tables and a pit toilet.

7 Lost Creek Reservoir

Location: About 20 miles northeast of Morgan
Facilities: Vault toilets and a boat ramp
Sites: Dispersed
Fee: None
Elevation: 6,000 feet
Road conditions: Gravel
Management: Bureau of Reclamation, Provo Area Office, 302 East 1860 South, Provo, UT 84606-7317
Reservations: None
Activities: Boating, fishing, and picnicking
Season: Memorial Day through Labor Day
Finding the campground: From exit 111 off Interstate 84, about 8 miles east of Morgan, drive northeast on Lost Creek Road for an additional 12 miles or so to the reservoir.

About the campground: Lost Creek Dam and Reservoir are located on Lost Creek, about 12 miles upstream from its confluence with the Weber River. Once part of the Utah state park system, the reservoir is being temporarily managed by the Bureau of Reclamation. Management will probably change in the future.

Situated in an open setting, this is a wakeless lake of 300-plus acres. Conifers and grassy slopes surround the reservoir, where anglers vie for rainbow and cutthroat trout. Folks at the Bureau of Reclamation tell me that they have no on-site manager or law enforcement at the reservoir; thus, there have been some problems in the past.

8 Weber County Memorial Park

Location: Near Causey Reservoir, about 10 miles northeast of Huntsville
Facilities: Fire grates, picnic tables, pit toilets, and drinking water. Four group sites also have horseshoe pits, a volleyball court, and a softball diamond
Sites: 49
Fee: $ for county residents; $$ for non–county residents
Elevation: 5,200 feet
Road conditions: Paved, then gravel in the campground
Management: Weber County Parks and Recreation Department, 1181 North Fairgrounds Drive, Ogden, UT 84404; (801) 399–8491 or (800) 407–2757
Reservations: For group sites, call (801) 399–8491 or (800) 407–2757
Activities: Fishing, hiking, volleyball, softball, horseshoes, and picnicking
Season: May through October
Finding the campground: From the junction of Utah Highway 39 and 100 South in Huntsville, head east on UT 39 for 8.4 miles, then turn right (south) onto the paved road to Causey Reservoir; a sign points the way. You'll reach the campground after another 1.2 miles. The campground is just north of the reservoir.

About the campground: This county park is situated along the banks of the South Fork Ogden River, a short distance from Causey Reservoir, where you'll find trails for hikers leading from the north end of Causey Dam at Boy Scout Camp to Baldy Ridge, Bear Hollow, and Baldy Peak.

There are four large group areas, each with its own horseshoe pit, softball diamond, and volleyball court. Fees vary—call the above reservation number for more information. All sites, including the group sites, are on the grass, with some trees for shade. Single sites are scattered throughout the area, with some located near the river, which is popular with anglers targeting rainbow, cut-throat, and brown trout.

9 Willows

Location: In the Wasatch-Cache National Forest, about 8 miles northeast of Huntsville
Facilities: Fire grates, picnic tables, Dutch oven stands, vault toilets, and drinking water
Sites: 17
Fee: $$ for single sites; $$$ for double sites
Elevation: 5,200 feet
Road conditions: Paved to the campground, then gravel
Management: Ogden Ranger District, 507 25th Street, Ogden, UT 84401; (801) 625–5112
Reservations: None
Activities: Fishing and picnicking
Season: May through October
Finding the campground: From the junction of Utah Highway 39 and 100 South in Huntsville, head east on paved UT 39 for 7.5 miles; the campground is on the south side of the road.

About the campground: Located along the South Fork Ogden River, this campground is a great place for fishing for rainbow, brown, and cutthroat trout; relaxing; and enjoying the cottonwoods and wild roses that inhabit the place.

10 Upper Meadows

Location: In the Wasatch-Cache National Forest, approximately 8 miles northeast of Huntsville
Facilities: Fire grates, picnic tables, Dutch oven stands, vault toilets, and drinking water
Sites: 24
Fee: $$ for single sites; $$$ for double sites
Elevation: 5,200 feet
Road conditions: Gravel
Management: Ogden Ranger District, 507 25th Street, Ogden, UT 84401; (801) 625-5112
Reservations: None
Activities: Fishing and picnicking
Season: May through October
Finding the campground: From the junction of Utah Highway 39 and 100 South in Huntsville, head east on paved UT 39 for 7.4 miles, then turn right (south) onto a gravel road leading to both the Upper Meadows and Lower Meadows Campgrounds. Stay straight, then make a right (west) and parallel the river for 0.8 mile to the campground.

About the campground: Situated in beautiful Ogden Canyon and located along the South Fork Ogden River, this is a great place for trout fishing, relaxing, and enjoying the cottonwoods and other plants and trees that live here.

11 Lower Meadows

Location: In the Wasatch-Cache National Forest, about 7 miles northeast of Huntsville
Facilities: Fire grates, picnic tables, pit toilets, and drinking water
Sites: 8
Fee: $
Elevation: 5,200 feet
Road conditions: Paved to the campground, then gravel
Management: Ogden Ranger District, 507 25th Street, Ogden, UT 84401; (801) 625-5112
Reservations: None
Activities: Fishing and picnicking
Season: May through October
Finding the campground: From the junction of Utah Highway 39 and 100 South in Huntsville, head east on paved UT 39 for 7.4 miles, then turn right (south) onto a gravel road leading to both the Upper Meadows and Lower Meadows Campgrounds. The campground is to the left (east) after you turn onto the gravel road.

About the campground: Resting in cottonwoods and other lush vegetation, this small campground is located in beautiful Ogden Canyon, along the South Fork Ogden River. Though not as new as some of the other surrounding campgrounds, it's a nice place for trout fishing and relaxing.

12 Perception Park

Location: In the Wasatch-Cache National Forest, about 7 miles northeast of Huntsville
Facilities: Fire grates, picnic tables, vault toilets, and drinking water
Sites: 27
Fee: $$
Elevation: 5,200 feet
Road conditions: Paved
Management: Ogden Ranger District, 507 25th Street, Ogden, UT 84401; (801) 625-5112
Reservations: For the group areas call (800) 280-2267; fee
Activities: Fishing, hiking, and picnicking
Season: May through October
Finding the campground: From the junction of Utah Highway 39 and 100 South in Huntsville, travel east on paved UT 39 for 7.2 miles to the campground, which is on the south side of the road.

About the campground: The South Fork Ogden River, with its typical habitat of cottonwoods and a whole lot more, makes this a nice spot for camping. The forest service claims this is one of the nicest campgrounds providing barrier-free use around. Several spaces are wheelchair accessible, and an asphalt trail along the river allows for viewing of the rapids. In addition, there are several fishing docks throughout the campground with guardrails. From here, anglers may catch rainbow, brown, and cutthroat trout.

Three group areas, which must be reserved, offer a playground, a volleyball court, and horseshoe pits.

13 South Fork

Location: In the Wasatch-Cache National Forest, about 6 miles northeast of Huntsville
Facilities: Fire grates, picnic tables, Dutch oven stands, vault toilets, and drinking water
Sites: 43
Fee: $$ for single sites; $$$ for double sites
Elevation: 5,200 feet
Road conditions: Paved to the campground, then gravel
Management: Ogden Ranger District, 507 25th Street, Ogden, UT 84401; (801) 625-5112
Reservations: None
Activities: Fishing and picnicking
Season: May through October

Finding the campground: From the junction of Utah Highway 39 and 100 South in Huntsville, travel east on paved UT 39 for 6.4 miles to the campground, which is on the south side of the road.

About the campground: The South Fork Ogden River and its typical cottonwood habitat are yours for the asking at this campground. An entrance gate closes at 10:00 P.M. and opens at 7:00 A.M. If you like to fish, try catching rainbow, brown, and cutthroat trout.

14 Botts

Location: In the Wasatch-Cache National Forest, approximately 6 miles northeast of Huntsville
Facilities: Fire grates, picnic tables, vault toilets, and drinking water
Sites: 7
Fee: $$–$$$$
Elevation: 5,200 feet
Road conditions: Paved to the campground, then gravel
Management: Ogden Ranger District, 507 25th Street, Ogden, UT 84401; (801) 625–5112
Reservations: None
Activities: Fishing and picnicking
Season: May through October
Finding the campground: From the junction of Utah Highway 39 and 100 South in Huntsville, travel east on paved UT 39 for 5.9 miles to the campground, which is on the south side of the road.

About the campground: This small campground, which I'd recommend for tents and vans only, is found along the South Fork Ogden River and offers typical cottonwood habitat. It's a good place to fish for trout or to just plain relax.

15 Hobble

Location: In the Wasatch-Cache National Forest, about 6 miles northeast of Huntsville
Facilities: Fire grates, picnic tables, and vault toilets
Sites: 4
Fee: $
Elevation: 5,200 feet
Road conditions: Paved to the campground, then dirt
Management: Ogden Ranger District, 507 25th Street, Ogden, UT 84401; (801) 625–5112
Reservations: None
Activities: Fishing and picnicing
Season: May through October
Finding the campground: From the junction of Utah Highway 39 and 100 South in Huntsville, travel east on paved UT 39 for 5.6 miles to the campground, which is on the north side of the road.

About the campground: This small campground, which I'd recommend for tents and vans only (the sites are very small), is located across the highway from the South Fork Ogden River and offers typical cottonwood and box elder habitat. Drinking water is not available, but it is found at the other campgrounds in the area.

16 Magpie

Location: In the Wasatch-Cache National Forest, about 5 miles northeast of Huntsville
Facilities: Fire grates, picnic tables, drinking water, and vault toilets
Sites: 9
Fee: $$-$$$$
Elevation: 5,200 feet
Road conditions: Paved to the campground, then gravel
Management: Ogden Ranger District, 507 25th Street, Ogden, UT 84401; (801) 625-5112
Reservations: None
Activities: Fishing and picnicking
Season: May through October
Finding the campground: From the junction of Utah Highway 39 and 100 South in Huntsville, travel east on paved UT 39 for 5.2 miles to the campground, which is on the south side of the road.

About the campground: Tucked away in a mix of cottonwoods and box elders, with the South Fork Ogden River flowing nearby, this recently renovated campground is a nice place for RVers who would like to do some trout fishing or relaxing.

17 Jefferson Hunt

Location: In the Wasatch-Cache National Forest, approximately 2 miles south of Huntsville
Facilities: Fire grates, picnic tables, Dutch oven stands, drinking water, and vault and pit toilets
Sites: 27
Fee: $
Elevation: 5,000 feet
Road conditions: Gravel
Management: Ogden Ranger District, 507 25th Street, Ogden, UT 84401; (801) 625-5112
Reservations: None
Activities: Fishing, swimming, boating, and picnicking
Season: June through September
Finding the campground: From the junction of Utah Highway 39 and 100 South in Huntsville, go south on paved UT 39 West for 1.4 miles. At a sign reading JEFFERSON HUNT, go right (north) onto the paved (later gravel) road for an additional 0.2 mile.

About the campground: Both open and shady sites exist in this campground, with cottonwoods, willows, and Russian olives among the trees.

The campground is on the southeast end of Pineview Reservoir, where the South Fork of the Ogden River meets the reservoir, and is an excellent base from which to enjoy water sports such as windsurfing, swimming, and boating. The reservoir is also a great place for fishing. Anglers may catch rainbow, brown, and cutthroat trout, along with bullhead catfish, largemouth and smallmouth bass, bluegills, crappie, yellow perch, whitefish, and tiger muskies.

18 Anderson Cove

Location: In the Wasatch-Cache National Forest, approximately 2 miles southwest of Huntsville
Facilities: Fire grates, picnic tables, Dutch oven stands, drinking water, sewage disposal station, vault toilets, horseshoe pit, volleyball court, public telephone, ice machine, and soda pop machine
Sites: 70
Fee: $$ for single sites; $$$$ for double sites
Elevation: 5,000 feet
Road conditions: Paved
Management: Ogden Ranger District, 507 25th Street, Ogden, UT 84401; (801) 625–5112
Reservations: Call (877) 444–6777 or TDD (877) 833–6777; fee
Activities: Fishing, swimming, boating, mountain biking, and picnicking
Season: May through September 21
Finding the campground: From the junction of Utah Highway 39 and 100 South in Huntsville, go south and then west on paved UT 39 West for 2.3 miles.

About the campground: Lots of grass and a bounty of shade trees are the norm at this lovely campground, located along the south shore of Pineview Reservoir. Nearly all water activities are popular, as is fishing. Anglers may catch rainbow, brown, and cutthroat trout, along with bullhead catfish, largemouth and smallmouth bass, bluegills, crappie, yellow perch, whitefish, and tiger muskies. There are two group sites—both cost $115 a day.

There are some mountain bike trails nearby. Check out Gregg Bromka's Falcon book *Mountain Biking Utah* for more information.

19 North Fork Park

Location: Along the North Fork Ogden River, about 10 miles northeast of North Ogden
Facilities: Fire grates, picnic tables, flush toilets, drinking water, and horse corrals. Six group sites also have horseshoe pits and volleyball poles.
Sites: 181
Fee: $ for county residents; $$ for non-county residents

Elevation: 6,200 feet
Road conditions: Paved to the campground, then gravel
Management: Weber County Parks and Recreation, 1181 North Fairgrounds Drive, Ogden, UT 84404; (801) 399-8491 or (800) 407-2757
Reservations: For group sites only, call (801) 399-8491 or (800) 407-2757
Activities: Fishing, hiking, mountain biking, horseback riding, volleyball, softball, horseshoes, and picnicking
Season: May through October
Finding the campground: From the junction of Washington Boulevard and North Ogden Canyon Road in North Ogden, go east on North Ogden Canyon Road for about 7 miles. Turn left and head north-northwest on North Fork Road to the campground.

About the campground: There are six group areas here, each with its own horseshoe pit and volleyball poles. Fees vary—call the above reservation number for more information. Several trails for nonmotorized vehicles are in the area, including the Ben Lommond Peak Trail, which begins here at the south end of the park near the horse corrals. This is one of the most popular and heavily used trails in the Ogden area, so be prepared for a crowd. Scenic vistas are your just reward for making the hike; it's 7.6 miles long and gains 2,880 feet.

20 Fort Buenaventura State Park

Location: In downtown Ogden
Facilities: Fire grates, picnic tables, chemical toilets, and a horseshoe pit
Sites: 1 group site
Fee: $$$$
Elevation: 4,300 feet
Road conditions: Paved
Management: Fort Buenaventura State Park, 2450 A Avenue, Ogden, UT 84401-2203; (801) 621-4808
Reservations: In the Salt Lake area, call (801) 322-3770; elsewhere, (800) 322-3770; fee
Activities: Fishing (for kids 13 and under), canoeing, and picnicking
Season: April through November
Finding the campground: From exit 345 off Interstate 15 in Ogden, drive east on 24th Street. There are signs pointing the way to the state park. After 1 mile, turn right (south) onto paved A Avenue and follow it for just 0.2 mile before turning left (east) onto a paved road that leads to the park.

About the campground: Though this campsite is in downtown Ogden, you'll hardly know it in this lush setting of box elders and cottonwoods. Though water isn't available in the campground, it's found nearby at the picnic area.

While visiting the campground, be sure to check out Fort Buenaventura as well; it was re-created in 1980 on its original site. Mountain Men Rendezvous are enacted at the fort on special occasions.

Campers enjoy the water activities at Willard Bay State Park.

21 | South Marina: Willard Bay State Park

Location: About 8 miles north of Ogden
Facilities: Fire grates, picnic tables, flush toilets, showers, drinking water, and boat ramps and docks
Sites: Dispersed
Fee: $$
Elevation: 4,200 feet
Road conditions: Paved
Management: Willard Bay State Park, 900 West 650 North, #A, Willard, UT 84340-9999; (435) 734-9494
Reservations: None
Activities: Fishing, swimming, boating, waterskiing, bird-watching, and picnicking
Season: April through October
Finding the campground: From exit 354 off Interstate 15, north of Ogden and just south of Willard, drive south on Utah Highway 126 for a short distance, then make a right (west) onto 4000 North. Signs for the state park point the way. After 1.4 miles, turn right (north) onto 2000 West. You'll reach the entrance station in an additional 0.8 mile.

About the campground: Located in one of two recreation areas along the east shore of Willard Bay, the South Marina Campground has open grassy sites with some scattered trees for shade. Designated sites are nonexistent; instead you will find dispersed camping, with access to Willard Bay, which rests atop the Great Salt Lake floodplain.

Anglers may hook kokanee salmon, largemouth bass, bluegills, crappie, yellow perch, and walleye.

22 Willow Creek: Willard Bay State Park

Location: About 15 miles north of Ogden
Facilities: Fire grates, picnic tables, flush toilets, sewage disposal station, showers, drinking water, and boat ramps and docks
Sites: 62
Fee: $$
Elevation: 4,200 feet
Road conditions: Paved
Management: Willard Bay State Park, 900 West 650 North, #A, Willard, UT 84340-9999; (435) 734-9494
Reservations: In the Salt Lake area, call (801) 322-3770; elsewhere, (800) 322-3770; fee
Activities: Fishing, swimming, boating, waterskiing, bird-watching, and picnicking
Season: Year-round
Finding the campground: From exit 360 off Interstate 15 in Willard, head south on the west side of the interstate. The entrance station is just off the interstate.

About the campground: Dense vegetation and an array of trees—including maple, box elder, cottonwood, and Russian olive—provide the setting for this popular campground. A sandy beach and a nature trail are bonuses for those who opt to camp here. A marina offers rentals and snacks, as well as boat ramps and boat docks.

Though it may seem as though fishing, boating, and other water-related activities are favorites, birding is also popular: More than 200 species can be observed at or near the park. Still, anglers may snag kokanee salmon, largemouth bass, bluegills, crappie, yellow perch, and walleye.

23 Box Elder

Location: In the Wasatch-Cache National Forest, just south of Mantua
Facilities: Fire grates, picnic tables, flush toilets, and drinking water
Sites: 28
Fee: $
Elevation: 5,800 feet
Road conditions: Paved, then gravel in the campground
Management: Logan Ranger District, 1500 East Highway 89, Logan, UT 84321-4373; (435) 755-3620
Reservations: For single sites, call (877) 444-6777 or TDD (877) 833-6777; fee. For group sites, call (435) 755-3620
Activities: Fishing and picnicking

Season: May 15 through September
Finding the campground: Leave U.S. Highway 91 at the exit for Mantua and the Box Elder Campground. Follow the signs for 0.8 mile on pavement to the campground, which is on the south side of US 91. A gravel road leads into the campground.

About the campground: Box Elder Creek sings through the thick vegetation of cottonwoods and box elders in this campground, which is just west of Mantua Reservoir. Two overnight group areas provide for groups of one to twenty-five users, twenty-six to fifty users, and fifty-one to one hundred users. Fees vary, call for information.

24 Clear Creek

Location: In the Sawtooth National Forest, approximately 39 miles west of Snowville
Facilities: Fire grates, picnic tables, pit toilets, and drinking water
Sites: 14
Fee: None
Elevation: 6,700 feet
Road conditions: Gravel
Management: Burley Ranger District, 3650 South Overland Avenue, Burley, ID 83318; (208) 678–0430
Reservations: None
Activities: Hiking, off-highway driving, and picnicking.
Season: May through October.
Finding the campground: From Snowville, drive west on Interstate 84 for about 2 miles to exit 5, then continue west on Utah Highway 30 for another 16 miles. Now keep straight on Utah Highway 42; after an additional 7.5 miles, UT 42 becomes Idaho Highway 81. Go another 1.3 miles before turning left onto Strevell Road. Drive the maintained road for about 4 miles to the junction of Forest Road 001. Go south, driving the gravel road approximately 8 more miles to the campground.

About the campground: Set on the slopes of the Raft River Range, this is a great base from which to explore the area, though trails are pretty much non-existent. The grassy range runs east to west, which is quite rare in this part of the country.

Great Salt Lake Country

Great Salt Lake Country is just what its name implies—great. The place is also big, and it's remote: No doubt, it can feel mighty lonely out in its western realms. And while much of the place is accessible to visitors, the public isn't allowed at the following military-restricted areas—Dugway Proving Grounds, the Deseret Test Center, and the Wendover Range. Still, there are fourteen campgrounds to make exploring just that much easier.

Great Salt Lake Country, one of Utah's nine travel regions, is situated in the northern part of the state. Comprised of 7,487 square miles, the place consists of two counties, Tooele and Salt Lake, and three Utah geographic areas—Great Basin, Wasatch Front Cities, and the Rocky Mountain Province. Bordered on the west by Nevada, it is surrounded on three sides by various other Utah travel regions. These are the Golden Spike Empire to the north, Mountainland to the east, and Panoramaland to the south.

Utah's capital, Salt Lake City, rests at the base of the lovely Wasatch Mountains. Wasatch, an Indian word meaning "high mountain pass," aptly describes the Wasatch Range, for it offers many such passes during its 200-mile journey from central Utah to Idaho.

Salt Lake City is a short drive from several wonderful campgrounds. These sites make great bases from which to explore the city; if you're more interested in the great out-of-doors, they're wonderful spots from which to explore the mountains. Climbers will find some superb rocks to scale here. There are wide ranges of both sport and traditional climbs in both Big and Little Cottonwood Canyons. Hikers, backpackers, horseback riders, mountain bikers, and anglers will also find plenty to keep them busy.

There's another haven for outdoor enthusiasts in the Deseret Peak Wilderness Area, located in the Stansbury Mountain Range. Trails lead to a bevy of high alpine lakes and glacial cirques. From Deseret Peak, at 11,031 feet, there are wonderful views of the Wasatch Mountains, the Great Salt Lake, and the Great Salt Lake Desert. Six campgrounds—Cottonwood, Intake, Boy Scout, Lower Narrows, Upper Narrows, and Loop—make exploring possible.

Out in the desert you'll find stretches of the original Pony Express Trail and a campground. Simpson Springs is within walking distance of a restored Pony Express station, a tribute to the hardy riders who routinely covered the ten-day, 1,838-mile distance from St. Joseph, Missouri, to Sacramento, California. Riders stopped at stations such as the one found here every 12 miles or so: Each rider would change horses about six times a day.

Of the fourteen campgrounds found in this travel region, eleven are managed by the Wasatch-Cache National Forest. In addition, the Uinta National Forest oversees one, while the Bureau of Land Management manages two of them. Though most are closed in winter, two can be visited year-round. Simpson Springs is available for camping all year, as is Vernon Reservoir, though Vernon is officially open from June through October. Try Vernon Reservoir in winter—it can be a nice place to go ice fishing, another one of the many activities enjoyed in the area.

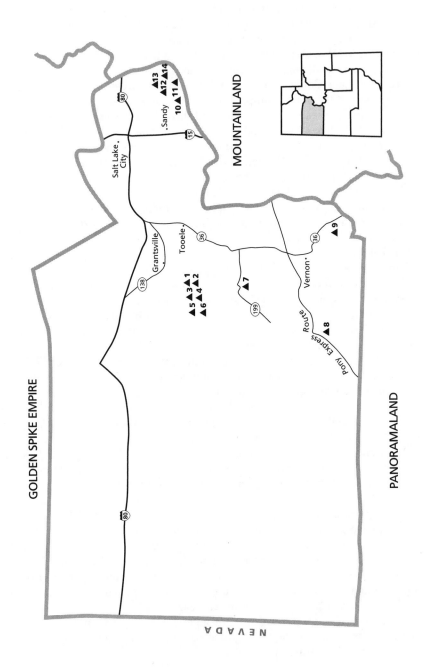

	Group sites	RV sites	Total sites	Max. RV length	Hookups	Toilets	Showers	Drinking water	Dump station	Pets	Wheelchair	Recreation	Fee($)	Season	Can reserve	Stay limit
1 Cottonwood			4			P				•		HCFM	$	May–Oct.15		7
2 Intake			4			P				•		HCFM	$	May–Sept.		7
3 Boy Scout	•	•	7	20		P				•		CMRFH	$	May–Sept.		7
4 Lower Narrows			3			P				•		CHRFM	$	May–Sept.		7
5 Upper Narrows	•		7			P				•		HCFM	$	May–Sept.		7
6 Loop		•	5	20		P				•		RHFCM	$	May–Sept.		7
7 Clover Springs	•	•	11	30		V				•	•	FRH	$	Apr.–Oct.		14
8 Simpson Springs		•	15	30		V				•		HOM	$			14
9 Vernon Reservoir		•	10			V	•			•		FOM		June–Oct.		14
10 Tanners Flat	•	•	39	20		F	•					FMHC	$$	May–Oct.	•	7
11 Albion Basin		•	25	25		V	•					HM	$$	July–Sept.	•	7
12 Jordan Pines	•		5			P	•					MCFH	$$$$	June–Sept.	•	7
13 Spruces	•	•	100	30		F	•		•			CMFH	$$	June–Sept.	•	7
14 Redman	•	•	49	20		P	•					MHFC	$$	June–Sept.		7

* Dispersed Camping—no designated sites **Hookups:** W = Water E = Electric S = Sewer **Toilets:** F = Flush V = Vault P = Pit C= Chemical **Recreation:** H = Hiking S = Swimming F = Fishing B = Boating L = Boat Launch O = Off-highway driving R = Horseback Riding C = Rock Climbing M = Mountain Biking **Maximum Trailer/RV length** given in feet. **Stay Limit** given in days. **Fee** given in dollars. If no entry under **Season,** campgound is open all year. If no entry under **Fee,** camping is free.

For more information, contact the Salt Lake Convention and Visitors Bureau at 90 South West Temple, Salt Lake City, UT 84101-1406; (801) 521–2822 or (800) 541–4955; fax (801) 355–9323; slcvb@saltlake.cvb.com.

1 Cottonwood

Location: In the Wasatch-Cache National Forest, about 9 miles southwest of Grantsville
Facilities: Fire pits, picnic tables, and pit toilets
Sites: 4
Fee: $
Elevation: 6,000 feet
Road conditions: Dirt
Management: Salt Lake Ranger District, 6944 South 3000 East, Salt Lake City, UT 84121; (801) 943–1794
Reservations: None
Activities: Fishing, mountain biking, hiking, rock climbing, and picnicking
Season: May through mid-October
Finding the campground: From Grantsville and Utah Highway 138 (Main Street), go south on West Street. Signs point the way to North and South Willow Canyon Roads. Drive for 5 miles on paved West Street, then turn right

An aspen grove in Wasatch-Cache National Forest.

(southwest) onto South Willow Canyon Road. It's narrow and paved, then turns to gravel after 3.3 miles; continue another 0.7 mile to the Cottonwood Campground, which is on the south side of the road.

About the campground: Box elders, dogwoods, and a whole lot more serve to shade this small shady place, with South Fork Willow Creek singing along its border. With a mere four sites, this would make a nice camping spot for a small group. Fishing and mountain biking are the most popular activities here, but farther up the canyon are rock climbing and hiking opportunities.

This is a tents-only kind of place with absolutely no place to turn trailers around; RVers should head up the canyon to the Loop Campground. Water isn't available here in the campground, but you can get it at the guard station just west of the Intake Campground.

2 Intake

Location: In the Wasatch-Cache National Forest, about 10 miles southwest of Grantsville
Facilities: Fire pits, picnic tables, and pit toilets
Sites: 4
Fee: $
Elevation: 6,300 feet

Road conditions: Dirt
Management: Salt Lake Ranger District, 6944 South 3000 East, Salt Lake City, UT 84121; (801) 943-1794
Reservations: None
Activities: Rock climbing, fishing, mountain biking, hiking, and picnicking
Season: May through September
Finding the campground: From Grantsville and Utah Highway 138 (Main Street), go south on West Street. Signs point the way to North and South Willow Canyon Roads. Drive for 5 miles on paved West Street, then turn right (southwest) onto South Willow Canyon Road. It's narrow and paved, then turns to gravel after 3.3 miles; continue another 1.4 miles to the Intake Campground, which is on the south side of the road.

About the campground: Box elders and miniature roses make this a shady place. Like most of the campgrounds here in the canyon, it's small and delightful, but recommended for tents only, because there's no place to turn trailers around. RVers should head up to the Loop Campground, where they'll find a little more room.

South Fork Willow Creek flows through the campground, making this a fun place for fishing. Mountain bikers can head up the canyon on their bicycles, while rock climbers will find some sport routes just up the canyon at the narrows. Hikers and horseback riders will find trails up the canyon at the Boy Scout and Loop Campgrounds.

Water isn't provided here in the campground, but it's available at the guard station just west of the campground.

3 Boy Scout

Location: In the Wasatch-Cache National Forest, about 10 miles southwest of Grantsville
Facilities: Fire pits, picnic tables, and pit toilets
Sites: 7
Fee: $
Elevation: 6,500 feet
Road conditions: Dirt
Management: Salt Lake Ranger District, 6944 South 3000 East, Salt Lake City, UT 84121; (801) 943-1794.
Reservations: None
Activities: Rock climbing, hiking, horseback riding, fishing, mountain biking, and picnicking
Season: May through September
Finding the campground: From Grantsville and Utah Highway 138 (Main Street), go south on West Street. Signs point the way to North and South Willow Canyon Roads. Drive for 5 miles on paved West Street, then turn right (southwest) onto South Willow Canyon Road. It's narrow and paved, then turns to gravel after 3.3 miles; continue another 2.0 miles to the Boy Scout Campground, which is on the south side of the road.

About the campground: A potpourri of deciduous trees and some pines shade this campground. There's a group site at space 6, a good place for trailers to turn around if the site is empty. South Fork Willow Creek flows through the campground, and hikers and horseback riders will find the Stansbury Front Trail, which leads 2.4 miles to Hickman Canyon.

If you'd rather do some rock climbing, check out the tough sport routes in the narrows, just up from the Upper Narrows Campground.

Water isn't available here in the campground, but it's provided at the guard station just west of the Intake Campground.

4 Lower Narrows

Location: In the Wasatch-Cache National Forest, about 11 miles southwest of Grantsville
Facilities: Fire pits, picnic tables, and pit toilets
Sites: 3
Fee: $
Elevation: 6,800 feet
Road conditions: Dirt
Management: Salt Lake Ranger District, 6944 South 3000 East, Salt Lake City, UT 84121; (801) 943–1794
Reservations: None
Activities: Rock climbing, hiking, horseback riding, fishing, mountain biking, and picnicking
Season: May through September
Finding the campground: From Grantsville and Utah Highway 138 (Main Street), go south on West Street. Signs point the way to North and South Willow Canyon Roads. Drive for 5 miles on paved West Street, then turn right (southwest) onto South Willow Canyon Road. It's narrow and paved, then turns to gravel after 3.3 miles; continue another 2.7 miles to the Lower Narrows Campground, which is on the south side of the road.

About the campground: Park off the road and walk into this small campground, with South Fork Willow Creek providing the opportunity for anglers to do a little fishing. With only three shady sites, this would make a nice place for a small group to meet and enjoy the outdoors.

From the Boy Scout Campground, there's a trail leading 2.4 miles to Hickman Canyon. It might be of interest for hikers and horseback riders. In addition, there are dirt roads for curious mountain bikers, and hard sport routes for rock climbers just up from the Upper Narrows Campground.

Water isn't available here in the campground, but you can get it at the guard station just west of the Intake Campground.

5 Upper Narrows

Location: In the Wasatch-Cache National Forest, about 11 miles southwest of Grantsville
Facilities: Fire pits, picnic tables, and pit toilets

Sites: 7
Fee: $
Elevation: 6,900 feet
Road conditions: Dirt
Management: Salt Lake Ranger District, 6944 South 3000 East, Salt Lake City, UT 84121; (801) 943-1794
Reservations: None
Activities: Rock climbing, hiking, horseback riding, fishing, mountain biking, and picnicking
Season: May through September
Finding the campground: From Grantsville and Utah Highway 138 (Main Street), go south on West Street. Signs point the way to North and South Willow Canyon Roads. Drive for 5 miles on paved West Street, then turn right (southwest) onto South Willow Canyon Road. It's narrow and paved, then turns to gravel after 3.3 miles; continue another 2.9 miles to the Upper Narrows Campground, which is on the south side of the road.

About the campground: Park off the road and walk into this small campground, with South Fork Willow Creek flowing alongside it. You'll find three shady sites near the parking area and another four shady sites just down a trail.

Hikers and horseback riders may want to check out the Stansbury Front Trail, which leads 2.4 miles to Hickman Canyon. It's back at the Boy Scout Campground. There are also trails leading from the Loop Campground, which is just up the canyon. Rock climbers will find twelve difficult sport routes at the narrows, which is just up from the campground.

Water isn't provided here in the campground, but it's available at the guard station just west of the Intake Campground.

6 Loop

Location: In the Wasatch-Cache National Forest, about 12 miles southwest of Grantsville
Facilities: Fire grates, picnic tables, and pit toilets
Sites: 5
Fee: $
Elevation: 7,400 feet
Road conditions: Dirt
Management: Salt Lake Ranger District, 6944 South 3000 East, Salt Lake City, UT 84121; (801) 943-1794
Reservations: None
Activities: Rock climbing, hiking, horseback riding, fishing, mountain biking, and picnicking
Season: May through September
Finding the campground: From Grantsville and Utah Highway 138 (Main Street), go south on West Street. Signs point the way to North and South Willow Canyon Roads. Drive for 5 miles on paved West Street, then turn right (southwest) onto South Willow Canyon Road. It's narrow and paved, then

turns to gravel after 3.3 miles; continue another 3.9 miles to the Loop Campground.

About the campground: Aspens, a variety of other deciduous trees, and conifers serve to shade these sites, some of which are partially open. It's a pretty place, with access to the Mill Fork Trailhead, which leads into the Deseret Peak Wilderness and offers exceptional hiking in the Stansbury Mountains.

Water is not available here in the campground, but you can get it at the guard station near the Intake Campground; you'll pass it en route to this campground.

---

7 Clover Springs

Location: On the north side of the Onaqui Mountains, about 23 miles southwest of Tooele
Facilities: Fire grates, picnic tables, vault toilets, horse feeding stations, and a horse trough
Sites: 11
Fee: $
Elevation: 6,000 feet
Road conditions: Paved to the campground, then gravel
Management: Bureau of Land Management, Salt Lake Field Office, 2370 South 2300 West, Salt Lake City, UT 84119; (801) 977–4300, UT-Salt_Lake@blm.gov
Reservations: None
Activities: Horseback riding, fishing, and hiking
Season: April through October
Finding the campground: Drive south from Tooele about 15 miles on Utah Highway 36, a paved road, and then head west on paved Utah Highway 199 for 7.8 miles to the campground, which is on the south side of the road.

About the campground: This is an equestrian-friendly campground, with sites 8 through 11 for visitors with horses. Sites offer horse feeding stations, and there's a horse water trough nearby. Junipers present what little shade they can in this pretty much open area.

Anglers may fish in the small stream here, while the area serves horseback riders and hikers as well.

---

8 Simpson Springs

Location: On the north side of the Simpson Mountains, about 58 miles southwest of Tooele
Facilities: Fire grates, picnic tables, and vault toilets
Sites: 15
Fee: $
Elevation: 5,100 feet
Road conditions: Gravel

Mike Vining at an old Pony Express Stop at Simpson Springs.

Management: Bureau of Land Management, Salt Lake Field Office, 2370 South 2300 West, Salt Lake City, UT 84119; (801) 977–4300, UT-Salt-Lake@blm.gov
Reservations: None
Activities: Hiking, off-highway driving, and mountain biking
Restrictions: Horses are not allowed in the campground
Season: Year-round
Finding the campground: Drive south from Tooele about 33 miles on paved Utah Highway 36, then head southwest on the Pony Express Trail National Scenic Backway, which is maintained gravel. Drive it for 24.7 miles to a Pony Express historic site and the campground.

About the campground: Located on the lower flank of the Simpson Mountains, there's a wide, sweeping view of the region north and west of here. It's Great Basin country, so expect juniper trees and sagebrush and not a whole lot more.

There's water at the campground, but it's posted as unsafe to drink. This could change in the future, but you should carry water just in case. It's a safe way to go anytime you're in a remote area such as this.

You'll see a restored Pony Express station near the campground, as well as the remains of a stone cabin built with stones from the original Pony Express station.

9 Vernon Reservoir

Location: In the Uinta National Forest, about 6 miles southeast of Vernon
Facilities: Fire pits, covered picnic tables, drinking water, and vault toilets
Sites: 10
Fee: None
Elevation: 6,500 feet
Road conditions: Gravel
Management: Spanish Fork Ranger District, 44 West 400 North, Spanish Fork, UT 84121; (801) 798–3571
Reservations: None
Activities: Fishing, off-highway driving, mountain biking, and picnicking
Season: June through October
Finding the campground: Drive south from Vernon on Utah Highway 36, then turn right (southeast) onto Forest Road 005. A sign points the way to Benmore. Travel the maintained gravel road for about 6 miles to the campground.

About the campground: Powerboats are not allowed on the lake, but folks with a canoe or rowboat are welcome to cruise around to their hearts' content. Situated in a pinyon-juniper setting, the campground is open with very little vegetation. The road to the reservoir is accessible most of the year, making this a good place to go ice fishing come winter. Please note that although you can camp in winter, the water is turned off because of freezing conditions.

10 Tanners Flat

Location: In the Wasatch-Cache National Forest, about 4 miles east of Sandy
Facilities: Fire grates, picnic tables, drinking water, and flush toilets
Sites: 39
Fee: $$
Elevation: 7,200 feet
Road conditions: Paved
Management: Salt Lake Ranger District, 6944 South 3000 East, Salt Lake City, UT 84121; (801) 943–1794
Reservations: Call (877) 444–6777 or TDD (877) 833–6777; fee
Activities: Rock climbing, hiking, mountain biking, fishing, and picnicking
Restrictions: No animals are allowed in the Little Cottonwood Canyon watershed
Season: May through October
Finding the campground: From the junction of Utah Highways 210 and 209, just east of Sandy, go east on UT 210 for 4.3 miles. The campground is on the right (south) side of the road.

About the campground: Aspens, a variety of other deciduous trees, and some conifers serve to shade these sites. Three group sites make this a popular spot for big groups, whereas some enjoy the park and walk-in sites, which are more private than those you just park and camp right next to. Little Cottonwood Creek is a favorite of anglers, and nearby areas offer a multitude of activities for rock climbers, hikers, and mountain bikers. Of special interest is a trail open to hiking and biking up White Pine Canyon; it's just up the road from the campground.

11 Albion Basin

Location: In the Wasatch-Cache National Forest, about 11 miles east of Sandy
Facilities: Fire grates, picnic tables, drinking water, and vault toilets
Sites: 25
Fee: $$
Elevation: 9,500 feet
Road conditions: Gravel
Management: Salt Lake Ranger District, 6944 South 3000 East, Salt Lake City, UT 84121; (801) 943-1794
Reservations: Call (877) 444-6777
Activities: Hiking, mountain biking, photography, and picnicking
Restrictions: No animals are allowed in the Little Cottonwood Canyon watershed
Season: July through September
Finding the campground: From the junction of Utah Highways 210 and 209, just east of Sandy, go east on UT 210 for approximately 11 miles. The road is paved for the first 8 miles or so, then turns to maintained gravel.

About the campground: Located in Little Cottonwood Canyon, the Albion Basin Campground is a good place from which to enjoy and explore the area. No doubt, the place is a photographer's paradise, especially in summer when it sees an explosion of wildflowers.

12 Jordan Pines

Location: In the Wasatch-Cache National Forest, about 13 miles southeast of Salt Lake City
Facilities: Fire grates, picnic tables, drinking water, and pit toilets
Sites: 5 group sites
Fee: $$$$
Elevation: 7,200 feet
Road conditions: Paved
Management: Salt Lake Ranger District, 6944 South 3000 East, Salt Lake City, UT 84121; (801) 943-1794
Reservations: Call (877) 444-6777 or TDD (877) 833-6777; fee
Activities: Rock climbing, hiking, mountain biking, fishing, and picnicking
Restrictions: No dogs or horses are allowed in Big Cottonwood Canyon; also, no ATVs at the campground.
Season: June through September
Finding the campground: From the junction of Utah Highways 210 and 190, about 4 miles southeast of Salt Lake City, travel east on UT 190 for 9.3 miles and make a right (south). Drive another 0.2 mile to the campground.

About the campground: Jordan Pines consists of five group sites—Lodgepole, Limber Grove, Pine Grove, Pinion Grove, and Ponderosa Pine—which can accommodate a number of people. The sites range from $50 to $150 and are available by reservation only.

Sites are both open and shady, with aspens and conifers making up most of the vegetation. Big Cottonwood Creek flows nearby, making this a nice spot for anglers, while there are nearby trails to delight hikers and a bounty of rock near the mouth of the canyon for rock climbers.

13 Spruces

Location: In the Wasatch-Cache National Forest, about 14 miles southeast of Salt Lake City
Facilities: Fire grates, picnic tables, drinking water, and flush toilets
Sites: 100
Fee: $$
Elevation: 7,400 feet
Road conditions: Paved
Management: Salt Lake Ranger District, 6944 South 3000 East, Salt Lake City, UT 84121; (801) 943-1794
Reservations: Call (877) 444-6777 or TDD (877) 833-6777; fee
Activities: Hiking, fishing, rock climbing, mountain biking, volleyball, softball, and picnicking
Restrictions: No dogs or horses are allowed in Big Cottonwood Canyon.
Season: June through September
Finding the campground: From the junction of Utah Highways 210 and 190, about 4 miles southeast of Salt Lake City, travel east on UT 190 for 9.8 miles to the campground, which is on the south side of the road.

About the campground: This is a nice campground in a lush forest of aspen and conifers, with some meadow thrown in for good measure. There are volleyball courts for the three overnight group areas, which have a limit of fifty people and cost $85 each.

Hikers will find a multitude of trails nearby, while anglers will find good fishing in Big Cottonwood Creek and climbers will find both traditional and sport routes in the canyon.

14 Redman

Location: In the Wasatch-Cache National Forest, about 17 miles southeast of Salt Lake City
Facilities: Fire grates, picnic tables, drinking water, and pit toilets
Sites: 49
Fee: $$
Elevation: 8,300 feet
Road conditions: Paved to the campground, then gravel
Management: Salt Lake Ranger District, 6944 South 3000 East, Salt Lake City, UT 84121; (801) 943-1794

Reservations: For group sites only, call (877) 444-6777 or TDD (877) 833-6777; fee

Activities: Rock climbing, mountain biking, hiking, fishing, and picnicking

Restrictions: No dogs or horses are allowed in Big Cottonwood Canyon

Season: June through September

Finding the campground: From the junction of Utah Highways 210 and 190, about 4 miles southeast of Salt Lake City, travel east on UT 190 for 13.1 miles to the campground, which is on the south side of the road.

About the campground: A mix of aspens, conifers, and meadow makes this a nice place to camp, with tiny streams trickling through the area. Sites are first come, first served, but the group sites are available by reservation.

Hiking trails are found in the canyon, as is good fishing in Big Cottonwood Creek. The place is also a mecca for rock climbers, who come to participate in both traditional and sport climbing.

Mountainland

Mountainland is, well, chock-full of mountains. Of course, if you spend time in the place, you'll find that the region is more than just mountains. It's an area of unique diversity, one of those places where there is virtually something for everyone. You'll find things to do whether you're interested in hot-air ballooning, snowmobiling, horseback riding, sailing, windsurfing, and other water-related activities, rock climbing, hiking, backpacking, bird-watching, wildlife watching, biking, and more.

Mountainland is the second smallest of Utah's travel regions, with 5,054 square miles tucked away in the northern part of the state. Bordered on the north by Wyoming and the state travel region called Bridgerland, the region snuggles up to Dinosaurland to the east, Castle Country and Panoramaland to the south, and Great Salt Lake Country and the Golden Spike Empire to the west. The region consists of three state geographic areas: the Great Basin, Wasatch Front Cities, and Rocky Mountain Province. It also includes all of Summit, Wasatch, and Utah Counties.

Located in the heart of the Rockies, Mountainlands is an easily accessible place, traversed north to south by Interstate 15 and east to west by Interstate 80. Driving is a pleasure here, for a number of roads have been designated Scenic Byways and Scenic Backways. In summer, drive the Mount Nebo Scenic Byway, a paved delight, and you'll climb to more than 9,000 feet while enjoying breathtaking views of Utah Valley and the Wasatch Mountains. Provo Canyon Scenic Byway is another must-see. Open year-round, this paved route winds past Bridal Veil Falls to Deer Creek Reservoir and on to Heber Valley. Another must-do is Mirror Lake Scenic Byway. It passes through heavily forested mountain terrain, climbing to 10,687 feet in its 65-mile length. It is closed in winter.

Mountainland might be a small travel region, but it is not small on campgrounds. You'll find sixty-one campgrounds in a potpourri of settings, most of them excellent places from which to explore the region.

There are fifty-three national forest campgrounds, thirty of which are found in the Wasatch-Cache National Forest. The Uinta National Forest manages the remaining twenty-three campgrounds. In addition, one city-managed campground—Jolley's Ranch—and one county-managed campground—Nunns Park—add to the riches found here. And, there are six state park campgrounds, two of which are found at Jordanelle Reservoir. With the exception of Wasatch Mountain State Park, Utah's largest state park with 22,000 acres, all of the state parks provide a wonderful place from which to enjoy a multitude of water sports. In fact, in Utah Lake State Park you'll find the largest freshwater lake in the state.

Fortunately, there are campgrounds close to Timpanogos Cave National Monument. A definite must-see, the cave is located deep inside majestic Mount Timpanogos. Here, visitors will have to earn seeing the beautiful cave formations: A 1.5-mile trail climbs more than 1,000 feet in elevation to the cave entrance. Be sure to pay for your ticket at the visitor center before climbing to the cave.

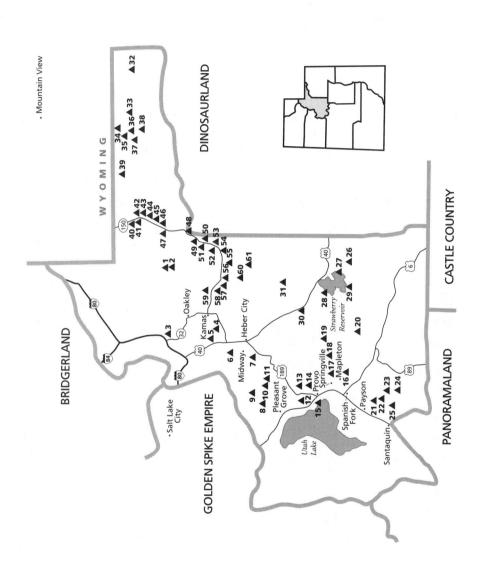

		Group sites	RV sites	Total sites	Max. RV length	Hookups	Toilets	Showers	Drinking water	Dump station	Pets	Wheelchair	Recreation	Fee($)	Season	Can reserve	Stay limit
1	Smith and Morehouse		•	34	45		V		•		•		MFBLH	$$	6/20–9/15	•	7
2	Ledgefork		•	73	50		V		•		•		MFBLH	$$	6/20–9/15	•	7
3	Rockport State Park	•	•	105	40	WE	VF	•	•	•	•	•	SFBL	$–$$		•	14
4	Rock Cliff			51			F	•	•			•	FMH	$$			14
5	Hailstone		•	177		WE	F	•	•	•	•	•	SFBL	$$–$$$$		•	14
6	Wasatch Mountain S.P.		•	139	30	WES	F	•	•	•	•	•	RHF	$$–$$$$	Apr.–Oct.	•	14
7	Deer Creek State Park	•	•	35	35		PF	•	•	•	•		BFSL	$$		•	14
8	Little Mill	•	•	79	28		F		•		•		CHF	$$	June–Sept.	•	14
9	Granite Flat	•	•	55	34		CV		•		•	•	MHF	$$–$$$$	June–Sept.	•	14
10	Timpooneke	•	•	33	28		V		•		•		MHF	$$	June–Sept.	•	14
11	Mount Timpanogos	•	•	29	25		F		•		•		H	$$	June–Sept.	•	14
12	Nunns Park		•	16			CF		•		•		FHM	$	May–Oct. 15	•	7
13	Hope		•	24	25		V		•		•		M	$	June–Sept.	•	14
14	Rock Canyon	•		4			P		•		•		MOH		May–Sept.		14
15	Utah Lake State Park		•	55	40	WE	F	•	•	•	•	•	SFBLM	$$–$$$$		•	14
16	Whiting	•	•	27	28		V		•		•		HR	$$	May–Oct.	•	14
17	Jolley's Ranch	•	•	46	35	WE	F		•		•		FM	$$	Apr.–Oct. 15		7
18	Cherry	•	•	18	35		P		•		•		RCMFH	$$–$$$$	May–Oct.	•	14
19	Balsam	•	•	13	30		P		•		•		RMFH	$$	May–Oct.	•	14
20	Diamond		•	61			F		•		•	•	FH	$$–$$$$	May–Oct.	•	14
21	Maple Lake			6			V				•		FH	$	June–Oct.		14
22	Maple Bench			10			V		•		•		HF	$	May–Oct.		14
23	Payson Lakes		•	98	25		F		•		•	•	HFB	$$	June–Oct.	•	14
24	Blackhawk	•	•	50	35		F		•	•	•		HR	$$	June–Oct.	•	14
25	Tinney Flat	•	•	16	30		FV		•		•		FCH	$$	June–Oct.	•	14
26	Aspen Grove		•	54	40		F		•		•		FBL	$$	May–Oct.	•	16
27	Soldier Creek	•	•	166	40		F		•	•	•	•	FBL	$$	May–Oct.	•	16
28	Strawberry Bay	•	•	354	40	WES	F		•	•	•	•	FBLHM	$$–$$$$	May–Oct.	•	16
29	Renegade Point		•	62	40		F		•		•		FBLHM	$$	May–Oct.		16
30	Lodgepole			51	30		F		•	•	•		H	$$	June–Oct.		16
31	Currant Creek	•	•	99	35		F		•	•	•	•	BRMFHL	$$	May–Oct.	•	16

* Dispersed Camping—no designated sites **Hookups:** W = Water E = Electric S = Sewer **Toilets:** F = Flush V = Vault P = Pit C= Chemical **Recreation:** H = Hiking S = Swimming F = Fishing B = Boating L = Boat Launch O = Off-highway driving R = Horseback Riding C = Rock Climbing M = Mountain Biking **Maximum Trailer/RV length** given in feet. **Stay Limit** given in days. **Fee** given in dollars. If no entry under **Season,** campgound is open all year. If no entry under **Fee,** camping is free.

		Group sites	RV sites	Total sites	Max. RV length	Hookups	Toilets	Showers	Drinking water	Dump station	Pets	Wheelchair	Recreation	Fee($)	Season	Can reserve	Stay limit
32	Hoop Lake	•		44	15		V		•		•		FHR	$	June 15–Sept.		14
33	Henrys Fork Trailhead	•		5	20		V				•		FRH		June–Oct.		14
34	Stateline Reservoir	•		41	32		V	•	•		•	•	FBL	$	June 15–Sept.	•	14
35	Bridger Lake	•		30			V	•			•	•	HMFBL	$	June 15–Sept.	•	14
36	Marsh Lake	•		34	25		V	•			•		LMFHB	$	June 15–Sept.	•	14
37	China Meadows	•		8	20		V				•		FROMH	$	June 15–Sept.		14
38	Trailhead	•		13	30		V				•		RFH	$	June 15–Sept.		14
39	Little Lyman Lake	•		10	16		V	•			•		FHO	$	June 15–Sept.		14
40	East Fork Bear River	•		7	20		V	•			•		FMO	$	June–Sept.		14
41	Bear River	•		4	20		V	•			•		FMO	$	June–Sept.		14
42	Christmas Meadows	•		11	20		V	•			•		RFH	$	June–Sept.	•	14
43	Stillwater	•		18	30		P	•			•		F	$	June–Oct.	•	14
44	Hayden Fork	•		9	20		P	•			•		F	$	June–Sept.		14
45	Beaver View	•		18	30		V	•			•		F	$	June–Sept.		14
46	Sulphur	•		21	30		V	•			•		F	$	June–Oct.		14
47	Butterfly Lake	•		20	30		P	•			•		RBFH	$	July–Sept.		7
48	Mirror Lake	•		79	40		V	•			•	•	RLFHB	$$–$$$$	July–Sept.	•	7
49	Moosehorn	•		33	20		P	•			•		FBH	$	July–Sept.	•	7
50	Lost Creek	•		35			P	•			•		FB	$$	July–Sept.	•	7
51	Lilly Lake	•		14	30		V	•			•		FB	$$	July–Sept.		7
52	Trial Lake	•		60	26		V	•			•		FH	$$	July–Sept.	•	7
53	Cobblerest	•		18			V	•			•		FH	$$	June–Sept.		7
54	Shady Dell	•		20			V	•			•		FH	$$	June–Oct.		7
55	Soapstone	•		34			VP	•			•		F	$$	June–Oct.	•	7
56	Lower Provo River	•		10			V	•			•		RFHM	$	June–Sept.	•	7
57	Shingle Creek	•		21	30		V	•			•		FOMH	$$	May–Oct.		7
58	Taylors Fork	•		11	20		V	•			•		HMOF	$	May–Oct.		7
59	Yellow Pine	•		33	32		V				•		MFRH	$	May–Oct.		16
60	Mill Hollow	•		28	40		V	•			•		FHM	$$	June–Sept.		16
61	Wolf Creek	•	•	6	25		P	•			•			$$	July–Sept.		16

* Dispersed Camping—no designated sites **Hookups:** W = Water E = Electric S = Sewer **Toilets:** F = Flush V = Vault P = Pit C= Chemical **Recreation:** H = Hiking S = Swimming F = Fishing B = Boating L = Boat Launch O = Off-highway driving R = Horseback Riding C = Rock Climbing M = Mountain Biking **Maximum Trailer/RV length** given in feet. **Stay Limit** given in days. **Fee** given in dollars. If no entry under **Season**, campgound is open all year. If no entry under **Fee,** camping is free.

There's also a campground near the Sundance Resort, founded in 1969 by Robert Redford. In winter both alpine and Nordic skiing are popular; in summer enchanting musicals are performed in an outdoor theater amid spectacular mountain scenery.

Throughout Mountainland you'll have the opportunity to view wildlife. The region's many lakes, streams, and rivers are stocked with fish ranging from cutthroat and rainbow trout to mackinaw and brown trout, walleye, bluegills, and striped bass. The meadows and mountains are home to moose, elk, mule deer, black bears, mountain lions, mountain goats, bobcats, and a variety of birds, including grouse, partridge, and others too numerous to mention.

For more information on Mountainland, write or call the folks at 586 East 800 North, Orem, UT 84097; (801) 229–3800; fax (801) 229–3801.

1 Smith and Morehouse

Location: In the Wasatch-Cache National Forest, about 13 miles northeast of Oakley
Facilities: Fire grates, picnic tables, drinking water, vault toilets, and a boat launch at nearby Smith and Morehouse Reservoir
Sites: 34
Fee: $$
Elevation: 7,800 feet
Road conditions: Gravel to the campground, then paved
Management: Kamas Ranger District, 50 East Center Street, P.O. Box 68, Kamas, UT 84036; (435) 783–4338
Reservations: Call (877) 444–6777 or TDD (877) 833–6777; fee
Activities: Fishing, boating, hiking, mountain biking, and picnicking
Restrictions: ATVs are not permitted.
Season: June 20 through mid-September
Finding the campground: From the small settlement of Oakley and the junction of Utah Highway 32 and Weber Canyon Road, drive northeast on paved Weber Canyon Road for 11.8 miles. Make a right (south) onto Forest Road 33, a gravel road. A sign points the way to the Smith and Morehouse Recreation Area. After 1.8 miles, you'll reach the campground.

About the campground: Set among aspens and pines, shaded sites and beautiful scenes make this a favorite place to visit. Nearby, Smith and Morehouse Reservoir allows visitors to fish, go boating, and more. The area is also a favorite for hikers and mountain bikers.

2 Ledgefork

Location: In the Wasatch-Cache National Forest, approximately 15 miles northeast of Oakley
Facilities: Fire grates, picnic tables, drinking water, vault toilets, and a boat launch at nearby Smith and Morehouse Reservoir
Sites: 73
Fee: $$

Elevation: 7,700 feet
Road conditions: Gravel to the campground, then paved
Management: Kamas Ranger District, 50 East Center Street, P.O. Box 68, Kamas, UT 84036; (435) 783-4338
Reservations: Call (877) 444-6777 or TDD (877) 833-6777; fee
Activities: Fishing, boating, mountain biking, hiking, and picnicking
Restrictions: ATVs are not permitted
Season: June 20 through mid-September
Finding the campground: From the small settlement of Oakley and the junction of Utah Highway 32 and Weber Canyon Road, drive northeast on paved Weber Canyon Road for 11.8 miles. Make a right (south) onto Forest Road 33, a gravel road. A sign points the way to the Smith and Morehouse Recreation Area. You'll pass the Smith and Morehouse Campground and Smith and Morehouse Reservoir before reaching the campground at 3.8 miles.

About the campground: As at the Smith and Morehouse Campground, which is located nearby, these campsites are set among aspens and pines, with plenty of shade and beautiful scenery. Smith and Morehouse Reservoir is close to the campground and allows you to fish and go boating. The area is also a favorite of hikers and mountain bikers.

3 Rockport State Park

Location: About 40 miles east of Salt Lake City
Facilities: Fire grates, picnic tables, electric and water hookups, flush and vault toilets, showers, drinking water, sewage disposal station, boat ramp and boat docks
Sites: 105
Fee: $ without hookups; $$ with hookups
Elevation: 6,100 feet
Road conditions: Paved
Management: Rockport State Park, 9040 North State Highway 302, Peoa, UT 84061-9701; (435) 336-2241
Reservations: In the Salt Lake area, call (801) 322-3770; elsewhere, (800) 322-3770; fee
Activities: Fishing, swimming, sailing, waterskiing, boating, birding, and picnicking. In winter, cross-country skiing and ice fishing are popular
Season: Year-round
Finding the campground: About 8 miles south of Coalville, leave Interstate 80 at exit 156 and head south on Utah Highway 32. After 5 miles, turn left (east) onto Utah Highway 302; you'll reach the park entrance after another 0.3 mile.

About the campground: Eight campgrounds here offer everything from primitive sites with vault toilets to water and electric hookups along with hot showers. Listing the campgrounds from north to south, Cottonwood has twenty shady sites; Hawthorne is a group camping area; and Crandalls has a total of nine sites, one of which is wheelchair accessible. There are twenty-four sites at Twin Coves, thirty-four sites with water and electricity at Juniper, and four tent sites, available by reservation only, at Cedar Point.

All these campgrounds are located along the shore of, or very near, scenic Rockport Reservoir. Spanning more than 500 acres, the reservoir is a popular place for water sports, fishing, bird-watching, and sunbathing. Most of the sites are partially shaded, and those that aren't offer covered picnic tables. Vault toilets are the norm at all but the Juniper Campground, where you will find flush toilets and hot showers.

Two campgrounds are found on the north end of Rockport Reservoir, just below the dam: Old Church is a group site, whereas Riverside offers eleven sites and one group site.

4 Rock Cliff: Jordanelle State Park

Location: About 14 miles northeast of Heber City
Facilities: Fire grates, picnic tables, flush toilets, showers, drinking water, fish cleaning station, and a small boat access ramp
Sites: 51
Fee: $$
Elevation: 6,200 feet
Road conditions: Paved
Management: Jordanelle State Park, P.O. Box 309, Heber City, UT 84032-0309; (435) 783-3030
Reservations: In the Salt Lake area, call (801) 322-3770; elsewhere, (800) 322-3770; fee
Activities: Fishing, hiking, mountain biking, and picnicking
Restrictions: Pets are not allowed
Season: Year-round
Finding the campground: From the junction of U.S. Highway 40 and Utah Highway 32, about 6 miles north of Heber City, drive north then east on UT 32 for 7.7 miles. The campground turnoff is on the north side of the highway; the entrance station is another 0.6 mile ahead.

About the campground: With its beautiful wetlands setting, this certainly has to be one of the most beautiful of all the Utah state parks. RVs are not allowed—in fact, cars aren't even allowed, at least not next to each campsite. Instead, campers park and walk into one of several walk-in campgrounds. Sites have all the usual amenities, and there are showers and flush toilets; you just have to walk to get to them.

Pets are not allowed in the campground due to the plentiful animal life found here. Birds are especially plentiful, with nearly 200 different species passing through or residing in the area. The tall cottonwoods and aspens of the beautiful riparian area at Rock Cliff are home to owls, kestrels, woodpeckers, hawks, and eagles, as well as a variety of hummingbirds. Ospreys nest in the area, and in winter bald eagles can be found roosting in the woodlands.

The Nature Center is certainly one of the highlights of the area, with an elevated boardwalk and interpretive area accessible for those in wheelchairs (some of the campsites are accessible, too).

5 | Hailstone: Jordanelle State Park

Location: About 9 miles north of Heber City

Facilities: Fire grates, picnic tables, flush toilets, showers, drinking water, sewage disposal station, water and electric hookups at the RV sites, public telephone, soda pop machines, mini laundries, boat ramp and boat docks, fish cleaning station, and a marina with a restaurant, store, and rentals

Sites: 177

Fee: $$ for walk-ins and tent sites; $$$ for RV sites

Elevation: 6,200 feet

Road conditions: Paved

Management: Jordanelle State Park, P.O. Box 309, Heber City, UT 84032; (435) 649-9540

Reservations: In the Salt Lake area, call (801) 322-3770; elsewhere, (800) 322-3770; fee

Activities: Fishing, swimming, boating, birding, hiking, and picnicking

Season: Year-round

Finding the campground: From Heber City, drive north on U.S. Highway 40 for about 8 miles to exit 8 (Mayflower) and a sign pointing the way to the state park. From the exit, it's another mile to the entrance station.

About the campground: A mix of wide-open sites should delight those camping on the west shore of scenic Jordanelle Reservoir. The place is popular with those who enjoy fishing, boating, water sports, swimming, hiking, and

RVs camped at Jordanelle Reservoir in Jordanelle State Park.

mountain biking. There are three separate campgrounds at Hailstone; one with water and electric hookups for RVers, another for car camping, and yet another for walk-in tent campers.

Dogs are allowed in the campground (on a leash, of course) but are not permitted on public beaches or adjacent waters.

6 Wasatch Mountain State Park

Location: About 3 miles northwest of Midway
Facilities: Fire grates, picnic tables, flush toilets, showers, water, electric, and sewer hookups, drinking water, sewage disposal station, public telephone, and a golf course
Sites: 139
Fee: $$ with water and electric; $$$ with full hookups
Elevation: 6,000 feet
Road conditions: Paved
Management: Wasatch Mountain State Park, P.O. Box 10, Midway, UT 84049-0010; (435) 654-1791; golf course (435) 654-0532 or (801) 266-0268
Reservations: In the Salt Lake area, call (801) 322-3770; elsewhere, (800) 322-3770; fee
Activities: Golfing, fishing, and hiking
Season: April through October
Finding the campground: From the junction of Utah Highways 113 and 224 in Midway, drive northwest on UT 224 for 2.2 miles to the visitor center. Signs point the way to the campground, which you will reach in another mile.

About the campground: Nestled away in beautiful Heber Valley and tucked up against the Wasatch Mountains, you'll find three wonderful campground loops to satisfy all your needs. Tents are not allowed at the Mahogany and Cottonwood Loops; most of the sites offer full hookups (though some are lacking sewer hookups) for RVers. Sites are fairly open, but some offer plenty of shade as well. The Oak Hollow Loop offers tent sites with water and electricity at each site. Vegetation is thick, so sites are pretty private.

In addition to the 122 sites listed above, there's a seventeen-site group-camping area at the Little Deer Creek Camp. It's 10 miles up a dirt road, the last 3 miles of which require high-clearance vehicles. You'll find water and flush toilets, but no showers or electricity.

A USGA-sanctioned golf course is a major attraction here. Other activities include hiking and horseback riding.

7 Deer Creek State Park

Location: About 12 miles northeast of Provo
Facilities: Fire grates, picnic tables, flush and pit toilets, showers, drinking water, sewage disposal station, public telephone, and a boat ramp
Sites: 35
Fee: $$

Elevation: 5,400 feet
Road conditions: Paved
Management: Deer Creek State Park, P.O. Box 257, Midway, UT 84049-0257; (435) 654-0171
Reservations: In the Salt Lake area, call (801) 322-3770; elsewhere, (800) 322-3770; fee
Activities: Fishing, swimming, boating, birding, and picnicking
Restrictions: Dogs are allowed only in the campground, not on the beach or in the water
Season: Year-round
Finding the campground: From the junction of Utah Highway 52 and U.S. Highway 189 in Provo, travel northeast on US 189 for 12 miles to the campground, which is on the left (north) side of the road.

About the campground: Deer Creek Reservoir lies in the southwest corner of lovely Heber Valley, and this campground lies at the south end of the lake. The place is a mecca for outdoor enthusiasts, especially those who enjoy water sports such as boating, windsurfing, swimming, sailboating, and more. A fish cleaning station is available, and two concessionaires provide a restaurant, boat rentals, gasoline, and other items.

A separate tenting area is available for those who want to camp away from RVs. Though close enough to showers and flush toilets, a pit toilet is provided for this section as well.

8 Little Mill

Location: In the Uinta National Forest, about 9 miles northeast of Pleasant Grove
Facilities: Fire grates, picnic tables, drinking water, and flush toilets
Sites: 79
Fee: $$
Elevation: 6,000 feet
Road conditions: Paved
Management: Pleasant Grove Ranger District, 390 North 100 East, Pleasant Grove, UT 84062; (801) 342-5240
Reservations: Call (877) 444-6777 or TDD (877) 833-6777; fee
Activities: Hiking, rock climbing, fishing, and picnicking
Season: June through September
Finding the campground: From the junction of Utah Highways 146 and 92, approximately 5 miles north of Pleasant Grove, travel east on UT 92 for 4.1 miles to the campground, which is on the right (south) side of the road. The North Mill Group Area is only 0.2 mile beyond, on the same side of the road.

About the campground: A shady, one-way road parallels the American Fork River for about 1 mile through this lengthy campground, with a forest of box elders, maples, and conifers to keep things cool. While some folks come to relax and fish, others come to enjoy nearby Timpanogos Cave National Monument, and some come to hike.

The place is especially favored among rock climbers, who try their best to stick to nearby walls. In fact, this campground offers several favorite rock climbing areas of its own. Diversion Wall is located just behind campsite 64 and offers an abundance of higher-level moderate to difficult routes. Campsites 42 and 33 also have routes, though climbing at campsite 33 isn't allowed when the site is occupied.

9 Granite Flat

Location: In the Uinta National Forest, about 13 miles northeast of Pleasant Grove
Facilities: Fire grates, picnic tables, drinking water, and both chemical and vault toilets
Sites: 55
Fee: $$ for single sites; $$$$ for double sites
Elevation: 6,800 feet
Road conditions: Paved
Management: Pleasant Grove Ranger District, 390 North 100 East, Pleasant Grove, UT 84062; (801) 342-5240
Reservations: Call (877) 444-6777 or TDD (877) 833-6777; fee
Activities: Hiking, mountain biking, fishing, softball, and picnicking
Season: June through September
Finding the campground: From the junction of Utah Highways 146 and 92, approximately 5 miles north of Pleasant Grove, travel east on UT 92 for 5.2 miles to a fork. Turn left (north) onto Utah Highway 144 for 3.2 miles.

About the campground: Granite Flat is a delight for large groups, with three large areas—Stonemason, Handshaker, and Sandwagon—to satisfy just about everyone's needs. In addition to these three sites, there are many single and double sites, most of which are located in the shady realms of conifers, aspens, and other deciduous trees. Hikers will find the Box Elder Trailhead here, while anglers will find good fishing at both Silver Lake Flat and Tibble Fork Reservoirs, located nearby. There's also a nice intermediate 8-mile mountain bike ride from Tibble Fork Reservoir past the campground and on up to Silver Lake Flat Reservoir.

10 Timpooneke

Location: In the Uinta National Forest, about 14 miles northeast of Pleasant Grove
Facilities: Fire grates, picnic tables, drinking water, and vault toilets
Sites: 33
Fee: $$
Elevation: 7,400 feet
Road conditions: Part paved; part gravel
Management: Pleasant Grove Ranger District, 390 North 100 East, Pleasant Grove, UT 84062; (801) 342-5240
Reservations: Call (877) 444-6777 or TDD (877) 833-6777; fee

Activities: Hiking, mountain biking, fishing, photography, and picnicking
Restrictions: Horses are not allowed in the campground
Season: June through September
Finding the campground: From the junction of Utah Highways 146 and 92, approximately 5 miles north of Pleasant Grove, travel east on UT 92 for 8.7 miles to the campground, which is on the right (south). If you're looking for the group site, you'll find the Altamont Group Area 0.2 mile prior to the campground, on the left (north) side of the road. The site is available by reservation only.

About the campground: Situated on the north side of Mount Timpanogos, a beautiful mountain in the Wasatch Range, this shady campground offers a forest of deciduous trees and conifers, as well as a creek that flows through the campground and offers anglers the opportunity to fish for their meals. The Altamont Group Area is found nearby and offers the same amenities for large groups.

Gravel roads are fun for mountain bikers, while the Timpooneke Trail leads to the top of Mount Timpanogos—at 11,750 feet the highest point in the Mount Timpanogos Wilderness. The trail is about 9 miles long and gains almost 4,900 feet in elevation.

11 Mount Timpanogos

Location: In the Uinta National Forest, about 12 miles northeast of Provo
Facilities: Fire grates, picnic tables, drinking water, and flush toilets
Sites: 29
Fee: $ $
Elevation: 6,800 feet
Road conditions: Paved
Management: Pleasant Grove Ranger District, 390 North 100 East, Pleasant Grove, UT 84062; (801) 342–5240
Reservations: Call (877) 444–6777 or TDD (877) 833–6777; fee
Activities: Hiking, photography, and picnicking
Restrictions: ATVs are not permitted
Season: June through September
Finding the campground: From the junction of U.S. Highway 189 and Utah Highway 52 on the north end of Provo, travel northeast on US 189 for 6.9 miles to the junction of Utah Highway 92. There's a sign reading SUNDANCE AND ASPEN GROVE at the junction. Now go north on UT 92 for 5 miles. The campground is on the right (east) side of the sometimes steep, narrow, winding paved road. The Theater in the Pines Group Area is reached just prior to the campground, but on the left (west) side of the road.

About the campground: Maples and other trees add to the thick ground vegetation to make this a shady place to camp, though the sites are relatively small. If you're in need of a group site, you'll find a spot for up to 150 tents just prior to entering the campground. Called Theater in the Pines, it's available by reservation only.

Nearby trails lead to a variety of places, including Mount Timpanogos—at 11,750 feet the highest point in the Mount Timpanogos Wilderness. A 9-mile trail takes off from the Aspen Grove Trailhead to climb about 4,900 vertical feet. It's a nice hike, with the view from the summit being one you won't soon forget.

12 Nunns Park

Location: About 3 miles north of Provo
Facilities: Fire grates, picnic tables, drinking water, and both flush and chemical toilets
Sites: 16
Fee: $
Elevation: 5,000 feet
Road conditions: Paved
Management: Utah County Parks, 2855 South State Street, Provo, UT 84606; (801) 370–8624.
Reservations: Call (801) 370–8640
Activities: Mountain biking, hiking, fishing, and picnicking
Season: May through mid-October
Finding the campground: From the junction of Utah Highway 52 and U.S. Highway 189 in Provo, travel northwest on US 189 for 3.2 miles to the campground, which is on the left (north) side of the road.

About the campground: Just off US 189, this pretty campground is shaded with box elder and other trees and offers the song of the Provo River, which flows alongside it. Bicyclists and hikers will find a 13-mile path of asphalt and hard-packed dirt and gravel, which follows the Provo River from the campground to Utah Lake State Park. The river also offers anglers a place to wet a line and nonanglers a place to cool their feet.

13 Hope

Location: In the Uinta National Forest, about 7 miles northeast of Provo
Facilities: Fire grates, picnic tables, drinking water, and vault toilets
Sites: 24
Fee: $
Elevation: 6,600 feet
Road conditions: Paved to the campground, then gravel
Management: Spanish Fork Ranger District, 44 West 400 North, Spanish Fork, UT 84660; (801) 342–5260
Reservations: Call (877) 444–6777 or TDD (877) 833–6777; fee
Activities: Mountain biking and picnicking
Season: June through September
Finding the campground: From the junction of Utah Highway 52 and U.S. Highway 189 in Provo, drive east on US 189 for 1.8 miles to Squaw Peak Road. Now travel south on Squaw Peak Road, a paved road that climbs and winds

its way up the mountain for 4.5 miles to the campground turnoff, which is on the left (north). Follow it another 0.3 mile to the campground.

About the campground: Lush vegetation of box elder, maple, and oak makes for a shady campground best suited for small trailers, tent trailers, and tents. It's a spot where some come just to relax, while others use it as a base from which to explore the surrounding areas. A bike ride along Squaw Peak Road begins here; see Gregg Bromka's *Mountain Biking Utah* for more information.

14 Rock Canyon

Location: In the Uinta National Forest, about 11 miles northeast of Provo
Facilities: Fire grates, picnic tables, drinking water, and pit toilets
Sites: 4
Fee: None
Elevation: 6,900 feet
Road conditions: Dirt
Management: Pleasant Grove Ranger District, 390 North 100 East, Pleasant Grove, UT 84062; (801) 342–5240
Reservations: Call the ranger district for information
Activities: Hiking, off-highway driving, mountain biking, and picnicking
Season: May through September
Finding the campground: From the junction of Utah Highway 52 and U.S. Highway 189 in Provo, drive east on US 189 for 1.8 miles to Squaw Peak Road. Now travel south on Squaw Peak Road, a paved road that climbs and winds its way up the mountain, then down into Rock Canyon. The road turns to gravel after 4.5 miles and isn't recommended for trailers or autos. Travel another 4.3 miles to the campground, keeping right (west) when you come to a fork just prior to the campground.

About the campground: An abundance of trees and other vegetation shade this campground, which offers group sites. There are four sites and numerous four-wheel-drive roads for mountain bikers and ATVers; be sure not to get lost! Also, Rock Canyon Trail travels 6 miles from the campground to the mouth of Rock Canyon at the end of North Temple Drive in Provo. Contact the Pleasant Grove Ranger District for more information regarding reserving a site.

15 Utah Lake State Park

Location: About 3 miles west of Provo
Facilities: Fire grates, picnic tables, water and electric hookups, flush toilets, showers, drinking water, sewage disposal station, public telephone, soda pop machines, boat ramp and boat docks
Sites: 55
Fee: $$ for single sites; $$$$ for double sites
Elevation: 4,500 feet
Road conditions: Paved

Management: Utah Lake State Park, 4400 West Center, Provo, UT 84601-9715; (801) 375-0731
Reservations: In the Salt Lake area, call (801) 322-3770; elsewhere, (800) 322-3770; fee
Activities: Fishing, swimming, boating, ice skating, mountain biking, hiking, birding, and picnicking
Season: Year-round
Finding the campground: From exit 268B off Interstate 15 travel west on Center Street, also known as Utah Highway 114 West, for 2.6 miles to the state park.

About the campground: Located along the east shore of Utah Lake, Utah's largest natural freshwater lake, this is a wonderful place to relax and play. The confluence of the Provo River and Utah Lake is found here, providing fabulous river and lakefront water play. Best of all, there are wonderful views of the Cedar Valley Mountains and the majestic Wasatch Range to gaze at while you enjoy a number of activities. These include swimming, fishing, waterskiing, sailing, canoeing, kayaking, and ice skating in winter. Bicyclists and hikers will find a 13-mile path made of asphalt and hard-packed dirt and gravel, which follows the Provo River from the state park to Bridal Veil Falls.

16 Whiting

Location: In the Uinta National Forest, about 3 miles east of Mapleton
Facilities: Fire grates, picnic tables, drinking water, and vault toilets
Sites: 27
Fee: $$
Elevation: 5,500 feet
Road conditions: Paved
Management: Spanish Fork Ranger District, 44 West 400 North, Spanish Fork, UT 84660; (801) 342-5260
Reservations: Call (877) 444-6777 or TDD (877) 833-6777; fee
Activities: Hiking, horseback riding, and picnicking
Season: May through October
Finding the campground: From the junction of Main Street and 400 North in Mapleton, follow the sign to the Whiting Campground via 400 North. You'll drive 2.7 miles east to the campground.

About the campground: Maple, box elder, and some other types of vegetation shade this campground, complete with three horse camping units. There are also two group sites that accommodate from 100 to 200 people, a stream, and a hiking and horseback riding trail. Call the ranger district for more information regarding the group sites.

17 Jolley's Ranch

Location: About 6 miles east of Springville
Facilities: Fire grates, picnic tables, drinking water, water and electric hookups, and flush toilets

Sites: 46
Fee: $$
Elevation: 5,100 feet
Road conditions: Paved to the campground, then gravel
Management: Springville City Parks Department, 50 South Main, Springville, UT 84663; (801) 489-2770
Reservations: None except for groups; call (801) 489-2714
Activities: Fishing, mountain biking, and picnicking
Season: April through mid-October
Finding the campground: From the junction of 400 South (Utah Highway 77) and U.S. Highway 89 (Main Street) in Springville, head east on 400 South. After 1.3 miles, turn right onto Canyon Road (also known as Hobble Creek Road) and continue on the paved road for 4.7 miles to a fork. Now keep right (east) on Right Fork Hobble Creek, a paved road, for an additional 0.4 mile to the campground, which is on the south side of the highway.

About the campground: A city-owned establishment, this campground offers a break to local residents, charging them just over half the nonresident fee. Though no reservations are taken for single sites, they're a must for the group site.

Hobble Creek meanders through the grassy, shaded park, with box elder, oak, and maple trees adding to the scene. There are water and electric hookups at each of the sites.

18 Cherry

Location: In the Uinta National Forest, about 7 miles east of Springville
Facilities: Fire grates, picnic tables, drinking water, pit toilets, and volleyball court
Sites: 18
Fee: $$ for single sites; $$$$ for double sites
Elevation: 5,200 feet
Road conditions: Paved
Management: Spanish Fork Ranger District, 44 West 400 North, Spanish Fork, UT 84660; (801) 342-5260
Reservations: Call (877) 444-6777 or TDD (877) 833-6777; fee
Activities: Fishing, hiking, mountain biking, rock climbing, horseback riding, and picnicking
Season: May through October
Finding the campground: From the junction of 400 South (Utah Highway 77) and U.S. Highway 89 (Main Street) in Springville, head east on 400 South. After 1.3 miles, turn right onto Canyon Road (also known as Hobble Creek Road) and continue on the paved road for 4.7 miles to a fork. Now keep right (east) on Right Fork Hobble Creek, a paved road, for an additional 1.4 miles to the campground, which is on the south side of the highway.

About the campground: Hobble Creek sings through this shady campground, with box elders, maples, and cottonwoods making up the majority of the tree species. Four group sites and fourteen single sites make this a plus for groups. Call the ranger district for more information.

Hiking and horseback riding are popular here, with the Left Fork Days Canyon Trailhead starting at the campground; it leads 7 miles to Packard Canyon. Rock climbers will find several routes (5.11 to 5.12) on a limestone crag about 1.4 miles east of the campground entrance.

19 Balsam

Location: In the Uinta National Forest, about 13 miles east of Springville
Facilities: Fire grates, picnic tables, drinking water, and pit toilets
Sites: 13
Fee: $$
Elevation: 5,900 feet
Road conditions: Paved
Management: Spanish Fork Ranger District, 44 West 400 North, Spanish Fork, UT 84660; (801) 342-5260
Reservations: Call (877) 444-6777 or TDD (877) 833-6777; fee
Activities: Fishing, hiking, horseback riding, mountain biking, and picnicking
Season: May through October
Finding the campground: From the junction of 400 South (Utah Highway 77) and U.S. Highway 89 (Main Street) in Springville, head east on 400 South. After 1.3 miles, turn right onto Canyon Road (also known as Hobble Creek Road) and continue on the paved road for 4.7 miles to a fork. Now keep right (east) on Right Fork Hobble Creek, a paved road, for an additional 6.7 miles to the campground, which is on the south side of the highway.

About the campground: As with the other campgrounds found in this area, Hobble Creek makes its appearance, but this time it shows up in a forest of conifers, as well as cottonwoods, box elders, and more. There are horseback riding and hiking trails in the nearby area.

20 Diamond

Location: In the Uinta National Forest, about 17 miles east of Spanish Fork
Facilities: Fire grates, picnic tables, drinking water, and flush toilets
Sites: 61
Fee: $$ for single sites, $$$$ for double sites
Elevation: 5,200 feet
Road conditions: Paved
Management: Spanish Fork Ranger District, 44 West 400 North, Spanish Fork, UT 84660; (801) 342-5260
Reservations: Call (877) 444-6777 or TDD (877) 833-6777; fee
Activities: Fishing, hiking, and picnicking
Season: May through October
Finding the campground: From Spanish Fork, drive southeast on U.S. Highway 6/89 for approximately 11 miles to Diamond Fork Canyon Road. Turn northeast onto the paved road and continue 5.8 miles to the campground.

About the campground: The Diamond Fork River and an abundance of deciduous trees make for a pleasant setting in this semi-open area. It's a popular place for fishing, hiking, and just plain relaxing. Recently renovated, the campground offers all the latest amenities.

21 Maple Lake

Location: In the Uinta National Forest, approximately 8 miles southeast of Payson
Facilities: Two picnic tables and a vault toilet
Sites: 6
Fee: $
Elevation: 6,400 feet
Road conditions: Paved to the campground, then gravel
Management: Spanish Fork Ranger District, 44 West 400 North, Spanish Fork, UT 84660; (801) 342-5260
Reservations: None
Activities: Hiking, fishing, and picnicking
Season: June through October
Finding the campground: From the junction of 100 North and 600 East in Payson, travel east on 600 East, following signs for the Mount Nebo Scenic Loop. After 6.6 miles, you'll reach the campground turnoff, which is on the right (west); drive another 1.1 miles up a narrow, winding road to the campground.

About the campground: Thick vegetation surrounds Maple Lake, a small lake that's popular for fishing and best for tents, because there isn't room for much else. Though most sites lack a picnic table, you will find tables at two of them. Conifers, oaks, and maples shade the densely vegetated sites. Hikers can choose between two trails—the Shoreline Trail is 0.25 mile, while another trail leads 3 miles to Red Lake.

Pay for your site at the Maple Bench Campground, which you'll pass en route to Maple Lake.

22 Maple Bench

Location: In the Uinta National Forest, approximately 7 miles southeast of Payson
Facilities: Fire grates, picnic tables, drinking water, and vault toilets
Sites: 10
Fee: $
Elevation: 5,800 feet
Road conditions: Paved to the campground, then gravel
Management: Spanish Fork Ranger District, 44 West 400 North, Spanish Fork, UT 84660; (801) 342-5260
Reservations: None
Activities: Hiking and fishing at nearby Maple Lake, and picnicking
Season: May through October
Finding the campground: From the junction of 100 North and 600 East in Payson, travel east on 600 East, following signs for the Mount Nebo Scenic

Loop. After 6.6 miles, you'll reach the campground turnoff, which is on the right (west); drive another 0.3 mile to a fork, and keep left to enter the campground. (The right fork leads 0.8 mile up a narrow, winding road to Maple Lake.)

About the campground: Turns are tight in this small campground, so you'd do best to bring nothing larger than a tent trailer or regular tent. Oaks and maples shade the small sites, which make a good base from which to explore the surrounding area.

23 Payson Lakes

Location: In the Uinta National Forest, approximately 13 miles southeast of Payson
Facilities: Fire grates, picnic tables, drinking water, and flush toilets
Sites: 98
Fee: $$
Elevation: 8,000 feet
Road conditions: Paved
Management: Spanish Fork Ranger District, 44 West 400 North, Spanish Fork, UT 84660; (801) 342-5260
Reservations: Call (877) 444-6777 or TDD (877) 833-6777; fee
Activities: Hiking, fishing, boating, and picnicking
Season: June through October
Finding the campground: From the junction of 100 North and 600 East in Payson, travel east on 600 East, following signs for the Mount Nebo Scenic Loop. After 12.8 miles, you'll reach the campground turnoff, which is on the right (west).

About the campground: Lush vegetation, including aspens and conifers, provides privacy for the small sites found here at Big East Lake, one of three Payson Lakes. Fishing is a popular activity, as are rafting and boating, though powerboats are not permitted.

Three group sites are available at Box Lake, another of the Payson Lakes, which also provides access for those interested in fishing. Contact the ranger district for more information. Hikers will find a trailhead across the road from the campground turnoff. It leads to Loafer Mountain and Santaquin Peak. See Dave Hall's *Hiking Utah* for more information.

24 Blackhawk

Location: In the Uinta National Forest, approximately 16 miles southeast of Payson
Facilities: Fire grates, picnic tables, drinking water, flush toilets, and a sewage disposal station
Sites: 50
Fee: $$
Elevation: 8,000 feet
Road conditions: Paved

Management: Spanish Fork Ranger District, 44 West 400 North, Spanish Fork, UT 84660; (801) 342-5260
Reservations: Call (877) 444-6777 or TDD (877) 833-6777; fee
Activities: Hiking, horseback riding, and picnicking
Season: June through October
Finding the campground: From the junction of 100 North and 600 East in Payson, travel east on 600 East, following signs for the Mount Nebo Scenic Loop. After 14.5 miles, you'll reach the campground turnoff on the left (east). Travel another 1.6 miles to the campground.

About the campground: Open meadows merge with a mix of conifers and deciduous trees such as oaks, maples, and aspens, making this a delightful place to camp. It's a mecca for group sites, with Loops A, B, C, and most of D dedicated wholly to groups. Call the ranger district for additional information. There are single sites in Loop E, which is also the place for those with horses. A trailhead provides access to Blackhawk and Loafer Mountain.

25 Tinney Flat

Location: In the Uinta National Forest, approximately 7 miles southeast of Santaquin
Facilities: Fire grates, picnic tables, drinking water, and both flush and vault toilets
Sites: 16
Fee: $$
Elevation: 7,000 feet
Road conditions: Paved
Management: Spanish Fork Ranger District, 44 West 400 North, Spanish Fork, UT 84660; (801) 342-5260
Reservations: Call (877) 444-6777 or TDD (877) 833-6777; fee
Activities: Fishing, rock climbing, hiking, and picnicking
Season: June through October
Finding the campground: From exit 248 off Interstate 15 in Santaquin, go southwest on Highland Drive, a frontage road. After 1.1 miles the road ends; make a left (southeast) onto Canyon Road and drive another 5.7 miles to the campground.

About the campground: Nestled in thick trees on the north slope of Mount Nebo, this campground can be quite busy. There's lots to do in the area, with access to three trails just up the road. There are also some bolted sport routes for rock climbers prior to reaching the campground.

26 Aspen Grove

Location: In the Uinta National Forest, about 39 miles southeast of Heber City
Facilities: Fire grates, picnic tables (some of which are covered), drinking water, flush toilets, boat ramp, and a marina with gas, ice, camping and fishing supplies, plus boat slip and boat rentals

Sites: 54
Fee: $$
Elevation: 7,800 feet
Road conditions: Paved
Management: Heber Ranger District, 2460 South Highway 40, Heber City, UT 84032; (801) 342–5200
Reservations: Call (877) 444–6777 or TDD (877) 833–6777; fee
Activities: Fishing, boating, photography, and picnicking
Restrictions: OHVs are not permitted
Season: May through October
Finding the campground: From the junction of U.S. Highways 189 and 40 in Heber City, drive southeast on US 40 for 32.9 miles, then go south at the sign for Aspen Grove and Soldier Creek Dam. Travel paved Forest Road 090 for 5.7 miles to the campground. A marina and boat ramp are found just prior to the campground.

About the campground: Overlooking the southeast corner of 17,000-acre Strawberry Reservoir, this campground offers both shaded and open sites. Loop A is shaded with aspens and conifers, while Loop B is more open and provides a view of the lake.

Anglers should enjoy fishing the bountiful waters of Strawberry Reservoir; species include cutthroat and rainbow trout, as well as some kokanee salmon and brook trout. Sailing is popular, too, with predictable daily winds often gliding sailboats or sailboards across Strawberry Reservoir. Hardy water-skiers don wet suits when skiing across the cold waters found at this elevation.

27 Soldier Creek

Location: In the Uinta National Forest, about 34 miles southeast of Heber City
Facilities: Fire grates, picnic tables (most of which are covered), drinking water, flush toilets, sewage disposal station, boat ramp, and a marina with boat and automobile gas (including propane), boat rentals, boat slip rentals, deep moorage rentals, dry boat storage, camping and fishing supplies, a soda pop machine, and a public telephone
Sites: 166
Fee: $$
Elevation: 7,800 feet
Road conditions: Paved
Management: Heber Ranger District, 2460 South Highway 40, Heber City, UT 84032; (801) 342–5200
Reservations: Call (877) 444–6777 or TDD (877) 833–6777; fee. For group use or long-term camping, call (435) 548–2554 or (801) 255–0879
Activities: Fishing, boating, photography, and picnicking
Restrictions: OHVs are not permitted
Season: May through October
Finding the campground: From the junction of U.S. Highways 189 and 40 in Heber City, drive southeast on US 40 for 31.7 miles, then go south at the

sign for Soldier Creek Recreation Complex. Travel the paved road for 2.5 miles to the campground.

About the campground: Four campground loops, all of which are open and offer wonderful views of the reservoir and surrounding mountains, overlook the southeast corner of 17,000-acre Strawberry Reservoir. Loop C has been set aside for long-term camping, and there are also sites for groups as well; for more information on both group and monthly sites, call the numbers under Reservations, above.

Anglers should enjoy fishing the bountiful waters of Strawberry Reservoir; species include cutthroat and rainbow trout, as well as some kokanee salmon and brook trout. Sailing is popular, too, with predictable daily winds often gliding sailboats or sailboards across Strawberry Reservoir. Hardy water-skiers don wet suits when skiing across the cold waters found at this elevation.

28 Strawberry Bay

Location: In the Uinta National Forest, about 26 miles southeast of Heber City

Facilities: Fire grates; picnic tables (some of which are covered); drinking water; flush toilets; water, sewer, and electric hookups; sewage disposal station; boat ramp; and a marina with boat and automobile gas (including propane); boat rentals; boat slip rentals; deep moorage rentals; dry boat storage; camping and fishing supplies; a soda pop machine; public telephones; and a cafe and lodge.

Sites: 354

Fee: $$ without hookups; $$$$ with hookups

Elevation: 7,700 feet

Road conditions: Paved

Management: Heber Ranger District, 2460 South Highway 40, Heber City, UT 84032; (801) 342-5200

Reservations: Call (877) 444-6777 or TDD (877) 833-6777; fee. For group use or long-term camping, call (435) 548-2554 or (801) 255-0879

Activities: Fishing, boating, mountain biking, hiking, photography, and picnicking

Restrictions: OHVs are not permitted

Season: May through October

Finding the campground: From the junction of U.S. Highways 189 and 40 in Heber City, drive southeast on US 40 for 22.4 miles, then go south at the sign for Strawberry Bay. There's a visitor center and a nature trail near the junction. Continue south on the paved road another 4 miles to the campground entrance, which is on the east side of the road.

About the campground: Eight campground loops and a large overflow serve up wonderful views of Strawberry Reservoir and the surrounding mountains. Sites are open, with wildflowers all around come summer. Most of the loops offer the same amenities, though Loop B does have full-hookup sites and Loop A has been set aside for long-term camping. Campers wishing to stay here can pay for a month at a time. There are also group sites at the 17,000-acre reservoir. Call the numbers under Reservations, above, for more information.

Anglers will find several species of fish at the reservoir, including cutthroat and rainbow trout, as well as kokanee salmon and brook trout. Other popular outdoor activities include sailing; predictable daily winds often glide sailboats or sailboards across Strawberry Reservoir. Hardy water-skiers need to wear wet suits, because the water is cold at this elevation. Hikers and mountain bikers will be happy to find plenty of trails and roads to explore in the surrounding areas.

29 Renegade Point

Location: In the Uinta National Forest, about 36 miles southeast of Heber City

Facilities: Fire grates, picnic tables, drinking water, and flush toilets. The marina, which is located just east of the campground, offers a small store with camping and fishing supplies, small-boat rentals, and boat slip rentals

Sites: 62

Fee: $$

Elevation: 7,800 feet

Road conditions: Paved

Management: Heber Ranger District, 2460 South Highway 40, Heber City, UT 84032; (801) 342–5200

Reservations: None

Activities: Fishing, boating, mountain biking, hiking, photography, and picnicking

Restrictions: OHVs are not permitted

Season: May through October

Finding the campground: From the junction of U.S. Highways 189 and 40 in Heber City, drive southeast on US 40 for 22.4 miles, then go south at the sign for Strawberry Bay. There's a visitor center and a nature trail near the junction. Continue south on the paved road another 13.8 miles to the campground entrance, which is on the west side of the road.

About the campground: Tucked away on the southwest end of 17,000-acre Strawberry Reservoir, there are two campground loops for folks wishing to camp here. Sites are open and offer nice views of the reservoir and mountains.

A marina is located just past the campground and provides a place for campers to launch or rent boats. Anglers will find several species of fish at the reservoir, including cutthroat and rainbow trout, as well as kokanee salmon and brook trout. Other popular outdoor activities include sailing; predictable daily winds often glide sailboats or sailboards across Strawberry Reservoir. Hardy water-skiers should wear wet suits, because the water is cold at this high-elevation lake. Fortunately, hikers and mountain bikers will find plenty of trails and roads to explore in the surrounding areas.

30 Lodgepole

Location: In the Uinta National Forest, about 16 miles southeast of Heber City

Facilities: Fire grates, picnic tables, drinking water, flush toilets, and a sewage disposal station

Sites: 51

Fee: $$

Elevation: 7,700 feet

Road conditions: Paved

Management: Heber Ranger District, 2460 South Highway 40, Heber City, UT 84032; (801) 342-5200

Reservations: Call (877) 444-6777 or TDD (877) 833-6777; fee

Activities: Hiking and picnicking

Season: June through October

Finding the campground: From the junction of U.S. Highways 189 and 40 in Heber City, drive southeast on US 40 for 15.5 miles to the campground, which is on the south side of the road.

About the campground: Shady sites are common here, where aspens and a variety of conifers grow tall and stout. Hikers should check out Foreman Hollow Trail, located in Upper Daniels Canyon. It's a 3-mile loop with wonderful views of Strawberry Reservoir, Strawberry Peak, and Twin Peaks. Interpretive signs offer interesting facts about the wildlife and the vegetation. See Dave Hall's *Hiking Utah* for more information about other hikes in the area.

31 Currant Creek

Location: In the Uinta National Forest, about 59 miles southeast of Heber City

Facilities: Fire grates, picnic tables, drinking water, flush toilets, sewage disposal station, boat ramp, fishing pier (wheelchair accessible), horse feeders in Loop C, and a public telephone

Sites: 99

Fee: $$

Elevation: 8,000 feet

Road conditions: Paved in the campground; gravel for the previous 19 miles.

Management: Heber Ranger District, 2460 South Highway 40, Heber City, UT 84032; (801) 342-5200

Reservations: Call (877) 444-6777 or TDD (877) 833-6777; fee

Activities: Fishing, boating, hiking, horseback riding, mountain biking, and picnicking

Season: May through October

Finding the campground: From the junction of U.S. Highways 189 and 40 in Heber City, drive southeast on US 40 for 40.1 miles. At a sign for the Currant Creek Recreation Area, go north on gravel Forest Road 471 for 17.4 miles, eventually curving around the north side of Currant Creek Reservoir. Here you'll reach a fork; keep left (southwest) to the campground, which you will reach in another 1.6 miles. The road is paved upon entering the campground.

About the campground: This campground is in a wonderful setting of aspens and conifers, with the trees shading most of the sites. Located on the southwest shore of Currant Creek Reservoir, several campground loops combine to offer a total of 99 sites, with Loop C offering space for horses as well. Here, in addition to a pretty setting, there are horse feeders.

Besides horseback riding, there are plenty of opportunities for hiking and mountain biking. For those who want to walk in the campground, a 1-mile-long interpretive trail is both beautiful and informative, and there's also a trail to a fishing pier, accessible to folks in wheelchairs. Hopeful anglers may catch rainbow, brook, and cutthroat trout.

32 Hoop Lake

Location: In the Wasatch-Cache National Forest, about 33 miles southeast of Mountain View, Wyoming
Facilities: Fire grates, picnic tables, drinking water, and vault toilets
Sites: 44
Fee: $
Elevation: 9,000 feet
Road conditions: Dirt
Management: Mountain View Ranger District, P.O. Box 129, Mountain View, WY 82939; (307) 782–6555
Reservations: None
Activities: Fishing, hiking, horseback riding, wildlife watching, and picnicking
Season: Mid-June through September
Finding the campground: From Mountain View, take Wyoming Highway 414 southeast for 23.6 miles, then take gravel Uinta County Road 264 south for 3.2 miles. A sign points the way to Hoop Lake and Hole-in-the-Rock. Upon reaching Forest Road 058, a dirt road, continue south, then east, an additional 6.5 miles to the campground. On a special note, the dirt road leading to the campground can be very slick when wet.

About the campground: Fishing for both cutthroat and rainbow trout is popular in this high-mountain setting along the south shore of Hoop Lake Reservoir. Hikers and horseback riders will be happy to know that the place also offers access into the High Uinta Wilderness.

33 Henrys Fork Trailhead

Location: In the Wasatch-Cache National Forest, about 30 miles southeast of Mountain View, Wyoming
Facilities: Fire grates, picnic tables, and vault toilets
Sites: 5
Fee: None

Elevation: 9,400 feet
Road conditions: Dirt
Management: Mountain View Ranger District, P.O. Box 129, Mountain View, WY 82939; (307) 782-6555
Reservations: None
Activities: Fishing, hiking, horseback riding, wildlife watching, and picnicking
Restrictions: Horses are not allowed in the campground
Season: June through October
Finding the campground: From the junction of Wyoming Highways 410 and 414 in Mountain View, drive south on paved WY 410 for 7 miles, then continue south on gravel Uinta County Road 246 (which later becomes Forest Road 072) for another 12.2 miles. There's a sign pointing the way to the Wasatch National Forest. At this point you'll reach the junction with Forest Road 017, which is on the left (east). A sign states HENRYS FORK. Continue southeast on it for 7 miles to the junction of Forest Road 077; proceed right (south) on FR 077 for an additional 3.4 miles to the campground.

About the campground: Popular with hikers heading off into the High Uinta Wilderness, most of whom are bound for Kings Peak, the highest point in Utah, this is not the place to go if you're wanting to get away from it all. Why? Because if you camp here, you literally camp at the trailhead, cars all around, hikers coming and going. It's a great place to camp, however, if you're heading off into the wilderness the next day. For those who do decide to camp here, there's fishing for cutthroat trout in the lovely waters of Henrys Fork. Wildlife is plentiful, with opportunities to see moose and other animals.

34 Stateline Reservoir

Location: In the Wasatch-Cache National Forest, about 22 miles south of Mountain View, Wyoming
Facilities: Fire grates, picnic tables, drinking water, vault toilets, boat ramp, and a sewage disposal station
Sites: 41
Fee: $
Elevation: 9,200 feet
Road conditions: Gravel to the campground, then paved
Management: Mountain View Ranger District, P.O. Box 129, Mountain View, WY 82939; (307) 782-6555
Reservations: Call (877) 444-6777 or TDD (877) 833-6777; fee
Activities: Fishing, boating, wildlife watching, and picnicking
Season: Mid-June through September
Finding the campground: From the junction of Wyoming Highways 410 and 414 in Mountain View, drive south on paved WY 410 for 7 miles, then continue south on gravel Uinta County Road 246 (which later becomes Forest Road 072) for another 15.1 miles to the campground. There's a sign pointing the way to the Wasatch National Forest. Though FR 072 is gravel, it turns to pavement in front of the campground.

About the campground: Aspens and conifers shade this campground, which sits on the shore of Stateline Reservoir. It's a nice place for outdoor enthusiasts, with anglers hoping to catch rainbow and cutthroat trout, as well as kokanee salmon.

35 Bridger Lake

Location: In the Wasatch-Cache National Forest, about 23 miles south of Mountain View, Wyoming
Facilities: Fire grates, picnic tables, drinking water, vault toilets, and a boat ramp
Sites: 30
Fee: $
Elevation: 9,400 feet
Road conditions: Gravel
Management: Mountain View Ranger District, P.O. Box 129, Mountain View, WY 82939; (307) 782–6555
Reservations: Call (877) 444–6777 or TDD (877) 833–6777; fee
Activities: Fishing, boating, hiking, mountain biking, wildlife watching, and picnicking
Season: Mid-June through September
Finding the campground: From the junction of Wyoming Highways 410 and 414 in Mountain View, drive south on paved WY 410 for 7 miles, then continue south on gravel Uinta County Road 246 (which later becomes Forest Road 072) for another 15.7 miles to the signed turnoff on your left; now go east on Forest Road 126 for 0.5 mile to the campground.

About the campground: Conifers shade this nice campground, and Bridger Lake provides a lovely backdrop for many of the sites. It's a good place for fishing or just plain relaxing. It's also a great base from which to explore the surrounding area.

36 Marsh Lake

Location: In the Wasatch-Cache National Forest, about 24 miles south of Mountain View, Wyoming
Facilities: Fire grates, picnic tables, drinking water, vault toilets, and a boat ramp
Sites: 34
Fee: $
Elevation: 9,400 feet
Road conditions: Gravel
Management: Mountain View Ranger District, P.O. Box 129, Mountain View, WY 82939; (307) 782–6555
Reservations: Call (877) 444–6777 or TDD (877) 833–6777; fee
Activities: Fishing, boating, hiking, mountain biking, wildlife watching, and picnicking
Season: Mid-June through September

Finding the campground: From the junction of Wyoming Highways 410 and 414 in Mountain View, drive south on paved WY 410 for 7 miles, then continue south on gravel Uinta County Road 246 (which later becomes Forest Road 072) for another 17.3 miles to the campground.

About the campground: This lovely place is divided into two distinct sites— East and West Marsh Lake—both of which offer spaces with views of Marsh Lake. The east side is shaded by conifers, while the west is partially shaded with aspens and conifers. The China Trail begins at West Marsh Lake and is a nice place to hike.

37 China Meadows

Location: In the Wasatch-Cache National Forest, about 26 miles south of Mountain View, Wyoming
Facilities: Fire grates, picnic tables, and vault toilets
Sites: 8
Fee: $
Elevation: 9,400 feet
Road conditions: Gravel
Management: Mountain View Ranger District, P.O. Box 129, Mountain View, WY 82939; (307) 782–6555
Reservations: None
Activities: Fishing, hiking, mountain biking, horseback riding, wildlife watching, off-highway driving, and picnicking
Season: Mid-June through September
Finding the campground: From the junction of Wyoming Highways 410 and 414 in Mountain View, drive south on paved WY 410 for 7 miles, then continue south on gravel Uinta County Road 246 (which later becomes Forest Road 072) for another 18.7 miles to a turnoff on the left (south) to the China Meadows and Trailhead Campgrounds. Travel the dirt road 0.1 mile to the campground.

About the campground: This small campground offers small sites that overlook China Lake and are shaded by conifers. It's a fine place for fishing, relaxing, and going for a hike or mountain bike ride. Some folks also enjoy off-highway driving in the area.

38 Trailhead

Location: In the Wasatch-Cache National Forest, about 26 miles south of Mountain View, Wyoming
Facilities: Fire grates, picnic tables, vault toilets, horse corrals, hitching posts, and a horse unloading ramp
Sites: 13
Fee: $
Elevation: 9,500 feet
Road conditions: Rough dirt

Management: Mountain View Ranger District, P.O. Box 129, Mountain View, WY 82939; (307) 782–6555
Reservations: None
Activities: Fishing, hiking, horseback riding, wildlife watching, and picnicking
Season: Mid-June through September
Finding the campground: From the junction of Wyoming Highways 410 and 414 in Mountain View, drive south on paved WY 410 for 7 miles, then continue south on gravel Uinta County Road 246 (which later becomes Forest Road 072) for another 18.7 miles to a turnoff on the left (south) to the China Meadows and Trailhead Campgrounds. Travel the rough, dirt road 0.7 mile to the campground.

About the campground: A wonderful place for those with horses (and even those without), this campground offers shady conifers as well as horse corrals, a loading and unloading ramp, and hitching posts. The campground is a good place from which to enter the High Uintas Wilderness, with access to the Red Castle Lake area.

39 Little Lyman Lake

Location: In the Wasatch-Cache National Forest, about 66 miles northeast of Kamas

Mike Vining camping in the High Uintas Wilderness in the Wasatch-Cache National Forest.

Facilities: Fire grates, picnic tables, drinking water, and vault toilets
Sites: 10
Fee: $
Elevation: 9,200 feet
Road conditions: Dirt and gravel
Management: Evanston Ranger District, 1565 Highway 150 South, Suite A, Evanston, WY 82930; (307) 789–3194
Reservations: None
Activities: Fishing, off-highway driving, hiking, wildlife watching, and picnicking
Season: Mid-June through September
Finding the campground: From the junction of Utah Highways 32 and 150 in Kamas, go southeast then northeast on UT 150, a scenic toll road, for 48.6 miles to Forest Road 058 (North Slope Road). Drive the maintained gravel road (before reaching the campground, it's rough and bumpy) for 16.7 miles, then turn north onto Forest Road 070. A sign points the way to the campground, which you'll reach via another rough road, in 0.4 mile.

About the campground: Shady sites among conifers overlook Lyman Lake, where the fishing is good. Nearby, hikers can explore West Fork Blacks Creek, which offers an excellent journey into the northwestern portion of the High Uintas Wilderness.

40 East Fork Bear River

Location: In the Wasatch-Cache National Forest, about 48 miles northeast of Kamas
Facilities: Fire grates, picnic tables, drinking water, and vault toilets
Sites: 7
Fee: $
Elevation: 8,400 feet
Road conditions: Paved to the campground, then gravel
Management: Evanston Ranger District, 1565 Highway 150 South, Suite A, Evanston, WY 82930; (307) 789–3194
Reservations: None
Activities: Fishing, off-highway driving, mountain biking, wildlife watching, and picnicking
Season: June through September
Finding the campground: From the junction of Utah Highways 32 and 150 in Kamas, go southeast then northeast on UT 150, a scenic toll road, for 48.4 miles to the campground, which is on the west side of the road.

About the campground: A small campground with lodgepoles and aspens providing some shade, this spot is not suitable for large RVs. Situated along the Bear River, just below the East Fork confluence, this is a place for fishing and also a good base from which ATVers can enjoy the Wolverine ATV Trail, which is nearby. The trail is a 10-mile loop with impressive views.

41 Bear River

Location: In the Wasatch-Cache National Forest, about 48 miles northeast of Kamas
Facilities: Fire grates, picnic tables, drinking water, and vault toilets
Sites: 4
Fee: $
Elevation: 8,400 feet
Road conditions: Paved to the campground, then gravel
Management: Evanston Ranger District, 1565 Highway 150 South, Suite A, Evanston, WY 82930; (307) 789-3194
Reservations: None
Activities: Fishing, off-highway driving, mountain biking, wildlife watching, and picnicking
Season: June through September
Finding the campground: From the junction of Utah Highways 32 and 150 in Kamas, go southeast then northeast on UT 150, a scenic toll road, for 48.3 miles to the campground, which is on the west side of the road.

About the campground: A small place, with lodgepoles and aspens providing some shade among a mere four semi-open spaces, this campground is not suitable for large RVs. It would be a nice spot, however, for four sets of friends. Situated along the Bear River, upstream from the East Fork confluence, this is a good base from which to fish and from which ATVers can enjoy the nearby Wolverine ATV Trail, a 10-mile loop with impressive views.

42 Christmas Meadows

Location: In the Wasatch-Cache National Forest, about 50 miles northeast of Kamas
Facilities: Fire grates, picnic tables, drinking water, and vault toilets
Sites: 11
Fee: $
Elevation: 8,900 feet
Road conditions: Gravel
Management: Evanston Ranger District, 1565 Highway 150 South, Suite A, Evanston, WY 82930; (307) 789-3194
Reservations: Call (877) 444-6777 or TDD (877) 833-6777; fee
Activities: Fishing, hiking, horseback riding, wildlife watching, and picnicking
Season: June through September
Finding the campground: From the junction of Utah Highways 32 and 150 in Kamas, go southeast then northeast on UT 150, a scenic toll road, for 45.9 miles to the junction of Forest Road 057, which is on the east side of the road. A sign points the way to Christmas Meadows. Continue another 4.2 miles on gravel FR 057 to reach the campground. A trailhead is just beyond.

About the campground: A lovely semi-open setting of aspens and conifers provides more than enough shade; there's also a wonderful view up the Stillwater drainage of the Bear River to Spread Eagle and Amethyst Mountains. A trail offers three destinations: West Basin, with Kermsuh Lake; Middle Basin, with McPheters and Ryder Lakes; and Amethyst Basin, containing Amethyst and Ostler Lakes. See Dave Hall's *Hiking Utah* for additional information. Look for moose and other animal life as you hike, ride horses, fish, or just plain relax at this splendid place. As the camp host said, "You're in paradise now!"

43 Stillwater

Location: In the Wasatch-Cache National Forest, about 46 miles northeast of Kamas
Facilities: Fire grates, picnic tables, drinking water, and pit toilets
Sites: 18
Fee: $
Elevation: 8,500 feet
Road conditions: Paved to the campground, then gravel
Management: Evanston Ranger District, 1565 Highway 150 South, Suite A, Evanston, WY 82930; (307) 789-3194
Reservations: Call (877) 444-6777 or TDD (877) 833-6777; fee
Activities: Fishing, wildlife watching, and picnicking
Season: June through October
Finding the campground: From the junction of Utah Highways 32 and 150 in Kamas, go southeast then northeast on UT 150, a scenic toll road, for 45.6 miles to the campground, which is on the east side of the road.

Stillwater Fork at the Christmas Meadow campground in the Wasatch-Cache National Forest.

About the campground: A lovely semi-open setting of aspens and lodgepoles provides shade, while the Bear River sings and gives anglers the opportunity to fish for whitefish and both rainbow and cutthroat trout. For added appeal, some sites rest on the bank along the river, near where the Stillwater Fork and Hayden Fork join the Bear.

44 Hayden Fork

Location: In the Wasatch-Cache National Forest, about 42 miles northeast of Kamas
Facilities: Fire grates, picnic tables, drinking water, and pit toilets
Sites: 9
Fee: $
Elevation: 8,900 feet
Road conditions: Paved to the campground, then gravel
Management: Evanston Ranger District, 1565 Highway 150 South, Suite A, Evanston, WY 82930; (307) 789-3194
Reservations: None
Activities: Fishing, wildlife watching, and picnicking
Season: June through September
Finding the campground: From the junction of Utah Highways 32 and 150 in Kamas, go southeast then northeast on UT 150, a scenic toll road, for 42.4 miles to the campground, which is on the east side of the road.

About the campground: There are two sections to this small campground, with five sites gracing the banks of Bear River and another four above on a small bluff. The hill is too steep for trailers, which should stay below. Typical vegetation shades all of the sites here, where the fishing is fine and the animal life is plentiful.

45 Beaver View

Location: In the Wasatch-Cache National Forest, about 42 miles northeast of Kamas
Facilities: Fire grates, picnic tables, drinking water, and vault toilets
Sites: 18
Fee: $
Elevation: 9,000 feet
Road conditions: Paved to the campground, then gravel
Management: Evanston Ranger District, 1565 Highway 150 South, Suite A, Evanston, WY 82930; (307) 789-3194
Reservations: None
Activities: Fishing, wildlife watching, and picnicking
Season: June through September
Finding the campground: From the junction of Utah Highways 32 and 150 in Kamas, go southeast then northeast on UT 150, a scenic toll road, for 41.9 miles to the campground, which is on the east side of the road.

About the campground: Lodgepole and other typical mountain vegetation do their best to shade the sites here, a place where visitors have the chance to see a beaver pond and lodge and hopefully the cute critters themselves. Sites overlook the Hayden Fork Bear River and offer fine fishing and fun exploring.

46 Sulphur

Location: In the Wasatch-Cache National Forest, about 39 miles northeast of Kamas
Facilities: Fire grates, picnic tables, drinking water, and vault toilets
Sites: 21
Fee: $
Elevation: 9,100 feet
Road conditions: Paved to the campground, then gravel
Management: Evanston Ranger District, 1565 Highway 150 South, Suite A, Evanston, WY 82930; (307) 789-3194
Reservations: None
Activities: Fishing, wildlife watching, and picnicking
Season: June through October
Finding the campground: From the junction of Utah Highways 32 and 150 in Kamas, go southeast then northeast on UT 150, a scenic toll road, for 38.9 miles to the campground, which is on the east side of the road.

About the campground: Lodgepoles and aspens grace this high-elevation campground, while meadows provide wildflowers and wide-open spaces. Sites are semi-open so you shouldn't feel closed in. Nearby is the Hayden Fork Bear River, a good place for fishing and having fun.

47 Butterfly Lake

Location: In the Wasatch-Cache National Forest, about 34 miles northeast of Kamas
Facilities: Fire grates, picnic tables, drinking water, and pit toilets
Sites: 20
Fee: $
Elevation: 10,300 feet
Road conditions: Paved to the campground, then gravel
Management: Kamas Ranger District, 50 East Center Street, P.O. Box 68, Kamas, UT 84036; (435) 783-4338
Reservations: None
Activities: Fishing, boating, hiking, horseback riding, wildlife watching, and picnicking
Restrictions: ATVs are not permitted
Season: July through September
Finding the campground: From the junction of Utah Highways 32 and 150 in Kamas, go southeast then northeast on UT 150, a scenic toll road, for 34 miles to the campground, which is on the west side of the road.

About the campground: Lodgepole pines shade the small, uneven sites at this campground, which rests on the shore of Butterfly Lake. Nonmotorized boats are welcome. Campers come to fish, float, and just plain relax.

48 Mirror Lake

Location: In the Wasatch-Cache National Forest, about 31 miles east of Kamas
Facilities: Fire grates, picnic tables, Dutch oven stands, drinking water, vault toilets, boat ramp, and horse feeding stations
Sites: 79
Fee: $$ for single sites; $$$$ for double and triple sites
Elevation: 10,200 feet
Road conditions: Paved to the campground, then gravel
Management: Kamas Ranger District, 50 East Center Street, P.O. Box 68, Kamas, UT 84036; (435) 783-4338
Reservations: Call (877) 444-6777 or TDD (877) 833-6777; fee
Activities: Fishing, boating, hiking, horseback riding, wildlife watching, and picnicking
Restrictions: ATVs are not permitted
Season: July through September
Finding the campground: From the junction of Utah Highways 32 and 150 in Kamas, go southeast then northeast on UT 150, a scenic toll road, for 31.3 miles to the campground, which is on the east side of the road.

About the campground: Conifers shade the sites at this busy campground, with its lovely, often mirrored view of the nearby mountains. The largest campground on the Mirror Lake Highway, it's also a good place from which to access the Highline Trail. Rainbow and brook trout inhabit the waters and delight anglers. Hikers will find the Shoreline Trail—a gentle 1.5-mile loop around the lake that's accessible to wheelchairs, with views of Bald Mountain and Hayden Peak. Boats can be launched by hand, though motorboats are not permitted.

49 Moosehorn

Location: In the Wasatch-Cache National Forest, about 31 miles east of Kamas
Facilities: Fire grates, picnic tables, drinking water, and pit toilets
Sites: 33
Fee: $
Elevation: 10,400 feet
Road conditions: Paved to the campground, then gravel
Management: Kamas Ranger District, 50 East Center Street, P.O. Box 68, Kamas, UT 84036; (435) 783-4338
Reservations: Call (877) 444-6777 or TDD (877) 833-6777; fee
Activities: Fishing, boating, hiking, wildlife watching, and picnicking
Restrictions: ATVs are not permitted

Season: July through September
Finding the campground: From the junction of Utah Highways 32 and 150 in Kamas, go southeast then northeast on UT 150, a scenic toll road, for 30.6 miles to the campground, which is on the west side of the road.

About the campground: Conifers shade the uneven sites at this not-so-roomy campground. Some of the sites overlook Moosehorn Lake, with a lovely peak in the background. Nonmotorized boats are welcome.

If you want to hike, look for the Bald Mountain Trailhead at nearby Bald Mountain Pass. The Bald Mountain Trail is a National Recreation Trail recognized for its outstanding scenery. It leads 2 miles and offers spectacular views of the High Uintas. Watch for mountain goats along the way. There's also the Fehr Lake Trail, an easy hike that leads to Fehr, Shepard, and Hoover Lakes.

50 Lost Creek

Location: In the Wasatch-Cache National Forest, about 27 miles east of Kamas
Facilities: Fire grates, picnic tables, drinking water, and pit toilets
Sites: 35
Fee: $$
Elevation: 9,800 feet
Road conditions: Paved
Management: Kamas Ranger District, 50 East Center Street, P.O. Box 68, Kamas, UT 84036; (435) 783–4338
Reservations: Call (877) 444–6777 or TDD (877) 833–6777; fee
Activities: Fishing, boating, wildlife watching, and picnicking
Restrictions: ATVs are not permitted
Season: July through September
Finding the campground: From the junction of Utah Highways 32 and 150 in Kamas, go southeast then northeast on UT 150, a scenic toll road, for 26.7 miles to the campground, which is on the south side of the road.

About the campground: Some of the sites here overlook Lost Lake, a nice place for canoeing and kayaking. Nonmotorized boats are welcome. Conifers are interspersed with meadows, offering semi-open sites. Anglers may fish for rainbow trout in the lake.

51 Lilly Lake

Location: In the Wasatch-Cache National Forest, about 27 miles east of Kamas
Facilities: Fire grates, picnic tables, drinking water, and vault toilets
Sites: 14
Fee: $$
Elevation: 9,800 feet
Road conditions: Paved
Management: Kamas Ranger District, 50 East Center Street, P.O. Box 68, Kamas, UT 84036; (435) 783–4338

Reservations: None
Activities: Fishing, boating, wildlife watching, and picnicking
Restrictions: ATVs are not permitted
Season: July through September
Finding the campground: From the junction of Utah Highways 32 and 150 in Kamas, go southeast then northeast on UT 150, a scenic toll road, for 26.5 miles to the campground, which is on the north side of the road.

About the campground: Lilly Lake is a nice place for canoeing and kayaking, with conifers providing shade for those who'd rather relax and enjoy the scenery. Nonmotorized boats are welcome.

52 Trial Lake

Location: In the Wasatch-Cache National Forest, about 26 miles east of Kamas
Facilities: Fire grates, picnic tables, drinking water, and vault toilets
Sites: 60
Fee: $$
Elevation: 9,800 feet
Road conditions: Paved
Management: Kamas Ranger District, 50 East Center Street, P.O. Box 68, Kamas, UT 84036; (435) 783-4338
Reservations: Call (877) 444-6777 or TDD (877) 833-6777; fee
Activities: Fishing, hiking, wildlife watching, and picnicking
Restrictions: ATVs are not permitted
Season: July through September
Finding the campground: From the junction of Utah Highways 32 and 150 in Kamas, go southeast then northeast on UT 150, a scenic toll road, for 25.5 miles to the turnoff for the campground, which is on the north side of the road. A sign points the way. Drive the paved road another 0.4 mile to the campground.

About the campground: Conifers and meadow, along with mountains and beautiful Trial Lake, join to make this a very nice place to camp. Some sites rest in the shady trees and do not provide a view of the lake, while others are situated along the lakeshore, with varying amounts of shade. Anglers can fish for rainbow trout, while hikers will find a trail leading to Three Divide Lakes, as well as many others. See Dave Hall's *Hiking Utah* for additional information.

53 Cobblerest

Location: In the Wasatch-Cache National Forest, about 19 miles southeast of Kamas
Facilities: Fire grates, picnic tables, drinking water, and vault toilets
Sites: 18
Fee: $$

Elevation: 8,300 feet
Road conditions: Paved
Management: Kamas Ranger District, 50 East Center Street, P.O. Box 68, Kamas, UT 84036; (435) 783–4338
Reservations: None
Activities: Fishing, hiking, wildlife watching, and picnicking
Restrictions: ATVs are not permitted
Season: June through September
Finding the campground: From the junction of Utah Highways 32 and 150 in Kamas, go southeast on UT 150, a scenic toll road, for 19.1 miles to the campground, which is on the south side of the road.

About the campground: Pines and spruce serve to shade the sites found here, with the lovely Provo River singing close by. Anglers may try for rainbow, cutthroat, brown, and brook trout.

54 Shady Dell

Location: In the Wasatch-Cache National Forest, about 17 miles southeast of Kamas
Facilities: Fire grates, picnic tables, drinking water, and vault toilets
Sites: 20
Fee: $$
Elevation: 8,200 feet
Road conditions: Paved
Management: Kamas Ranger District, 50 East Center Street, P.O. Box 68, Kamas, UT 84036; (435) 783–4338
Reservations: None
Activities: Fishing, hiking, wildlife watching, and picnicking
Restrictions: ATVs are not permitted
Season: June through October
Finding the campground: From the junction of Utah Highways 32 and 150 in Kamas, go southeast on UT 150, a scenic toll road, for 16.9 miles to the campground, which is on the south side of the road.

About the campground: Conifers and aspens provide both shady and semi-open sites for those who visit this campground. It's a nice place from which to explore the area, or just relax and enjoy your surroundings. Anglers will find the bountiful Provo River nearby, with opportunities to catch rainbow, cutthroat, brown, and brook trout.

55 Soapstone

Location: In the Wasatch-Cache National Forest, about 16 miles southeast of Kamas
Facilities: Fire grates, picnic tables, drinking water, and vault and pit toilets
Sites: 34
Fee: $$

Elevation: 8,200 feet
Road conditions: Paved
Management: Kamas Ranger District, 50 East Center Street, P.O. Box 68, Kamas, UT 84036; (435) 783–4338
Reservations: Call (877) 444–6777 or TDD (877) 833–6777; fee
Activities: Fishing, wildlife watching, and picnicking
Restrictions: ATVs are not permitted
Season: June through October
Finding the campground: From the junction of Utah Highways 32 and 150 in Kamas, go southeast on UT 150, a scenic toll road, for 15.8 miles to the campground, which is on the south side of the road.

About the campground: Conifers and aspens provide both shady and semi-open sites for those who visit this campground. Anglers will find the bountiful Provo River nearby: Bounties include rainbow, cutthroat, brown, and brook trout.

56 Lower Provo River

Location: In the Wasatch-Cache National Forest, about 11 miles southeast of Kamas
Facilities: Fire grates, picnic tables, drinking water, and vault toilets
Sites: 10
Fee: $
Elevation: 7,500 feet
Road conditions: Gravel
Management: Kamas Ranger District, 50 East Center Street, P.O. Box 68, Kamas, UT 84036; (435) 783–4338
Reservations: Call (877) 444–6777 or TDD (877) 833–6777; fee
Activities: Fishing, hiking, horseback riding, mountain biking, wildlife watching, and picnicking
Restrictions: ATVs are not permitted
Season: June through September
Finding the campground: From the junction of Utah Highways 32 and 150 in Kamas, go southeast on UT 150, a scenic toll road, for 10.7 miles to its junction with Forest Road 053, which is on the south side of the road. A sign points the way to the campground, which you'll reach via paved, then gravel, FR 053 in 0.6 mile.

About the campground: Conifers and the lovely Provo River grace this campground, with the Scenic Byway Trail close at hand. Open to nonmotorized vehicles, including mountain bikes, horses, foot travel, and wheelchairs, the trail extends for several miles.

Those with group camping in mind should check out the Pine Valley Group Campground. Open by reservation only, there are three group areas among aspens and conifers. The campground is located just prior to Lower Provo.

57 Shingle Creek

Location: In the Wasatch-Cache National Forest, about 10 miles southeast of Kamas

Facilities: Fire grates, picnic tables, drinking water, and vault toilets

Sites: 21

Fee: $$

Elevation: 7,400 feet

Road conditions: Paved to the campground, then gravel

Management: Kamas Ranger District, 50 East Center Street, P.O. Box 68, Kamas, UT 84036; (435) 783–4338

Reservations: None

Activities: Fishing, off-highway driving, mountain biking, hiking, and picnicking

Season: May through October

Finding the campground: From the junction of Utah Highways 32 and 150 in Kamas, go southeast on UT 150, a scenic toll road, for 9.5 miles to the campground, which is on the south side of the highway.

About the campground: Open to off-highway vehicles, this campground offers shady and semi-open sites. Aspens and conifers do the honors. Shingle Creek flows through the area, providing opportunities for anglers. The Shingle Creek Trailhead is 0.3 mile away. The trail is rated as moderate to difficult and leads to Shingle Lake, which is less than 6 miles away. Mountain bikers will want to ride the Beaver Creek Trail, which is part of the Taylor Fork ATV Trail system. See Gregg Bromka's *Mountain Biking Utah* for additional information.

58 Taylors Fork

Location: In the Wasatch-Cache National Forest, about 9 miles southeast of Kamas

Facilities: Fire grates, picnic tables, drinking water, and vault toilets

Sites: 11

Fee: $

Elevation: 7,400 feet

Road conditions: Paved to the campground, then gravel

Management: Kamas Ranger District, 50 East Center Street, P.O. Box 68, Kamas, UT 84036; (435) 783–4338

Reservations: None

Activities: Fishing, off-highway driving, mountain biking, hiking, and picnicking

Season: May through October

Finding the campground: From the junction of Utah Highways 32 and 150 in Kamas, go southeast on UT 150, a scenic toll road, for 9.1 miles to the campground, which is on the south side of the highway.

About the campground: Open to off-highway vehicles, this campground offers conifers, aspens, and open meadow. There are shady and semi-open sites along Beaver Creek. There are also some designated sites, as well as dispersed camping. Designated sites are not very long; trailers and motor homes should head to the dispersed sites.

The Taylor Fork–Cedar Hollow ATV Trail is here. It's 22 miles of linked trails, a difficult route through aspen-conifer forests ranging from 7,200 to 8,600 feet. The Beaver Creek Trail is part of that system and is a must-do for mountain bikers of all levels.

---

59 Yellow Pine

Location: In the Wasatch-Cache National Forest, about 7 miles southeast of Kamas
Facilities: Fire grates, picnic tables, and vault toilets
Sites: 33
Fee: $
Elevation: 7,300 feet
Road conditions: Paved to the campground, then gravel
Management: Kamas Ranger District, 50 East Center Street, P.O. Box 68, Kamas, UT 84036; (435) 783–4338
Reservations: None
Activities: Fishing, hiking, mountain biking, horseback riding, and picnicking
Restrictions: ATVs are not permitted
Season: May through October
Finding the campground: From the junction of Utah Highways 32 and 150 in Kamas, go southeast on UT 150, a scenic toll road, for 6.8 miles to the campground, which is on the north side of the highway.

About the campground: Yellow Pine Creek flows near the campground, a place decorated in oaks and pines. Hikers and horseback riders will find the Yellow Pine Trailhead close by. It leads to Yellow Pine Lakes, about 4 miles away, and continues beyond. In addition, the Beaver Creek Trail is across the highway: a good trail for mountain bikers of all levels. It's also part of the larger Taylor Fork–Cedar Hollow ATV Trail system, so be prepared for motorized vehicles. Another trail, the 8-mile Scenic Byway, is an easy interpretive trail and fun for everyone.

---

60 Mill Hollow

Location: In the Uinta National Forest, about 34 miles northeast of Heber City
Facilities: Fire grates, picnic tables, drinking water, and vault toilets
Sites: 28
Fee: $ $
Elevation: 8,800 feet
Road conditions: Gravel

Management: Heber Ranger District, 2460 South Highway 40, Heber City, UT 84032; (801) 342-5200
Reservations: None
Activities: Fishing, hiking, mountain biking, and picnicking
Season: June through September
Finding the campground: From the junction of U.S. Highway 40 and Utah Highway 32, about 6 miles north of Heber City, go north then east on UT 32 for 10.4 miles to its junction with Utah Highway 35. Keep straight at the junction, continuing east on UT 35, which is paved then becomes gravel, for 15.1 miles. At this point, turn right (south) onto Forest Road 054; follow the gravel road 2.9 miles to the Mill Hollow Reservoir and campground.

About the campground: It's no wonder that Mill Hollow is a favorite among campers—it sits along the shore of Mill Hollow Reservoir, where the trout fishing is fine. It's also a lovely place from which to take a hike. Look for the Mill Hollow Trail and the Lakeshore Trail before checking further. For other nearby hikes, check out *Hiking Utah*, Dave Hall's Falcon book, for more information. If mountain biking is more your thing, read about a nice loop in Gregg Bromka's *Mountain Biking Utah*.

Campsites are shady, with a forest of mostly conifers decorating the scene. Some of the sites overlook the reservoir, where floating, rafting, and kayaking are preferred. Motorboats are not allowed.

61 Wolf Creek

Location: In the Uinta National Forest, about 36 miles northeast of Heber City
Facilities: Fire grates, picnic tables, drinking water, and pit toilets
Sites: 6
Fee: $$
Elevation: 9,400 feet
Road conditions: Gravel
Management: Heber Ranger District, 2460 South Highway 40, Heber City, UT 84032; (801) 342-5200
Reservations: None
Activities: Picnicking
Season: July through September
Finding the campground: From the junction of U.S. Highway 40 and Utah Highway 32, about 6 miles north of Heber City, go north then east on UT 32 for 10.4 miles to its junction with Utah Highway 35. Keep straight at the junction, continuing east on UT 35, which is paved then becomes gravel, for 19.7 miles to the campground.

About the campground: Set among conifers with plenty of shade, this is a place from which to explore the region. There's not a whole lot more to do at the campground except to relax and enjoy it and its surroundings.

Dinosaurland

Dinosaurs once roamed the Utah travel region known as Dinosaurland. Today visitors roam as well, seeing evidence of that time and more, for this region is enhanced by more than just bones and fossils. Dinosaurland is a land of high mountains, bountiful lakes, trophy-class fishing, great mountain biking, superb hiking, serene float trips, wonderful opportunities for horseback riding, and grand vistas.

Comprised of 8,424 square miles, Dinosaurland is located in northeastern Utah and bordered by the states of Wyoming and Colorado, as well as the Utah travel regions known as Mountainland, Castle Country, and Canyonlands. The area consists of three distinct geologic areas: from north to south, the Uinta Mountains, the Uinta Basin, and the East Tavaputs Plateau. Three counties—Daggett, Duchesne, and Uintah—call the region home.

The High Uintas, the highest mountain range in Utah, stand guard over the area, with Kings Peak, the highest point in Utah, a favorite goal for many backpackers. In addition, there's an abundance of things to do and see in the Flaming Gorge area, and at Dinosaur National Monument there are about 2,000 dinosaur bones to look and wonder at.

Forty-nine campgrounds, some of which are open year-round, make this an easy place to explore. You'll find sites anyplace from the high alpine forest to the dry lowlands. There are three state park campgrounds, three Bureau of Land Management (BLM) campgrounds, fourteen national recreation area campgrounds, two national monument campgrounds, and twenty-seven national forest campgrounds.

The three state parks—Starvation, Steinaker, and Red Fleet—all offer water sports and fishing. Two of the BLM sites—Bridge Hollow and Indian Crossing—encourage the history buff to visit. Here visitors can stop, just as Butch Cassidy and the Sundance Kid once did, at the John Jarvie Ranch. Now a historic site, the ranch is located on the Green River in Browns Park. The thirty-five-acre site contains the Jarvies' first residence, an original stone house, and a two-room dugout. There is also a replica of the general store, originally built in 1881.

For the most part the national forest campgrounds promise shade and a multitude of activities, from hiking, backpacking, mountain biking, and horseback riding to fishing, boating, and swimming.

One national monument and one national recreation area exist in Dinosaurland. Dinosaur National Monument offers a wealth of dinosaur bones shown in relief on a 200-foot-long wall just waiting to be examined. North of the monument is the Flaming Gorge National Recreation Area, a popular place with boaters and anglers and for those who want nothing more to do than relax and enjoy the stunning scenes found there. Anglers are attracted by the world-record fish that have come from the 91-mile-long reservoir. Species include mackinaw (lake) trout, rainbow trout, smallmouth bass, and kokanee salmon.

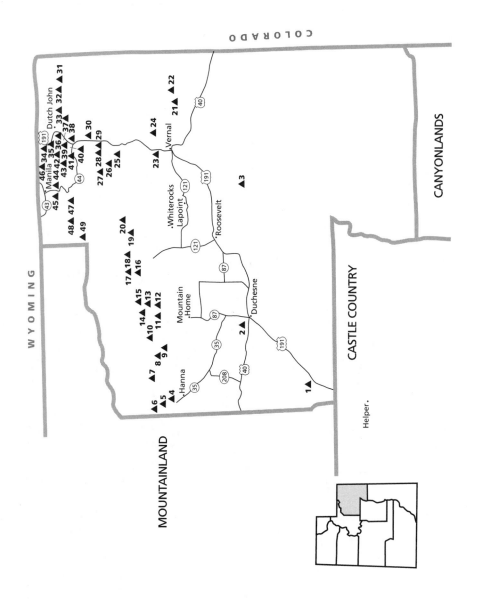

		Group sites	RV sites	Total sites	Max. RV length	Hookups	Toilets	Showers	Drinking water	Dump station	Pets	Wheelchair	Recreation	Fee($)	Season	Can reserve	Stay limit
1	Avintaquin	•	•	25	22		V				•			$	June–Sept.		16
2	Starvation State Park		•	54	30		F	•	•	•	•		LBSOF	$$		•	14
3	Pelican Lake			12			V				•		FL				14
4	Aspen Grove		•	32	22		V		•		•		RHFM	$–$$	June–Sept.		16
5	Hades		•	17	22		V		•		•		RHFM	$–$$	June–Sept.		16
6	Iron MIne	•	•	27	22		V		•		•		RHFM	$–$$	June–Sept.	•	16
7	Upper Stillwater	•	•	19			F		•		•		FHRMLB	$$–$$$$	June–Sept.	•	16
8	Yellow Pine	•	•	29	30		F		•	•	•		FH	$$–$$$$	June–Sept.	•	16
9	Miners Gulch	•	•	5	27		V				•		FH	$$$$	June–Sept.	•	16
10	Moon Lake	•	•	58	25		F		•		•		FHR	$	June–Sept.	•	16
11	Yellowstone	•	•	14	22		V		•		•		FO	$	June–Sept.		16
12	Bridge			4	15		V		•		•		F	$	June–Sept.		16
13	Reservoir		•	5	20		V		•		•		F	$	June–Sept.		16
14	Riverview		•	19	22		V		•		•		FHR	$	June–Sept.		16
15	Swift Creek		•	11	22		V		•		•		FHR	$	June–Sept.		16
16	Uinta Canyon		•	24	35		V				•		FHR	$	June–Sept.		16
17	Wandin		•	6	15		V				•		FHR	$	June–Sept.		16
18	Pole Creek Lake		•	19	22		V				•		F	$	July–Sept.		16
19	Whiterocks		•	21	30		V				•		F	$	May–Sept.		16
20	Paradise Park		•	15	22		V				•		FHR	$	June–Sept.		16
21	Split Mountain	•		4	35		V		•		•		FBLH	$$$$		•	14
22	Green River		•	88	35		F		•		•		FHB	$$			14
23	Steinaker State Park		•	29	35		F	•	•	•	•	•	FBSLH	$		•	14
24	Red Fleet State Park		•	38	35		F	•	•	•	•		FBSLH	$			14
25	Iron Springs	•		2			V		•		•		M	$$$$	June–Labor Day	•	16
26	Kaler Hollow			5			P				•		FM		June–Sept.		16
27	Oaks Park		•	11	20		V				•		FBM	$	June–Sept.		14
28	East Park		•	21	25		PV		•		•		FBLM	$	June–Sept.		16

* Dispersed Camping—no designated sites **Hookups:** W = Water E = Electric S = Sewer **Toilets:** F = Flush V = Vault P = Pit C= Chemical **Recreation:** H = Hiking S = Swimming F = Fishing B = Boating L = Boat Launch O = Off-highway driving R = Horseback Riding C = Rock Climbing M = Mountain Biking **Maximum Trailer/RV length** given in feet. **Stay Limit** given in days. **Fee** given in dollars. If no entry under **Season,** campgound is open all year. If no entry under **Fee,** camping is free.

	Group sites	RV sites	Total sites	Max. RV length	Hookups	Toilets	Showers	Drinking water	Dump station	Pets	Wheelchair	Recreation	Fee($)	Season	Can reserve	Stay limit
29 Red Springs		•	13	25		V	•		•				$$–$$$	June–Sept.		16
30 Lodgepole		•	35	35		F	•	•	•				$$	May 15–Sept. 15	•	16
31 Bridge Hollow	•	•	13	20		V	•		•			FBM	$			14
32 Indian Crossing	•	•	21	20		V	•	•	•			FBM	$			14
33 Dripping Springs	•	•	25	45		FV	•		•	•	•	BFHM	$$–$$$$		•	16
34 Antelope Flat	•	•	50			F	•	•	•			SBFL	$$–$$$$	May 15–	•	16
35 Mustang Ridge		•	73			VF	•	v	•	•		SLBF	$$–$$$$	May 15–Sept. 15	•	16
36 Deer Run		•	19	25		FV	•	•	•	•		SLBFHM	$$–$$$$	Apr.–Oct. 15	•	16
37 Cedar Springs		•	21	30		V	•	•	•			SLBFHM	$$–$$$$	May–Oct. 15	•	16
38 Firefighters Memorial		•	93	45		F	•	•	•	•	•	HM	$$	May 15–Sept. 15	•	16
39 Greendale West		•	8	45		V	•		•			HM	$$	May–Sept.		16
40 Skull Creek		•	17	40		V	•		•			HM	$$	May 15–Sept. 15		16
41 Greens Lake	•	•	21	40		V	•		•			HMF	$$	May 15–Oct.		16
42 Canyon Rim		•	18			V	•		•			HM	$$	May 15–Sept. 15	•	16
43 Red Canyon		•	8	30		V	•		•			HM	$$	May 15–Sept. 15		16
44 Willows/Mann's		•	*			VP			•			F	$			16
45 Carmel Family		•	15			V			•			F	$			16
46 Lucerne Valley	•	•	165			F	•	•	•	•	•	BLSFM	$$	May–Sept. 15	•	16
47 Deep Creek		•	17	30		V			•			MFOH	$	May–Sept. 15		16
48 Browne Lake			8			V			•			RFBHM	$	May 15–Sept. 15		16
49 Spirit Lake		•	24	20		V			•			FBRHM	$	June–Sept. 15		16

* Dispersed Camping—no designated sites **Hookups:** W = Water E = Electric S = Sewer **Toilets:** F = Flush V = Vault P = Pit C = Chemical **Recreation:** H = Hiking S = Swimming F = Fishing B = Boating L = Boat Launch O = Off-highway driving R = Horseback Riding C = Rock Climbing M = Mountain Biking **Maximum Trailer/RV length** given in feet. **Stay Limit** given in days. **Fee** given in dollars. If no entry under **Season,** campgound is open all year. If no entry under **Fee,** camping is free.

Below the reservoir is the Green River, one of the finest tailwater fisheries in the world. It's a prime fly-fishing destination, offering ample populations of rainbow, brown, and cutthroat trout.

There are many scenic drives in the area, with the Sheep Creek Geologic Loop Tour a particularly impressive ride. Besides bighorn sheep, you'll see dramatic geology that includes jagged rock spires and the dramatic Uinta Fault.

Wildlife is abundant in the region, with pronghorn antelope, elk, deer, moose, and bighorn sheep sometimes visible. Near the water look for river otters, and be sure to watch for bald eagles come winter. In summer ospreys nest in the area, while marmots frequent grassy slopes. Numerous species of birds are common all year.

For more information, contact the Dinosaurland Travel Region at 25 East Main, Vernal, UT 84078; (435) 789-6932 or (800) 477-5558; fax (435) 789-7465; dinomaster@dinoland.com.

1 Avintaquin

Location: In the Ashley National Forest, about 19 miles northeast of Helper
Facilities: Fire grates, picnic tables, and vault toilets
Sites: 25
Fee: $
Elevation: 8,800 feet
Road conditions: Dirt
Management: Duchesne Ranger District, P.O. Box 981, Duchesne, UT 84021; (435) 738-2482
Reservations: None except for the group area; call (877) 444-6777 or TDD (877) 833-6777; fee
Activities: Picnicking
Restrictions: ATVs are prohibited
Season: June through September
Finding the campground: From the junction of U.S. Highways 6 and 191, about 3 miles north of Helper, go northeast on US 191 for 14.4 miles to the turnoff for Reservation Ridge Road (Forest Road 147); it's on the left (west) side of the highway. The paved road turns to dirt in 0.2 mile; follow FR 147 a total of 1.2 miles from US 191.

About the campground: Conifers and aspens serve to shade these high-elevation sites. Sites are not reservable, though if you are interested in the group area, you will have to reserve it. Call for more information.

2 Starvation State Park

Location: About 4 miles northwest of Duchesne
Facilities: Fire grates, picnic tables, flush toilets, showers, drinking water, sewage disposal station, fish cleaning station, a boat ramp, and a public telephone
Sites: 54

Fee: $$
Elevation: 5,700 feet
Road conditions: Paved
Management: Starvation State Park, P.O. Box 584, Duchesne, UT 84021-0584; (435) 738-2326
Reservations: In the Salt Lake area, call (801) 322-3770; elsewhere, (800) 322-3770; fee
Activities: Fishing, swimming, boating, water activities, off-highway driving, and picnicking
Season: Year-round
Finding the campground: From Duchesne, go west on U.S. Highway 40, then turn right (northwest) at the sign pointing the way to Starvation Reservoir. The campground is about 4 miles up the road.

About the campground: With 23 miles of shoreline, Starvation Reservoir is a popular place for water sports and fishing. Views of the Uinta Mountains add to the scene. There are two developed campgrounds: Mountain View and Beach. Beach is popular for tent camping. Four primitive campgrounds—Knight Hollow, Juniper Point, Indian Bay, and Rabbit Gulch—are located around the reservoir. They offer vault toilets; drinking water is not available at these sites.

This is one of Utah's best fisheries for walleye; other species include small-mouth bass and brown trout. Wildlife watching is popular too, with mule deer, prairie dogs, beavers, badgers, and rabbits living in the park. Coyotes, foxes, bobcats, and elk live in the area and are seen on occasion. Off-highway driving is allowed only in the Knight Hollow area designated open to OHV use.

3 Pelican Lake

Location: On BLM land, about 25 miles southwest of Vernal
Facilities: Fire grates, picnic tables, vault toilets, and a boat launch
Sites: 12
Fee: None
Elevation: 4,800 feet
Road conditions: Maintained gravel
Management: Bureau of Land Management, Vernal Field Office, 170 South 500 East, Vernal, UT 84078; (435) 781-4400; UT-Vernal@blm.gov
Reservations: None
Activities: Fishing, bird-watching in spring, and picnicking
Season: Year-round
Finding the campground: From Vernal, drive approximately 15 miles southwest on U.S. Highway 40/191, then go south on Utah Highway 88 for about 10 miles to the southwest end of the lake. The campground is located here.

About the campground: Located on the south shore of the lake, this is a favorite with anglers, who vie for largemouth bass and bluegills. It's also a favorite with birders, who come to watch the large numbers of birds often seen here.

4 Aspen Grove

Location: In the Ashley National Forest, about 9 miles northwest of Hanna
Facilities: Fire grates, picnic tables, drinking water, and vault toilets
Sites: 32
Fee: $ for single sites; $$ for double sites
Elevation: 7,000 feet
Road conditions: Paved
Management: Duchesne Ranger District, P.O. Box 981, Duchesne, UT 84021; (435) 738-2482
Reservations: None
Activities: Hiking, mountain biking, horseback riding, fishing, and picnicking
Season: June through September
Finding the campground: From Hanna, go northwest about 6 miles via paved Utah Highway 35, then turn right (north) onto the paved road paralleling the North Fork Duchesne River. You'll reach the campground after 2.7 miles.

About the campground: Located along the North Fork Duchesne River, aspen and spruce serve to shade this campground, though you'll find some semi-open sites if you desire.

5 Hades

Location: In the Ashley National Forest, about 12 miles northwest of Hanna
Facilities: Fire grates, picnic tables, drinking water, and vault toilets
Sites: 17
Fee: $ for single sites; $$ for double sites
Elevation: 7,400 feet
Road conditions: Dirt
Management: Duchesne Ranger District, P.O. Box 981, Duchesne, UT 84021; (435) 738-2482
Reservations: None
Activities: Hiking, mountain biking, horseback riding, fishing, and picnicking
Season: June through September
Finding the campground: From Hanna, go northwest about 6 miles via paved Utah Highway 35, then turn right (north) onto the paved road paralleling the North Fork Duchesne River. Reach the campground after approximately 6 miles. The pavement turns to gravel and dirt about 2 miles before the campground.

About the campground: This aspen- and conifer-blessed campground sits along the North Fork Duchesne River. Just north of the campground, hikers and horseback riders will find an access road leading to the Grand View Trailhead and eventually the High Uintas, a wonderful mountain range that stretches from west to east.

6 Iron Mine

Location: In the Ashley National Forest, about 14 miles northwest of Hanna
Facilities: Fire grates, picnic tables, drinking water, and vault toilets
Sites: 27
Fee: $ for single sites; $$ for double sites
Elevation: 7,500 feet
Road conditions: Dirt
Management: Duchesne Ranger District, P.O. Box 981, Duchesne, UT 84021; (435) 738-2482
Reservations: Call (877) 444-6777 or TDD (877) 833-6777; fee
Activities: Hiking, mountain biking, horseback riding, fishing, and picnicking
Season: June through September
Finding the campground: From Hanna, go northwest about 6 miles via paved Utah Highway 35, then turn right (north) onto the paved road paralleling the North Fork Duchesne River. Reach the campground after driving another 7.6 miles. The pavement turns to gravel and dirt a few miles prior to the campground.

About the campground: Aspens and conifers serve to shade these sites, with access to mountain biking, hiking, and horseback riding trails. This is a place to explore to your heart's content.

7 Upper Stillwater

Location: In the Ashley National Forest, about 23 miles northwest of Mountain Home
Facilities: Fire grates, picnic tables, drinking water, flush toilets, and a boat ramp
Sites: 19
Fee: $$ for single sites; $$$ for double sites; $$$$ for group sites
Elevation: 8,000 feet
Road conditions: Paved
Management: Duchesne Ranger District, P.O. Box 981, Duchesne, UT 84021; (435) 738-2482
Reservations: Call (877) 444-6777 or TDD (877) 833-6777; fee
Activities: Hiking, mountain biking, horseback riding, boating, fishing, and picnicking
Season: June through September
Finding the campground: From Mountain Home, go west on 6750N (some maps call this Forest Road 134) for 23.4 miles to the campground.

About the campground: Located just below Upper Stillwater Dam, the music of Rock Creek is available for all campers to hear. Hikers will find a trail leading to both the Yellow Pine and Miners Gulch Campgrounds, which are down the canyon 4 and 5 miles, respectively. There's also a trail for hikers and horseback riders leading up Rock Creek and into the High Uintas Wilderness.

8 Yellow Pine

Location: In the Ashley National Forest, about 19 miles northwest of Mountain Home
Facilities: Fire grates, picnic tables, drinking water, flush toilets, and a sewage disposal station
Sites: 29
Fee: $$ for single sites; $$$ for double sites; $$$$ for group sites
Elevation: 7,600 feet
Road conditions: Paved
Management: Duchesne Ranger District, P.O. Box 981, Duchesne, UT 84021; (435) 738-2482
Reservations: Call (877) 444-6777 or TDD (877) 833-6777; fee
Activities: Hiking, fishing, and picnicking
Restrictions: ATVs are prohibited
Season: June through September
Finding the campground: From Mountain Home, go west on 6750N (some maps call this Forest Road 134) for 19.3 miles to the campground.

About the campground: Sites are spread out among aspens, pines, and conifers, with Rock Creek flowing nearby. There's a trail leading from here on up to the Upper Stillwater Dam and Campground. In addition, you'll find a trail leading down the canyon to Miners Gulch. Hikers are bound to enjoy both trails.

9 Miners Gulch

Location: In the Ashley National Forest, about 18 miles northwest of Mountain Home
Facilities: Fire grates, picnic tables, and vault toilets
Sites: 5
Fee: $$$$
Elevation: 7,500 feet
Road conditions: Paved
Management: Duchesne Ranger District, P.O. Box 981, Duchesne, UT 84021; (435) 738-2482
Reservations: Call (877) 444-6777 or TDD (877) 833-6777; fee
Activities: Hiking, fishing, and picnicking
Restrictions: ATVs are prohibited
Season: June through September
Finding the campground: From Mountain Home, go west on 6750N (some maps call this Forest Road 134) for 18.3 miles to the campground.

About the campground: Situated on flat terrain, with lodgepole pine, ponderosa pine, and quaking aspen decorating the grounds, this is a group area with room for five to seven RVs; the maximum length is 27 feet. Anglers can look for cutthroat, brown, and rainbow trout in Rock Creek. Hikers can look for the Rock Creek Trailhead about 7 miles away; it leads into the High Uintas

Wilderness. Also, a pleasant trail leads from the campground to the Upper Stillwater Campground.

10 Moon Lake

Location: In the Ashley National Forest, about 11 miles northwest of Mountain Home
Facilities: Fire grates, picnic tables, drinking water, and flush toilets
Sites: 58
Fee: $
Elevation: 8,100 feet
Road conditions: Paved
Management: Roosevelt Ranger District, 244 West Highway 40, Roosevelt, UT 84066; (435) 722-5018
Reservations: Call (877) 444-6777 or TDD (877) 833-6777; fee
Activities: Hiking, horseback riding, fishing, and picnicking
Restrictions: No ATVs or horses in the campground; 25-foot trailer restriction in the area
Season: June through September
Finding the campground: From Mountain Home, go north on 21000 West for 0.8 mile to a T intersection, then make a right (east) onto 7500N. The road curves back to the north almost immediately; continue another 10 miles to the campground.

About the campground: Located across the road from Moon Lake, a beautiful lake with the High Uintas filling the background, this is a nice spot from which to explore the area. While horses are not allowed in the campground, they are allowed on the nearby trails. Hikers and horseback riders will also find the trailheads for both Fish Creek and Lake Fork in the near vicinity. Among the tall pines there are also two group sites, which make this a nice spot for family reunions. Just across the road you'll find a store, cabins, and boat rentals.

11 Yellowstone

Location: In the Ashley National Forest, about 12 miles northeast of Mountain Home
Facilities: Fire grates, picnic tables, drinking water, and vault toilets
Sites: 14
Fee: $
Elevation: 7,700 feet
Road conditions: Gravel
Management: Roosevelt Ranger District, 244 West Highway 40, Roosevelt, UT 84066; (435) 722-5018
Reservations: None
Activities: Fishing, off-highway driving, and picnicking
Season: June through September

Finding the campground: From Mountain Home, go north on 21000 West for 0.8 mile to a T junction, then make a right (east) onto 7500N. The road curves back to the north almost immediately; continue another 4.4 miles to a road junction. Turn right (northeast); you're now traveling a gravel road to Yellowstone Canyon. You'll reach the campground after an additional 6.7 miles.

About the campground: Yellowstone Creek flows through this aspen- and conifer-graced campground. Anglers will find excellent fishing, while other campers will find nothing more—or less—than a great place to relax and enjoy their surroundings. ATVers should enjoy the Yellowstone ATV Trail, which is nearby.

12 Bridge

Location: In the Ashley National Forest, about 14 miles northeast of Mountain Home
Facilities: Fire grates, picnic tables, drinking water, and vault toilets
Sites: 4
Fee: $
Elevation: 7,700 feet
Road conditions: Gravel.
Management: Roosevelt Ranger District, 244 West Highway 40, Roosevelt, UT 84066; (435) 722–5018
Reservations: None
Activities: Fishing and picnicking
Season: June through September
Finding the campground: From Mountain Home, go north on 21000 West for 0.8 mile to a T junction, then make a right (east) onto 7500N. The road curves back to the north almost immediately; continue another 4.4 miles to a road junction. Turn right (northeast); you're now traveling a gravel road to Yellowstone Canyon. You'll reach the campground after an additional 8.4 miles.

About the campground: Set among aspens and conifers, with Yellowstone Creek singing nearby, this is a popular spot for anglers who fish the creek, and ATVers who ride the Yellowstone ATV Trail. Though trailers are allowed, there is a 15-foot limit. Note that this is not really the best place for trailers; the campground is small and more suited for tents and tent trailers.

13 Reservoir

Location: In the Ashley National Forest, about 16 miles northeast of Mountain Home
Facilities: Fire grates, picnic tables, drinking water, and vault toilets
Sites: 5
Fee: $
Elevation: 7,900 feet
Road conditions: Gravel
Management: Roosevelt Ranger District, 244 West Highway 40, Roosevelt, UT 84066; (435) 722–5018

Reservations: None
Activities: Fishing and picnicking
Season: June through September
Finding the campground: From Mountain Home, go north on 21000 West for 0.8 mile to a T junction, then make a right (east) onto 7500N. The road curves back to the north almost immediately; continue another 4.4 miles to a road junction. Turn right (northeast); you're now traveling a gravel road to Yellowstone Canyon. You'll reach the campground after an additional 10.8 miles.

About the campground: Like the other campgrounds along this route, this one is more enchanting because of Yellowstone Creek, which flows nearby. In addition to the creek, there's a dam, with the upstream waters fun for playing and fishing. A fishing dock adds a nice touch. The campground is small and best for tents and tent trailers—aspens and conifers serve to partially shade the sites.

14 Riverview

Location: In the Ashley National Forest, about 17 miles northeast of Mountain Home
Facilities: Fire grates, picnic tables, drinking water, and vault toilets
Sites: 19
Fee: $
Elevation: 8,000 feet
Road conditions: Gravel

Yellowstone Creek at Riverview Campground.

Management: Roosevelt Ranger District, 244 West Highway 40, Roosevelt, UT 84066; (435) 722-5018
Reservations: None
Activities: Fishing, hiking, horseback riding, and picnicking
Season: June through September
Finding the campground: From Mountain Home, go north on 21000 West for 0.8 mile to a T junction, then make a right (east) onto 7500N. The road curves back to the north almost immediately; continue another 4.4 miles to a road junction. Turn right (northeast); you're now traveling a gravel road to Yellowstone Canyon. You'll reach the campground after an additional 12.0 miles.

About the campground: Stretched out along the east bank of Yellowstone Creek, with aspens and conifers to shade all the sites, this is a favorite place for anglers and campers who just want to relax and have fun. It also provides close access to the trailhead at Swift Creek, which leads into the High Uintas Wilderness.

15 Swift Creek

Location: In the Ashley National Forest, about 18 miles northeast of Mountain Home
Facilities: Fire grates, picnic tables, drinking water, vault toilets, and a horse loading ramp
Sites: 11
Fee: $
Elevation: 8,100 feet
Road conditions: Gravel
Management: Roosevelt Ranger District, 244 West Highway 40, Roosevelt, UT 84066; (435) 722-5018
Reservations: None
Activities: Fishing, hiking, horseback riding, and picnicking
Season: June through September
Finding the campground: From Mountain Home, go north on 21000 West for 0.8 mile to a T junction, then make a right (east) onto 7500N. The road curves back to the north almost immediately; continue another 4.4 miles to a road junction. Turn right (northeast); you're now traveling a gravel road to Yellowstone Canyon. You'll reach the campground after an additional 12.9 miles.

About the campground: Set among aspens and conifers, this campground is located at a trailhead leading into the High Uintas Wilderness. There's a horse loading ramp for those who want to ride into the wilderness, and nice campsites for those who'd like to day hike into the lovely region. A backpack trip is best, however. For more information, see Dave Hall's Falcon book *Hiking Utah*.

16 Uinta Canyon

Location: In the Ashley National Forest, about 25 miles northwest of Roosevelt

Facilities: Fire grates, picnic tables, nonpotable water, and vault toilets
Sites: 24
Fee: $
Elevation: 7,600 feet
Road conditions: Gravel
Management: Roosevelt Ranger District, 244 West Highway 40, Roosevelt, UT 84066; (435) 722-5018
Reservations: None
Activities: Hiking, horseback riding, fishing, and picnicking
Season: June through September
Finding the campground: From the junction of U.S. Highway 40/191 and Utah Highway 121 in Roosevelt, travel north on UT 121. There are signs for Uinta Canyon. UT 121 heads east after 10.1 miles, but you should stay straight (north) on 2000 West. After another 8.4 miles, you'll reach a fork; keep right to Uinta Canyon. (A left would take you to Yellowstone Canyon.) Drive an additional 4 miles to another fork; go right again, continuing follow signs for Uinta Canyon. After another 2.2 miles, the road turns to gravel; the campground is 0.7 mile beyond.

About the campground: Conifers serve to shade the sites here along the Uinta River. Though there is water, it was nonpotable when we checked out the campground. Fortunately, the cost was reduced due to the inconvenience. Check with the ranger district for more information. On another note, look for the nearby trail that provides for horseback riders and hikers access into the lovely High Uintas Wilderness. Anglers fish for rainbow, cutthroat, brown, and brook trout.

If you're looking for a group site, you'll find Uinta River just up the road. It's a reservable site. Call (877) 444-6777 or TDD (877) 833-6777 for more information; there's a fee.

17 Wandin

Location: In the Ashley National Forest, about 27 miles northwest of Roosevelt
Facilities: Fire grates, picnic tables, and vault toilets
Sites: 6
Fee: $
Elevation: 7,800 feet
Road conditions: Gravel
Management: Roosevelt Ranger District, 244 West Highway 40, Roosevelt, UT 84066; (435) 722-5018
Reservations: None
Activities: Hiking, horseback riding, fishing, and picnicking
Season: June through September
Finding the campground: From the junction of U.S. Highway 40/191 and Utah Highway 121 in Roosevelt, travel north on UT 121. There are signs for Uinta Canyon. UT 121 heads east after 10.1 miles, but you should stay straight (north) on 2000 West. After another 8.4 miles, you'll reach a fork; keep right

to Uinta Canyon. (A left would take you to Yellowstone Canyon.) Drive an additional 4 miles to another fork; go right again, continuing to follow signs for Uinta Canyon. After another 2.2 miles, the road turns to gravel; the campground is 2.1 miles beyond.

About the campground: Conifers and aspens partially shade this small campground, which is used by tenters and those with small trailers. It's located along the Uinta River, and there's also a spring just up the road. Don't leave without seeing Smokey Spring! A nearby trail leads horseback riders and hikers into the lovely High Uintas Wilderness. If you enjoy fishing, expect to find rainbow, cutthroat, brown, and brook trout.

18 Pole Creek Lake

Location: In the Ashley National Forest, about 34 miles north of Roosevelt
Facilities: Fire grates, picnic tables, and vault toilets
Sites: 19
Fee: $
Elevation: 10,000 feet
Road conditions: Gravel
Management: Roosevelt Ranger District, 244 West Highway 40, Roosevelt, UT 84066; (435) 722–5018
Reservations: None
Activities: Fishing and picnicking
Season: July through September
Finding the campground: From the junction of U.S. Highway 40/191 and Utah Highway 121 in Roosevelt, travel north on UT 121. There are signs for Uinta Canyon. UT 121 heads east after 10.1 miles, but you should stay straight (north) on 2000 West. After another 8.4 miles, you'll reach a fork; keep right to Uinta Canyon. (A left would take you to Yellowstone Canyon.) Drive an additional 4 miles to another fork; go right again and, after crossing a bridge over the river, stay right on the Elkhorn Loop, which is gravel. The road is rough and narrow for the first few miles. You'll reach a fork after 3.6 miles; keep straight (north). Continue an additional 8 miles to the northeast to the campground.

About the campground: Conifers shade this high-elevation campground, with Pole Creek Lake adding to the southern vista. It's a nice place for fishing and relaxing and exploring to your heart's content.

19 Whiterocks

Location: In the Ashley National Forest, about 14 miles north of Whiterocks
Facilities: Fire grates, picnic tables, and vault toilets
Sites: 21
Fee: $
Elevation: 7,400 feet
Road conditions: Gravel

Management: Vernal Ranger District, 355 North Vernal Avenue, Vernal, UT 84078; (435) 789–1181
Reservations: None
Activities: Fishing and picnicking
Season: May through September
Finding the campground: From the Elkhorn Guard Station, which is a few miles north of Whiterocks (Whiterocks is approximately 18 miles northeast of Roosevelt), go south for 1 mile on a paved road, then east on a paved road for another 2.3 miles. Now turn north onto the gravel road for 6.5 miles; a sign points the way to the campground.

About the campground: Spruce, conifer, and aspen serve to shade this campground, with the Whiterocks River singing a tune nearby. It's a nice place for fishing (rainbow, cutthroat, and brook trout inhabit these waters), relaxing, and just plain enjoying the sights and sounds of the forest.

20 Paradise Park

Location: In the Ashley National Forest, 25 miles northwest of Lapoint
Facilities: Fire grates, picnic tables, and vault toilets
Sites: 15
Fee: $
Elevation: 9,800 feet
Road conditions: Gravel
Management: Vernal Ranger District, 355 North Vernal Avenue, Vernal, UT 84078; (435) 789–1181
Reservations: None
Activities: Fishing, hiking, horseback riding, and picnicking
Season: June through September
Finding the campground: From Lapoint and the Utah Highway 121 and 11500 East junction, on the east side of town, go north on paved 11500 East. A sign points the way to Paradise. You'll reach a fork after 6.9 miles; keep left (northwest) to reach Paradise Reservoir. This road is known as Mosby Canyon Road. After another 8.5 miles, the road turns to dirt. Drive an additional 9.6 miles, climbing to the campground entrance and continuing beyond to reach the reservoir.

About the campground: Located in a high-mountain setting, there's an overflow camping area in addition to the main campground. There's also a trailhead leading into the High Uintas Wilderness, so this is a great place for hikers and horseback riders. It's popular among anglers, too, because there are fish (rainbow and brook trout) to be had in Paradise Park Reservoir.

21 Split Mountain: Dinosaur National Monument

Location: About 22 miles east of Vernal
Facilities: Fire grates, picnic tables, vault toilets, drinking water, a boat launch, and a public telephone

Sites: 4 group sites
Fee: $$$$
Elevation: 4,800 feet
Road conditions: Paved
Management: Dinosaur National Monument, Quarry Visitor Center, Box 128, Jensen, UT 84035; (435) 789-2115
Reservations: Sites must be reserved; call 435-781-7759; fee
Activities: Fishing, boating, hiking, photography, and picnicking
Season: Year-round
Finding the campground: From Vernal, head south then east on U.S. Highway 40 for about 12 miles, then go north on Utah Highway 149 for 6 miles to the entrance station and visitor center. Continue 2.6 miles to the campground turnoff, which is on the left (north) side of the road. You'll reach the campground in another 1.1 miles.

About the campground: Situated among cottonwoods, with the Green River meandering nearby and Split Mountain jutting straight into the heavens, this is a beautiful place to stay. There are four group sites, all of which are located near a day-use area that's a popular put-in point for rafters. Hikers will want to check out the trail.

For many campers, the best thing about staying here is the chance to see dinosaur bones, and lots of them. Don't miss the Dinosaur Quarry; it's the only place in the park to see dinosaur bones. The quarry is open every day of the year except for Thanksgiving, Christmas, and New Year's.

Though the campground is open all year, the water is shut off from fall through spring. When that happens, camping is free.

22 Green River: Dinosaur National Monument

Location: About 23 miles east of Vernal
Facilities: Fire grates, picnic tables, flush toilets, drinking water, and a public telephone
Sites: 88
Fee: $$
Elevation: 4,800 feet
Road conditions: Paved
Management: Dinosaur National Monument, Quarry Visitor Center, Box 128, Jensen, UT 84035; (435) 789-2115
Reservations: None
Activities: Fishing, boating, hiking, photography, and picnicking
Season: Year-round
Finding the campground: From Vernal, head south then east on U.S. Highway 40 for about 12 miles, then go north on Utah Highway 149 for 6 miles to the entrance station and visitor center. Continue, now traveling east, then south, 4.1 miles to the campground turnoff, which is on the left (east) side of the road. You'll reach the campground in another 0.4 mile.

About the campground: Huge cottonwoods decorate these partially open sites, with the Green River wandering along the campground border. A hiking trail leads 1.8 miles from this campground to the one at Split Mountain, another beautiful area with yet another trail to hike.

Of course, you won't want to miss seeing dinosaur bones—and lots of them. Be sure to tour the Dinosaur Quarry; it's the only place in the park to see dinosaur bones. The quarry is open every day of the year except for Thanksgiving, Christmas, and New Year's.

The campground is open year-round, though the water is shut off from fall through spring. Fortunately, camping is free when that happens.

23 Steinaker State Park

Location: About 7 miles north of Vernal
Facilities: Fire grates, picnic tables (some covered), flush toilets, drinking water, sewage disposal station, boat launch, fish cleaning station, soda pop machines, and a public telephone
Sites: 29
Fee: $
Elevation: 5,500 feet
Road conditions: Paved
Management: Steinaker State Park, 4335 North Highway 191, Vernal, UT 84078-7800; (435) 789–4432
Reservations: In the Salt Lake area, call (801) 322–3770; elsewhere, (800) 322–3770; fee
Activities: Fishing, swimming, boating, waterskiing, wildlife watching, hiking, and picnicking
Restrictions: Dogs are not allowed on the beach
Season: Year-round
Finding the campground: From Vernal, and the junction of U.S. Highways 40 and 191, go north on US 191 for 5.6 miles, then turn left (west) at the signed junction. Continue another 1.8 miles on the paved road to the campground.

About the campground: With sites overlooking Steinaker Reservoir and cottonwoods and junipers to partially shade them, this campground is certainly an extra-nice place to stay. Visitors come to this desert oasis to fish, to enjoy various water sports, and sometimes to set up a base camp from which to explore the surrounding area.

When it's full, Steinaker Reservoir covers 780 surface acres and is up to 130 feet deep. Water temperatures reach seventy degrees in July, making the park a water recreation paradise. It's also one of Utah's prime fisheries, with rainbow trout, largemouth bass, and an occasional brown trout. Many wildlife species live in the park, including mule deer, rabbits, porcupines, and birds such as golden eagles and ospreys. Elk make rare appearances.

24 Red Fleet State Park

Location: About 12 miles northeast of Vernal
Facilities: Fire grates, covered picnic tables, flush toilets, drinking water, sewage disposal station, boat launch, fish cleaning station, and a public telephone

Sites: 38
Fee: $
Elevation: 5,600 feet
Road conditions: Paved
Management: Red Fleet State Park, 8750 North Highway 191, Vernal, UT 84078-7800; (435) 789–4432
Reservations: None
Activities: Fishing, swimming, boating, hiking, wildlife watching, and picnicking
Season: Year-round
Finding the campground: From Vernal and the junction of U.S. Highways 40 and 191, go north on US 191 for 10.2 miles, then turn right (east) at the signed junction. Continue another 1.9 miles on the paved road to the campground.

About the campground: Hillside sites seem to stand guard over 650-acre Red Fleet Reservoir, named for the three large Navajo sandstone outcrops that jut up from the water like a fleet of ships. Known by local boaters as Little Lake Powell, spectacular sandstone cliffs and secluded sandy beaches await visitors who enjoy water-oriented activities. Anglers target rainbow and brown trout, bluegills, and bass, while other visitors go waterskiing and swimming. Swimmers should use caution; the water may be extremely deep just offshore.

In addition to present-day animal life, you can see dinosaur tracks made 190 to 200 million years ago. Preserved in rock, the tracks are on the shore immediately across the reservoir from the boat ramp. Contact a ranger for directions and the best viewing areas.

25 Iron Springs

Location: In the Ashley National Forest, about 24 miles north of Vernal
Facilities: Fire grates, picnic tables, drinking water, and vault toilets
Sites: 2 group sites
Fee: $$$$
Elevation: 8,700 feet
Road conditions: Gravel
Management: Vernal Ranger District, 355 North Vernal Avenue, Vernal, UT 84078; (435) 789–1181
Reservations: Call (877) 444–6777 or TDD (877) 833–6777; fee
Activities: Mountain biking and picnicking
Season: June through Labor Day
Finding the campground: From Vernal, go north on U.S. Highway 191 for about 19 miles to a paved road heading northwest. This is Forest Road 018, also known as the Red Cloud Loop. Drive it 3.3 miles to another junction; continue left (west) on FR 018, which is now gravel, for 1.4 miles to the campground.

About the campground: Open by reservation only, this campground is set amid conifers and aspens but overlooks a vast meadow. Two group sites serve a maximum of one hundred people each. It's a nice base from which to go mountain biking. The East Park Loop, a 32-mile ride, is a particular favorite, touring some of the highlights of this lovely region.

26 Kaler Hollow

Location: In the Ashley National Forest, about 28 miles northwest of Vernal
Facilities: Fire grates, picnic tables, and pit toilets
Sites: 5
Fee: None
Elevation: 8,700 feet
Road conditions: Gravel
Management: Vernal Ranger District, 355 North Vernal Avenue, Vernal, UT 84078; (435) 789–1181
Reservations: None
Activities: Fishing, mountain biking, and picnicking
Season: June through September
Finding the campground: From Vernal, go north on U.S. Highway 191 for about 19 miles to a paved road heading northwest. This is Forest Road 018, also known as the Red Cloud Loop. Drive it 3.3 miles to another junction; continue left (west) on FR 018, which is now gravel, for 5.9 miles to the campground.

About the campground: Located in a previously logged area, these sites are nothing special, but they are free, and they make a good base from which to explore the area. The East Park Loop Mountain Bike Ride circles about 32 miles throughout this area, passing by this spot along the way. There's also a mountain bike ride described by Gregg Bromka in his book *Mountain Biking Utah*. The open sites rest near a small creek where anglers might wet a line.

27 Oaks Park

Location: In the Ashley National Forest, about 32 miles northwest of Vernal
Facilities: Fire grates, picnic tables, and vault toilets
Sites: 11
Fee: $
Elevation: 9,200 feet
Road conditions: Dirt
Management: Vernal Ranger District, 355 North Vernal Avenue, Vernal, UT 84078; (435) 789–1181
Reservations: None
Activities: Fishing, boating, mountain biking, and picnicking
Season: June through September
Finding the campground: From Vernal, go north on U.S. Highway 191 for about 19 miles to a paved road heading northwest. This is Forest Road 018, also known as the Red Cloud Loop. Drive it 3.3 miles to another junction; continue left (west) on FR 018, which is now gravel, for 8.8 miles to the signed campground turnoff. Now go right (northeast) for another 0.9 mile to the campground.

About the campground: Located in a previously logged area, there are some conifers to partially shade these sites near Oaks Park Reservoir. You'll find plenty of dirt roads for mountain biking or walking, while anglers vie for rainbow trout. Mountain bikers should check out the East Park Loop Mountain Bike Ride. It's about 32 miles long and passes near the campground. There's also a mountain bike ride described by Gregg Bromka in his book *Mountain Biking Utah.*

28 East Park

Location: In the Ashley National Forest, about 28 miles northwest of Vernal
Facilities: Fire grates, picnic tables, drinking water, both vault and pit toilets, and a gravel boat ramp
Sites: 21
Fee: $
Elevation: 9,000 feet
Road conditions: Paved to the campground, then gravel
Management: Vernal Ranger District, 355 North Vernal Avenue, Vernal, UT 84078; (435) 789–1181
Reservations: None
Activities: Fishing, boating, mountain biking, and picnicking
Season: June through September
Finding the campground: From Vernal, go north on U.S. Highway 191 for about 19 miles to a paved road heading northwest. This is Forest Road 018, also known as the Red Cloud Loop. Drive it 3.3 miles, then stay straight on Forest Road 020 (FR 018 takes off to the west) for a total of 8.4 miles to the signed campground turnoff. Turn right (east) onto the gravel road for an additional 0.7 mile to the campground.

About the campground: Situated in a previously logged area, this partially shaded campground overlooks East Park Reservoir. Conifers add to the scene. There's a gravel boat ramp for boaters, and this is a fine place for mountain biking as well. The East Park Loop, a 32-mile bike ride, passes through here. Anglers have the opportunity to catch rainbow and brook trout.

29 Red Springs

Location: In the Ashley National Forest, about 30 miles north of Vernal
Facilities: Fire grates, picnic tables, drinking water, and vault toilets
Sites: 13
Fee: $$ for single sites; $$$$ for double sites
Elevation: 8,100 feet
Road conditions: Paved
Management: Vernal Ranger District, 355 North Vernal Avenue, Vernal, UT 84078; (435) 789–1181
Reservations: None
Activities: Picnicking
Season: June through September

Finding the campground: From Vernal, go north on U.S. Highway 191 for about 30 miles to the campground, which is on the left (west) side of the road.

About the campground: Aspens and conifers offer a shady place to camp. There's not much else to do in the campground but relax and enjoy, though it makes a good stopover en route to your next destination.

30 Lodgepole

Location: In the Ashley National Forest, about 31 miles north of Vernal
Facilities: Fire grates, picnic tables, drinking water, flush toilets, a sewage disposal station, and wastewater disposal stations
Sites: 35
Fee: $$
Elevation: 8,100 feet
Road conditions: Paved
Management: Vernal Ranger District, 355 North Vernal Avenue, Vernal, UT 84078; (435) 789-1181
Reservations: Call (877) 444-6777 or TDD (877) 833-6777; fee
Activities: Picnicking
Season: Mid-May through mid-September
Finding the campground: From Vernal, go north on U.S. Highway 191 for about 30.5 miles to the campground, which is on the right (east) side of the road.

About the campground: Semi-open, with aspens and lodgepole pines calling the place home, this is a nice campground with shade, though there isn't much to do here except relax and enjoy. If that's not enough, you can explore Flaming Gorge National Recreation Area; it's close by.

31 Bridge Hollow

Location: In Browns Park, about 31 miles east of Dutch John
Facilities: Fire grates, picnic tables, drinking water, vault toilets, and a public telephone
Sites: 13
Fee: $
Elevation: 5,500 feet
Road conditions: Gravel
Management: Bureau of Land Management, Vernal Field Office, 170 South 500 East, Vernal, UT 84078; (435) 781-4400; UT-Vernal@blm.gov
Reservations: None except for the group sites; call (435) 781-4400
Activities: Fishing, rafting, mountain biking, photography, and picnicking
Season: Year-round; the water is turned off from October through April
Finding the campground: From Dutch John, go west then north on U.S. Highway 191. Soon after crossing into Wyoming, turn right (east) onto Wyoming County Road 700. The turnoff is 8.9 miles from Dutch John and is signed. The road is both paved and gravel along the way. After 11 miles, you'll

reach a fork; go right (southeast) to Browns Park. Drive another 9.1 miles (at one point descending a 14 percent grade) to the turnoff for both the Indian Crossing and Bridge Hollow Campgrounds. You'll reach Bridge Hollow after 1.5 miles.

About the campground: The Green River flows near this campground, and huge junipers and cottonwoods shade most of it. The site is a short walk from the John Jarvie Historic Ranch, which is open for tours on a daily basis from May through October, 10:00 A.M. to 5:00 P.M. There are some original structures, each more than a hundred years old, at the ranch. You'll see a stone house, a two-room dugout, a blacksmith shop and corral, and a replica of the original general store, which was built in 1881. It's furnished with numerous artifacts from the Jarvie period. In addition, there's a cemetery and a museum.

32 Indian Crossing

Location: In Browns Park, about 31 miles east of Dutch John
Facilities: Fire grates, picnic tables (most covered), drinking water, sewage disposal station, vault toilets, and a raft ramp
Sites: 21
Fee: $
Elevation: 5,500 feet
Road conditions: Gravel
Management: Bureau of Land Management, Vernal Field Office, 170 South 500 East, Vernal, UT 84078; (435) 781-4400; UT-Vernal@blm.gov
Reservations: None except for the group site; call 435-781-4400
Activities: Fishing, rafting, mountain biking, photography, and picnicking
Season: Year-round; the water is turned off from October through April
Finding the campground: From Dutch John, go west then north on U.S. Highway 191. Soon after crossing into Wyoming, turn right (east) onto Wyoming County Road 700. The turnoff is 8.9 miles from Dutch John and is signed. The road is both paved and gravel along the way. After 11 miles, you'll reach a fork; go right (southeast) to Browns Park. Drive another 9.1 miles (at one point descending a 14 percent grade) to the turnoff for both the Indian Crossing and Bridge Hollow Campgrounds. You'll reach Indian Crossing after 2.1 miles.

About the campground: Situated above the lovely Green River, the campground is a short walk from the Jarvie Historic Ranch. The ranch is open for tours on a daily basis from May through October, 10:00 A.M. to 5:00 P.M.

Blessed with sagebrush and other desert vegetation, with riparian growth along the river, this is a good place from which to observe wildlife. Deer frequent the campground, as do many kinds of birds, including hummingbirds. It's also a place from which some folks begin rafting.

Though the campground can accommodate large RVs, the road leading to the campground is recommended for smaller RVs, mostly because of the steep 14 percent grade. You'll have to determine whether or not you want to drive down there.

33 Dripping Springs: Flaming Gorge National Recreation Area

Location: In the Flaming Gorge National Recreation Area, about 2 miles southeast of Dutch John
Facilities: Fire grates, picnic tables, drinking water, and flush and vault toilets
Sites: 25
Fee: $$ for single sites; $$$$ for double sites
Elevation: 6,200 feet
Road conditions: Paved
Management: Flaming Gorge Ranger District, P.O. Box 279, Manila, UT 84046; (435) 784–3445
Reservations: Call (877) 444–6777 or TDD (877) 833–6777; fee
Activities: Fishing, rafting, hiking, mountain biking, and picnicking
Season: Year-round
Finding the campground: From Dutch John, drive east then southeast on the first paved road (Forest Road 075) for about 2 miles to the campground.

About the campground: Situated on flat terrain, with pinyon, juniper, and sagebrush the dominant vegetation, this campground offers little shade. The area tends to be windy and dusty, but the folks who come to fish, hike, bike, and raft don't seem to mind too much.

In addition to twenty-one sites, there are four group areas, which must be reserved. The sites require a minimum of fifteen people and a maximum of sixty.

Little Hole Boat Ramp on the Green River is about 3 miles east of the campground. Rafters use the area, while others hike 7 miles from the Little Hole Trailhead at the boat ramp to the other end of the trail, Flaming Gorge Dam.

34 Antelope Flat: Flaming Gorge National Recreation Area

Location: In the Flaming Gorge National Recreation Area, about 10 miles northwest of Dutch John
Facilities: Fire grates, picnic tables (some covered), drinking water, flush toilets, sewage disposal station, fish cleaning station, and a boat ramp
Sites: 50
Fee: $$ for single sites; $$$$ for double sites
Elevation: 6,200 feet
Road conditions: Paved
Management: Flaming Gorge Ranger District, P.O. Box 279, Manila, UT 84046; (435) 784–3445
Reservations: Call (877) 444–6777 or TDD (877) 833–6777; fee
Activities: Fishing, boating, swimming, wildlife watching, photography, and picnicking
Season: Mid-May through mid-September

Finding the campground: From Dutch John, go northwest on U.S. Highway 191 for 4.6 miles. At the signed junction, go west on paved Forest Road 145 to the campground; you'll reach it in another 4.9 miles.

About the campground: Antelope Flat is located on sagebrush flats overlooking the reservoir. Vegetation is mainly sage, with some small deciduous trees such as poplar, cottonwood, and so on. There are actually 120-plus sites here, but two loops are no longer used, so I've excluded them. You'll now find forty-six single-family sites plus four group sites. The group sites must be reserved.

In addition to nice views of the 91-mile-long reservoir, there's also the opportunity to fish for rainbow trout, kokanee salmon, smallmouth bass, and lake trout or mackinaw. This is also a good place from which to observe pronghorn, North America's fastest land mammal. The area tends to be hot and windy, so be prepared.

35 Mustang Ridge: Flaming Gorge National Recreation Area

Location: In the Flaming Gorge National Recreation Area, about 4 miles west of Dutch John
Facilities: Fire grates, picnic tables, drinking water, both flush and vault toilets, showers, and both a boat launch and swimming beach nearby
Sites: 73
Fee: $$ for single sites; $$$$ for double sites
Elevation: 6,200 feet
Road conditions: Paved
Management: Flaming Gorge Ranger District, P.O. Box 279, Manila, UT 84046; (435) 784-3445
Reservations: Call (877) 444-6777 or TDD (877) 833-6777; fee
Activities: Fishing, boating, swimming, wildlife watching, photography, and picnicking
Season: Mid-May through mid-September
Finding the campground: From Dutch John, go northwest on U.S. Highway 191 for 1.9 miles. At the signed junction, go south on paved Forest Road 184 for another 1.9 miles to the campground.

About the campground: A thick forest of juniper and pinyon pine, with some sagebrush thrown in, makes this a moderately shady place to camp. There are some more open sites that offer nice views of the reservoir, but these can be hot at times. Noncampers should note that you can come into the campground and take a shower for a fee.

The area is close to a boat ramp and boat trailer parking, as well as an undeveloped swimming area. Flaming Gorge Reservoir is 91 miles long and covers 42,000 acres. It's premiere trophy lake trout region, and you can expect to find rainbow trout, kokanee salmon, and smallmouth bass.

36 Deer Run: Flaming Gorge National Recreation Area

Location: In the Flaming Gorge National Recreation Area, about 5 miles southwest of Dutch John
Facilities: Fire grates, picnic tables, drinking water, both flush and vault toilets, showers, and a sewage disposal station (it's close by); a boat ramp, marina, and fish cleaning station are nearby, too
Sites: 19
Fee: $$ for single sites; $$$$ for double sites
Elevation: 6,200 feet
Road conditions: Paved
Management: Flaming Gorge Ranger District, P.O. Box 279, Manila, UT 84046; (435) 784-3445
Reservations: Call (877) 444-6777 or TDD (877) 833-6777; fee
Activities: Fishing, boating, swimming, hiking, mountain biking, wildlife watching, photography, and picnicking
Season: April through mid-October
Finding the campground: From Dutch John, go southwest on U.S. Highway 191 for 4.2 miles, then turn right (north) onto paved Forest Road 183. A sign points the way to the Cedar Spring Recreation Complex. Continue 0.4 mile to the campground turnoff, which is on the west side of the road.

About the campground: Rolling terrain with tall pinyon pine and juniper trees is offered at this campground. Promising only moderate amounts of shade, this place can be hot at times. Please note that noncampers can come into the campground and shower for a fee.

There's plenty to do in the area. A nearby marina offers boat rentals, groceries, gas, mooring, and guided fishing excursions, while there are hiking and mountain biking trails a short distance away.

37 Cedar Springs: Flaming Gorge National Recreation Area

Location: In the Flaming Gorge National Recreation Area, about 5 miles southwest of Dutch John
Facilities: Fire grates, picnic tables, drinking water, and vault toilets. In addition, there's a sewage disposal station, a fish cleaning station, a boat ramp, and a marina nearby
Sites: 21
Fee: $$ for single sites; $$$$ for double sites
Elevation: 6,100 feet
Road conditions: Paved
Management: Flaming Gorge Ranger District, P.O. Box 279, Manila, UT 84046; (435) 784-3445
Reservations: Call (877) 444-6777 or TDD (877) 833-6777; fee
Activities: Fishing, boating, swimming, hiking, mountain biking, wildlife watching, photography, and picnicking

Season: May through mid-October
Finding the campground: From Dutch John, go southwest on U.S. Highway 191 for 4.2 miles, then make a right (north) onto paved Forest Road 183. A sign points the way to the Cedar Spring Recreation Complex. Continue 0.6 mile to the campground turnoff, which is on the west side of the road.

About the campground: Located between the Deer Run Campground and the marina—which offers boat rentals, groceries, gas, mooring, and guided fishing—this campground is set on rolling terrain, with pinyon pine, juniper, and sagebrush serving to decorate the place. It can be hot here, because there is only a moderate amount of shade.

Area activities abound. In addition to touring the dam, you'll find wonderful opportunities for fishing, mountain biking, hiking, and just plain relaxing at the 91-mile-long reservoir.

38 Firefighters Memorial: Flaming Gorge National Recreation Area

Location: In the Flaming Gorge National Recreation Area, about 6 miles southwest of Dutch John
Facilities: Fire grates, picnic tables, drinking water, flush toilets, and a sewage disposal station
Sites: 93
Fee: $$
Elevation: 6,900 feet
Road conditions: Paved
Management: Flaming Gorge Ranger District, P.O. Box 279, Manila, UT 84046; (435) 784–3445
Reservations: Call (877) 444–6777 or TDD (877) 833–6777; fee
Activities: Hiking, mountain biking, and picnicking
Season: Mid-May through mid-September
Finding the campground: From Dutch John, go southwest on U.S. Highway 191 for 6.2 miles to the campground turnoff, which is on the south side of the road.

About the campground: This campground, blessed with a mix of stately ponderosa pines and sage, is named for the memorial that shares a place on its grounds. A short walk leads from a two-car parking area to a simple memorial, dedicated to three firefighters who died in the late 1970s.

Across the highway you'll find the Bear Canyon–Bootleg Trail for hiking and biking, while just down the road there's the Flaming Gorge Lodge, with a motel, cafe, store, service station, and raft rentals.

39 Greendale West: Flaming Gorge National Recreation Area

Location: In the Flaming Gorge National Recreation Area, about 7 miles southwest of Dutch John

Facilities: Fire grates, picnic tables, drinking water, and vault toilets
Sites: 8
Fee: $$
Elevation: 7,000 feet
Road conditions: Paved
Management: Flaming Gorge Ranger District, P.O. Box 279, Manila, UT 84046; (435) 784–3445
Reservations: None
Activities: Hiking, mountain biking, and picnicking
Season: May through September
Finding the campground: From Dutch John, go southwest on U.S. Highway 191 for 6.9 miles to the campground turnoff, which is on the north side of the road.

About the campground: A small, ponderosa pine-blessed campground, this is a nice place for those who don't want to camp with crowds. If you're looking for a group site, check out the campground across the road; it's a group area with lots of room.

The campground is within walking distance of the Bear Canyon–Bootleg Trail, a nice trail for hikers and bikers. It's also close to the Flaming Gorge Lodge, which offers a motel, cafe, store, service station, and raft rentals.

40 Skull Creek: Flaming Gorge National Recreation Area

Location: In the Flaming Gorge National Recreation Area, about 12 miles southwest of Dutch John
Facilities: Fire grates, picnic tables, drinking water, and vault toilets
Sites: 17
Fee: $$
Elevation: 7,600 feet
Road conditions: Paved
Management: Flaming Gorge Ranger District, P.O. Box 279, Manila, UT 84046; (435) 784–3445
Reservations: None
Activities: Hiking, mountain biking, and picnicking
Season: Mid-May through mid-September
Finding the campground: From Dutch John, go southwest on U.S. Highway 191 for 8.8 miles to its junction with Utah Highway 44. Now drive northwest on UT 44 for another 2.7 miles to the campground turnoff, which is on the north side of the road.

About the campground: Aspens, ponderosa pines, and a variety of other conifers decorate this semi-open setting. The Canyon Rim Trail leads from this campground to three other campgrounds—Greendale, Greens Lake, and Canyon Rim. It's open to hikers and bicyclists. Quiet hikers may see moose, elk, or other animal life.

41 Greens Lake: Flaming Gorge National Recreation Area

Location: In the Flaming Gorge National Recreation Area, about 13 miles southwest of Dutch John
Facilities: Fire grates, picnic tables, drinking water, and vault toilets
Sites: 21
Fee: $$
Elevation: 7,400 feet
Road conditions: Paved
Management: Flaming Gorge Ranger District, P.O. Box 279, Manila, UT 84046; (435) 784–3445
Reservations: None, except call (877) 444-6777 for the group site
Activities: Hiking, mountain biking, fishing, and picnicking
Season: Mid-May through October
Finding the campground: From Dutch John, go southwest on U.S. Highway 191 for 8.8 miles to its junction with Utah Highway 44. Now drive northwest on UT 44 for another 3.5 miles to its junction with Forest Road 95. A sign points the way north to the Red Canyon Recreation Complex. You'll reach the campground turnoff after traveling another 0.5 mile; turn east and proceed yet another 0.5 mile to the campground.

About the campground: Lovely ponderosa pines and aspens decorate this semi-open setting, where there is plenty of shade. In addition to twenty family units, there's a group site, which must be reserved. Greens Lake is located at the edge of the campground near the Red Canyon Lodge, where you'll find cabins, a restaurant, horseback rides, a children's fishing pond, fishing supplies, and gas. Campers must ask permission from the resort before using the lake.

The Canyon Rim Trail leads from this campground to three others—Skull Creek, Greendale, and Canyon Rim. It's open to hikers and bicyclists. Quiet visitors may see wildlife, including moose and elk.

42 Canyon Rim: Flaming Gorge National Recreation Area

Location: In the Flaming Gorge National Recreation Area, about 14 miles southwest of Dutch John
Facilities: Fire grates, picnic tables, drinking water, and vault toilets
Sites: 18
Fee: $$
Elevation: 7,400 feet
Road conditions: Paved
Management: Flaming Gorge Ranger District, P.O. Box 279, Manila, UT 84046; (435) 784–3445
Reservations: Call (877) 444–6777 or TDD (877) 833–6777; fee
Activities: Hiking, mountain biking, photography, and picnicking
Season: Mid-May through mid-September
Finding the campground: From Dutch John, go southwest on U.S. Highway 191 for 8.8 miles to its junction with Utah Highway 44. Now drive northwest

on UT 44 for another 3.5 miles to its junction with Forest Road 95. A sign points the way north to the Red Canyon Recreation Complex. Drive FR 95 for an additional 1.6 miles to the campground.

About the campground: Aspens, ponderosa pines, and a variety of mountain vegetation offer scattered shade in this semi-open setting. The campground is close to the Red Canyon Visitor Center and the spectacular Red Canyon Overlook. From the overlook, you can gaze down on the reservoir 1,369 feet below. In addition, the Canyon Rim Trail leads from this campground to three others—Skull Creek, Greendale, and Greens Lake—and is open to hikers and bicyclists.

The Red Canyon Lodge is nearby, offering a restaurant, cabins, groceries, horseback rides, fishing supplies, and a children's fishing pond.

43 Red Canyon: Flaming Gorge National Recreation Area

Location: In the Flaming Gorge National Recreation Area, about 15 miles southwest of Dutch John
Facilities: Fire grates, picnic tables, drinking water, and vault toilets
Sites: 8
Fee: $$
Elevation: 7,400 feet
Road conditions: Paved
Management: Flaming Gorge Ranger District, P.O. Box 279, Manila, UT 84046; (435) 784–3445
Reservations: None
Activities: Hiking, mountain biking, photography, and picnicking
Season: Mid-May through mid-September
Finding the campground: From Dutch John, go southwest on U.S. Highway 191 for 8.8 miles to its junction with Utah Highway 44. Now drive northwest on UT 44 for another 3.5 miles to its junction with Forest Road 95. A sign points the way north to the Red Canyon Recreation Complex. Drive FR 95 for another 2.4 miles to the campground.

About the campground: Ponderosa pine and juniper provide shade in this campground, which was once a picnic area. The semi-open sites are within easy walking distance of the Red Canyon Visitor Center, which offers a wheelchair-accessible hiking trail and overlook. The campground is also close to the Red Canyon Lodge, which offers cabins, a restaurant, gas, canoe rentals, and fishing.

44 Willows/Mann's: Flaming Gorge National Recreation Area

Location: In the Flaming Gorge National Recreation Area, about 7 miles south of Manila
Facilities: Fire grates, picnic tables, and vault and pit toilets
Sites: Dispersed

Fee: $
Elevation: 7,200 feet
Road conditions: Paved to the campground, then gravel
Management: Flaming Gorge Ranger District, P.O. Box 279, Manila, UT 84046; (435) 784–3445
Reservations: None
Activities: Fishing and picnicking
Season: Year-round
Finding the campground: From Manila, drive south on Utah Highway 44 for 6 to 7 miles to the campgrounds, which are located 0.4 mile apart.

About the campground: Fishing in Sheep Creek is about all there is to do from these dispersed sites, though they do provide a place from which you can explore the nearby sights of the Flaming Gorge Recreation Area. There are seven picnic tables at Willows, which is shaded partially by cottonwoods and spruce, with willows along the creek. At Mann's there are few trees and almost no shade. Still, both are located in beautiful Sheep Creek Valley.

45 Carmel Family: Flaming Gorge National Recreation Area

Location: In the Flaming Gorge National Recreation Area, about 7 miles south of Manila
Facilities: Fire grates, picnic tables, and vault toilets
Sites: 15
Fee: $
Elevation: 6,500 feet
Road conditions: Paved to the campground, then gravel
Management: Flaming Gorge Ranger District, P.O. Box 279, Manila, UT 84046; (435) 784–3445
Reservations: None
Activities: Fishing and picnicking
Season: Year-round
Finding the campground: From Manila and the junction of Utah Highways 44 and 43, drive south on UT 44 for 5.8 miles to its junction with Forest Road 218, also called Sheep Creek Geological Loop. Now go west on FR 218 for 0.8 mile to the campground.

About the campground: Cottonwoods and conifers shade these sites, some of which are semi-open, all of which provide close access to the Flaming Gorge National Recreation Area and the rest of Sheep Rock Geological Loop, a must-see. Be sure to pick up a copy of *Wheels in Time*, a geology brochure, at the ranger district and various visitor centers. In addition, anglers may want to try their luck at trout fishing along Sheep Creek.

46 Lucerne Valley: Flaming Gorge National Recreation Area

Location: In the Flaming Gorge National Recreation Area, about 8 miles east of Manila

View of Sheep Creek Geological Area.

Facilities: Fire grates, picnic tables (some covered), drinking water, flush toilets, sewage disposal station, and a marina with a boat ramp, fish cleaning station, grocery store, boat rentals, dry storage area, and a public telephone
Sites: 165
Fee: $$
Elevation: 6,100 feet
Road conditions: Paved
Management: Flaming Gorge Ranger District, P.O. Box 279, Manila, UT 84046; (435) 784-3445
Reservations: Call (877) 444-6777 or TDD (877) 833-6777; fee
Activities: Fishing, boating, swimming, mountain biking, wildlife watching, and picnicking
Restrictions: No ATVs or off-road motorcycles are allowed in the campground.
Season: May through mid-September
Finding the campground: From Manila and the junction of Utah Highways 44 and 43, drive east then northeast on UT 43 for 2.8 miles, where you'll cross into Wyoming. Continue on what is now Wyoming Highway 530 for another 1.1 miles. Then turn right (southeast) onto Forest Road 146 (Lucerne Valley Road); a sign points the way to the Lucerne Valley Complex and Marina. Continue into Utah, driving an additional 3.9 miles to the campground.

About the campground: Cottonwoods only partially shade this open area, with its lovely view of the reservoir. Pronghorn hang out in the campground, making this a great place for wildlife watching. In addition to 161 family units, there are 4 group sites, available by reservation only.

If you'd rather save a few dollars, try camping at the primitive site known as State Line Cove. It's located about 1 mile prior to Lucerne Valley. The cost is under $10, but the only amenities are vault toilets.

47 Deep Creek

Location: In the Ashley National Forest, about 21 miles south of Manila
Facilities: Fire grates, picnic tables, and vault toilets
Sites: 17
Fee: $
Elevation: 7,600 feet
Road conditions: Gravel
Management: Flaming Gorge Ranger District, P.O. Box 279, Manila, UT 84046; (435) 784-3445
Reservations: None
Activities: Fishing, hiking, mountain biking, off-highway driving, and picnicking
Season: Mid-May through mid-September
Finding the campground: From Manila, drive south on Utah Highway 44 for about 17 miles to its junction with Forest Road 539. A sign points the way to the campground. Drive west on FR 539 for 3.8 miles to the campground.

About the campground: Deep Creek flows near this campground, which provides both shade and semi-open sites. Conifers serve to shade the sites. Nearby Elk Park offers some nice hiking and mountain biking trails, including one strenuous trip that is nearly 20 miles round-trip. The trail passes this campground, as well as the one at Browne Lake. See Gregg Bromka's *Mountain Biking Utah,* or contact the forest service, for additional information.

48 Browne Lake

Location: In the Ashley National Forest, about 22 miles southwest of Manila
Facilities: Fire grates, picnic tables, and vault toilets
Sites: 8
Fee: $
Elevation: 8,400 feet
Road conditions: Rough dirt
Management: Flaming Gorge Ranger District, P.O. Box 279, Manila, UT 84046; (435) 784–3445
Reservations: None
Activities: Fishing, boating, horseback riding, hiking, mountain biking, and picnicking
Season: Mid-May through mid-September
Finding the campground: From Manila and the junction of Utah Highways 44 and 43, drive south on UT 44 for 5.8 miles to its junction with Forest Road 218, also called Sheep Creek Geological Loop. Go west, then south, on FR 218. The road is mostly paved, but it does have sections of gravel. After 10 miles, you'll reach the junction of Forest Road 221 and make a right (west); after another 4.8 miles, turn left (southeast) at the sign and continue 1.8 miles to the campground.

About the campground: Situated near Browne Lake and offering views of Leidy Peak and other fine places, this tents-only site has the usual amenities. Just outside the shady campground there are places for dispersed camping, which means RVs can park there.

Trailheads abound in the area, leading to such places as Elk Park, Weyman Park, Anson Lake, Spirit Lake, and Leidy Peak. Some of them allow mountain bikes, but all were designed for hikers and horseback riders. On a historical note, you may want to check out the Ute Mountain Fire Lookout Tower at 8,834 feet; it's open seasonally to the public.

49 Spirit Lake

Location: In the Ashley National Forest, about 33 miles southwest of Manila
Facilities: Fire grates, picnic tables, and vault toilets. Spirit Lodge offers cabins, meals, showers, groceries, rowboat and canoe rentals, and horse rentals
Sites: 24
Fee: $
Elevation: 10,200 feet

Road conditions: Dirt
Management: Flaming Gorge Ranger District, P.O. Box 279, Manila, UT 84046; (435) 784–3445
Reservations: None
Activities: Fishing, boating, horseback riding, hiking, mountain biking, and picnicking
Season: June through mid-September
Finding the campground: From Manila and the junction of Utah Highways 44 and 43, drive south on UT 44 for 5.8 miles to its junction with Forest Road 218, also called Sheep Creek Geological Loop. Go west, then south, on FR 218. The road is mostly paved, but it does have sections of gravel. After 10 miles, you'll reach the junction of Forest Road 221 and make a right (west); after another 10.8 miles, you'll reach a junction. Turn south onto Forest Road 1 and drive another 6.4 miles to the campground.

About the campground: This campground is best suited for tents and tent trailers, because its sites are pretty small. The high alpine lake setting is lovely, but the place can be quite muddy during a heavy rain. Conifers offer plenty of shade, and the forest service reports that there are plenty of mosquitoes, too.

There are several trailheads in the area, with many alpine lakes being just a half-day hike from the campground. Look for a 3-mile round-trip trail that begins between the campground and the lodge. It ascends moderately to Tamarack Lake, with a side trail leading to Jessen Lake. For a longer outing, see *Hiking Utah* by Dave Hall.

Panoramaland

Panoramaland is a vast and varied place, with everything from barren deserts to towering forested mountains, high alpine tundra, an array of rock monoliths, wide valleys, and perhaps a human-made lake or two.

Located in central Utah in the geologic regions known as the Great Basin and Rocky Mountain Province, this is the second largest of Utah's nine travel regions. Comprised of a whopping 17,043 square miles, Panoramaland consists of five counties—Juab, Millard, Sanpete, Sevier, and Piute. The region is bordered by the state of Nevada to the west, and by the state travel regions known as Color Country to the south, Canyonlands and Castle Country to the east, and Mountainland and Great Salt Lake Country to the north.

Thirty-four campgrounds offer base sites from which to explore everything from Mount Nebo—at 11,928 feet the highest point in the region—to the white-sand dunes of the Little Sahara Recreation Area, a favorite with campers who thrill to off-highway driving. Mountains are abundant in this land, with most of the public campgrounds found in the Fishlake and Manti-La Sal National Forests. In addition, there are two in the Uinta National Forest and one in the Dixie National Forest. The remaining campgrounds are managed by various agencies, including the Bureau of Land Management, the National Park Service, and Utah state parks.

There are five state parks in the region, each one a sharp contrast to the others. Fremont Indian State Park offers the Castle Rock Campground in addition to a treasure trove of rock art and archaeological sites. Visitors to this wonderful park discover the riches of Clear Creek Canyon. Indoor activities include a video program that introduces visitors to the Fremont Indians. Outside are twelve interpretive trails, one accessible to wheelchairs, that lead to various pictographs and petroglyphs. The state park also offers a wide assortment of special activities, many of which are for children. The annual Easter egg hunt is one such popular event.

In contrast, Yuba State Park provides an unlimited array of water activities, including swimming, sailing, Jet Skiing, waterskiing, and a whole lot more. Yuba State Park also boasts a first in the Utah state parks system. If you have a boat, check out the boat-in-only Eagle View Campground. Each site offers a covered picnic table, food preparation table, barbecue grill, fire pit, tent pads, and solar lighting.

The area's other state parks are Piute, Otter Creek, and Palisade. Though their settings vary, all three offer warm waters that draw swimmers as well as water-skiers, Jet Skiers, and those with nothing more than boating on their minds.

An assortment of forest campgrounds make this a fun place to visit. Look for an abundance of sites along the shores of Fish Lake, where anglers fish to their hearts' content, photographers while away the hours making images, and campers come to just relax. At Maple Canyon folks hike and climb on conglomerate, an amazing mix of rock that ends up a great climbing surface.

Some campgrounds are found at or near Skyline Drive, a magnificent 100-mile byway that follows the crest of the Wasatch Plateau. Winding through

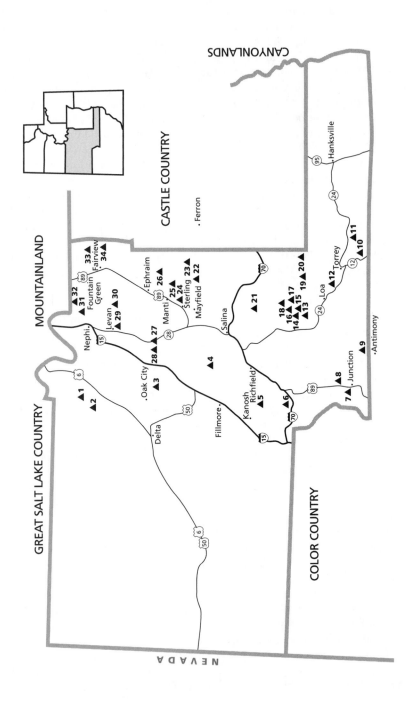

#	Name	Group sites	RV sites	Total sites	Max. RV length	Hookups	Toilets	Showers	Drinking water	Dump station	Pets	Wheelchair	Recreation	Fee($)	Season	Can reserve	Stay limit
1	White Sands		•	99	40		FV		•		•		O	$			14
2	Oasis		•	114	40		FV	•	•	•	•		O	$			14
3	Oak Creek	•	•	23	28		FP		•		•		F	$	May–Oct.		14
4	Maple Grove	•	•	22			V	•			•	•	FH	$	May 21–Oct. 30		14
5	Adelaide	•		8			FV		•		•		F	$	May–Oct.		14
6	Castle Rock-Fremont Indian State Park	•	•	31			CF		•		•	•	HM	$	May–Oct. 15	•	14
7	City Creek	•	•	5	24		V		•		•		FRH	$	May 21–Oct. 20		14
8	Piute State Park	•	•	*			V				•						14
9	Otter Creek State Park	•	•	61	40		F	•	•	•	•	•	SFBLO	$–$$		•	14
10	Singletree	•	•	31	35		VF		•		•		H	$	May 20–Sept. 15	•	14
11	Fruita	•	•	70	35		PF	•	•		•	•	MHC	$$			14
12	Sunglow	•	•	9			F		•		•			$			14
13	Doctor Creek	•	•	32			F	•	•	•	•	•	BMHF	$–$$$$	Memorial–Labor Day	•	10
14	Mackinaw		•	67			F	•	•		•	•	BMHF	$–$$$	Memorial–Labor Day	•	10
15	Bowery Creek	•	•	43			F		•		•	•	BMHF	$–$$$$	Memorial–Labor Day	•	10
16	Frying Pan	•	•	12			F		•		•	•	MH	$	Memorial–Labor Day	•	14
17	Piute		•	48			P				•		FMH	$	Memorial–Labor Day		60
18	Tasha Equestrian	•	•	11			F		•		•		R		Memorial–Labor Day		14
19	Elkhorn	•	•	7	22		V		•		•		HRM	0–$$$$	June 15–Sept.		14
20	Cathedral Valley			6			V				•		H				14
21	Gooseberry (Salina)	•	•	7			C		•		•		F	$–$$$$	May–Nov.		16
22	Twelve Mile Flat	•	•	16			V		•		•		HM	$	June–Oct.	•	16
23	Ferron Reservoir	•	•	30			P		•		•		BLMFH	$	June 15–Sept. 20	•	16
24	Palisade State Park	•	•	54	40		F	•	•	•	•	•	FSBL	$$		•	14
25	Manti Community	•	•	9	25		V		•		•		FM	$	June–Oct.	•	16
26	Lake Hill	•	•	11	30		P		•		•		HFM	$	June–Oct.	•	16

* Dispersed Camping—no designated sites **Hookups:** W = Water E = Electric S = Sewer **Toilets:** F = Flush V = Vault P = Pit C= Chemical **Recreation:** H = Hiking S = Swimming F = Fishing B = Boating L = Boat Launch O = Off-highway driving R = Horseback Riding C = Rock Climbing M = Mountain Biking **Maximum Trailer/RV length** given in feet. **Stay Limit** given in days. **Fee** given in dollars. If no entry under **Season**, campground is open all year. If no entry under **Fee,** camping is free.

	Group sites	RV sites	Total sites	Max. RV length	Hookups	Toilets	Showers	Drinking water	Dump station	Pets	Wheelchair	Recreation	Fee($)	Season	Can reserve	Stay limit
27 Painted Rocks: Yuba State Park	•		*			V				•		SFBLMO	$			14
28 Oasis: Yuba State Park	•	•	27	40		F	•	•	•	•	•	SFBLMO	$$		•	14
29 Chicken Creek	•	•	8	25		P	•		•			F	$	May–Oct.	•	16
30 Maple Canyon	•		13			P				•		HCM	$	May–Oct.	•	16
31 Ponderosa		•	22	25		V	•		•	•		HF	$–$$	May–Oct.	•	16
32 Bear Canyon	•		9	30		F	•		•			HF	$	May–Oct.		16
33 Gooseberry Reservoir	•	•	10	25		P	•		•			FMO	$	June 15– Sept. 15	•	16
34 Flat Canyon	•	•	13	30		P			•			F	$	June 15– Sept. 15	•	16

* Dispersed Camping—no designated sites **Hookups:** W = Water E = Electric S = Sewer **Toilets:** F = Flush V = Vault P = Pit C= Chemical **Recreation:** H = Hiking S = Swimming F = Fishing B = Boating L = Boat Launch O = Off-highway driving R = Horseback Riding C = Rock Climbing M = Mountain Biking **Maximum Trailer/RV length** given in feet. **Stay Limit** given in days. **Fee** given in dollars. If no entry under **Season**, campgound is open all year. If no entry under **Fee**, camping is free.

desert and mountains, several other scenic highways are must-travels, including Utah Highways 12, 24, and 28.

Capitol Reef is the only national park in the region. Here, magnificent scenery and fascinating history combine to make this one of the country's most unusual national parks. It's also a wonderful place for rock climbers. The park is open all year and is a must-see for all who come to this wonderful area.

For more information on the Panoramaland Travel Region, send your request to P.O. Box 71, Nephi, UT 84648; call (435) 623–5203 or (800) 748–4361; or fax (435) 623–4609.

1 White Sands: Little Sahara Recreation Area

Location: In the Little Sahara Recreation Area, about 40 miles northeast of Delta
Facilities: Fire grates, picnic tables, drinking water, and both flush and vault toilets
Sites: 99
Fee: $
Elevation: 5,000 feet
Road conditions: Paved to the campground, then hard-packed sand
Management: Bureau of Land Management, Fillmore Field Office, 35 East 500 North, Fillmore, UT 84631; (435) 743–3100; UT-Fillmore@blm.gov
Reservations: None
Activities: Off-highway driving, playing on the sand dunes, photography, and picnicking

Season: Year-round; water is shut off in winter
Finding the campground: From Delta, drive U.S. Highway 6 northeast for about 32 miles to Jericho Junction and make a left (west) at the sign pointing the way to the Little Sahara Recreation Area. Take the paved road 4.4 miles to another paved road, and make a left (southwest). In another 1.7 miles, you'll reach the visitor center. Follow more signs an additional 2.1 miles to the campground.

About the campground: Located in the sand and juniper trees of one of Utah's largest dune fields, this is a popular place for off-highway driving. Be sure to use a whip flag and stay on constructed roads and trails. There's also a fenced in sand-play area for kids.

If you have a large group, check out the Jericho and Sand Mountain areas. Group-use fees are $50 for one to forty people, then 75 cents for each additional person over the age of twelve.

2   Oasis: Little Sahara Recreation Area

Location: In the Little Sahara Recreation Area, about 43 miles northeast of Delta
Facilities: Fire grates, picnic tables, drinking water, sewage disposal station, and both flush and vault toilets
Sites: 114
Fee: $
Elevation: 5,000 feet
Road conditions: Paved
Management: Bureau of Land Management, Fillmore Field Office, 35 East 500 North, Fillmore, UT 84631; (435) 743-3100; UT-fillmore@blm.gov
Reservations: None
Activities: Off-highway driving, playing on the sand dunes, photography, and picnicking
Season: Year-round; water shut off in winter
Finding the campground: From Delta, drive U.S. Highway 6 northeast for about 32 miles to Jericho Junction and make a left (west) at the sign pointing the way to the Little Sahara Recreation Area. Take the paved road 4.4 miles to another paved road, and make a left (southwest). In another 1.7 miles, you'll reach the visitor center. Follow more signs an additional 5.2 miles to the campground.

About the campground: Located in the sand and juniper trees of the Little Sahara Recreation Area, one of Utah's largest dune fields, this campground is popular with the ATV and motorcycle crowd. Be sure to use a whip flag and stay on constructed roads and trails.

If you have a large group, check out the Jericho and Sand Mountain areas. These sites are designed for group use; fees are $50 for one to forty people, and 75 cents per person after that.

3 Oak Creek

Location: In the Fishlake National Forest, approximately 4 miles southeast of Oak City
Facilities: Fire grates, picnic tables, drinking water, and both flush and pit toilets
Sites: 23
Fee: $
Elevation: 5,900 feet
Road conditions: Paved
Management: Fillmore Ranger District, 390 South Main, Fillmore, UT 84631; (435) 743-5721
Reservations: None except for the group sites. Groups can call (877) 444-6777 or TDD (877) 833-6777; fee
Activities: Fishing and picnicking
Season: May through October
Finding the campground: From the junction of Utah Highway 125 and Center Street in Oak City (look for a sign reading FOREST CAMP), go east on Center, which becomes Canyon Road. The paved road leads mostly southeast for 4.2 miles to the campground.

About the campground: Cottonwoods, maples, and box elders shade this lovely campground, with Oak Creek flowing nearby. There are two units— Lower Loop and Upper Loop—both of which offer the same amenities.

4 Maple Grove

Location: In the Fishlake National Forest, approximately 16 miles northwest of Salina
Facilities: Fire grates, picnic tables, drinking water, and vault toilets
Sites: 22
Fee: $
Elevation: 6,400 feet
Road conditions: Paved
Management: Fillmore Ranger District, 390 South Main, Fillmore, UT 84631; (435) 743-5721
Reservations: For the group sites only, call (877) 444-6777 or TDD (877) 833-6777; fee
Activities: Fishing, hiking, and picnicking
Season: May 21 through October 30
Finding the campground: From the junction of U.S. Highways 50 and 89 in downtown Salina, go west on US 50, eventually heading northwest. After 12.6 miles, turn left (west) at the signed, paved road. Drive another 3.7 miles to the campground.

About the campground: If you like trees, and lots of them, then this is the place for you. Shaded by dense groves of box elders, maples, conifers, and even a few oaks and junipers, these canopied sites lie along a creek that offers fishing for rainbow trout. The three group sites must be reserved. Hikers will find the Rock Canyon Trail nearby.

5 Adelaide

Location: In the Fishlake National Forest, approximately 5 miles southeast of Kanosh
Facilities: Fire grates, picnic tables, drinking water, and both flush and vault toilets
Sites: 8
Fee: $
Elevation: 5,500 feet
Road conditions: Gravel
Management: Fillmore Ranger District, 390 South Main, Fillmore, UT 84631; (435) 743-5721
Reservations: None except for the group sites. Groups can call (877) 444-6777 or TDD (877) 833-6777; fee
Activities: Fishing and picnicking
Season: May through October
Finding the campground: From Main Street and 300 South (Forest Road 106) in Kanosh, drive southeast for 5 miles to the campground.

About the campground: Located along Corn Creek in a posted flash-flood area, this is a place to avoid come big thunderstorms. Box elders, cottonwoods, and maples shade the grassy sites found here, with plenty of room to fish, read a book, or just plain relax.

6 Castle Rock: Fremont Indian State Park

Location: About 24 miles southwest of Richfield
Facilities: Fire grates, picnic tables, chemical and flush toilets, and drinking water
Sites: 31
Fee: $
Elevation: 6,500 feet
Road conditions: Maintained gravel
Management: Fremont Indian State Park, 11550 West Clear Creek Canyon Road, Sevier, UT 84766-9999; (435) 527-4631
Reservations: In the Salt Lake area, call (801) 322-3770; elsewhere, (800) 322-3770; fee
Activities: Hiking, mountain biking, picnicking, and photography. Three trails provide access to the 260-mile Paiute ATV Trail
Season: May through mid-October. You can also camp in winter; facilities are limited but the fee is reduced.
Finding the campground: From Richfield, travel southwest on Interstate 70 for about 23 miles, getting off at exit 17. The visitor center and museum are about 1 mile to the right (east). Reach the campground by heading south,

crossing over the interstate, and driving Forest Road 478 for 1.3 miles. Signs point the way to both places.

About the campground: Campsites are situated among juniper and oak, with Joe Lott Creek singing nearby. The campground snuggles up to an amazing medley of mud towers, a conglomeration of volcanic ash from seventeen-million-year-old explosions in the Tushar Mountains area.

The campground is also near the museum at Fremont Indian State Park. Here you'll learn all about Clear Creek Canyon's treasury of rock art and archaeological sites. A video program introduces you to the Fremont Indians. In addition, twelve interpretive trails, one accessible to wheelchairs, lead you to various pictographs and petroglyphs.

The state park offers a wide assortment of special activities, many of them for children—for instance, an annual Easter egg hunt. There are also many activities related to learning about the Indians who once lived here. Contact the state park for further information.

7 City Creek

Location: In the Fishlake National Forest, about 5.5 miles northwest of Junction

Facilities: Fire grates, picnic tables, drinking water, and vault toilets

Sites: 5

Fee: None

Elevation: 7,600 feet

Road conditions: Paved and gravel

Management: Beaver Ranger District, 575 South Main, Beaver, UT 84713; (435) 438–2436

Reservations: None

Activities: Fishing, horseback riding, hiking, and picnicking

Season: May 21 through October 20

Finding the campground: From Junction, travel northwest on Utah Highway 153, which is paved for about 5 miles then turns to maintained gravel. You'll reach the campground in 5.5 miles.

About the campground: City Creek flows near this campground set among cottonwood, ponderosa pine, pinyon pine, and juniper trees; it makes a nice base for anglers, hikers, and horseback riders. There are hiking opportunities on both the North and South Forks of City Creek. Anglers can expect fish up to 9 inches in length. Wild rainbow trout are the most common species; the South Fork offers the greatest success rate.

8 Piute State Park

Location: About 6 miles north of Junction

Facilities: Fire grates, a few picnic tables, boat launch, dock, and vault toilets

Sites: Dispersed

Fee: None

Elevation: 5,900 feet
Road conditions: Maintained gravel
Management: Piute State Park, P.O. Box 43, Antimony, UT 84712-0043; (435) 624–3268
Reservations: None
Activities: Fishing, boating, swimming, waterskiing, rockhounding, mountain biking, and picnicking
Season: Year-round
Finding the campground: From Junction, travel north on U.S. Highway 89 for 6.2 miles to signed Piute State Park. A wide, gravel road leads right (east) for 0.5 mile to its end at the reservoir.

About the campground: Piute Reservoir, one of Utah's largest artificial lakes at 3,300 acres, is the setting for this state park. It offers primitive camping with a couple of toilets, a few picnic tables, a boat ramp, a dock, and little more in the way of amenities. Still, the primitive conditions may be just fine for those who enjoy fishing for trout, boating, water sports, rockhounding, or riding the local dirt roads on a mountain bike.

9 Otter Creek State Park

Location: About 60 miles south of Richfield
Facilities: Fire grates, picnic tables, drinking water, flush toilets, showers, public telephone, fish cleaning station, boat launch, loading docks, sewage disposal station, and horseshoes on loan
Sites: 30 developed; 31 overflow
Fee: $$ for developed sites; $ for overflow sites
Elevation: 6,400 feet
Road conditions: Paved
Management: Otter Creek State Park, P.O. Box 43, Antimony, UT 84712-0043; (435) 624–3268
Reservations: In the Salt Lake area, call (801) 322–3770; elsewhere, (800) 322–3770; fee
Activities: Fishing, boating, waterskiing, bird-watching, off-highway driving, picnicking, ice skating, and ice fishing
Season: Year-round
Finding the campground: From the old mining town of Antimony, travel north for about 4 miles on Utah Highway 22.

About the campground: Located on the south end of Otter Creek Reservoir, the campground and surrounding areas are good places to look for both resident and migratory bird life, including ospreys, bald eagles, ducks, geese, and swans. The reservoir offers some of the state's finest year-round rainbow trout fishing. There are also cutthroat and brown trout. The lake's record is a sixteen-pound, seven-ounce brown trout.

Hookups are nonexistent, but there are wooden windscreens, and shade trees for privacy. Overflow camping areas are found to the west and east sides of the main campground.

Three ATV trails originate in the park, including the popular Paiute ATV Trail, which is a 260-mile loop over three mountain ranges and through rugged canyons and deserts.

10 Singletree

Location: In the Dixie National Forest, approximately 12 miles southeast of Torrey
Facilities: Fire grates, picnic tables, nonpotable water, vault and flush toilets, volleyball area, and horseshoe area
Sites: 31
Fee: $
Elevation: 8,600 feet
Road conditions: Paved
Management: Escalante Ranger District, 755 West Main, P.O. Box 246, Escalante, UT 84726; (435) 826-5400
Reservations: Call (877) 444-6777 or TDD (877) 833-6777 to reserve the group site; fee
Activities: Hiking and picnicking
Restrictions: ATVs are not allowed
Season: May 20 through mid-September
Finding the campground: From Torrey, drive south on Utah Highway 12 for 11.7 miles. You'll see the campground and turnoff on your left.

About the campground: Embraced by ponderosa pines, with Singletree Creek singing its way through the center of the campground, this is a great spot for relaxing. There's also a nice view east to the Henry Mountains from the east edge of the campground. The Singletree Falls Trail leads 1 mile from the campground to the waterfall.

11 Fruita: Capitol Reef National Park

Location: About 1 mile south of the visitor center
Facilities: Fire grates, picnic tables, drinking water, flush and pit toilets, sewage disposal station, and public telephone
Sites: 70
Fee: $$
Elevation: 5,500 feet
Road conditions: Paved
Management: Capitol Reef National Park, HCR 70, Box 15, Torrey, UT 84775; (435) 425-3791; Care_Interpretation@nps.gov
Reservations: The group campsite is open from April through October 20, except Tuesday and Wednesday. Write or fax your request to (435) 425-3026
Activities: Hiking, mountain biking, rock climbing, picnicking, scenic driving, and photography
Restrictions: Generator use allowed only from 9:00 A.M. to 11:00 A.M. and 4:00 P.M. to 6:00 P.M.
Season: Year-round

Finding the campground: From the visitor center, about 11 miles east of Torrey off Utah Highway 24, go south about 1 mile to the campground.

About the campground: An oasis in the desert, the campground is blanketed with grass and lovely trees that provide shade come summer. Nearby you'll find Fruita's historic orchards, harvested for almost a century. The legacy lives on, for the National Park Service preserves the orchards, replacing old trees with historical varieties. Fruit is available throughout most of the summer and fall. You may eat as much fruit as you wish in an orchard open for public harvest—you must purchase it at a self-pay station. A scale for weighing fruit and plastic bags are provided.

When you're done gorging on fruit, you'll find a multitude of trails to explore and a lovely scenic drive; rock climbing is popular as well. If you're climbing, please note that you must use colored chalk; white chalk is not permitted.

12 Sunglow

Location: In the Fishlake National Forest, about 1 mile east of Bicknell and 7 miles west of Torrey
Facilities: Fire grates, picnic tables, drinking water, and flush toilets
Sites: 9
Fee: $
Elevation: 7,500 feet
Road conditions: Dirt
Management: Loa Ranger District, 138 South Main, P.O. Box 129, Loa, UT 84747; (435) 836–2811
Reservations: None
Activities: Picnicking
Season: Year-round
Finding the campground: From the center of the small town of Bicknell, drive east on Utah Highway 24 for about 1 mile. Turn left (north) onto a paved road (there's a sign for Sunglow) and drive 1 mile before the road turns to dirt. Continue another 0.2 mile to the campground.

About the campground: Partially surrounded by red rock and tucked away in a box canyon of sorts, this site is decorated with juniper and cottonwood trees. A small creek flows through the campground, which is open all year, though the water is turned off from October through April.

13 Doctor Creek: Fish Lake Recreation Area

Location: In the Fishlake National Forest, about 20 miles northwest of Loa
Facilities: Fire grates, picnic tables, drinking water, flush toilets, and sewage disposal station
Sites: 32
Fee: $ for single sites; $$$$ for group sites
Elevation: 8,900 feet

A bighorn lamb.

Road conditions: Paved
Management: Loa Ranger District, 138 South Main, P.O. Box 129, Loa, UT 84747; (435) 836-2811
Reservations: Call (877) 444-6777 or TDD (877) 833-6777; fee
Activities: Fishing, boating, mountain biking, hiking, wildlife watching, photography, and picnicking
Restrictions: ATVs are not allowed in the campground
Season: Memorial Day through Labor Day
Finding the campground: From Loa, travel northwest on Utah Highway 24 for 12.9 miles to its junction with Utah Highway 25. Make a right (northeast) onto paved UT 25 and drive 7.2 miles to a turnoff on the right (southeast) for the campground. Pass the sewage disposal station, and continue 0.3 mile to the fee station.

About the campground: Located near the southern shore of Fish Lake, this beautiful campground is set among aspens. There's plenty to do in the area, with many hiking and mountain biking trails nearby, including one along the lakeshore. There are also three resorts in the area; they offer showers, self-service laundries, limited groceries, dining facilities, boat rentals, and boat ramps. There are also Sunday church services at Fish Lake Lodge.

14 Mackinaw: Fish Lake Recreation Area

Location: In the Fishlake National Forest, approximately 22 miles northwest of Loa
Facilities: Fire grates, picnic tables, drinking water, public telephone, flush toilets, and showers
Sites: 67
Fee: $ for single sites; $$$ for double sites
Elevation: 8,900 feet
Road conditions: Paved
Management: Loa Ranger District, 138 South Main, P.O. Box 129, Loa, UT 84747; (435) 836-2811.
Reservations: Call (877) 444-6777 or TDD (877) 833-6777; fee
Activities: Fishing, boating, mountain biking, hiking, wildlife watching, photography, and picnicking
Restrictions: ATVs are not allowed in the campground
Season: Memorial Day through Labor Day
Finding the campground: From Loa, travel northwest on Utah Highway 24 for 12.9 miles to its junction with Utah Highway 25. Make a right (northeast) onto paved UT 25 and drive 9.1 miles to a turnoff on the left (north) for the campground. There are two more entrances 0.2 and 0.4 mile farther down the road.

About the campground: Located amid a wonderful grove of aspens, the campground is situated across the highway from the west shore of Fish Lake. There's a multitude of things to do in the area. For example, hiking and mountain biking trails abound; there's even one that parallels the lakeshore. In addition, there are three resorts in the area that offer boat rentals and boat ramps, showers, self-service laundries, limited groceries, and dining facilities. There are also Sunday church services at Fish Lake Lodge.

15 Bowery Creek: Fish Lake Recreation Area

Location: In the Fishlake National Forest, about 23 miles northwest of Loa
Facilities: Fire grates, picnic tables, drinking water, and flush toilets
Sites: 43
Fee: $ for single sites; $$$ for double sites, $$$$ for group sites
Elevation: 8,900 feet
Road conditions: Paved
Management: Loa Ranger District, 138 South Main, P.O. Box 129, Loa, UT 84747; (435) 836–2811
Reservations: Call (877) 444–6777 or TDD (877) 833–6777; fee
Activities: Fishing, boating, mountain biking, hiking, wildlife watching, photography, and picnicking
Restrictions: ATVs are not allowed in the campground
Season: Memorial Day through Labor Day
Finding the campground: From Loa, travel northwest on Utah Highway 24 for 12.9 miles to its junction with Utah Highway 25. Make a right (northeast) onto paved UT 25 and drive 9.9 miles to the campground turnoff on the left (north).

About the campground: Located among aspens and pines, the campground rests across the highway from the west shore of Fish Lake. There are many activities to enjoy in the region. For instance, hiking and mountain biking trails abound; there's even one that parallels the lakeshore and follows part of the Old Spanish Trail. Three nearby resorts offer boat rentals and boat ramps, showers, self-service laundries, limited groceries, and dining facilities. There are also Sunday church services at Fish Lake Lodge.

16 Frying Pan: Fish Lake Recreation Area

Location: In the Fishlake National Forest, approximately 28 miles northwest of Loa
Facilities: Fire grates, picnic tables, drinking water, and flush toilets
Sites: 12
Fee: $
Elevation: 8,900 feet
Road conditions: Paved
Management: Loa Ranger District, 138 South Main, P.O. Box 129, Loa, UT 84747; (435) 836–2811
Reservations: Call (877) 444–6777 or TDD (877) 833–6777; fee
Activities: Mountain biking, hiking, wildlife watching, photography, and picnicking
Restrictions: ATVs are not allowed in the campground
Season: Memorial Day through Labor Day

Finding the campground: From Loa, travel northwest on Utah Highway 24 for 12.9 miles to its junction with Utah Highway 25. Make a right (northeast) onto paved UT 25 and drive 14.9 miles to the campground turnoff on the left (north).

About the campground: Located among aspens and pines, the campground is tucked away on the north side of the road. There are many activities to enjoy in the area; hiking and mountain biking are especially popular. You can even enjoy fishing at nearby Fish Lake and Johnson Reservoir. In addition, three resorts offer boat rentals and boat ramps, showers, self-service laundries, limited groceries, and dining facilities. There are also Sunday church services at Fish Lake Lodge.

17 Piute

Location: In the Fishlake National Forest, about 24 miles north of Loa
Facilities: Pit toilets
Sites: 48
Fee: $
Elevation: 8,900 feet
Road conditions: Paved
Management: Loa Ranger District, 138 South Main, P.O. Box 129, Loa, UT 84747; (435) 836–2811
Reservations: None
Activities: Mountain biking, hiking, and fishing
Season: Memorial Day through Labor Day
Finding the campground: From Loa, travel north-northeast on paved Utah Highway 72 for about 10 miles. Upon reaching the junction, turn left (northwest) onto Gooseberry-Fremont Road (a sign says that this is Route 3268) and continue 13.6 miles to the campground.

About the campground: Sometimes known as the Piute Parking Campground, this forty-eight-site area is in the open, with close access to fishing at Johnson Reservoir. The sites are set up parking-lot style, with paved slabs and pit toilets all there is to offer. Still, it's an inexpensive place to set up a base camp for fishing, mountain biking, and hiking. See Gregg Bromka's Falcon book *Mountain Biking Utah* for more information.

18 Tasha Equestrian

Location: In the Fishlake National Forest, about 25 miles north of Loa
Facilities: Fire grates, picnic tables, drinking water, flush toilets, horse corrals, tie racks for horses, and a horse unloading ramp
Sites: 11
Fee: None
Elevation: 8,900 feet
Road conditions: Dirt

Management: Loa Ranger District, 138 South Main, P.O. Box 129, Loa, UT 84747; (435) 836–2811
Reservations: None
Activities: Horseback riding
Season: Memorial Day through Labor Day
Finding the campground: From Loa, travel north-northeast on paved Utah Highway 72 for about 10 miles. Upon reaching the junction, turn left (north-west) onto Gooseberry-Fremont Road (a sign calls this Route 3268) and continue 14.2 miles to the campground turnoff, which is on the right (north) side of the road. Follow the dirt road 0.7 mile to the campground.

About the campground: Managed by the forest service, this campground is cleaned and maintained by the Central Utah Backcountry Horsemen under an adoption agreement. It's a horses-only kind of place, so if you don't have a horse you won't be staying here. It's an excellent base for those with horses, with many nearby trails leading up Tasha Canyon and Mytoge Mountain. The campground is tucked away amid pines and aspens. There are several sets of corrals throughout the campground. Each site has a tie rack for the horses, as well as the usual amenities.

19 Elkhorn

Location: In the Fishlake National Forest, about 20 miles northeast of Loa
Facilities: Fire grates, picnic tables, drinking water, vault toilet
Sites: 7
Fee: None for single; $$$$ for the group site
Elevation: 9,800 feet
Road conditions: Dirt
Management: Loa Ranger District, 138 South Main, P.O. Box 129, Loa, UT 84747; (435) 836–2811
Reservations: None except for the group site; fee. Call (435) 836–2811
Activities: Hiking, horseback riding, and mountain biking
Season: Mid-June through September
Finding the campground: From Loa, travel north-northeast on paved Utah Highway 72 for about 12 miles. At this point, make a right (east) onto Forest Road 206, which is gravel. A sign says it's 8 miles to the campground. As you continue, the road narrows to a singletrack with turnouts; its surface is dirt with a sprinkling of gravel. Stay on FR 206, driving 4.6 miles to a fork; continue on FR 206 to the campground in less than 4 miles.

About the campground: Set in a forest of spruce, fir, and aspen, this small, isolated campground makes a good base from which to explore a number of nearby hiking, biking, and horseback trails.

20 Cathedral Valley: Capitol Reef National Park

Location: About 39 miles north of the visitor center
Facilities: Fire grates, picnic tables, and vault toilets

Temple of the Sun and the Moon, Cathedral Valley, Capitol Reef National Park.

Sites: 6
Fee: None
Elevation: 7,000 feet
Road conditions: Dirt and sand; high-clearance or four-wheel-drive vehicles are recommended and often required. Road conditions change due to rain or snow; check with the visitor center for current conditions.
Management: Capitol Reef National Park, HCR 70, Box 15, Torrey, UT 84775; (435) 425–3791; Care_Interpretation@nps.gov
Reservations: None
Activities: Hiking, picnicking, and photography
Season: Year-round
Finding the campground: From the visitor center, about 11 miles east of Torrey, continue east on Utah Highway 24 for another 11.7 miles. Make a left at the small sign onto River Ford Road (also known as Hartnet Road), a dirt road, to a fork at 25.4 miles. Straight (west) would lead to Thousand Lake Mountain; keep right (north) for 0.3 mile to the campground, which is on the left (west).

If you'd rather not ford the river, continue east on UT 24 for an additional 6.7 miles to Caineville Wash Road; follow it about 29 miles to the campground.

About the campground: Spacious sites sit among a partially open forest of pinyon and juniper on the flanks of Thousand Lake Mountain. From here, there are views of the mountain as well as into the eastern reaches of Capitol

Reef. This primitive, bring-your-own-water campground is suitable for tenters.

Hikers with map and compass in hand can explore to their hearts' content, while photographers will find an endless array of images to make.

21 Gooseberry (Salina)

Location: In the Fishlake National Forest, about 16 miles southeast of Salina
Facilities: Fire grates, picnic tables, drinking water, and chemical toilets
Sites: 7
Fee: $ for single sites; $$$$ for a group (up to 40 people)
Elevation: 7,800 feet
Road conditions: Dirt
Management: Loa Ranger District, 138 South Main, P.O. Box 129, Loa, UT 84747; (435) 836–2811
Reservations: For the group site only, call (435) 896–9233; fee
Activities: Fishing and picnicking
Season: May through November
Finding the campground: From Salina, head east on Interstate 70 for about 7 miles to Gooseberry Road, exit 61. Head south on Gooseberry Road, which is paved for about 6.0 miles then turns to a one-lane dirt road with turnouts. You'll reach the campground, which is on your right, after another 3.3 miles of dirt road.

About the campground: A pretty setting with aspens all around, there's a group site as well as several single sites. The host told us that some folks try their luck fishing in Gooseberry Creek. He claims the fish are small but "good tasting."

22 Twelve Mile Flat

Location: In the Manti–La Sal National Forest, approximately 19 miles east of Mayfield
Facilities: Fire grates, picnic tables, drinking water, and vault toilets
Sites: 16
Fee: $
Elevation: 9,800 feet
Road conditions: Dirt
Management: Sanpete Ranger District, 540 North Main Street, P.O. Box 692, Ephraim, UT 84627; (435) 283–4151
Reservations: Call (877) 444–6777 or TDD (877) 833–6777; fee
Activities: Hiking, mountain biking, photography, and picnicking
Season: June through October
Finding the campground: From the junction of Main Street and Canyon Road in downtown Mayfield, head east on paved Canyon Road. After 1.7 miles, the road becomes gravel. Continue approximately 17 miles to the campground.

About the campground: There are fourteen single sites and two group areas—which hold sixty-plus people in each unit—at this lovely campground set among Engelmann spruce and subalpine fir. One group site holds up to seventy-five people; call for more information.

23 Ferron Reservoir

Location: In the Manti–La Sal National Forest, about 26 miles west of Ferron
Facilities: Fire grates, boat launch, picnic tables, drinking water, and pit toilets
Sites: 30
Fee: $
Elevation: 9,500 feet
Road conditions: Gravel
Management: Ferron Ranger District, 115 West Canyon Road, P.O. Box 310, Ferron, UT 84523; (435) 384–2372
Reservations: Call (877) 444–6777 or TDD (877) 833–6777; fee
Activities: Fishing, boating, hiking, mountain biking, and picnicking
Season: Mid-June through September 20
Finding the campground: From the junction of Utah Highway 10 and Canyon Road in downtown Ferron, head west on paved Canyon Road. Signs for Millstate State Park and Ferron Reservoir point the way. Travel 4.3 miles before the road turns to gravel; later the road is signed FOREST ROAD 22. Continue another 21.7 miles (sometimes encountering steep grades on the one-lane road with turnouts) to Ferron Reservoir and a fork. You'll find six campsites in 0.5 mile if you make a right (north) and then a left (west). There are more sites if you head left (west) at the lake; you'll find six sites after 0.2 mile and another eighteen sites after yet another 0.5 mile.

About the campground: This campground is managed in three sections, one (six sites) on the northeast side of the lake, and two sections (one with six sites, the other with eighteen) on the west side of the lake. A group site holds up to fifty people; call for more information.

Conifers and some aspens shade most of the sites, many of which overlook lovely Ferron Reservoir. Near the eighteen-site section you'll find a 0.5-mile-long nature trail. The trailhead is near site 24. Mountain bikers will find plenty of roads and trails for biking. For more information, see *Mountain Biking Utah,* by Gregg Bromka. It's a Falcon guide.

24 Palisade State Park

Location: About 2 miles northeast of Sterling
Facilities: Fire grates, picnic tables, flush toilets, showers, sewage disposal station, boat launch and docks, golf course and clubhouse, and drinking water
Sites: 54
Fee: $$
Elevation: 5,868 feet
Road conditions: Paved
Management: Palisade State Park, 2200 Palisade Road, P.O. Box 650070, Sterling, UT 84665-0070; (435) 835–PARK. Golf course (435) 835–GOLF

Reservations: In the Salt Lake area, call (801) 322-3770; elsewhere, (800) 322-3770; fee
Activities: Nonmotorized boating, swimming, fishing, golfing, ice fishing and ice skating (in winter), and picnicking
Season: Year-round
Finding the campground: From the north end of Sterling, turn right (east) off U.S. Highway 89 onto paved Palisades Road. A sign points the way. You'll reach the park entrance station after 1.6 miles.

About the campground: Landscaped with grass and a variety of deciduous trees, this state park offers three separate campground units spread out along the north, east, and south ends of Palisade Lake. The northernmost section is known as Arapeen, the eastern side is called Pioneer, and the south section is named Sanpitch.

In summer folks come to this lovely area to swim, go boating, do some fishing, indulge in some golfing, or just plain relax. In winter visitors come to skate on the frozen lake or to drop a line into a hole in the lake to do some ice fishing.

25 Manti Community

Location: In the Manti–La Sal National Forest, approximately 6 miles east of Manti
Facilities: Fire grates, picnic tables, drinking water, and vault toilets
Sites: 9
Fee: $
Elevation: 7,400 feet
Road conditions: Dirt
Management: Sanpete Ranger District, 540 North Main Street, P.O. Box 692, Ephraim, UT 84627; (435) 283-4151
Reservations: Call (877) 444-6777 or TDD (877) 833-6777; fee
Activities: Fishing, mountain biking, and picnicking
Season: June through October
Finding the campground: From Fifth South and Main in Manti, head east on paved Fifth South. After 0.8 mile, the road turns to gravel and later dirt; it can be very bumpy. The road also turns into Forest Road 045 as you continue. You'll reach the campground, which is on your right, in another 5.2 miles.

About the campground: Set amid a forest of aspen, juniper, spruce, and other pines, this campground offers more than just woods. It's adjacent to Yearns Reservoir and the chance to fish for breakfast, lunch, or dinner.

A hiking and OHV trail is found at the Patton Trailhead, about 3 miles prior to the campground. There are many dirt roads and trails for mountain bikes as well. A group site for up to thirty people is available; call for additional information.

26 Lake Hill

Location: In the Manti–La Sal National Forest, about 8 miles east of Ephraim
Facilities: Fire grates, picnic tables, drinking water, and pit toilets
Sites: 11
Fee: $
Elevation: 8,400 feet
Road conditions: Dirt
Management: Sanpete Ranger District, 540 North Main Street, P.O. Box 692, Ephraim, UT 84627; (435) 283-4151
Reservations: Call (877) 444-6777 or TDD (877) 833-6777; fee
Activities: Fishing, hiking, mountain biking, and picnicking
Restrictions: No OHVs and no livestock
Season: June through October
Finding the campground: From the junction of Main and 400 South on the south end of Ephraim, travel east on 400 South for 0.4 mile, then turn right (south) onto 300 East. Signs for Ephraim Canyon point the way at both junctions. Road 400 South curves east after a short distance and becomes Canyon Road. The paved road turns to dirt and gravel, which is slippery when wet, after 2.2 miles. Continue another 5.2 miles to the campground entrance, which is on your right; travel an additional 0.3 mile to the fee station.

About the campground: Aspens and conifers shade the sites in this campground, which offers fishing at Lake Hill Reservoir. It's stocked with fish on a yearly basis. Hikers will find several trails in the area, and mountain bikers will find pathways for riding.

Most of the sites are fairly small, but a couple of them will hold an RV of about 30 feet. Anything much bigger is not recommended. A group site holds up to seventy-five people; call for more information.

27 Painted Rocks: Yuba State Park

Location: About 25 miles south of Nephi
Facilities: Fire grates, picnic tables, vault toilets, boat ramp, and courtesy docks
Sites: Dispersed
Fee: $
Elevation: 5,000 feet
Road conditions: Gravel
Management: Yuba State Park, P.O. Box 159, Levan, UT 84639-0159; (435) 758-2611
Reservations: None
Activities: Fishing, mountain biking, off-highway driving (in designated areas), boating, sailing, swimming, photography, and picnicking
Season: Year-round

Finding the campground: From Nephi, head south on paved Utah Highway 28 for about 10 miles to Levan; from there continue south another 14 miles or so via UT 28 to a sign pointing the way to Yuba Reservoir. Make a right (west) and drive 0.7 mile via a gravel road to the fee station.

About the campground: Open, dispersed sites along the eastern shore of 22-mile-long Yuba Reservoir (originally called Sevier Bridge Reservoir) make this a popular spot for those with fishing or boating on their minds. The water boasts a whopping seventy degree temperature in summer, making this a great place for activities such as waterskiing, boating, sailboarding, sailing, and swimming. Ancient rock art is also a draw, with the art at Painted Rocks accessible by boat only.

Anglers can enjoy year-round fishing—species include walleye, yellow perch, channel catfish, and northern pike. Other activities include mountain biking (there are many dirt roads to ride), rockhounding, and off-highway vehicle riding in designated areas just outside the park.

28 Oasis: Yuba State Park

Location: About 27 miles southwest of Nephi
Facilities: Fire grates, covered picnic tables, drinking water, showers, sewage disposal dump, flush toilets, and boat ramp
Sites: 27
Fee: $$
Elevation: 5,000 feet
Road conditions: Paved
Management: Yuba State Park, P.O. Box 159, Levan, UT 84639-0159; (435) 758-2611
Reservations: In the Salt Lake area, call (801) 322-3770; elsewhere, (800) 322-3770; fee
Activities: Fishing, mountain biking, off-highway driving (in designated areas), boating, sailing, swimming, photography, and picnicking
Season: Year-round
Finding the campground: Drive Interstate 15 south from Nephi for about 23 miles, getting off at exit 202. Continue south on the signed, paved road to Yuba Lake; you'll reach the entrance station on your left after another 4 miles.

About the campground: A sprinkling of deciduous trees, including cottonwoods, and a grand view across the 22-mile-long lake to Mount Nebo, the highest point in the Wasatch Range, make this a pleasant spot to camp. Located on the western shore of Yuba Reservoir (originally called Sevier Bridge Reservoir), this is a fine place to indulge in water activities such as waterskiing, boating, sailboarding, sailing, and swimming. The water warms to a whopping seventy degrees in summer.

Anglers can enjoy year-round fishing—species include walleye, yellow perch, channel catfish, and northern pike. Other activities include mountain biking (there are many dirt roads to ride), rockhounding, and off-highway vehicle riding in designated areas just outside the park.

29 Chicken Creek

Location: In the Manti–La Sal National Forest, about 6 miles southeast of Levan
Facilities: Fire grates, picnic tables, drinking water, and pit toilets
Sites: 8
Fee: $
Elevation: 6,200 feet
Road conditions: Dirt
Management: Sanpete Ranger District, 540 North Main Street, P.O. Box 692, Ephraim, UT 84627; (435) 283-4151
Reservations: Call (877) 444-6777 or TDD (877) 833-6777; fee
Activities: Fishing and picnicking
Season: May through October
Finding the campground: From the small town of Levan, go east on paved First South Street. There's a sign for the paved street, but not for the campground. After 1.5 miles, you'll reach a fork; go right (southeast) onto Chicken Creek Road (also known as Forest Road 101) for an additional 4.5 miles. This road is gravel, then turns to narrow dirt.

About the campground: Marmots inhabit this campground, which is decorated with junipers, oaks, maples, and conifers. Chicken Creek flows alongside the camp, offering some an opportunity to fish while others just plain sit and relax. A group site holds thirty-plus people and is 0.2 mile up Canyon Road from the main campground; call for additional information.

30 Maple Canyon

Location: In the Manti–La Sal National Forest, approximately 10 miles southwest of Fountain Green
Facilities: Fire grates, picnic tables, and pit toilets
Sites: 13
Fee: $
Elevation: 6,800 feet
Road conditions: Gravel
Management: Sanpete Ranger District, 540 North Main Street, P.O. Box 692, Ephraim, UT 84627; (435) 283-4151
Reservations: Call (877) 444-6777 or TDD (877) 833-6777; fee
Activities: Rock climbing, mountain biking, hiking, bird-watching, photography, and picnicking
Season: May through October
Finding the campground: From Fountain Green (about 14.0 miles southeast of Nephi), head west on 400 South. A sign reading MAPLE CANYON points the way. After 0.5 mile, the paved road curves south and becomes West Side Road. Continue another 5.5 miles and make a right (west) onto Freedom Road. After an additional 0.5 mile, the road curves north and later west; it turns into a gravel one-lane with turnouts. You'll reach the campground in another 3 miles.

About the campground: Located in a narrow canyon on the eastern flank of the San Pitch Mountains—a small range—this campground is shaded by a thick grove of maple trees. Sites are not very long, so vans or tents are best. There's also a group site for up to forty people; call for more information.

The area is a popular spot for rock climbers, with more than 160 climbs ranging from an easy 5.4 to a very difficult 5.13C. It's also a place for engaging in some hikes; be sure to check out the one that leads to an arch. And in spring look for nesting birds along the trail.

31 Ponderosa

Location: In the Uinta National Forest, approximately 9 miles northeast of Nephi
Facilities: Fire grates, picnic tables, drinking water, and vault toilets
Sites: 22
Fee: $$ weekends; $ weekdays
Elevation: 6,200 feet
Road conditions: Paved
Management: Spanish Fork Ranger District, 44 West 400 North, Spanish Fork, UT 84660; (801) 342-5260
Reservations: Call (877) 444-6777 or TDD (877) 833-6777; fee
Activities: Fishing, hiking, and picnicking
Restrictions: ATVs are not allowed
Season: May through October
Finding the campground: From the junction of Utah Highway 132 and Interstate 15 in Nephi, drive east on UT 132 for 4.9 miles. Turn left (north) at the signed Mount Nebo Scenic Loop (Forest Road 048), a paved road; continue 3.4 miles to a fork. Go left (northwest) up the paved road leading to Bear Canyon. After 0.5 mile, you'll see the campground entrance on your left.

About the campground: Salt Creek sings through the campground, providing music to campers' ears and the opportunity to fish for trout. Ponderosa pines provide shade; in fact, the place was named for the pines that were planted here in 1914.

Hikers should note the trailhead for Andrews Ridge, which is another 0.7 mile up the road. An 8-mile trail leads from there to the top of Mount Nebo—at 11,928 feet the highest point in the Wasatch Range.

32 Bear Canyon

Location: In the Uinta National Forest, about 11 miles northeast of Nephi
Facilities: Fire grates, picnic tables, drinking water, and flush toilets
Sites: 9
Fee: $
Elevation: 6,800 feet
Road conditions: Paved
Management: Spanish Fork Ranger District, 44 West 400 North, Spanish Fork, UT 84660; (801) 342-5260

Reservations: Call (877) 444–6777 or TDD (877) 833–6777 for group sites only; fee
Activities: Fishing, hiking, and picnicking
Restrictions: ATVs are not allowed
Season: May through October
Finding the campground: From the junction of Utah Highway 132 and Interstate 15 in Nephi, drive east on UT 132 for 4.9 miles. Turn left (north) at the signed Mount Nebo Scenic Loop (Forest Road 048), a paved road; continue 3.4 miles to a fork. Go left (northwest) up the paved road leading to Bear Canyon. After 2.1 miles, you'll reach the end of the narrow road at the campground.

About the campground: Salt Creek divides this campground in half. On the west side you'll find three group sites, all of which must be reserved. These group sites, which have a capacity of fifty to seventy-five people, vary in cost; call for more information. Across the bridge there are six walk-in sites, which are not reservable. A mix of lofty conifers and deciduous trees shades the sites, especially the walk-ins.

Hikers will find the Bear Canyon Trailhead at the bridge. It's a 3-mile hike from here to Nebo Loop Road 015. If you'd rather be on top of things, it's just 0.9 mile back to the Andrews Ridge Trailhead. From here, an 8-mile trail leads to the top of Mount Nebo—at 11,928 feet the highest point in the Wasatch Range.

33 Gooseberry Reservoir

Location: In the Manti–La Sal National Forest, about 11 miles northeast of Fairview
Facilities: Fire grates, picnic tables, drinking water, and pit toilets
Sites: 10
Fee: $
Elevation: 8,400 feet
Road conditions: Gravel
Management: Ferron Ranger District, 115 West Canyon Road, P.O. Box 310, Ferron, UT 84523; (435) 384–2372
Reservations: Call (877) 444–6777 or TDD (877) 833–6777; fee
Activities: Fishing, off-highway travel, mountain biking, and picnicking
Season: Mid-June through mid-September
Finding the campground: From the junction of U.S. Highway 89 and Utah Highway 31 in Fairview, head northeast on UT 31, a paved road that climbs an 8 percent grade. After 8.4 miles, you'll reach the junction with Utah Highway 264 to Scofield. Turn left (east) onto UT 264, then curve immediately around to the north. You'll reach a large parking area with vault toilets and a sign for Skyline Drive—a 100-mile-long Scenic Byway that follows the crest of the Wasatch Plateau—after 0.2 mile. The road turns to gravel as you continue south for an additional 0.2 mile to a road leading right (northeast) to the signed Gooseberry Campground; reach the campground via Forest Road 224 in another 3.5 miles.

Campers at Gooseberry Campground in Manti-La Sal National Forest.

About the campground: Set in a grove of aspens and conifers, this campground offers some sites with a nice view of Gooseberry Lake. There are several dirt roads to explore, by either ATV or mountain bike. One of the roads leads to the ninety-acre lake where anglers vie for stocked rainbow trout and wild cutthroats. Wildlife-watchers should keep an eye out for abundant animal life, including the usually elusive badger.

34 Flat Canyon

Location: In the Manti–La Sal National Forest, approximately 13 miles northeast of Fairview
Facilities: Fire grates, picnic tables, and pit toilets
Sites: 13
Fee: $
Elevation: 8,800 feet
Road conditions: Paved
Management: Ferron Ranger District, 115 West Canyon Road, P.O. Box 310, Ferron, UT 84523; (435) 384–2372
Reservations: For the group site only, call (877) 444–6777 or TDD (877) 833–6777; fee
Activities: Fishing and picnicking
Season: Mid-June through mid-September
Finding the campground: From the junction of U.S. Highway 89 and Utah Highway 31 in Fairview, head northeast on UT 31, a paved road that climbs

an 8 percent grade. After 8.4 miles, you'll reach the junction with Utah Highway 264 to Scofield. Turn left (east) onto paved UT 264, then curve immediately around to the north. You'll reach a large parking area with vault toilets and a sign for Skyline Drive—a 100-mile-long Scenic Byway that follows the crest of the Wasatch Plateau—after 0.2 mile. Continue driving UT 264 another 4.2 miles to the campground, which is on your right.

About the campground: Shaded by thick pines, this small campground has a group site that overlooks Boulger Reservoir, a fine place for fishing. The site holds up to fifty people. If you drive, it's just over a mile away. Other nearby fishing spots include Electric Lake and Beaver Dam Reservoir, both about 2 miles distant.

Castle Country

Barren, bleak, and *unoccupied* are probably the words most often used to describe what is known as Castle Country, but the place is much more than that to those who spend time exploring its lovely realms. Travel around the region and you'll find a world of towering sandstone walls and monoliths, strange formations—some of which do indeed look like castles—and a whole lot more. In addition, there are quiet oases of cottonwoods and water that attract a variety of animal life, tall forests and open meadows where you can find moose and solitude, and places where ancient drawings and etchings lure visitors from all around. In addition to being what I'd rather call remote and unencumbered, Castle Country embraces part of the Manti–La Sal National Forest, where cool, lush, high-elevation refuges provide places for folks to come and fish, ride their OHVs, hike, ride horseback, photograph some vistas that beg to be captured on film, or just sit and enjoy the shade and scenery.

One of Utah's nine travel regions, Castle Country is located pretty much in the heart of the state, with just a little push to the east. Bordered by four state travel regions—Dinosaurland, Mountainland, Panoramaland, and Canyonlands—it encompasses all of Emery and Carbon Counties for a total of 5,915 square miles. Comprised of five distinct geologic areas—the Wasatch Plateau, the San Rafael Swell, the East Tavaputs Plateau, the San Rafael Desert, and the Mancos Shale Lowlands—its sixteen campgrounds are found in a potpourri of settings. Sites range from the cool realms of the national forest to the water-blessed likes of several state parks, to the strange pillars and knobs of Goblin State Park, and the amazing sandstone pillars and walls of the San Rafael Swell.

Fortunately, there's a campground at the San Rafael Swell. Located along the San Rafael River and close (you can see some of the routes from there) to hundreds of climbs, the place is a marvelous geologic wonder. Though there are moderate routes for climbers, the majority of climbs are for the more experienced. The San Rafael Swell is also a popular place to view prehistoric rock art—the Buckhorn Wash Pictograph Panel is a must-see. It's believed to have been created about 2,000 years ago by members of the Barrier Canyon Culture. Distinctive features of this culture include life-sized anthropomorphic figures that lack arms and legs. Broad shoulders, tapered trunks, and bug eyes are also characteristic. In addition, you'll see rays, crowns, and dots above the figures' heads, with many of the figures accompanied by birds, insects, snakes, and dogs.

At the very southern edge of Castle Country you'll find Goblin Valley State Park, with its unique sandstone formations and numerous claims to fame: The state park has been featured in various films, including *City Slickers II.*

The northwest corner of the region offers the most campgrounds, with the state park system contributing three lake-blessed sites. Visitors to Millsite, Huntington, and Scofield all have the opportunity to fish, engage in various water sports, and so on.

There's no doubt that Castle Country offers a wide variety of activities to enjoy and wonderful places to see on a year-round basis. Though some of the

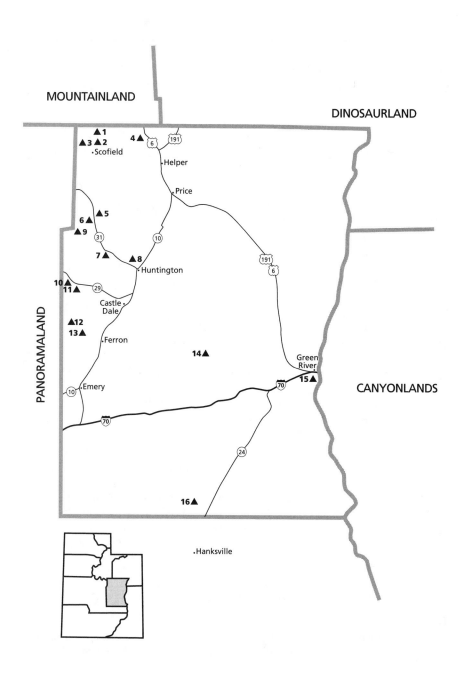

MOUNTAINLAND

DINOSAURLAND

▲1
▲3 ▲2
4▲ 🛢6 191
•Scofield
•Helper
•Price
6▲ ▲5
▲9 31
10
7▲ ▲8
•Huntington
191
6
10▲ 29
11▲
Castle•
Dale
▲12
13▲
•Ferron
14▲
Green
River•
15▲
10 •Emery
70
CANYONLANDS
70
24
16▲
PANORAMALAND
•Hanksville

	Group sites	RV sites	Total sites	Max. RV length	Hookups	Toilets	Showers	Drinking water	Dump station	Pets	Wheelchair	Recreation	Fee($)	Season	Can reserve	Stay limit
1 Madsen Bay		•	36			F		•	•	•		FBHSL	$	May–Oct.	•	14
2 Mountain View		•	34	22		F	•	•	•	•		FBHSL	$$	May–Oct.	•	14
3 Fish Creek			7			V				•		MFH		May–Oct.		14
4 Price Canyon		•	18	25		V		•		•		H	$	June–Oct.		14
5 Old Folks Flat	•	•	8	30		F		•		•		FH	$	June–Sept. 15	•	16
6 Forks of Huntington	•	•	6	20		V		•		•		FH	$	June–Sept. 15		16
7 Bear Creek		•	26	35		FP		•		•		F	$	May 20–Oct.		
8 Huntington State Park	•	•	22			F	•	•	•	•	•	FSHBL	$$		•	14
9 Indian Creek		•	12			P		•		•		F	$	July–Sept.		16
10 Joes Valley		•	49			V		•		•		FBLM	$–$$	May 25–Oct. 25	•	16
11 Joes Valley Boat Ramp		•	12	38		V		•		•	•	FBLM	$	May 25–Oct. 25	•	16
12 Ferron Canyon	•	•	4	20		P				•		F		May–Oct.		16
13 Millsite State Park	•	•	20			F	•	•	•	•	•	FBLSH	$$		•	14
14 San Rafael Bridge		•	12	35		P				•		HCM	$			14
15 Green River State Park	•	•	40	45		F	•	•	•	•	•	BFL	$$		•	14
16 Goblin Valley S.P.	•	•	21	30		F	•	•	•	•		HM	$$		•	14

* Dispersed Camping—no designated sites **Hookups:** W = Water E = Electric S = Sewer **Toilets:** F = Flush V = Vault P = Pit C = Chemical **Recreation:** H = Hiking S = Swimming F = Fishing B = Boating L = Boat Launch O = Off-highway driving R = Horseback Riding C = Rock Climbing M = Mountain Biking **Maximum Trailer/RV length** given in feet. **Stay Limit** given in days. **Fee** given in dollars. If no entry under **Season**, campgound is open all year. If no entry under **Fee**, camping is free.

campgrounds are closed in winter, the areas can still be visited and enjoyed by those with a desire to engage in winter sports.

For more information, contact the Castle Country Travel Region in Carbon County at P.O. Box 1037, Price, UT 84501; (435) 637-3009 or (800) 842-0789; fax (435) 637-7010; cctr@afnetinc.com. Or you can get in touch with the folks in Emery County at Green River City, UT 84525; (435) 564-3600 or (888) 564-3600

1 Madsen Bay: Scofield State Park

Location: About 7 miles north of Scofield
Facilities: Fire grates, picnic tables, flush toilets, sewage disposal station, drinking water, fish cleaning station, boat ramp, and a soda pop machine
Sites: 36
Fee: $
Elevation: 7,600 feet

Road conditions: Paved
Management: Scofield State Park, P.O. Box 166, Price, UT 84501-0166; (435) 448-9449 (summer) or (435) 637-8497 (winter)
Reservations: In the Salt Lake area, call (801) 322-3770; elsewhere, (800) 322-3770; fee
Activities: Fishing, boating, swimming, waterskiing, hiking, photography, and picnicking
Restrictions: OHV use is prohibited
Season: May through October
Finding the campground: From the junction of U.S. Highway 6 and Utah Highway 96, about 17 miles northwest of Helper, head west and then south on UT 96 for 8.9 miles to the campground turnoff, which is on the west side of the road.

About the campground: One of two campgrounds at Scofield State Park, Madson Bay sits in the open on the north shore of Scofield Lake and offers the largest sites. A forested tent-camping area and a wildlife interpretive area are located a short distance away.

Located in the Manti–La Sal Mountains of the Wasatch Plateau, this 2,800-acre lake is an excellent place for boating and is known for its year-round fishing potential. One of Utah's prime fisheries, the cool waters are ideal for rainbow and cutthroat trout as well as crawfish. Below Scofield Dam, a footbridge leads to hiking and fishing areas along Lower Fish Creek.

2 Mountain View: Scofield State Park

Location: About 6 miles north of Scofield
Facilities: Fire grates, picnic tables, flush toilets, showers, sewage disposal station, drinking water, fish cleaning station, boat ramp, and a public telephone
Sites: 34
Fee: $$
Elevation: 7,600 feet
Road conditions: Paved
Management: Scofield State Park, P.O. Box 166, Price, UT 84501-0166; (435) 448-9449 (summer) or (435) 637-8497 (winter)
Reservations: In the Salt Lake area, call (801) 322-3770; elsewhere, (800) 322-3770; fee
Activities: Fishing, boating, swimming, waterskiing, hiking, photography, and picnicking
Restrictions: OHV use is prohibited
Season: May through October
Finding the campground: From the junction of U.S. Highway 6 and Utah Highway 96, about 17 miles northwest of Helper, head west and then south on UT 96 for 10.5 miles to the campground turnoff, which is on the west side of the road.

About the campground: The smaller of the two campgrounds at Scofield State Park, Mountain View's campers rest parking-lot-style next to their neighbors.

The small sites are partially shaded with aspens and conifers, and there's a boat ramp nearby. The plus to this campground is that it offers a shower, whereas the other one, Madsen Bay, does not.

Located in the Manti–La Sal Mountains of the Wasatch Plateau, this 2,800-acre lake is an excellent place for boating and is known for its year-round fishing potential. One of Utah's prime fisheries, the cool waters are ideal for rainbow and cutthroat trout as well as crawfish. Below Scofield Dam, a footbridge leads to hiking and fishing areas along Lower Fish Creek.

3 Fish Creek

Location: In the Manti–La Sal National Forest, about 5 miles northwest of Scofield
Facilities: Fire grates, picnic tables, and a vault toilet
Sites: 7
Fee: None
Elevation: 7,700 feet
Road conditions: Dirt
Management: Price Ranger District, 599 West Price River Drive, Price, UT 84501; (435) 637–2817
Reservations: None
Activities: Fishing, hiking, mountain biking, photography, and picnicking
Season: May through October
Finding the campground: From the small town of Scofield, go north on an unsigned paved road that follows along the east shore of Scofield Lake. You'll travel for 3.5 miles before the road turns to dirt. After another 0.2 mile, you'll reach a fork to the Fish Creek Trailhead; it's on the left (west). Drive this unmaintained road—which can be impassable when it's wet, and impassable to passenger cars at any time of year—for another 1.7 miles until it ends at the primitive campground and the trailhead.

About the campground: Though primitive, this spot makes a nice place for tent campers set on exploring the gentle realms of the Fish Creek drainage. It's also a wonderful place for anglers set on catching trout.

Aspens and conifers decorate the periphery of the campground, which is in a mostly open setting and provides good views of Fish Creek. Look for animal life while you are here. Bears live in the area, so be sure to keep a clean camp; there are also opportunities to observe moose, elk, mule deer, mountain lions, beavers, and a whole lot more.

4 Price Canyon

Location: About 13 miles northwest of Helper
Facilities: Fire grates, picnic tables, drinking water, and vault toilets
Sites: 18
Fee: $
Elevation: 7,800 feet
Road conditions: Paved to the campground, then gravel

Management: Bureau of Land Management, Price Field Office, 125 South 600 West, Price, UT 84501; (435) 636-3600; UT-Price@blm.gov
Reservations: None
Activities: Hiking and picnicking
Season: June through October
Finding the campground: From the junction of U.S. Highways 191 and 6, about 3 miles north of Helper, drive northwest on US 6 for 6.7 miles to the Price Canyon Recreation Area turnoff, which is on the south side of the road. Travel this paved, winding, steep, and narrow road for 3.2 miles to a T junction. You'll find day-use sites to your right and overnight campsites to your left; the road is gravel at this point.

About the campground: Situated among oaks and pines, this is a nice, high-elevation campground with views of nearby mountains and canyons. There's an even better view from a 1-mile-long trail to a nearby butte. The Bristlecone Ridge Trail climbs past oak, mahogany, and both ponderosa and bristlecone pine trees, gaining more than 600 feet in its quest for the summit.

5 Old Folks Flat

Location: In the Manti–La Sal National Forest, about 21 miles northwest of Huntington
Facilities: Fire grates, picnic tables, drinking water, and flush toilets
Sites: 8
Fee: $
Elevation: 7,800 feet
Road conditions: Paved to the campground, then dirt
Management: Ferron Ranger District, 115 West Canyon Road, P.O. Box 310, Ferron, UT 84523; (435) 384-2372
Reservations: Call (877) 444-6777 or TDD (877) 833-6777; fee
Activities: Fishing, hiking, and picnicking
Season: June through mid-September
Finding the campground: From the junction of Utah Highways 10 and 31 in Huntington, travel northwest on paved UT 31 for 20.5 miles to the campground, which is on your right.

About the campground: Set among aspen and spruce, this small campground caters to those wanting group sites, though three single sites are available. A nature trail leads into the canyon, and the fishing in Huntington Creek is good for rainbow, cutthroat, and brown trout.

6 Forks of Huntington

Location: In the Manti–La Sal National Forest, approximately 18 miles northwest of Huntington
Facilities: Fire grates, picnic tables, drinking water, and vault toilets
Sites: 6
Fee: $

Elevation: 7,600 feet
Road conditions: Paved to the campground, then dirt
Management: Ferron Ranger District, 115 West Canyon Road, P.O. Box 310, Ferron, UT 84523; (435) 384–2372
Reservations: The group site must be reserved at (877) 444–6777 or TDD (877) 833–6777; fee
Activities: Fishing, hiking, and picnicking
Season: June through mid-September
Finding the campground: From the junction of Utah Highways 10 and 31 in Huntington, travel northwest on paved UT 31 for 17.7 miles to the campground, which is on your left.

About the campground: Sites are located along the rushing waters of Left Fork Huntington Creek. Fir and spruce serve to shade the small sites, accessible to only the smallest of RVs. Anglers can vie for trout, while hikers check out the Left Fork of Huntington Creek National Recreation Trail. The trail is 4.5 miles long and gains about 650 feet en route to the confluence of Scad Valley Creek. See *Hiking Utah* by Dave Hall for more information.

A group site accommodates up to forty people; call for more information.

7 Bear Creek

Location: About 9 miles northwest of Huntington
Facilities: Fire grates, picnic tables, drinking water, flush and pit toilets, and a volleyball court
Sites: 26
Fee: $
Elevation: 6,900 feet
Road conditions: Paved to the campground, then dirt
Management: Emery County Recreation Department, P.O. Box 531, Castle Dale, UT 84513; (435) 381–2108
Reservations: None
Activities: Fishing, volleyball, and picnicking
Restrictions: No ATVs or motorcycles
Season: May 20 through October
Finding the campground: From the junction of Utah Highways 10 and 31 in Huntington, travel northwest on paved UT 31 for 8.7 miles to the campground, which is on your left.

About the campground: Cottonwoods and other deciduous trees shade the campsites at this county park. There's a nice picnic area with green grass, and a volleyball court provides pleasure, too. Bear Creek flows only 30 feet from the campground and offers the chance to hook rainbow or brook trout.

8 Huntington State Park

Location: About 2 miles north of Huntington
Facilities: Fire grates, picnic tables, flush toilets, showers, drinking water,

sewage disposal station, public telephone, soda pop machines, boat ramp and boat docks
Sites: 22
Fee: $$
Elevation: 5,800 feet
Road conditions: Paved
Management: Huntington State Park, P.O. Box 1343, Huntington, UT 84528-1343; (435) 687-2491
Reservations: In the Salt Lake area, call (801) 322-3770; elsewhere, (800) 322-3770; fee
Activities: Fishing, swimming, boating, birding, hiking, and picnicking
Season: Year-round
Finding the campground: From the junction of Utah Highways 10 and 31 in Huntington, travel north on UT 10 for 1.7 miles to its junction with Road 302 on the left (west). Drive left on paved Road 302 for 0.3 mile to the entrance station on your left

About the campground: Green grass and shade trees blanket the north shore of Huntington Reservoir, one of Utah's finest warm-water fisheries. Anglers can hook largemouth bass and bluegills. Crawdad fishing is especially popular with children.

Migrating birds will delight birders, while the boat ramp provides access for all types of watercraft. The warm water makes the reservoir a popular place for waterskiing and swimming. Service roads around the reservoir offer 2 miles of hiking and jogging trails. OHVs are not allowed to unload in the park; there are areas just outside the park, however, where they are permitted.

9 Indian Creek

Location: In the Manti–La Sal National Forest, about 25 miles northwest of Castle Dale
Facilities: Fire grates, picnic tables, drinking water, and pit toilets
Sites: 12
Fee: $
Elevation: 8,700 feet
Road conditions: Dirt
Management: Ferron Ranger District, 115 West Canyon Road, P.O. Box 310, Ferron, UT 84523; (435) 384-2372
Reservations: For group sites only, call (877) 444-6777 or TDD (877) 833-6777; fee
Activities: Fishing and picnicking
Season: July through September
Finding the campground: From the junction of Utah Highways 10 and 29, about 2 miles north of Castle Dale, head northwest on paved UT 29 for 11.7 miles to a junction. Now turn right (north) onto Cottonwood Canyon Road (also known as Forest Road 040). The paved road turns to gravel in a few miles and eventually downgrades to a one-lane dirt road with turnouts. A sign claims the campground is 10 miles away; it's actually 13 miles from UT 29 to the site.

About the campground: Blessed with aspens, this high-elevation site caters to groups, though you'll find seven single sites, too. Five group areas can handle from thirty to seventy-five people each. Reservations are mandatory for the group sites, but are not taken for single sites. Cost for group sites vary; call for more information.

10 Joes Valley

Location: In the Manti–La Sal National Forest, approximately 22 miles northwest of Castle Dale

Facilities: Fire grates, picnic tables, drinking water, and vault toilets, with a boat ramp, fish cleaning station, and marina nearby. The marina offers boat rentals, a cafe, and fishing tackle

Sites: 49

Fee: $ for single sites; $$ for double sites

Elevation: 7,200 feet

Road conditions: Paved

Management: Ferron Ranger District, 115 West Canyon Road, P.O. Box 310, Ferron, UT 84523; (435) 384–2372

Reservations: Call (877) 444–6777 or TDD (877) 833–6777; fee

Activities: Fishing, waterskiing, boating, mountain biking, and picnicking

Season: May 25 through October 25

Finding the campground: From the junction of Utah Highways 10 and 57, about 2 miles south of Castle Dale, drive northwest on paved UT 57 for 6.7 miles to its junction with Utah Highway 29. Now turn left (west) onto UT 29 for an additional 14.8 miles to the end of UT 29. Turn left onto Forest Road 170 and drive 0.1 mile to the campground entrance, which is on your left.

About the campground: Situated on a bluff overlooking Joes Valley Reservoir and nearly surrounded by mountains, this campground is decorated with juniper, pinyon pine, and ponderosa pine trees. The lake offers anglers the chance to hook rainbow and cutthroat trout, and gives water enthusiasts the opportunity to enjoy a multitude of water sports.

11 Joes Valley Boat Ramp

Location: In the Manti–La Sal National Forest, about 22 miles northwest of Castle Dale

Facilities: Fire grates, picnic tables, drinking water, vault toilets, plus a boat ramp and fish cleaning station. The local marina offers boat rentals, a cafe, and fishing tackle

Sites: 12

Fee: $

Elevation: 7,100 feet

Road conditions: Paved

Management: Ferron Ranger District, 115 West Canyon Road, P.O. Box 310, Ferron, UT 84523; (435) 384–2372

Reservations: Call (877) 444–6777 or TDD (877) 833–6777; fee
Activities: Fishing, waterskiing, boating, mountain biking, and picnicking
Season: May 25 through October 25
Finding the campground: From the junction of Utah Highways 10 and 57, about 2 miles south of Castle Dale, drive northwest on paved UT 57 for 6.7 miles to its junction with Utah Highway 29. Now turn left (west) onto UT 29 for an additional 14.8 miles to the end of UT 29. Turn left onto Forest Road 170 and drive 0.7 mile past the marina to the end of the road and parking area.

About the campground: If you opt to use this campground, you'll be close to the west side of the lake, but you'll sit parking-lot-style next to your neighbors.

The lake offers anglers the chance to hook rainbow and cutthroat trout. It also gives water enthusiasts the opportunity to enjoy a multitude of water sports.

12 Ferron Canyon

Location: In the Manti–La Sal National Forest, approximately 9 miles northwest of Ferron
Facilities: Fire grates, picnic tables, and pit toilets
Sites: 4
Fee: None
Elevation: 6,500 feet
Road conditions: Paved to the campground, then dirt
Management: Ferron Ranger District, 115 West Canyon Road, P.O. Box 310, Ferron, UT 84523; (435) 384–2372
Reservations: None
Activities: Fishing and picnicking
Season: May through October
Finding the campground: From the junction of Utah Highway 10 and Canyon Road in downtown Ferron, head west on paved Canyon Road. Signs for Millstate State Park and Ferron Reservoir point the way. Travel 9.4 miles to the campground, which is on your right. (The road turns to gravel after traveling 4.3 miles.)

About the campground: Located along Ferron Creek, where trout fishing is popular, this tiny campground might be full when you find it. Three single sites and a small group site are partially shaded by conifers.

13 Millsite State Park

Location: About 4 miles west of Ferron
Facilities: Fire grates, picnic tables, flush toilets, showers, drinking water, sewage disposal station, boat ramp and boat docks
Sites: 20
Fee: $$
Elevation: 6,100 feet

Jet skiers at Millsite Reservoir, Millsite State Park.

Road conditions: Paved
Management: Millsite State Park, P.O. Box 1343, Huntington, UT 84528-1343; (435) 687–2491
Reservations: In the Salt Lake area, call (801) 322–3770; elsewhere, (800) 322–3770; fee
Activities: Fishing, swimming, boating, hiking, and picnicking. Surrounding areas offer unlimited mountain biking opportunities as well as the chance to do some golfing
Season: Year-round
Finding the campground: From the junction of Utah Highway 10 and Canyon Road in downtown Ferron, head west on paved Canyon Road. Signs for the state park and Ferron Reservoir point the way. Travel 4.3 miles to the campground entrance, which is on your right.

About the campground: Located on the southwest shore of Millsite Reservoir, a 435-acre jewel with majestic cliffs towering 2,000 feet above, campsites are shaded by a smattering of poplar trees and landscaped lawns. However, a large natural section contains native plants with a nature trail interpreting vegetation.

Water activities are popular, with visitors indulging in swimming, sailing, Jet Skiing, and waterskiing. Anglers fish from a boat or the shoreline, netting cutthroat and rainbow trout. OHVs are not allowed in the park, but there are many areas nearby in which to travel off road. Golfers will find Ferron City's challenging nine-hole golf course adjacent to the park. Wildlife is abundant, especially in winter, when you enjoy ice fishing while gaining the chance to see deer, elk, and moose.

14 San Rafael Bridge

Location: In the San Rafael Swell, about 49 miles northwest of Green River
Facilities: Fire grates, picnic tables, and pit toilets
Sites: 12
Fee: $
Elevation: 5,100 feet
Road conditions: Gravel
Management: Bureau of Land Management, Price Field Office, 125 South 600 West, Price, UT 84501; (435) 636-3600; UT-Price@blm.gov
Reservations: None
Activities: Hiking, rock climbing, mountain biking, photography, and picnicking
Season: Year-round
Finding the campground: From Green River, drive Interstate 70 west for approximately 29 miles, getting off at ranch exit 129. A sign points the way to Buckhorn Draw, the Buckhorn Wash Pictograph Panel, and the Wedge Overlook. Note that the gravel road immediately curves around to the east and parallels the interstate for a few miles before heading north; it may be impassable during wet weather. After 18.9 miles, you'll reach the campground and a bridge over the San Rafael River.

About the campground: Located on the south side of the river, this is a nice spot with tent pads and plenty of room, though you'll want to beware of biting flies in early summer.

The San Rafael Swell is an excellent place for hiking (with map and compass in hand), mountain biking, or rock climbing. There are many climbs here, ranging from moderate to very difficult, and from traditional climbs to sport routes.

A must-see is the Buckhorn Wash Pictograph Panel, which is about 5 miles across the bridge and up Buckhorn Wash. The pictographs, fine art by the Barrier Canyon Culture, are believed to have been made 2,000 or more years ago. Distinctive features of this culture include life-sized anthropomorphic figures lacking arms or legs. These figures have broad shoulders, tapered trunks, and bug eyes. There are dots, rays, and crowns above their heads, and are accompanied by birds, insects, snakes, and dogs.

15 Green River State Park

Location: About 0.5 mile south of Green River
Facilities: Fire grates, picnic tables, flush toilets, showers, public telephone, sewage disposal station, boat launch, and drinking water
Sites: 40
Fee: $$

Elevation: 4,100 feet
Road conditions: Paved
Management: Green River State Park, P.O. Box 637, Green River, UT 84525-0637; (435) 564-3633. Golf clubhouse (435) 564-8882
Reservations: In the Salt Lake area, call (801) 322-3770; elsewhere, (800) 322-3770; fee
Activities: Fishing, rafting, wildlife watching, golfing, and picnicking
Season: Year-round
Finding the campground: From the junction of Main Street and Green River Boulevard in Green River, head south on paved Green River Boulevard for 0.4 mile; make a left at the signed entrance.

About the campground: Shaded by stately cottonwoods and lush Russian olive trees, this campground is a haven for those interested in watching wildlife (look for owls, egrets, beavers, and much more), rafting the Green River, playing a little golf, or using the site as a base camp to explore other nearby areas. The campground is a favorite embarkation point for river trips through Labyrinth and Stillwater Canyons. In addition, a nine-hole golf course is challenging and fun for all levels of golfers.

16 Goblin Valley State Park

Location: About 31 miles north of Hanksville
Facilities: Fire grates, picnic tables, flush toilets, showers, sewage disposal station, and drinking water
Sites: 21
Fee: $$
Elevation: 5,200 feet
Road conditions: Maintained gravel
Management: Goblin Valley State Park, P.O. Box 637, Green River, UT 84525-0637; (435) 564-3633
Reservations: In the Salt Lake area, call (801) 322-3770; elsewhere, (800) 322-3770; fee
Activities: Hiking, mountain biking, photography, and picnicking
Season: Year-round
Finding the campground: From the junction of Utah Highways 24 and 95 in Hanksville, drive north on UT 24 for 19.3 miles. Now turn left (west) where a sign points the way to Goblin Valley. This paved road is sometimes called Goblin Valley Road and is also known as Temple Mountain Road. Continue on it for 5.2 miles, then make another left (south) at another sign for Goblin Valley. Proceed on the maintained gravel road for 6.4 miles to the campground entrance station.

About the campground: Tenters and RVers line up parking-lot-style next to each other in this campground, with some of the park's unique rock sculptures complementing the scene. Goblin Valley is a fantasyland of eroded sandstone formations, some of which look like mushrooms, others suggesting mischievous folklore goblins. While mountain biking is permitted only on the roadways and not on park trails, there are plenty of nearby roads to explore. In addition, there are two marked trails here, as well as self-discovery hiking throughout the Valley of Goblins.

If you want to explore a wonderful slot canyon, drive 8.8 miles to the Wild Horse Canyon Trailhead; a hike up Wild Horse Canyon and down Bell Canyon makes a great 8-mile loop.

Color Country

Color Country is, well, full of color! It's a vast and varied place, where rainbow hues tend to be commonplace, and campers come to share in the glory.

Located in southwestern Utah, Color Country snuggles up to Arizona and Nevada to the south and west, while the state travel regions known as Panoramaland and Canyonlands sit to the north and east. One of the state's nine travel regions, Color Country encompasses a mix of five distinct counties—Beaver, Iron, Washington, Garfield, and Kane—for a total of 17,370 square miles. The largest of the state's travel regions, the place is comprised of a wonderful world of national parks, national monuments, national recreation areas, state parks, national forests, and other public lands. Fortunately, sixty-one public campgrounds provide a place to camp while exploring its realms.

The region stretches across two distinct geologic areas: the Great Basin and Colorado Plateau. Here you'll find tall mountains, shimmering lakes, sandstone cliffs, lofty plateaus, and deep, often narrow canyons. With this sort of geology, travelers can expect to wind up and down many a roadway. Sure, there are lots of straight and fairly level roads, but you'll find just as many—or perhaps even more—with 15-mile-per-hour turns and signs prompting drivers to use low gears instead of their brakes. No doubt, there may even come a time when you are poking up a 14 percent grade or two.

Zion National Park is probably the most visited place in this area, and while it's definitely worth a visit, it isn't the only place worthy of your time. Perhaps it's just the place everyone thinks they should see when they pass through southwest Utah. In addition to Zion, however, is one of Utah's finest national parks, Bryce Canyon. Here you'll find a fairyland of fun, a potpourri offering a remarkable display of fascinating orange, red, and pink hoodoos, and a whole lot more.

In addition to the national parks, campers have access (though in summer only) to the likes of Cedar Breaks National Monument: year-round (though it's often cold in winter) you can enjoy the great expanse of Utah's newest national monument, Grand Staircase–Escalante. Visitors to this big (1.7 million acres), awesome place can see time in the making, as they marvel at "stairsteps" leading from one geologic formation to the next.

Utah offers a number of wonderful state parks, many of them with campgrounds to make exploring just that much easier. In Snow Canyon, a place usually devoid of snow, mountain bikers bike, climbers climb, and hikers hike to their hearts' content, while at Quail Creek boaters fish and enjoy a variety of water sports. Utah's state parks offer something for just about everyone.

The southeast corner of Color Country is the setting of the Glen Canyon National Recreation Area, home to Lake Powell and the world's largest natural bridge. Spanning 275 feet across and standing 290 feet high, Rainbow Bridge is accessed by a strenuous backpack trip or an easy boat ride.

The national forests offer plenty to see and do as well. Here, you'll find camping throughout the Dixie National Forest: four distinct segments of forest offering a multitude of campgrounds and opportunities to enjoy the outdoors.

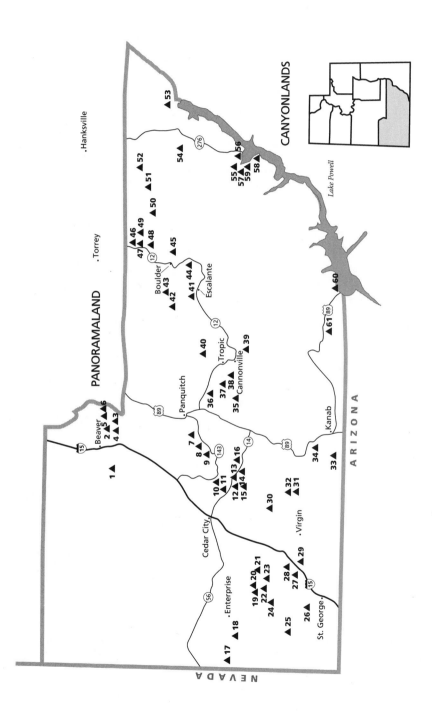

#	Campground	Group sites	RV sites	Total sites	Max. RV length	Hookups	Toilets	Showers	Drinking water	Dump station	Pets	Wheelchair	Recreation	Fee($)	Season	Can reserve	Stay limit
1	Minersville State Park	•	•	29	40	WE	F	•	•	•	•	•	SFBL	$$	Apr.–Oct.	•	14
2	Little Cottonwood		•	14	40		F		•		•	•	F	$$	Memorial Day–Sept.		14
3	Kents Lake	•	•	18	60		VF	•		•			SBF	$$	June 10–Sept. 30		14
4	Anderson Meadow		•	10	24		V	•		•			SBFH	$	June 10–Sept. 30		14
5	Little Reservoir		•	7	40		V	•		•	•		FH	$	Memorial Day–Sept.		14
6	Mahogany Cove		•	7	24		V	•		•			HM	$	Memorial Day–Sept.		14
7	White Bridge		•	29	24		FV	•	•	•			MFH	$$–$$$	mid-June–mid-Sept.	•	14
8	Panguitch Lake North	•	•	51	35		F	•	•	•		•	BLMSFH	$$–$$$	mid-June–mid-Sept.	•	14
9	Panguitch Lake South			18			F	•		•			BLMSFH	$	mid-June–mid-Sept.		14
10	Point Supreme		•	30	30		F	•		•	•		H	$$	mid-June–mid-Sept.		14
11	Cedar Canyon	•	•	19	24		V	•		•	•	•	HM	$–$$	mid-June–mid-Sept.	•	14
12	Deer Haven Organizational Camp	•		18			F	•		•	•	•	HM	$$$$	mid-June–mid-Sept.	•	14
13	Spruces		•	26	24		F	•		•	•	•	FBSHM	$$–$$$	mid-June–mid-Sept.		14
14	Navajo Lake		•	27	24		F	•	•	•	•	•	FBLSHM	$$–$$$	mid-June–mid-Sept.		14
15	Te-Ah		•	42	24		F	•	•	•			FBS	$$	mid-June–mid-Sept.		14
16	Duck Creek	•	•	95	35		VF	•	•	•		•	FHM	$$–$$$	mid-June–mid-Sept.	•	14
17	Pine Park			*			V			•			HO				14
18	Honeycomb Rocks		•	22	35		V	•		•			FBLMS	$	Memorial–Labor Day		14
19	Equestrian		•	18			FV	•	•	•			FBHR	$–$$	Memorial–Labor Day	•	14
20	Upper Pines	•		1	35		V	•	•	•			FBH	$$$$	Memorial–Labor Day	•	14
21	Pines	•	•	13	35		VF	•	•	•	•	•	FBH	$$–$$$$	Memorial–Labor Day		14
22	Blue Springs		•	20	20		V	•	•	•			FBH	$$–$$$$	Memorial–Labor Day	•	14

* Dispersed Camping—no designated sites **Hookups:** W = Water E = Electric S = Sewer **Toilets:** F = Flush V = Vault P = Pit C = Chemical **Recreation:** H = Hiking S = Swimming F = Fishing B = Boating L = Boat Launch O = Off-highway driving R = Horseback Riding C = Rock Climbing M = Mountain Biking **Maximum Trailer/RV length** given in feet. **Stay Limit** given in days. **Fee** given in dollars. If no entry under **Season,** campgound is open all year. If no entry under **Fee,** camping is free.

#	Campground	Group sites	RV sites	Total sites	Max. RV length	Hookups	Toilets	Showers	Drinking water	Dump station	Pets	Wheelchair	Recreation	Fee($)	Season	Can reserve	Stay limit
23	Juniper Park		•	23	25		V		•	•	•		HFB	$$–$$$$	Memorial–Labor Day		14
24	Baker Dam	•	•	19	45		V				•	•	FH	$	Mar. 15–Dec. 15		14
25	Gunlock State Park	•		*			V						FBLMS				14
26	Snow Canyon S.P.	•	•	34	40	WE	F	•	•	•	•	•	HRCM	$$		•	5
27	Red Cliffs Rec. Site		•	10	25		V	•		•	•		HM	$			14
28	Oak Grove			8			P	•		•			HR	$	Memorial–Labor Day		14
29	Quail Creek State Park	•	•	23	40		F	•		•	•		FSBL	$		•	14
30	Lava Point		•	6	16		V			•			H		June–Oct.		14
31	South		•	128			F	•	•	•	•		HC	$$			14
32	Watchman	•	•	153		E	F	•	•	•	•		HC	$$	Apr.–Oct.	•	14
33	Coral Pink Sand Dunes State Park	•	•	22	45		F	•	•	•	•		HO	$$		•	14
34	Ponderosa Grove	•	•	9	24		V	•		•			O	$			14
35	Kings Creek	•	•	38	45		VF	•	•	•			SBMH FOL	$	May 20–Labor Day	•	14
36	Red Canyon	•	•	37	40		F	•	•	•			MHR	$	May 20–Oct. 1		14
37	Sunset	•	•	110	30		F	•		•			HR	$$	May 15–Oct. 10		14
38	North		•	107	30		F	•		•			HR	$$			14
39	Kodachrome Basin S.P.	•	•	27	30		F	•	•	•	•	•	HRM	$$		•	14
40	Pine Lake	•	•	33	45		V	•		•	•		FHMO	$	May 20–Sept. 15		14
41	Escalante State Park	•	•	22	30		F	•	•	•	•	•	BLSHF	$$		•	14
42	Posey Lake	•	•	23	24		V	•		•			BLHF	$	May 20–Sept. 15	•	14
43	Blue Spruce			8	18		V	•		•			F	$	May 20–Sept. 15		14
44	Calf Creek	•	•	13	25		FV	•		•			HF	$			14
45	Deer Creek			7			V			•			HF	$			14
46	Upper Pleasant Creek		•	12	28		V	•		•			MHF	$	May 20–Sept. 15		14
47	Lower Pleasant Creek		•	5	20		V	•		•			MHF	$$	May 20–Sept. 15		14
48	Oak Creek		•	6	20		V	•		•			FHM	$–$$	May 20–Sept. 20		14

* Dispersed Camping—no designated sites **Hookups:** W = Water E = Electric S = Sewer **Toilets:** F = Flush V = Vault P = Pit C = Chemical **Recreation:** H = Hiking S = Swimming F = Fishing B = Boating L = Boat Launch O = Off-highway driving R = Horseback Riding C = Rock Climbing M = Mountain Biking **Maximum Trailer/RV length** given in feet. **Stay Limit** given in days. **Fee** given in dollars. If no entry under **Season,** campground is open all year. If no entry under **Fee,** camping is free.

	Group sites	RV sites	Total sites	Max. RV length	Hookups	Toilets	Showers	Drinking water	Dump station	Pets	Wheelchair	Recreation	Fee($)	Season	Can reserve	Stay limit
49 Lower Bowns			*			P						FM		May 20–Sept. 20		14
50 Cedar Mesa			5			V				•		H				14
51 McMillan Springs			10			V				•		M	$	May–Nov.		14
52 Lonesome Beaver	•		5			V				•		HM	$	May–Oct.		14
53 Dirty Devil River		•	*			C				•		FBS	$			14
54 Starr Springs		•	12	20		V				•		H	$	Apr.–Oct.		14
55 Bullfrog North		•	*			VC				•		SBF	$			14
56 Bullfrog South		•	*			VC				•		SBF	$			14
57 Stanton Creek		•	*			CV				•		SBFL	$			14
58 Bullfrog		•	85	35		F	•	•	•	•		SBFL	$$			14
59 Bullfrog RV		•	24		WES	F	•	•	•	•	•	SBFL	$$$–$$$$			14
60 Lone Rock		•	*			V				•		FBS	$			14
61 White House			5			V				•		H	$			14

* Dispersed Camping—no designated sites **Hookups:** W = Water E = Electric S = Sewer **Toilets:** F = Flush V = Vault P = Pit C = Chemical **Recreation:** H = Hiking S = Swimming F = Fishing B = Boating L = Boat Launch O = Off-highway driving R = Horseback Riding C = Rock Climbing M = Mountain Biking **Maximum Trailer/RV length** given in feet. **Stay Limit** given in days. **Fee** given in dollars. If no entry under **Season**, campgound is open all year. If no entry under **Fee**, camping is free.

In addition, you'll enjoy a small portion of the Fishlake National Forest in the northwest corner of the region.

Exploring is fun year-round in Color Country, though you will find the mountain campgrounds closed in winter. Of course, during winter you can always camp at one of the low-elevation campgrounds and explore high. For more information on things to see and do in Color Country, contact the travel council at P.O. Box 1550, St. George, UT 84771; (435) 628-4171 or (800) 233-8824; fax (435) 673-3540. Or get in touch with the travel council in Kanab at P.O. Box 728, Kanab, UT 84741; (800) 733-5263; fax (435) 644-5923; kanetrav@kaneutah.com.

1 Minersville State Park

Location: About 11 miles southwest of Beaver
Facilities: Fire grates, picnic tables, flush toilets, showers, electric and water hookups, sewage disposal station, fish cleaning station, public telephone, drinking water, and boat launch. There's also a large overflow area for primitive camping.
Sites: 29
Fee: $$

Elevation: 5,513 feet
Road conditions: Paved
Management: Minersville State Park, P.O. Box 1531, Beaver, UT 84713-1531; (435) 438-5472
Reservations: In the Salt Lake area, call (801) 322-3770; elsewhere, (800) 322-3770; fee
Activities: Swimming, boating, water sports, fishing, bird-watching, photography, and picnicking
Season: April through October
Finding the campground: From Beaver, travel west and then southwest on Utah Highway 21 for 11.2 miles

About the campground: Located between the Tushar and Mineral Mountains and surrounded by sagebrush and wild grass, with cottonwoods and willows growing near the water, Minersville Reservoir encompasses 1,130 acres. It's a wonderful place to swim, water-ski, kayak, and canoe. The reservoir is also one of Utah's prime fisheries, with the highlights being rainbow and cutthroat trout, as well as smallmouth bass.

The campground is a nice spot from which to enjoy all of the above activities. It also makes a good base from which you can make day trips into the nearby mountains. If you opt for a trailer space, you'll sit parking-lot-style next to your neighbor. The sites are nice, but too close together for some folks; tent spaces along the lakeshore offer a lot more room.

2 Little Cottonwood

Location: In the Fishlake National Forest, about 7 miles east of Beaver
Facilities: Fire grates, picnic tables, flush toilets, drinking water, paved path to the river for wheelchair access
Sites: 14
Fee: $$
Elevation: 6,500 feet
Road conditions: Paved
Management: Beaver Ranger District, 575 South Main Street, Beaver, UT 84713; (435) 438-2436
Reservations: None
Activities: Fishing and picnicking
Season: Memorial Day through September
Finding the campground: From Beaver, travel east on Utah Highway 153 (200 North Street) through Beaver Canyon and on to the Little Cottonwood Campground, which is on your right, just off the highway. You'll reach it after driving 6.8 miles.

About the campground: Situated on the banks of Beaver Creek, with pines and cottonwoods all around, the campground is a pleasant place to stay come summer. Fishing is popular here; a paved path makes it possible for the wheelchairbound to enjoy angling as well.

3 Kents Lake

Location: In the Fishlake National Forest, about 15 miles southeast of Beaver
Facilities: Fire grates, picnic tables, vault and flush toilets, and drinking water
Sites: 18
Fee: $$
Elevation: 8,800 feet
Road conditions: Maintained gravel
Management: Beaver Ranger District, 575 South Main Street, Beaver, UT 84713; (435) 438–2436
Reservations: None
Activities: Fishing, swimming, boating, and picnicking
Season: June 10 through September
Finding the campground: From Beaver, travel east on Utah Highway 153 (200 North Street) for 10.2 miles to Forest Road 137. Turn right (southeast) onto the gravel road and drive about 5 miles to the campground.

About the campground: Situated in a lush forest of aspen and fir and set amid spectacular mountain scenery, this campground promises good trout fishing at Kents Lake. A cool refuge come summer, it's a wonderful place to just sit and relax.

4 Anderson Meadow

Location: In the Fishlake National Forest, about 15 miles southeast of Beaver
Facilities: Fire grates, picnic tables, vault toilets, and drinking water
Sites: 10
Fee: $
Elevation: 9,400 feet
Road conditions: Maintained gravel
Management: Beaver Ranger District, 575 South Main Street, Beaver, UT 84713; (435) 438–2436
Reservations: None
Activities: Fishing, swimming, boating, hiking, and picnicking
Season: June 10 through September
Finding the campground: From Beaver, travel east on Utah Highway 153 (200 North Street) for 10.2 miles to Forest Road 137. Turn right (southeast) onto the gravel road and drive another 8 miles or so to the campground.

About the campground: Nestled in a mix of Engelmann spruce, aspen, and fir, the campground overlooks Anderson Meadow Reservoir. A potpourri of beautiful scenery, the reservoir offers trout fishing. Swimming is also a must-do if you can stand the frigid waters. If you'd rather stay on dry land, check out one of the nearby popular trails.

5 Little Reservoir

Location: In the Fishlake National Forest, about 11 miles east of Beaver
Facilities: Fire grates, picnic tables, vault toilets, and drinking water
Sites: 7
Fee: $
Elevation: 7,300 feet
Road conditions: Maintained gravel
Management: Beaver Ranger District, 575 South Main Street, Beaver, UT 84713; (435) 438-2436
Reservations: None
Activities: Fishing, hiking, bird-watching, and picnicking
Season: Memorial Day through September
Finding the campground: From Beaver, travel east on Utah Highway 153 (200 North Street) for 10.2 miles to Forest Road 137. Turn right (south) and drive the maintained gravel road less than 1 mile to the campground.

About the campground: Set amid spectacular mountain scenery, the campground is tucked away in a ponderosa pine forest mixed with pinyon, juniper, and scrub oak. About half of the sites are shaded. A small, four-acre lake and good fishing allow anglers to while away the hours or days. Hiking and bird-watching are also popular.

6 Mahogany Cove

Location: In the Fishlake National Forest, about 12 miles east of Beaver
Facilities: Fire grates, picnic tables, vault toilets, and drinking water
Sites: 7
Fee: $
Elevation: 7,500 feet
Road conditions: Paved
Management: Beaver Ranger District, 575 South Main Street, Beaver, UT 84713; (435) 438-2436
Reservations: None
Activities: Hiking, mountain biking, and picnicking
Season: Memorial Day through September
Finding the campground: From Beaver, travel east on Utah Highway 153 (200 North Street) through Beaver Canyon and on up to the Mahogany Cove Campground, which is right off the highway. You'll reach it after driving 11.4 miles.

About the campground: Set on a high bench overlooking Beaver Canyon, the campground offers plenty of its namesake—mountain mahogany. There's also ponderosa pine, juniper, Gambel oak, and cottonwood in the area. The views from this spot are nice. In fact, the campground's only downfall is its close proximity to the road. You won't find any trailheads leading from the campground, but you'll have access to some trails nearby. Explore to your heart's content. Mountain bikers should check out Gregg Bromka's *Mountain Biking Utah*, a Falcon guide, for a nearby ride.

7 White Bridge

Location: In the Dixie National Forest, about 12 miles southwest of Panguitch
Facilities: Fire grates, picnic tables, drinking water, vault and flush toilets, and sewage dump station
Sites: 29
Fee: $$ for single sites; $$$ for double sites
Elevation: 7,900 feet
Road conditions: Paved
Management: Cedar City Ranger District, 1789 North Wedgewood Lane, Cedar City, UT 84720; (435) 865-3200
Reservations: Call (877) 444-6777 or TDD (877) 833-6777; fee
Activities: Fishing, hiking, mountain biking, and picnicking
Season: Mid-June through mid-September
Finding the campground: From the junction of Utah Highway 143 and U.S. Highway 89 in Panguitch, travel southwest on UT 143 for 12.5 miles to the campground.

About the campground: This pleasant campground is just across a white bridge that spans Panguitch Creek. Campers can fish and wade in the creek. Junipers and cottonwoods provide campground shade. The forest service boasts of hiking and mountain biking opportunities adjacent to the campground. If you're itching to swim or boat, you can always travel to Panguitch Lake, about 5 miles southwest of the campground.

8 Panguitch Lake North

Location: In the Dixie National Forest, about 19 miles southwest of Panguitch
Facilities: Fire grates, picnic tables, boat launch, drinking water, Sunday church services, amphitheater, flush toilets, and a sewage dump station
Sites: 51
Fee: $$ for single sites; $$$ for double sites
Elevation: 8,400 feet
Road conditions: Paved
Management: Cedar City Ranger District, 1789 North Wedgewood Lane, Cedar City, UT 84720; (435) 865-3200
Reservations: Call (877) 444-6777 or TDD (877) 833-6777; fee
Activities: Fishing, boating, swimming, mountain biking, hiking, and picnicking
Season: Mid-June through mid-September
Finding the campground: From the junction of Utah Highway 143 and U.S. Highway 89 in Panguitch, travel southwest on UT 143 for 18.7 miles to the campground.

About the campground: Set among ponderosa pines, some of the sites at this spacious campground have a view of Panguitch Lake. The campground is on the southwest end of the 1,250-acre reservoir, which is especially popular for fishing. Rainbow trout are particularly outstanding, though German brown trout can also be caught in the lake and downstream in Panguitch Creek. Access to the lake is via UT 143. There are also excellent opportunities for hiking and mountain biking, according to the forest service.

9 Panguitch Lake South

Location: In the Dixie National Forest, about 19 miles southwest of Panguitch
Facilities: Fire grates, picnic tables, boat launch, drinking water, and flush toilets
Sites: 18
Fee: $
Elevation: 8,400 feet
Road conditions: Paved to the campground entrance, then dirt
Management: Cedar City Ranger District, 1789 North Wedgewood Lane, Cedar City, UT 84720; (435) 865–3200
Reservations: None
Activities: Picnicking, hiking, and mountain biking, plus fishing, boating, and swimming at nearby Panguitch Lake
Season: Mid-June through mid-September
Finding the campground: From the junction of Utah Highway 143 and U.S. Highway 89 in Panguitch, travel southwest on UT 143 for 18.7 miles to the campground.

About the campground: Set among ponderosa pines, these small sites are suitable for tents; trailers are not recommended. The campground is about 0.5 mile from Panguitch Lake, which is especially popular for fishing. Rainbow trout are outstanding, though German brown trout can also be caught in the lake and downstream in Panguitch Creek. The forest service says that mountain biking and hiking opportunities abound in the area.

10 Point Supreme: Cedar Breaks National Monument

Location: About 1.5 miles north of the south entrance
Facilities: Fire grates, picnic tables, drinking water, and flush toilets
Sites: 30
Fee: $$
Elevation: 10,350 feet
Road conditions: Paved
Management: Cedar Breaks National Monument, Box 749, Cedar City, UT 84720; (435) 586–9451; CEBR_superintendent@nps.gov
Reservations: None
Activities: Hiking, photography, and picnicking
Season: Usually mid-June through September

Finding the campground: From the south entrance of the monument, off Utah Highway 14, go north about 1.5 miles on a paved road.

About the campground: A great base from which to explore Cedar Breaks National Monument, this campground is located just east of the visitor center. Here, staff offer nature walks, geology talks, and campfire programs.

There are two easy hikes near the rim; in addition, you'll find a 5-mile-long scenic drive past four breathtaking overlooks. The season is short here; visit while you can.

11 Cedar Canyon

Location: In the Dixie National Forest, about 13 miles southeast of Cedar City
Facilities: Fire grates, picnic tables, drinking water, and vault toilets
Sites: 19
Fee: $ for single sites; $$ for double sites
Elevation: 8,100 feet
Road conditions: Paved
Management: Cedar City Ranger District, 1789 North Wedgewood Lane, Cedar City, UT 84720; (435) 865-3200
Reservations: Call (877) 444-6777 or TDD (877) 833-6777; fee
Activities: Hiking, mountain biking, and picnicking
Season: Mid-June through mid-September
Finding the campground: From the junction of Utah Highways 14 and 130 in downtown Cedar City, travel southeast on UT 14 for 12.3 miles.

About the campground: The Cedar Canyon Campground is located in a beautiful canyon by the same name. Campsites snuggle up to Crow Creek, while aspen, fir, and spruce add to the scene. If you want to see bristlecone pine trees, you can drive or bike about 5 miles southeast on UT 14. There's a trailhead on the south side of the road. The Bristlecone Pine Trail is an easy 0.5-mile loop and is wheelchair accessible. Some of the pines are 300 to 500 years old. From the trail there are excellent views of the North Fork of the Virgin River and the northern areas of Zion National Park.

12 Deer Haven Organizational Camp

Location: In the Dixie National Forest, about 17 miles southeast of Cedar City
Facilities: Fire grates, picnic tables, drinking water, and flush toilets
Sites: 18
Fee: $$$$
Elevation: 8,900 feet
Road conditions: Dirt
Management: Cedar City Ranger District, 1789 North Wedgewood Lane, Cedar City, UT 84720; (435) 865-3200
Reservations: Call (877) 444-6777 or TDD (877) 833-6777; fee

Activities: Hiking, mountain biking, and picnicking
Season: Mid-June through mid-September
Finding the campground: From the junction of Utah Highways 14 and 130 in downtown Cedar City, travel southeast on UT 14 for about 15 miles to Forest Road 052, also known as Webster Flat Road. Turn right (south) and continue approximately 3.0 more miles on a dirt road to the campground.

About the campground: Set in aspen trees at the base of Black Mountain, this campground is designed and constructed to accommodate group organizations. It can be used by reservation only. The site holds up to 200 people. Each campsite should be planned to accommodate up to three tents and ten to twelve people. Mountain biking and hiking opportunities abound in the area. Hikers will find an access trail to the Virgin River Rim Trail, a 32-mile journey along the rim between Strawberry Point and Woods Ranch, which is about 2 miles from the campground. It provides wonderful views of the Virgin River basin and Zion National Park.

13 Spruces

Location: In the Dixie National Forest, about 28 miles southeast of Cedar City
Facilities: Fire grates, picnic tables, drinking water, and flush toilets. Commercial boat rentals and launching at nearby Behmer Lodge and Landing (located between Spruces and Navajo Campgrounds) and Navajo Lake Lodge (located at the west end of the lake)
Sites: 26
Fee: $$ for single sites; $$$ for double sites
Elevation: 9,200 feet
Road conditions: Paved
Management: Cedar City Ranger District, 1789 North Wedgewood Lane, Cedar City, UT 84720; (435) 865–3200
Reservations: None
Activities: Fishing, swimming, boating, hiking, mountain biking, and picnicking
Season: Mid-June through mid-September
Finding the campground: From the junction of Utah Highways 14 and 130 in downtown Cedar City, travel southeast on UT 14 for about 25.6 miles to Forest Road 053 (Navajo Lake Road). Turn right (south) and follow the paved road approximately 1.5 miles to the campground, the first of three located along the road.

About the campground: Situated along the south shore of 3.5-mile-long Navajo Lake, the campground straddles Navajo Lake Road and is embraced by aspen, spruce, and fir. Anglers vie for rainbow trout as well as eastern brook and brown trout. Mountain bikers find plenty to do, while hikers have access to the 32-mile-long Virgin River Rim Trail. Hike this trail and you'll have wonderful views of Zion National Park and the Virgin River basin.

14 Navajo Lake

Location: In the Dixie National Forest, about 29 miles southeast of Cedar City
Facilities: Fire grates, picnic tables, drinking water, flush toilets, sewage disposal station (located 2 miles west), boat ramp (for a fee). Commercial boat rentals and launching at nearby Behmer Lodge and Landing (located between the Spruces and Navajo Campgrounds) and Navajo Lake Lodge (located at the west end of the lake).
Sites: 27
Fee: $$ for single sites; $$$ for double sites
Elevation: 9,200 feet
Road conditions: Paved
Management: Cedar City Ranger District, 1789 North Wedgewood Lane, Cedar City, UT 84720; (435) 865-3200
Reservations: None
Activities: Fishing, boating, swimming, hiking, mountain biking, and picnicking
Season: Mid-June through mid-September
Finding the campground: From the junction of Utah Highways 14 and 130 in downtown Cedar City, travel southeast on UT 14 for about 25.6 miles to Forest Road 053 (Navajo Lake Road). Turn right (south) and follow the paved road for about 3.5 miles to the second of three public campgrounds.

About the campground: Situated along the south shore of 3.5-mile-long Navajo Lake, the campground straddles Navajo Lake Road and is embraced by aspen, spruce, and fir. Here, anglers vie for rainbow trout, as well as eastern brook and brown trout. Mountain bikers ride to their hearts' content, and hikers find an access trail to the Virgin River Rim Trail. This trail spans about 32 miles and provides wonderful views of Virgin River basin and Zion National Park.

15 Te-Ah

Location: In the Dixie National Forest, about 30 miles southeast of Cedar City
Facilities: Fire grates, picnic tables, drinking water, flush toilets, and a sewage disposal station. Commercial boat rentals and launching are available at nearby Behmer Lodge and Landing (located between the Spruces and Navajo Campgrounds) and Navajo Lake Lodge (located at the west end of the lake).
Sites: 42
Fee: $$
Elevation: 9,200 feet
Road conditions: Paved
Management: Cedar City Ranger District, 1789 North Wedgewood Lane, Cedar City, UT 84720; (435) 865-3200
Reservations: Call (877) 444-6777 or TDD (877) 833-6777; fee
Activities: Fishing, hiking, boating, and picnicking
Season: Mid-June through mid-September

Finding the campground: From the junction of Utah Highways 14 and 130 in downtown Cedar City, travel southeast on UT 14 for about 25.6 miles to Forest Road 053 (Navajo Lake Road). Turn right (south) and follow the paved road for about 4.5 miles to the last of three public campgrounds.

About the campground: Unlike the two campgrounds you passed en route to Te-Ah, this site is situated about 1.5 miles from Navajo Lake. Still, it's a popular spot for anglers with trout on their minds. It's also an excellent place from which to observe wild turkeys and deer.

16 Duck Creek

Location: In the Dixie National Forest, about 28 miles southeast of Cedar City
Facilities: Fire grates, picnic tables, drinking water, flush and vault toilets, and sewage disposal station. There are also Sunday church services, an amphitheater, and a telephone across the street at the ranger station/visitor center.
Sites: 95
Fee: $$ for single sites; $$$ for double sites
Elevation: 8,600 feet
Road conditions: Paved
Management: Cedar City Ranger District, 1789 North Wedgewood Lane, Cedar City, UT 84720; (435) 865-3200
Reservations: Call (877) 444-6777 or TDD (877) 833-6777; fee. Reservations are required for all group sites
Activities: Fishing, hiking, mountain biking, and picnicking
Season: Mid-June through mid-September
Finding the campground: From the junction of Utah Highways 14 and 130 in downtown Cedar City, travel southeast on UT 14 for 28 miles. You'll see the campground on the north side of the road; a ranger station/visitor center sits on the south side.

About the campground: Fishing is popular both in the adjacent creek and in Duck Lake. Visit and you'll know exactly how the lake got its name: Ducks seem to enjoy the place as much as human visitors.

There are several hiking trails in the vicinity. The longest trail is the Lost Hunter Trail, a 3-mile loop with some nice views of the area. You're bound to enjoy the Singing Pines Interpretive Trail, which is just across the street, east of the ranger station/visitor center. Be sure to pick up an information sheet for the easy, 0.5-mile-loop; this trail introduces the trees through songs. The Old Ranger Interpretive Trail does a similar thing—only this time you'll learn about the forest from the eyes of an old ranger. This trail is the shortest of the three, a 0.3-mile loop through aspen, Douglas fir, and ponderosa pine.

17 Pine Park

Location: In the Dixie National Forest, about 26 miles southwest of Enterprise and 67 miles southwest of Cedar City

Facilities: Fire grates, picnic tables, and vault toilet
Sites: Dispersed camping
Fee: None
Elevation: 6,200 feet
Road conditions: One-lane, dirt
Management: Pine Valley Ranger District, 196 East Tabernacle, Room 40, St. George, UT 84770; (435) 688–3246
Reservations: None
Activities: Hiking, off-highway driving, and picnicking
Season: Year-round
Finding the campground: From Enterprise, go west on Utah Highway 219. After 8.3 miles, the road turns to maintained gravel and is eventually called Forest Road 300. Drive another 8.4 miles to Forest Road 017 and a sign for Pine Park. Go left (south) for 0.2 mile; when the road forks keep left (south) on Forest Road 001, which is a one-lane dirt road. The road ends at the campground in just over 9 miles. Though a sign warns of a narrow, rough road, it may allow access for those with two-wheel-drive and low-clearance vehicles.

About the campground: Just before reaching the campground, which is set among towering ponderosa pines and enhanced by a singing spring, you'll travel past a wonderful world of volcanic tuff formations. It's an amazing place to wander and photograph to your heart's content.

The small campground (RVs and trailers shouldn't attempt it) provides access to the South Boundary Trail, which is located in a 30,000-acre roadless area, so you're bound to find solitude. The trail is a true wilderness trail, which means it is often difficult to follow. You'll need a forest service map, topographic maps, and a compass before heading out. ATVs are popular in the area, too.

18 Honeycomb Rocks

Location: In the Dixie National Forest, about 12 miles southwest of Enterprise and 53 miles southwest of Cedar City
Facilities: Fire grates, covered picnic tables, vault toilets, drinking water, and a boat launch
Sites: 22
Fee: $
Elevation: 5,700 feet
Road conditions: Paved
Management: Pine Valley Ranger District, 196 East Tabernacle, Room 40, St. George, UT 84770; (435) 688–3246
Reservations: None
Activities: Fishing, swimming, boating, mountain biking, picnicking, and photography
Restrictions: Please note that the drinking water has a high sodium content.
Season: Memorial Day through Labor Day
Finding the campground: From Enterprise, go west on paved Utah Highway

219. After 7.1 miles, turn left (south) onto an unnamed paved road. A sign points the way to the campground and Enterprise Reservoirs. After another 5.6 miles, you'll find the campground, which is just across the road from the reservoir.

About the campground: There are plenty of activities at this scenic campground, where sites are nestled into an unusual series of welded tuff formations. Part of the Ox Valley Tuff formation of the late Miocene—which means they're about twelve to fifteen million years old—the porous volcanic rocks do look a bit like honeycombs, thus their name. The rest of the country is wide open, a place where sage and grass are predominant. An occasional pine or oak adds to the scene.

Rainbow trout thrive in both the lower and upper reservoirs. The larger of the two is Upper Enterprise Reservoir, where you'll find a paved boat ramp. It's also the closest water source to the campground.

19 Equestrian: Pine Valley Recreation Area

Location: In the Dixie National Forest, about 23 miles southeast of Enterprise
Facilities: Fire grates, picnic tables, flush and vault toilets, sewage disposal station, and drinking water
Sites: 18
Fee: $ to $$
Elevation: 6,800 feet
Road conditions: Paved
Management: Pine Valley Ranger District, 196 East Tabernacle, Room 40, St. George, UT 84770; (435) 688–3246
Reservations: Call (877) 444–6777 or TDD (877) 833–6777; fee
Activities: Horseback riding, hiking, fishing, boating, and picnicking
Season: Memorial Day through Labor Day
Finding the campground: From Enterprise, drive south on Utah Highway 18 for 13.6 miles, then turn left (east) onto paved Pine Valley Road E. Drive another 9.6 miles, passing through the small community of Pine Valley, en route to the Pine Valley Recreation Area. Just 0.2 mile after entering the recreation area, you'll see the campground turnoff.

About the campground: The campground is set among pines and firs, and offers a nice place for horse owners to camp with their four-legged friends. Portable stalls may be used with permission from the host. In addition, there's the opportunity to fish for rainbow and brook trout at Pine Valley Reservoir, which is about 0.7 mile farther up the road. A special ramp allows those in wheelchairs to fish as well. You can also fish in the Santa Clara River, which flows nearby.

Whether you want to hike or ride horses, there are plenty of nearby trails that allow access into the Pine Valley Mountain Wilderness Area, a region rich in pine, aspen, fir, and spruce. The granite spire known as Signal Peak stands more than 10,000 feet in elevation and is the highest point in the wilderness.

20 Upper Pines: Pine Valley Recreation Area

Location: In the Dixie National Forest, about 23 miles southeast of Enterprise
Facilities: Fire grates, picnic tables, vault toilets, sewage disposal station, and drinking water
Sites: 1
Fee: $$$$
Elevation: 6,800 feet
Road conditions: Paved
Management: Pine Valley Ranger District, 196 East Tabernacle, Room 40, St. George, UT 84770; (435) 688-3246
Reservations: Call (877) 444-6777 or TDD (877) 833-6777; fee
Activities: Hiking, fishing, boating, and picnicking
Season: Memorial Day through Labor Day
Finding the campground: From Enterprise, drive south on Utah Highway 18 for 13.6 miles, then turn left (east) onto paved Pine Valley Road E. Drive another 9.6 miles, passing through the small community of Pine Valley, en route to the Pine Valley Recreation Area. Less than 1 mile after entering the recreation area, you'll see the campground turnoff.

About the campground: Set among pines and firs, this group campground, with a capacity of fifty campers and eight vehicles, offers a nice place for just relaxing and enjoying the cool realms of the forest. In addition, there's the opportunity to fish for rainbow and brook trout at nearby Pine Valley Reservoir. A special ramp allows those in wheelchairs to fish as well. There's also fishing upstream and downstream in the Santa Clara River.

An abundance of nearby trails allow access into the Pine Valley Mountain Wilderness Area, a region rich in pine, aspen, fir, and spruce. The granite spire known as Signal Peak stands more than 10,000 feet in elevation and is the highest point in the wilderness.

21 Pines: Pine Valley Recreation Area

Location: In the Dixie National Forest, about 24 miles southeast of Enterprise
Facilities: Fire grates, picnic tables, flush and vault toilets, sewage disposal station, and drinking water
Sites: 13
Fee: $$ for single sites; $$$$ for double sites
Elevation: 6,800 feet
Road conditions: Paved
Management: Pine Valley Ranger District, 196 East Tabernacle, Room 40, St. George, UT 84770; (435) 688-3246
Reservations: None
Activities: Hiking, fishing, boating, and picnicking
Season: Memorial Day through Labor Day
Finding the campground: From Enterprise, drive south on Utah Highway 18 for 13.6 miles, then turn left (east) onto paved Pine Valley Road E. Drive another 9.6 miles, passing through the small community of Pine Valley, en route

to the Pine Valley Recreation Area. About 2 miles after entering the recreation area, you'll see the campground turnoff.

About the campground: The campground is set among pines and firs, and offers a nice place for simply relaxing and enjoying the cool realms of the forest. In addition, there's the opportunity to fish for rainbow and brook trout at Pine Valley Reservoir, which is nearby. A special ramp allows those in wheelchairs to fish as well. There's also fishing upstream and downstream in the Santa Clara River.

An abundance of nearby trails allow access into the Pine Valley Mountain Wilderness Area. Rich in pine, aspen, fir, and spruce, Signal Peak, a granite spire, stands more than 10,000 feet in elevation and is the highest point in the wilderness.

22 Blue Springs: Pine Valley Recreation Area

Location: In the Dixie National Forest, about 24 miles southeast of Enterprise
Facilities: Fire grates, picnic tables, vault toilets, and drinking water
Sites: 20
Fee: $$ for single sites; $$$$ for double sites
Elevation: 6,800 feet
Road conditions: Paved
Management: Pine Valley Ranger District, 196 East Tabernacle, Room 40, St. George, UT 84770; (435) 688-3246
Reservations: Call (877) 444-6777 or TDD (877) 833-6777; fee
Activities: Hiking, fishing, boating, and picnicking
Season: Memorial Day through Labor Day
Finding the campground: From Enterprise, drive south on Utah Highway 18 for 13.6 miles, then turn left (east) onto paved Pine Valley Road E. Drive another 9.6 miles, passing through the small community of Pine Valley, en route to the Pine Valley Recreation Area. About 2 miles after entering the recreation area, you'll see the campground turnoff.

About the campground: The campground is set among pines and firs, and offers a nice place for relaxing and enjoying the cool realms of the forest. In addition, there's the opportunity to fish for rainbow and brook trout at Pine Valley Reservoir, which is nearby. A special ramp allows those in wheelchairs to fish as well. There's also fishing upstream and downstream in the Santa Clara River.

An abundance of nearby trails allow access into the Pine Valley Mountain Wilderness Area, a region rich in pine, aspen, fir, and spruce. The granite spire known as Signal Peak stands more than 10,000 feet in elevation and is the highest point in the wilderness.

23 Juniper Park: Pine Valley Recreation Area

Location: In the Dixie National Forest, about 24 miles southeast of Enterprise
Facilities: Fire grates, picnic tables, vault toilets, sewage disposal station, and drinking water

Sites: 23
Fee: $$ for single sites; $$$$ for double sites
Elevation: 6,800 feet
Road conditions: Paved
Management: Pine Valley Ranger District, 196 East Tabernacle, Room 40, St. George, UT 84770; (435) 688–3246
Reservations: None
Activities: Hiking, fishing, boating, and picnicking
Season: Memorial Day through Labor Day
Finding the campground: From Enterprise, drive south on Utah Highway 18 for 13.6 miles, then turn left (east) onto paved Pine Valley Road E. Drive another 9.6 miles, passing through the small community of Pine Valley, en route to the Pine Valley Recreation Area. About 2 miles after entering the recreation area, you'll see the campground turnoff.

About the campground: The campground is set among pines and firs, and offers a nice place for simply enjoying the cool realms of the forest. In addition, campers can fish for rainbow and brook trout at nearby Pine Valley Reservoir. A special ramp allows those in wheelchairs to fish as well. There's also fishing upstream and downstream in the Santa Clara River.

An abundance of trails allow access into the Pine Valley Mountain Wilderness Area, a region rich in pine, aspen, fir, and spruce. The highest point in the wilderness is a granite spire known as Signal Peak; it stands more than 10,000 feet in elevation.

24 Baker Dam

Location: On the west side of the Pine Valley Mountains, about 25 miles north of St. George
Facilities: Fire grates, picnic tables, vault toilets, and a boat ramp
Sites: 19
Fee: $
Elevation: 5,000 feet
Road conditions: Paved to the campground, then gravel
Management: Bureau of Land Management, St. George Field Office, 345 East Riverside Drive, St. George, UT 84790; (435) 688–3200; UT-ST_George@blm.gov
Reservations: None
Activities: Fishing, hiking, and picnicking
Season: Mid-March to mid-December
Finding the campground: From Interstate 15 in St. George, travel northwest on Utah Highway 18. Just past mile marker 24, turn right (east) onto a wide, paved road. A sign points the way to Baker Dam Reservoir; you'll reach the campground in about 0.5 mile.

About the campground: Utah juniper trees decorate this lovely campground, while the nearby Pine Mountains provide a picturesque backdrop.

You can roam to your heart's content if you have a good map and compass, or opt for the short, but maintained, 0.2-mile trail.

Most people come here to relax and fish. One camp host claims that fourteen-pound cutthroat trout have been hooked here at the fifty-acre reservoir. Other species include rainbow, brook, and German brown trout.

Note that gate closes at 10:00 P.M. and opens at 8:00 A.M.

25 Gunlock State Park

Location: About 20 miles northwest of St. George
Facilities: Vault toilets, picnic tables, boat-launch ramp, and docks
Sites: Undeveloped; large RVs will fit almost anyplace
Fee: None
Elevation: 3,600 feet
Road conditions: Paved to the campground, then dirt
Management: Gunlock State Park, P.O. Box 140, Santa Clara, UT 84765-0140; (435) 628-2255
Reservations: None
Activities: Boating, water sports, swimming, fishing, mountain biking, and picnicking
Season: Year-round
Finding the campground: From Interstate 15 in St. George, travel north on Utah Highway 18 about 3 miles to its junction with Utah Highway 8 (Sunset Boulevard). Go left (west) on UT 8 for 5 miles. At this point UT 8 heads north; keep straight, now driving Old Highway 91. Go an additional 6 miles to a fork and stay right (north) for another 5.8 miles to the state park entrance.

About the campground: This primitive campground hugs the east shore of 266-acre Gunlock Reservoir, which is quite popular despite its lack of amenities. Boating and other water sports are favorites; fishing for quality largemouth bass, channel catfish, and bluegills is also a high priority for many visitors. Near the dam you'll find a parking area, a paved boat ramp, and docks. There's a red-sand beach across the lake. Reach it by boat or by walking across the dam. On a historical note, the road leading to Gunlock Lake is a part of the Old Spanish Trail, which once stretched from Santa Fe, New Mexico, to Los Angeles, California.

26 Snow Canyon State Park

Location: About 11 miles northwest of St. George
Facilities: Fire grates, picnic tables, flush toilets, showers, electric and water hookups, sewage disposal station, public telephone, drinking water, and a volleyball court
Sites: 34
Fee: $$
Elevation: 3,200 feet
Road conditions: Paved

Management: Snow Canyon State Park, P.O. Box 140, Santa Clara, UT 84765-0140; (435) 628-2255
Reservations: In the Salt Lake area, call (801) 322-3770; elsewhere, (800) 322-3770; fee
Activities: Hiking, rock climbing, mountain biking, horseback riding, picnicking, photography, and volleyball
Season: Year-round
Finding the campground: From Interstate 15 in St. George, travel north on Utah Highway 18 about 11 miles to the paved park road, which drops into the canyon. You'll reach the campground and entrance station in less than 3 miles.

About the campground: Set in Snow Canyon, a land of Navajo sandstone boasting shades of pink, red, and yellow, capped by black lava rock, the campground offers some shaded sites. If you dry-camp, you'll enjoy wide sites and privacy; opt for hookups and you'll sit parking-lot-style next to your neighbor. Reservations are not required, but they are advised.

Activities are abundant, with a volleyball court in the campground. There are also more than 15 miles of hiking trails, over a hundred rock climbing routes, and a 5-mile-long bike trail. More than 5 miles of horseback riding trails exist, too, in the 5-mile-long canyon. Cacti bloom in the spring; wildlife watching can be enjoyed all year, though summers are very hot.

27 Red Cliffs Recreation Site

Location: On the south end of the Pine Valley Mountains, approximately 15 miles northeast of St. George
Facilities: Fire grates, covered picnic tables, vault toilets, and drinking water
Sites: 10
Fee: $
Elevation: 3,240 feet
Road conditions: Paved, with two narrow, one-lane tunnels
Management: Bureau of Land Management, St. George Field Office, 345 East Riverside Drive, St. George, UT 84790; (435) 688-3200; UT-St_George@blm.gov
Reservations: None
Activities: Hiking, mountain biking, picnicking, and photography
Restrictions: Tunnels are restricted to vehicles less than 11 feet, 6 inches high and no wider than 12 feet. Visitors with long RVs should beware of steep dips and sharp curves.
Season: Year-round.
Finding the campground: From Interstate 15 and Leeds exits 22 and 23 (use exit 22 if you're northbound, exit 23 if you're southbound), about 15 miles northeast of St. George, go south on the frontage road for 2 to 3 miles to the signed Red Cliffs turnoff. Go right (west) and through two tunnels, crossing Quail Creek en route to the campground fee station, another 1.5 miles away.

About the campground: The campground at the Red Cliffs Recreation Site guards the mouth of one of many Utah redrock canyons. Cottonwood trees shade most of the ten sites, and three trails lead to three very different places. One leads a mere 0.8 mile to a lookout point; another travels across fairly open country to an Ancestral Puebloan archaeological site; and the longest leads a mile up Quail Creek, more if you're up to exploring on your own.

Red Cliffs is a busy place, so you shouldn't expect to have it to yourself. The hike up Quail Creek is especially popular, but there are good reasons for its popularity. Several deep pools offer the chance to cool off, while a slot canyon offers slickrock, alcoves, grottoes, and pictographs. Note that the campground gate closes at 10:00 P.M. and opens at 6:00 A.M.

28 Oak Grove

Location: In the Dixie National Forest, approximately 19 miles northeast of St. George
Facilities: Fire grates, picnic tables, pit toilets, and drinking water
Sites: 8
Fee: $
Elevation: 6,800 feet
Road conditions: One-lane with turnouts, maintained dirt; not recommended for trailers
Management: Pine Valley Ranger District, 196 East Tabernacle, Room 40, St. George, UT 84770; (435) 688–3246
Reservations: None
Activities: Hiking, horseback riding, and picnicking
Season: Memorial Day through Labor Day
Finding the campground: From Interstate 15 and Leeds exits 22 and 23 (use exit 22 if you're northbound, exit 23 if you're southbound), about 15 miles northeast of St. George, go northwest on Silver Reef Road. The road is paved until it becomes unsigned Forest Road 032. Continue 8.7 miles to the campground, which is at the end of the road.

About the campground: Situated in a forest of ponderosa pine, spruce, and Gambel and shrub live oak, this small campground provides a cool refuge come summer. Leeds Creek offers trout fishing, though dense shrubs make access difficult.

Hiking is none too easy, but it is available. The Oak Grove Trail begins at the campground and climbs a steady, steep grade through the beautiful Pine Valley Mountain Wilderness. A sign says the trail leads 3 miles to the Summit Trail, though it seems more like 4 miles to most people. Regardless of its length, it climbs just over 3,000 feet to the trail junction.

29 Quail Creek State Park

Location: About 12 miles northeast of St. George
Facilities: Fire grates, covered picnic tables, flush toilets, drinking water, public telephone, fish cleaning station, two boat ramps, and two covered group-use pavilions
Sites: 23

Fee: $
Elevation: 3,300 feet
Road conditions: Paved
Management: Quail Creek State Park, P.O. Box 1943, St. George, UT 84771-1943; (435) 879-2378
Reservations: In the Salt Lake area, call (801) 322-3770; elsewhere, (800) 322-3770; fee
Activities: Fishing, swimming, waterskiing, Jet Skiing, sailboarding, boating, and picnicking
Restrictions: The lake capacity is seventy boats year-round. From May 1 through Labor Day boats are restricted to launch by bow number. Odd-bow-numbered craft are allowed to launch on odd-numbered days, while even-bow-numbered craft launch on even-calendar numbered days.
Season: Year-round
Finding the campground: From the south (St. George area), drive northeast on Interstate 15 for about 8 miles to Utah Highway 9. Turn right (east) onto UT 9 for 2.6 miles to the park entrance via Utah Highway 318. You'll reach the campground and entrance station in 1.8 miles. If you're coming from the north, exit I-15 at Leeds exit 23 (about 15 miles northeast of St. George) and follow the frontage road south for 3.4 miles, then turn left and continue for about 1.5 miles.

About the campground: Excellent year-round camping can be had in this part of sunny, southwest Utah. In fact, during summer Quail Creek Reservoir boasts the warmest water in the state. It is an especially nice place to camp if you enjoy waterskiing, boating, swimming, or fishing for largemouth bass, catfish, bluegills, and rainbow trout. Reservations are not required, but they are advised.

30 Lava Point: Zion National Park

Location: North-central Zion National Park, about 20 miles north of Virgin
Facilities: Fire grates, picnic tables, and vault toilets
Sites: 6
Fee: None
Elevation: 7,890 feet
Road conditions: One-and-a-half-lane, gravel
Management: Zion National Park, SR 9, Springdale, UT 84767-1099; (435) 772-3256; ZION_park_information@nps.gov
Reservations: None
Activities: Hiking, picnicking, and photography
Restrictions: Generators are prohibited
Season: June through October
Finding the campground: From Utah Highway 9 in Virgin, drive north on Kolob Reservoir Road (called Kolob Terrace Road on park maps). The road is paved and climbs dramatically for wonderful views of Zion National Park and surrounding areas. After 20.2 miles, turn right (east) where a sign points the

way to the Lava Point Campground. Drive the dirt road less than 2 miles to the campground.

About the campground: Surrounded by aspen, ponderosa pine, Gambel oak, and white fir, the Lava Point Campground sits at just under 7,900 feet in elevation. Generators are not allowed, so you should enjoy a quiet time at this small campground.

For a magnificent view of the park and beyond, you can walk to the Lava Point Fire Lookout a few hundred yards to the east. Signs help identify Cedar Breaks National Monument to the north and Pink Cliffs to the northeast; if you look east, you'll see Zion Canyon Narrows. And if that isn't enough, gaze southeast and see the Sentinel and other grand features of Zion Canyon, and look south into Arizona. Nearby hiking trails lead to various points. In addition, you can fish at Kolob Reservoir, a high-country lake reached by driving another 3.5 miles north past the Lava Point turnoff via Kolob Reservoir Road.

31 South: Zion National Park

Location: Just north of the south entrance
Facilities: Fire grates, picnic tables, flush toilets, sewage disposal station, public telephone, utility sinks, and drinking water
Sites: 128
Fee: $$
Elevation: 3,950 feet
Road conditions: Paved
Management: Zion National Park, SR 9, Springdale, UT 84767-1099; (435) 772–3256; ZION_park_information@nps.gov
Reservations: None
Activities: Hiking, rock climbing, photography, and picnicking
Restrictions: If you enter the park from the west, you'll have no problems negotiating Utah Highway 9. Enter from the east, however, traveling what is also called Zion–Mt. Carmel Highway, and you'll have to travel through two narrow tunnels. The shorter is 530 feet long; the longer is 5,600 feet. Vehicles over 13 feet, 1 inch tall, single vehicles over 40 feet long, combined vehicles over 50 feet long, and pedestrians and bicyclists are prohibited. Vehicles over 7 feet, 10 inches wide and/or 11 feet, 4 inches high must travel through with one-way traffic. A fee is charged. Check with the park service for designated travel times.
Season: Year-round
Finding the campground: The campground is located off Utah Highway 9, just north of the south entrance station, about 2 miles north of Springdale.

About the campground: South Campground is the smaller of the two campgrounds located near the south entrance. Located along the North Fork Virgin River, campsites are shaded compliments of netleaf hackberries and Fremont cottonwoods. The campground fills by early to midafternoon during the peak spring-through-fall season, so you should arrive early if you hope to camp here.

Activities abound here in Zion National Park. Some folks come to sit by the river and read a book, some to hike a short trail, others to hoist a heavy backpack and head for Zion's backcountry. Still others come to climb one of Zion's monoliths. While most of the big-wall climbs are in the difficult range—5.10 and above—there's a wonderful 5.8 climb on the northwest side of Mount Spry. Check with the backcountry office for more information.

32 Watchman: Zion National Park

Location: At the south entrance station
Facilities: Fire grates, picnic tables, flush toilets, sewage disposal station, public telephone, utility sinks, and drinking water; some sites have electric hookups
Sites: 153
Fee: $$
Elevation: 3,900 feet
Road conditions: Paved
Management: Zion National Park, SR 9, Springdale, UT 84767-1099; (435) 772-3256; ZION_park_information@nps.gov
Reservations: All sites must be reserved at (800) 365-2267 or visit the Web site at reservations.nps.gov\
Activities: Hiking, rock climbing, picnicking, and photography
Restrictions: If you enter the park from the west, you'll have no problems negotiating Utah Highway 9. Enter from the east, however, traveling what is also called Zion–Mt. Carmel Highway, and you'll have to travel through two narrow tunnels. The shorter is 530 feet long; the longer is 5,600 feet. Vehicles over 13 feet, 1 inch tall, single vehicles over 40 feet long, combined vehicles over 50 feet long, and pedestrians and bicyclists are prohibited. Vehicles over 7 feet, 10 inches wide and/or 11 feet, 4 inches high must travel through with one-way traffic. A fee is charged. Check with the park service for designated travel times.
Season: April through October
Finding the campground: The campground is located off Utah Highway 9, at the entrance station, about 1 mile north of Springdale.

About the campground: Named for The Watchman, a famous rock formation that stretches 6,545 feet into the heavens, this campground is situated on a bench above the North Fork Virgin River. Hackberry, ash, and cottonwood serve to shade campers. Closed in winter, the campground was recently renovated in order to make room for the new park shuttle system, which went into effect in 2000. The campground fills by early to midafternoon during the peak spring-through-fall season, so you should make plans to arrive early if you want to camp here.

Hiking, climbing, and photography opportunities abound. A popular hike begins at the Grotto Picnic Area and ascends some steep switchbacks before traveling through the magnificent realms of Refrigerator Canyon. It then ascends a series of short switchbacks—called Walter's Wiggles—to Scott Lookout. From there you'll have to decide whether or not to ascend the steep,

500-foot-high, knife-edged sandstone rib to Angel's Landing. Steps, human-made depressions cut into the rock, and thick chains may help calm the nerves of those who are afraid of heights. Children and hikers who are seriously afraid of heights should stay below. Atop Angel's Landing, about 1,500 feet above the valley floor, you'll thrill to close-up views of the likes of the Great White Throne and Zion Canyon.

33 Coral Pink Sand Dunes State Park

Location: About 22 miles west of Kanab
Facilities: Fire grates, picnic tables, drinking water, public telephone, ice machine, showers, flush toilets, and sewage disposal station
Sites: 22
Fee: $$
Elevation: 6,000 feet
Road conditions: Paved
Management: Coral Pink Sand Dunes State Park, P.O. Box 95, Kanab, UT 84741-0095; (435) 648–2800
Reservations: In the Salt Lake area, call (801) 322–3770; elsewhere, (800) 322–3770; fee
Activities: Off-highway vehicle driving, hiking, photography, and picnicking
Season: Year-round
Finding the campground: From Kanab, drive north on U.S. Highway 89 for 8.2 miles, then turn left (west) onto signed Hancock Road, which is paved. Drive 9.3 miles to its end at another paved road. A sign points left (southwest) to the state park, which you'll reach in another 4.2 miles. The park is on the left (east) side of the road.

About the campground: This is a great place for those with OHVs, which are especially popular with weekend folks. Weekdays find most people happy to hike and photograph the dunes. A short boardwalk trail allows access via wheelchair. In addition, there is one wheelchair-accessible shower.

The ranger station sells ATV flags (which are mandatory), T-shirts, and an assortment of other items. There's also the "From Around the World Sand Collection," which offers sands from many different parts of the world; check it out.

34 Ponderosa Grove

Location: About 15 miles northwest of Kanab
Facilities: Fire grates, picnic tables, drinking water, and vault toilets
Sites: 9
Fee: $
Elevation: 6,300 feet
Road conditions: Paved, then the campground road is gravel
Management: Bureau of Land Management, Kanab Field Office, 318 North First East, Kanab, UT 84741; (435) 644–4600; UT-Kanab@blm.gov
Reservations: None

Activities: Off-highway vehicle driving and picnicking
Season: Year-round
Finding the campground: From Kanab, drive north on U.S. Highway 89 for 8.2 miles, then turn left (west) onto signed Hancock Road, which is paved. Drive 7.3 miles to the campground turnoff, which is on the right side of the road.

About the campground: This is a popular place for those with OHVs. The campground, in a lovely setting of Utah junipers and ponderosa pines, provides access to Coral Pink Sand Dunes State Park, just 4 miles southwest.

35 Kings Creek

Location: In the Dixie National Forest, approximately 26 miles southeast of Panguitch
Facilities: Fire grates, picnic tables, flush and vault toilets, sewage disposal station, drinking water, and boat ramp
Sites: 38
Fee: $
Elevation: 8,000 feet
Road conditions: Maintained gravel
Management: Powell Ranger District, P.O. Box 80, Panguitch, UT 84759; (435) 676-9300
Reservations: Call (435) 676-9300; fee
Activities: Hiking, fishing, boating, swimming, mountain biking, access to the Fremont ATV Trail, and picnicking
Season: May 20 through Labor Day
Finding the campground: From the junction of Utah Highway 12 and U.S. Highway 89, about 7 miles south of Panguitch, travel east on UT 12 for 10.8 miles. At this point, head south on Forest Road 087, a gravel road also known as East Fork of the Sevier Road, for another 7 miles to Forest Road 572. Make a right (west) onto gravel FR 572, passing Tropic Reservoir and reaching the campground in less than 1 mile.

About the campground: A ponderosa pine forest blankets the west shore of Tropic Reservoir, where the campground is located, making this a nice spot for boating, trout fishing, swimming, hiking, off-highway driving, or just plain relaxing. Nearby, the East Fork of the Sevier River offers fishing opportunities for brook, cutthroat, brown, and rainbow trout.

Several hiking trails of varying difficulty begin at the campground. Mountain bikers may want to check out *Mountain Biking Utah;* Gregg Bromka's book describes a ride from the campground. ATVers should sample the Fremont ATV Trail. This popular ATV trail, which is about 60 miles long, starts near the campground and ends in Circleville, connecting with other ATV trails—East Fork, the Great Western Trail, and the Casto Canyon—along the way.

The group area (which can accommodate 1 to 150 people) is available by reservation only; fees vary. Contact the forest service for more information.

36 Red Canyon

Location: In the Dixie National Forest, about 11 miles southeast of Panguitch
Facilities: Fire grates, picnic tables, showers, flush toilets, sewage disposal station, and drinking water
Sites: 37
Fee: $
Elevation: 7,400 feet
Road conditions: Paved
Management: Powell Ranger District, P.O. Box 80, Panguitch, UT 84759; (435) 676-9300
Reservations: None
Activities: Hiking, mountain biking, horseback riding, and picnicking
Season: May 20 through October 1
Finding the campground: From the junction of Utah Highway 12 and U.S. Highway 89, about 7 miles south of Panguitch, travel east on scenic UT 12 for 3.8 miles. The campground is on the right (south) side of the highway.

About the campground: Situated in a mini Bryce Canyon–like setting, with its own collection of hoodoos and spires, Red Canyon is a nice place to camp if you don't mind being next to the highway.

There are several trails in the area; the most popular one takes off from the visitor center, located just west of the campground. The Pink Ledges Trail loops about 0.5 mile, with signs to identify the most common trees and plants.

37 Sunset: Bryce Canyon National Park

Location: South of the entrance station
Facilities: Fire grates, picnic tables, drinking water, public telephone, and flush toilets
Sites: 110
Fee: $$
Elevation: 8,000 feet
Road conditions: Paved
Management: Bryce Canyon National Park, P.O. Box 170001, Bryce Canyon, UT 84717-0001; (435) 834-5322; BRCA_superintendent@nps.gov
Reservations: None
Activities: Hiking, horseback riding, picnicking, and photography
Restrictions: Trailers are not permitted beyond Sunset Campground. Campers should leave their trailers at their campsite. Motor homes and trailers are not permitted to park in spaces designated for buses.
Season: Mid-May through October 10
Finding the campground: The campground entrance is just over 1 mile south of the entrance station and visitor center, on the west side of the road.

About the campground: Open during the busy days of summer, this campground is near Sunset Point. It provides access to one of the most beautiful

View from Fairyland Point Bryce in Canyon National Park.

places in all the world—Bryce Canyon. An amazing array of hoodoos and other unique formations makes this canyon, which is really an amphitheater, a great place for hiking. There are approximately 50 miles of trails here. If you don't enjoy hiking, you can explore the park by automobile. To do so, drive the 18-mile park road along Plateau Rim to Yovimpa and Rainbow Points. Thirteen pullouts offer views you won't soon forget.

38 | North: Bryce Canyon National Park

Location: The north end of the park
Facilities: Fire grates, picnic tables, drinking water, flush toilets, and a sewage disposal station (there's a fee)
Sites: 107
Fee: $$
Elevation: 8,000 feet
Road conditions: Paved
Management: Bryce Canyon National Park, P.O. Box 170001, Bryce Canyon, UT 84717-0001; (435) 834–5322; BRCA_superintendent@nps.gov
Reservations: None
Activities: Hiking, horseback riding, picnicking, and photography
Restrictions: Trailers are not permitted beyond Sunset Campground. Campers should leave their trailers at their campsite. Motor homes and trailers are not permitted to park in spaces designated for buses.
Season: Year-round.

Finding the campground: The campground entrance is just south of the entrance station and visitor center, on the east side of the road.

About the campground: Open all year, this campground provides access to one of the most beautiful places in all the world—Bryce Canyon. Its amazing array of hoodoos and other unique formations makes this a great place for hiking and exploring; about 50 miles of trails are found here. If you prefer, you can explore by automobile, driving the 18-mile park road along the Plateau Rim to Yovimpa and Rainbow Points. Thirteen pullouts offer views you won't soon forget.

39 Kodachrome Basin State Park

Location: Approximately 9 miles south of Cannonville
Facilities: Fire grates, picnic tables, drinking water, public telephone, soda pop machine, flush toilets, showers, and a sewage disposal station. Trailhead Station, located in the center of the park, offers information, film, food, ice, and supplies. You can also arrange for guided horseback and stagecoach rides. Phone (435) 679–8536 for additional information.
Sites: 27
Fee: $$
Elevation: 5,800 feet
Road conditions: Paved
Management: Kodachrome Basin State Park, P.O. Box 238, Cannonville, UT 84718; (435) 679–8562
Reservations: In the Salt Lake area, call (801) 322–3770; elsewhere, (800) 322–3770; fee
Activities: Hiking, horseback riding, mountain biking, photography, and picnicking
Restrictions: Limited generator use; two hours maximum
Season: Year-round
Finding the campground: From Utah Highway 12 in Cannonville, head south on the paved road (known as Cottonwood Canyon Road). Signs point the way to Kodachrome Basin. You'll reach the self-serve entrance station after 7.7 miles. Travel another 1 mile to the campground.

About the campground: This is one of Utah's nicest state parks, where campsites are partially surrounded by unique red- and white-tinged rock formations. It should be no surprise that the National Geographic Society conceived the name of this place, which practically begs to be photographed.

There are plenty of hiking trails to keep you occupied. All have their own attractions: Of particular interest is the nature trail, a paved, wheelchair-accessible path where visitors learn about the native vegetation and geology.

40 Pine Lake

Location: In the Dixie National Forest, about 17 miles northeast of Bryce Canyon National Park

Facilities: Fire grates, picnic tables, vault toilets, sewage disposal station, and drinking water
Sites: 33
Fee: $
Elevation: 8,300 feet
Road conditions: Maintained gravel
Management: Escalante Ranger District, 755 West Main, P.O. Box 246, Escalante, UT 84726; (435) 826-5400
Reservations: None except for group sites. Call (877) 444-6777 or TDD (877) 833-6777; fee
Activities: Hiking, fishing, mountain biking, off-highway driving, and picnicking
Season: May 20 through mid-September
Finding the campground: From the junction of Utah Highway 12, Utah Highway 63, and John Valley Road (a sign says this is Route 1660), drive northeast on John Valley Road for 10.7 miles. At this point, there's a sign pointing the way to the campground; make a right (east) onto Forest Road 132, which is maintained gravel. Follow it, driving an additional 6 miles or so to the campground.

About the campground: Located on the east side of Pine Lake, the campground is in a lovely setting of ponderosa pine trees. Fishing is popular here, though motorized boats are not allowed. There is some hiking in the area, as well as an ATV trail.

41 Escalante State Park

Location: About 1 mile west of Escalante
Facilities: Fire grates, covered picnic tables, drinking water, boat ramp, canoe rentals, public telephone, soda machines, sewage disposal station, showers, and flush toilets
Sites: 22
Fee: $$
Elevation: 6,000 feet
Road conditions: Paved
Management: Escalante State Park, P.O. Box 350, Escalante, UT 84726-0350; (435) 826-4466
Reservations: In the Salt Lake area, call (801) 322-3770; elsewhere, (800) 322-3770; fee
Activities: Fishing, boating, swimming, water sports, hiking, and picnicking
Season: Year-round
Finding the campground: From Escalante, travel west on scenic Utah Highway 12 for about 1.5 miles. You'll see the park entrance on the right (north) side of the road; continue 0.7 mile to the fee station/visitor center.

About the campground: If you like petrified wood, chukars calling, and a lake nearby, then you'll like this Utah state park. Wide Hollow Reservoir, 130 acres in size, offers fishing as well as Jet Skiing, waterskiing, and the like. Two interpretive trails allow hikers to learn all about the colorful petrified wood and dinosaur bones found in this park, once called Escalante Petrified Forest; hike the trails here and you'll quickly learn where it got that name. Collecting is not permitted in the park and should be discouraged elsewhere.

42 Posey Lake

Location: In the Dixie National Forest, approximately 16 miles northwest of Escalante
Facilities: Fire grates, picnic tables, drinking water, boat ramp, fish cleaning station, and vault toilets
Sites: 23
Fee: $
Elevation: 8,600 feet
Road conditions: Maintained gravel
Management: Escalante Ranger District, 755 West Main, P.O. Box 246, Escalante, UT 84726; (435) 826–5400
Reservations: Call (877) 444–6777 or TDD (877) 833–6777; fee
Activities: Fishing, boating, hiking, and picnicking
Restrictions: ATVs are not permitted
Season: May 20 through mid-September
Finding the campground: From Escalante, travel east on Utah Highway 12 for about 1.0 mile to the turnoff for Hells Backbone Road (called 300 East here, and later Forest Road 153), which is on the left (north). You'll travel on paved road for the first 3.5 miles, then maintained gravel. After another 10 miles, you'll reach a fork in the road; FR 153 continues to the right (north), while Forest Road 154 heads left (west). Keep left on FR 154 and you'll reach Posey Lake after 1.8 miles.

About the campground: The south shore of Posey Lake is the setting for this campground, with ponderosa pine and aspen trees all around. Anglers vie for both rainbow and brook trout, while hikers, mountain bikers, and horseback riders can travel 1 mile and 385 feet up (2 miles round-trip) to the Posey Lake Lookout, a historic landmark. Access to the nice view is via a trailhead across from campsite 14. Another trail, the Posey Lake Spur Trail, is 1.2 miles long and begins in the campground near the boat dock on the south side of the lake; it ends at John Allen Bottom on the Great Western Trail.

43 Blue Spruce

Location: In the Dixie National Forest, about 20 miles north of Escalante
Facilities: Fire grates, picnic tables, drinking water, and vault toilets
Sites: 8
Fee: $
Elevation: 8,000 feet
Road conditions: Maintained gravel, then dirt
Management: Escalante Ranger District, 755 West Main, P.O. Box 246, Escalante, UT 84726; (435) 826–5400

Reservations: None
Activities: Fishing in a nearby stream, and picnicking
Season: May 20 through mid-September
Finding the campground: From Escalante, travel east on Utah Highway 12 for about 1.0 mile to the turnoff for Hells Backbone Road (called 300 East here, and later Forest Road 153), which is on the left (north). You'll travel on paved road for the first 3.5 miles, then maintained gravel. After another 10 miles, you'll reach a fork in the road; Forest Road 153 continues to the right (north), while Forest Road 154 heads left (west). Keep right on FR 153, and you'll reach the campground turnoff in 4.6 miles. The turnoff is to the left (north) on Forest Road 145, a narrow dirt and gravel road. Travel 0.5 mile to the campground. Please note that this is a tents-only kind of place; sites are small and trailer turnaround space is nonexistent.

About the campground: As its name implies, this campground is set among blue spruce, with some aspen and ponderosa pine as well. You can use the site as a base from which to explore several nearby trails; anglers can fish for trout in a nearby stream.

Just west of the campground look for the Blue Springs Trail; it's 1.5 miles long. Other nearby trails include the Box Trail, about 0.5 mile southwest, along with the Jubilee Trail, Auger Hole Trail, and West Fork Trail.

44 Calf Creek: Grand Staircase–Escalante National Monument

Location: About 16 miles northeast of Escalante
Facilities: Fire grates, picnic tables, drinking water, and vault and flush toilets
Sites: 13
Fee: $
Elevation: 5,400 feet
Road conditions: Paved
Management: Bureau of Land Management, Escalante Interagency Office, P.O. Box 225, Escalante, UT 84726; (435) 826–5600; UT-Escalante@blm.gov
Reservations: None
Activities: Fishing, hiking, and picnicking
Season: Year-round
Finding the campground: From Escalante, travel southeast then northeast on scenic Utah Highway 12 for about 16 miles. A sign points the way to the campground entrance, which is on the left (west) side of the road; go 0.2 mile to the entrance.

About the campground: If you have a vehicle less than 25 feet long, you'll be able to indulge in the cottonwoods and oaks of this scenic campground, located in the much larger Grand Staircase–Escalante National Monument. Tucked into a canyon along Calf Creek, anglers can wet a line while hikers enjoy the trail to Lower Calf Falls. It's an interpretive trail, so with guide in

Calf Creek Falls at Grand Staircase–Escalante.

hand you can learn all about the native vegetation, see amazing pictographs and Indian ruins, and know that the gorgeous falls are 126 feet high.

45 Deer Creek: Grand Staircase–Escalante National Monument

Location: About 6 miles southeast of Boulder
Facilities: Fire grates, picnic tables, and vault toilets
Sites: 7
Fee: $
Elevation: 5,800 feet
Road conditions: Paved to the campground, then dirt
Management: Bureau of Land Management, Escalante Interagency Office, P.O. Box 225, Escalante, UT 84726; (435) 826–5600; UT-Escalante@blm.gov
Reservations: None
Activities: Fishing, hiking, and picnicking
Season: Year-round
Finding the campground: At the south end of Boulder, go east on Boulder-Bullfrog Scenic Road, also known as the Burr Trail. Though this portion of the road is paved, it is not recommended for trailer traffic due to numerous sharp curves. You'll reach the campground after 6.3 miles. Please note that a trailer turnaround is nonexistent.

About the campground: Located in the grand expanse of Grand Stair-case–Escalante National Monument, these small sites are set along Deer Creek, where there is fishing. A trailhead is just across the road; it leads south through Deer Creek Canyon.

46 Upper Pleasant Creek

Location: In the Dixie National Forest, approximately 17 miles southeast of Torrey
Facilities: Fire grates, picnic tables, drinking water, and vault toilets
Sites: 12
Fee: $
Elevation: 8,700 feet
Road conditions: Paved
Management: Escalante Ranger District, 755 West Main, P.O. Box 246, Escalante, UT 84726; (435) 826–5400
Reservations: None
Activities: Hiking, mountain biking, fishing, and picnicking
Restrictions: ATVs are not allowed
Season: May 20 through mid-September
Finding the campground: From Torrey, drive south on scenic Utah Highway 12 for 16.8 miles. You'll see the campground and turnoff on the left (east) side of the road.

About the campground: The upper portion of two side-by-side campgrounds (known as Upper and Lower Pleasant Creek), this campground is set in a forest of ponderosa pines. There's fishing at Pleasant Creek, as well as access to many trails nearby. Hikers should check out the Pleasant Creek Trailhead, which includes access to the Great Western Divide Trail. It's off UT 12, 0.4 mile to the north.

47 Lower Pleasant Creek

Location: In the Dixie National Forest, about 17 miles southeast of Torrey
Facilities: Fire grates, picnic tables, drinking water, and vault toilets
Sites: 5
Fee: $
Elevation: 8,700 feet
Road conditions: Paved
Management: Escalante Ranger District, 755 West Main, P.O. Box 246, Escalante, UT 84726; (435) 826–5400
Reservations: None
Activities: Hiking, mountain biking, fishing, and picnicking
Restrictions: ATVs are not allowed
Season: May 20 through mid-September
Finding the campground: From Torrey, drive south on scenic Utah Highway 12 for 16.9 miles. You'll see the campground and turnoff on the left (east) side of the road.

About the campground: The lower portion of two side-by-side campgrounds (known as Upper and Lower Pleasant Creek), this campground is set in a forest of ponderosa pines. Trailer turnaround is tight here—if your vehicle is longer than 20 feet, you should check out the Upper Pleasant Creek Campground. There's fishing at Pleasant Creek, as well as access to many trails nearby. Check out the Pleasant Creek Trailhead, which includes access to the Great Western Divide Trail; it's off UT 12, 0.5 mile to the north.

48 Oak Creek

Location: In the Dixie National Forest, approximately 18 miles south of Torrey
Facilities: Fire grates, picnic tables, drinking water, and vault toilets
Sites: 6
Fee: $ for single sites; $$ for double sites
Elevation: 8,800 feet
Road conditions: Paved
Management: Escalante Ranger District, 755 West Main, P.O. Box 246, Escalante, UT 84726; (435) 826–5400
Reservations: None
Activities: Fishing, mountain biking, hiking, and picnicking
Season: May 20 through September 20
Finding the campground: From Torrey, drive south on scenic Utah Highway 12 for 18 miles; turn left (east) at the campground sign and travel 0.1 mile to the campground.

About the campground: Small RVs (there's a 20-foot maximum here) should note that there's little room to turn around at the end of this campground, set in a forest of ponderosa pine, spruce, and aspen, Oak Creek provides music nearby. Hikers and bikers looking for a trail needn't look far; the High Ranger Trailhead is just across the street.

49 Lower Bowns

Location: In the Dixie National Forest, about 21 miles southeast of Torrey
Facilities: Pit toilets
Sites: Dispersed
Fee: None
Elevation: 7,400 feet
Road conditions: Dirt; not recommended for passenger vehicles
Management: Escalante Ranger District, 755 West Main, P.O. Box 246, Escalante, UT 84726; (435) 826–5400
Reservations: None.
Activities: Fishing, mountain biking, bird-watching, and picnicking
Season: May 20 through September 20
Finding the campground: From Torrey, drive south on scenic Utah Highway 12 for 17 miles to a turnoff for Lower Bowns Reservoir. Make a left (east) onto

Forest Road 181, a narrow dirt road that can be impassable in wet weather. Reach the reservoir in 3.8 miles.

About the campground: This is a tents-only type of place, because there is absolutely no room for trailers or motor homes to turn around. Sites are dispersed, shaded by pinyon pines, and embraced by the sagebrush found around the reservoir. The fishing for rainbow (and occasionally cutthroat) trout can be good; bird-watching is fun, too. A bike ride is described in the Falcon book *Mountain Biking Utah,* by Gregg Bromka.

50 Cedar Mesa: Capitol Reef National Park

Location: About 30 miles southeast of the visitor center
Facilities: Fire grates, picnic tables, and vault toilets
Sites: 5
Fee: None
Elevation: 5,400 feet
Road conditions: Dirt and sand; usually passable to passenger vehicles, but high-clearance vehicles are recommended. Road conditions change due to rain or snow and sometimes require a four-wheel-drive vehicle; check at the visitor center for current conditions.
Management: Capitol Reef National Park, HCR 70, Box 15, Torrey, UT 84775; (435) 425–3791; CARE_interpretation@nps.gov
Reservations: None
Activities: Hiking, photography, and picnicking
Season: Year-round
Finding the campground: From the visitor center, about 11 miles east of Torrey, continue east on Utah Highway 24 for 8.9 miles. Make a right, driving Notom-Bullfrog Road (it's paved at first, then turns to dirt and sand) for 21.1 miles. At this point, go right (west) on a short spur road leading to the campground.

About the campground: Excellent views of Red Canyon and the wide mesas east of Waterfold Mesa are yours from broad Cedar Mesa, where the campground is located. Tucked away in a forest of juniper trees, the campground provides access to Red Canyon. Travel both by trail and cross-country to the canyon and a huge amphitheater, which is partially surrounded by lofty cliffs of reddish orange Wingate sandstone.

51 McMillan Springs

Location: In the Henry Mountains, about 53 miles southwest of Hanksville
Facilities: Fire grates, picnic tables, and vault toilets
Sites: 10
Fee: $
Elevation: 8,400 feet
Road conditions: One-lane, dirt; high-clearance vehicles recommended
Management: Bureau of Land Management, Henry Mountain Field Station, P.O. Box 99, Hanksville, UT 84734; (435) 542–3461; UT-Hanksville@blm.gov

Reservations: None
Activities: Mountain biking and picnicking
Season: May through November
Finding the campground: From the junction of Utah Highway 24 and Notom-Bullfrog Road, about 28 miles west of Hanksville, head south on paved Notom-Bullfrog Road, which later turns to dirt and sand. Drive it about 8 miles to Sandy Ranch; head left (east) on a dirt road. A sign may point the way to McMillan Springs. Continue approximately 17 miles to the campground, merging onto Bull Creek Pass National Backcountry Byway a couple of miles prior to the campground. When you reach the byway, head left (northeast).

About the campground: McMillan Springs is a scenic campground set among a forest of lofty ponderosa pines. A local herd of bison hangs out in the area, making this a popular spot for wildlife watching. The Henry Mountains are home to one of the few free-roaming herds of bison in the continental U.S. Transplanted from Yellowstone National Park in 1941, the original herd of 18 now tops out at about 300 animals. Lucky visitors may also see mule deer, pronghorn antelope, bighorn sheep, elk, and mountain lions.

Though you can reach the campground by traveling to the Lonesome Beaver Campground and continuing another 10 miles or so, you'd have to wait until July to do this, because the 10,485-foot Bull Creek Pass is often closed by snow until then. Use the above route via Notom-Bullfrog Road when snow prevails.

52 Lonesome Beaver

Location: In the Henry Mountains, about 21 miles southwest of Hanksville
Facilities: Fire grates, picnic tables, and vault toilets
Sites: 5
Fee: $
Elevation: 8,300 feet
Road conditions: One-lane, dirt; winding with steep grades. High-clearance vehicles are recommended
Management: Bureau of Land Management, Henry Mountain Field Station, P.O. Box 99, Hanksville, UT 84734; (435) 542–3461; UT-Hanksville@blm.gov
Reservations: None
Activities: Hiking, mountain biking, and picnicking
Season: May through October
Finding the campground: From the junction of Utah Highway 24 and Henry Mountain Access Road (100 East) in Hanksville, head south on Henry Mountain Access Road. The road is paved for 0.4 mile, then turns to maintained gravel, and eventually deteriorates to a one-lane dirt road. As you climb in elevation, the road becomes winding and very steep. Trailers are not recommended; no doubt drivers would have trouble making some of the tight turns. Reach the campground after a total of 21.3 miles. You'll see the Dandelion Flat Picnic Area about 0.4 mile prior to the campground.

About the campground: There's lots of shade in this campground, with aspen, spruce, and pine all around. Bull Creek does a little singing near the camp, which is best suited for tenters.

This is a nice base for a classic Utah bike ride. This grueling, 20-mile loop is described in Gregg Bromka's book *Mountain Biking Utah.* You can also hike to the top of Mount Ellen from several areas, including Bull Creek Pass, about 4 miles farther. Please note, that the pass is at 10,485 feet and usually only open from early June through late October.

53 Dirty Devil River: Glen Canyon National Recreation Area

Location: About 44 miles southeast of Hanksville
Facilities: Chemical toilets
Sites: Dispersed
Fee: $
Elevation: 3,800 feet
Road conditions: One-lane, dirt
Management: Glen Canyon National Recreation Area, P.O. Box 1507, Page, AZ 86040-1507; (520) 608–6404; GLCA_CHVC@nps.gov
Reservations: None
Activities: Fishing, boating, water sports, swimming, picnicking, and photography
Season: Year-round
Finding the campground: From Hanksville, travel south then southeast on Utah Highway 95 for 43.8 miles.

About the campground: Several areas of dispersed, shadeless sites are found along the sandstone-blessed shores of the Dirty Devil River. There are magnificent views of the surrounding areas, as well as the chance to indulge in the water sport of your choice. Also, anglers may want to fish while photographers make lasting images of the place.

54 Starr Springs

Location: In the Henry Mountains, approximately 47 miles south of Hanksville
Facilities: Fire grates, picnic tables, and vault toilets
Sites: 12
Fee: $
Elevation: 6,300 feet
Road conditions: Maintained gravel (one-lane upon entering the campground)
Management: Bureau of Land Management, Henry Mountain Field Station, P.O. Box 99, Hanksville, UT 84734; (435) 542–3461; UT-Hanksville@blm.gov
Reservations: None
Activities: Hiking and picnicking
Season: April through October
Finding the campground: From the junction of Utah Highways 95 and 24 in Hanksville, head south on UT 95 for 25.8 miles. At this point, continue right (south) on paved Utah Highway 276 toward Bullfrog. Drive another 16.9 miles to the turnoff for Starr Springs Recreation Site and turn right (northwest) on the well-maintained gravel road for 3.9 miles to the campground.

About the campground: Situated in a forest of oak and juniper at the base of Mount Hillers, the campground provides access to the Panorama Knoll Nature Trail, which is across from the fee station and picnic area. A short loop trail gives hikers access to a viewpoint. On another note, about 0.5 mile prior to reaching the campground, there are old ranch ruins for visitors to see and photograph, though you shouldn't pass beyond the fenced enclosure.

55 Bullfrog North: Glen Canyon National Recreation Area

Location: About 7 miles northwest of the north entrance station near Bullfrog
Facilities: Vault and chemical toilets
Sites: Dispersed
Fee: $
Elevation: 3,800 feet
Road conditions: One-lane, dirt
Management: Glen Canyon National Recreation Area, P.O. Box 1507, Page, AZ 86040-1507; (520) 608–6404; GLCA_CHVC@nps.gov
Reservations: None
Activities: Fishing, boating, water sports, swimming, picnicking, and photography
Season: Year-round
Finding the campground: From the north entrance fee station, about 63 miles south of Hanksville, travel north on Utah Highway 276 for 3.1 miles, then make a left (west) onto Burr Trail Scenic Backway, a paved road. Drive it 3.5 miles to the campground turnoff on the left (southwest). Continue 0.4 mile to the campground.

About the campground: There are many dispersed, though shadeless, sites along this inlet of Bullfrog Bay. The views are wonderful from here, and there are many opportunities to engage in the water sport of your choice. The fishing is also good: The lake is known for its largemouth, smallmouth, and striped bass, as well as crappie and walleye.

56 Bullfrog South: Glen Canyon National Recreation Area

Location: About 6 miles northwest of the north entrance station near Bullfrog
Facilities: Vault and chemical toilets
Sites: Dispersed
Fee: $
Elevation: 3,800 feet
Road conditions: One-lane, dirt
Management: Glen Canyon National Recreation Area, P.O. Box 1507, Page, AZ 86040-1507; (520) 608–6404; GLCA_CHVC@nps.gov
Reservations: None
Activities: Fishing, boating, water sports, swimming, picnicking, and photography
Season: Year-round

Finding the campground: From the north entrance fee station, about 63 miles south of Hanksville, travel north on Utah Highway 276 for 3.1 miles, then make a left (west) onto Burr Trail Scenic Backway, a paved road. Drive it 2 miles to the campground turnoff on the left (southwest). Continue 0.7 mile to the campground.

About the campground: Dispersed, shadeless sites are abundant along this inlet of Bullfrog Bay, where the views are wonderful. There are ample opportunities to indulge in the water sport of your choice. The fishing is good, too: The lake is known for its largemouth, smallmouth, and striped bass, as well as crappie and walleye.

57 Stanton Creek: Glen Cayon National Recreation Area

Location: About 2 miles southeast of the north entrance station near Bullfrog
Facilities: Boat launch, vault and chemical toilets
Sites: Dispersed
Fee: $
Elevation: 3,800 feet
Road conditions: One-lane, dirt
Management: Glen Canyon National Recreation Area, P.O. Box 1507, Page, AZ 86040-1507; (520) 608–6404; GLCA_CHVC@nps.gov
Reservations: None
Activities: Fishing, boating, water sports, swimming, picnicking, and photography
Season: Year-round
Finding the campground: From the north entrance fee station, about 63 miles south of Hanksville, travel south on Utah Highway 276 for 0.2 mile, then make a left (east) on a maintained gravel road that turns to dirt. Continue another 2 miles to the campground.

About the campground: Dispersed, shadeless sites are abundant along this inlet, across from Halls Crossing. From here, campers enjoy fishing for various game fish, such as largemouth, smallmouth, and striped bass. Broad bays offer plenty of space for waterskiing and for the houseboats that ply the lovely waters of Lake Powell.

58 Bullfrog: Glen Canyon National Recreation Area

Location: About 2 miles southwest of the north entrance station near Bullfrog
Facilities: Fire grates, picnic tables, flush toilets, sewage disposal station, public telephone, soda pop machine, and drinking water; a boat launch is nearby.
Sites: 85
Fee: $$
Elevation: 3,900 feet
Road conditions: Paved
Management: Glen Canyon National Recreation Area, P.O. Box 1507, Page, AZ 86040-1507; (520) 608-6404; GLCA_CHVC@nps.gov

Reservations: None
Activities: Fishing, boating, water sports, swimming, picnicking, and photography
Season: Year-round
Finding the campground: From the north entrance fee station, about 63 miles south of Hanksville, travel south on Utah Highway 276 for 1.2 miles to the visitor center. Continue straight (southwest) for another 0.3 mile to the campground entrance, which is on the left (south).

About the campground: An assortment of deciduous trees provides some shade in the campground, which is near a boat ramp and not too far from the marina where there are boat rentals, a store, and a fast-food restaurant. There's also a ferry: The *John Atlantic Burr* travels between Bullfrog and Halls Crossing and saves 145 road miles. Lake Powell visitors have plenty to do— water sports, boating, fishing, and photography are perhaps the most popular activities.

59 Bullfrog RV: Glen Canyon National Recreation Area

Location: About 2 miles southwest of the north entrance station near Bullfrog
Facilities: Fire grates, picnic tables, flush toilets, showers, electric, water, and sewer hookups, sewage disposal station, boat ramp, public telephone, soda pop machine, and drinking water
Sites: 24
Fee: $$$ to $$$$
Elevation: 3,900 feet
Road conditions: Paved
Management: Glen Canyon National Recreation Area, P.O. Box 1507, Page, AZ 86040-1507; (520) 608–6404; GLCA_CHVC@nps.gov
Reservations: None
Activities: Fishing, boating, water sports, swimming, picnicking, and photography
Season: Year-round
Finding the campground: From the north entrance fee station, about 63 miles south of Hanksville, travel south on Utah Highway 276 for 1.2 miles to the visitor center. At the corner, turn right (west) toward the marina; you'll see the RV campground a short distance down on your right.

About the campground: Full hookups, hot showers, and some shade trees will delight those who like plenty of amenities. On a hill overlooking the lovely waters of Lake Powell, the campground is near the marina, where campers can sign up for a boat tour of the lake. If you have your own boat, you'll find a boat ramp nearby. There's also a ferry: The *John Atlantic Burr* travels between Bullfrog and Halls Crossing and saves 145 road miles. Activities abound here, with water sports, boating, fishing, and photography perhaps the most popular.

60 | Lone Rock: Glen Canyon National Recreation Area

Location: About 63 miles east of Kanab
Facilities: Vault toilets
Sites: Undeveloped beach camping; large RVs are okay
Fee: $
Elevation: 3,700 feet
Road conditions: Paved to the beach, then sand
Management: Glen Canyon National Recreation Area, P.O. Box 1507, Page, AZ 86040-1507; (520) 608–6404; GLCA_CHVC@nps.gov
Reservations: None
Activities: Boating, swimming, waterskiing, fishing, photography, and picnicking
Season: Year-round
Finding the campground: From Kanab, drive northeast on U.S. Highway 89 for 62.7 miles, then turn left (east) onto Lone Rock Road. The beach and campground are 2 miles farther.

About the campground: Dispersed camping is the norm here at Lone Rock Beach, which is along the southwest shore of Wahweap Bay at Lake Powell. It's a beautiful spot, and whereas the place is primitive, there are all sorts of amenities at Wahweap Resort, about 5 miles southeast across the Arizona border.

61 | White House: Grand Staircase–Escalante National Monument

Location: About 45 miles east of Kanab
Facilities: Fire grates, picnic tables, and vault toilets
Sites: 5
Fee: $
Elevation: 4,400 feet
Road conditions: Gravel and sand
Management: Bureau of Land Management, Kanab Field Office, 318 North First East, Kanab, UT 84741; (435) 644–4600; UT-Kanab@blm.gov
Reservations: None
Activities: Hiking, photography, and picnicking
Season: Year-round
Finding the campground: From Kanab, drive east on U.S. Highway 89 for 42.6 miles. At this point, turn right (south) at the sign for Paria Canyon–Vermillion Cliffs. There's a fee station and ranger station just after you turn. Continue 2 miles on the combination gravel and sand road to the campground. You'll have to park your vehicle and walk in to each site.

About the campground: Tucked up against vermilion cliffs, this campground is set in a beautiful spot and makes a good base from which to explore the area. Better yet, spend several days backpacking into Paria Canyon and be entranced by numerous narrow, twisting slot canyons. Please note that if you want to backpack, you'll have to obtain a hiking permit. Contact the managing agency for more information.

The Painted Hills of Paria at sunset.

Canyonlands

Utah is an outdoor kind of place, and the Canyonlands travel region is no exception when it comes to enjoying the great out-of-doors. There are many favored activities; some of the more popular use camera equipment, mountain bikes, rock climbing paraphernalia, hiking boots, fishing poles, rafts, kayaks, canoes, powerboats, and off-road vehicles.

Photographers will find a multitude of scenes worthy of their film, while mountain bikers will enjoy a wide range of terrain, including slickrock, a particular favorite. Rock climbers will find everything from traditional finger crack and crack climbs to bolted slab friction, while hikers will enjoy just as much variety in trails—or even more. In addition, anglers will find many a fine fishing hole; rafters; kayakers, and canoeists will no doubt thrill to the likes of the Green, Colorado, and San Juan Rivers; boaters will enjoy the twisting canyons of Lake Powell; and off-road enthusiasts will discover many a track to follow.

In Canyonlands, visitors find it all. The countryside offers up everything from desert to mountains, narrow slot canyons, wide vistas, lengthy Lake Powell, and all things in between. Part of the geologic region known as the Colorado Plateau, it's a paradise for photographers and other artists; in fact, it's a paradise of sorts for all who come to visit.

Grand and San Juan Counties make up Canyonlands, the third largest of Utah's nine travel regions. Scattered over 11,414 square miles, the region is bordered on the north by Dinosaurland, on the west by the Green River, on the east and south by the respective states of Colorado and Arizona.

A total of twenty-nine public campgrounds features sites ranging from the lofty realms of the LaSal and Abajo Mountain, to the desert oasis at Sand Island (it's located on the banks of the San Juan River), and the natural-bridge-blessed kingdom of Natural Bridges National Monument. In addition, there are wonderful views from Dead Horse Point State Park, a maze of hiking trails and a bevy of climbing routes in and near both Canyonlands and Arches National Parks, and the water-sports-oriented waters of Lake Powell and the Colorado River. Ancient Indian ruins are common in this part of the country, with Hovenweep National Monument and Natural Bridges National Monument particularly nice spots from which to easily explore them. All of the campsites are managed by either the National Park Service, the Bureau of Land Management, the U.S. National Forest Service, or the state park system.

The region can be visited at any time of year, though you'll find some of the higher campgrounds closed come winter. Still, you can always camp low and go high to cross-country ski in the LaSal and Abajo Mountains. Of course, even some of the lower-elevation campgrounds have the water turned off during winter months. Fortunately, camp fees are usually reduced, thus this is a good time to save money and avoid the summer crowds. Speaking of crowds, most of the national park campgrounds fill early from about March through October; plan accordingly.

CANYONLANDS

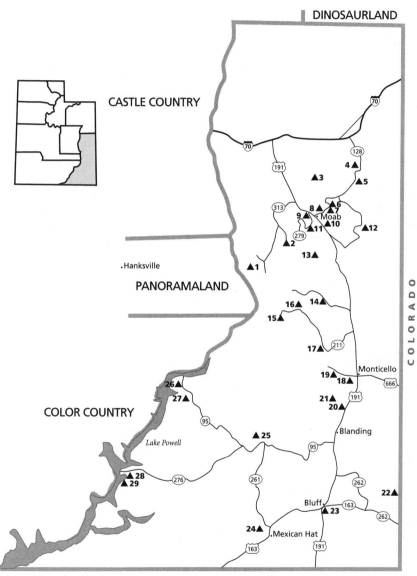

DINOSAURLAND

CASTLE COUNTRY

DINOSAURLAND

70

128

191

4 ▲

▲3

▲5

313

8 ▲▲6

▲7

9 ▲ Moab

▲10

▲11

279

2 ▲

▲12

13 ▲

. Hanksville

▲1

PANORAMALAND

16 ▲ 14 ▲

15 ▲

17 ▲ 211

19 ▲ 18 ▲ Monticello

26 ▲

27 ▲

21 ▲ 20 ▲ 191

COLOR COUNTRY

95

▲ 25 Blanding

Lake Powell

95

28 ▲ 29 ▲

276

261

262

22 ▲

Bluff 163

23 ▲

24 ▲ . Mexican Hat

262

163

191

COLORADO

ARIZONA

		Group sites	RV sites	Total sites	Max. RV length	Hookups	Toilets	Showers	Drinking water	Dump station	Pets	Wheelchair	Recreation	Fee($)	Season	Can reserve	Stay limit
1	Willow Flat		•	12	23		V				•		MHO	$			7
2	Dead Horse Point S.P.	•	•	22		E	F		•	•	•	•	H	$$		•	14
3	Devils Garden	•	•	56	35		F		•		•	•	CHM	$$			7
4	Dewey Bridge		•	7	34		V				•		HMOLB	$			14
5	Hittle Bottom		•	12	20		V				•		LBOM	$			14
6	Big Bend Rec. Site	•	•	22	30		V				•		OHM	$			14
7	Hal Canyon/Oak Grove		•	18	20		V				•		OHM	$			14
8	Goose Island	•	•	18	30		V				•		OHM	$			14
9	Jay Cee Park			6			V				•		CHM	$			14
10	Sand Flats Rec. Area	•	•	147	30		P				•		CMOH	$			14
11	Kane Creek			37			V				•		MCH	$			14
12	Warner Lake	•	•	20	25		P		•		•		MHFR	$	June–Oct.		16
13	Hatch Point		•	10	25		V		•		•		HM	$$			14
14	Wind Whistle	•	•	18	20		V		•		•		H	$$			14
15	Squaw Flat	•	•	29	30		FV		•		•		HMCO	$$			7
16	Hamburger Rock		•	7	25		P				•		CHM				14
17	Newspaper Rock Rec. Site			*			V				•		CH				14
18	Dalton Springs		•	17	30		V		•		•		HF	$	Memorial–Labor Day		16
19	Buckboard	•	•	12	25		V		•		•		HF	$	Memorial–Labor Day		16
20	Devil's Canyon	•	•	33	30		V		•		•		H	$$	Memorial–Labor Day		16
21	Nizhoni	•	•	23	40		V		•		•	•	HF	$	Memorial–Labor Day		16
22	Hovenweep N.M.		•	31	25		F		•		•	•	HM	$$			7
23	Sand Island		•	23			V				•		BLF	$			14
24	Goosenecks State Res.		•	4			V				•						14
25	Natural Bridges N.M.		•	13	26		V		•		•		H	$$			7
26	Hite		•	*			F		•	•	•		SBFL	$			14
27	Farley Canyon		•	*			CV				•		SBF	$			14
28	Halls Crossing		•	65	35		F		•	•	•		SBFL	$$$			14
29	Halls Crossing RV		•	32	35	WES	F		•	•	•		SBFL	$$$$			14

* Dispersed Camping—no designated sites **Hookups:** W = Water E = Electric S = Sewer **Toilets:** F = Flush V = Vault P = Pit C= Chemical **Recreation:** H = Hiking S = Swimming F = Fishing B = Boating L = Boat Launch O = Off-highway driving R = Horseback Riding C = Rock Climbing M = Mountain Biking **Maximum Trailer/RV length** given in feet. **Stay Limit** given in days. **Fee** given in dollars. If no entry under **Season,** campgound is open all year. If no entry under **Fee,** camping is free.

For more information contact the Canyonlands Travel Region North in Moab at P.O. Box 550, Moab, UT 84532; (435) 259-1370 or (800) 635-6622; fax (435) 259-1376; pseep@grand.state.ut.us. You can also contact the Canyonlands Travel Region South in Monticello at P.O. Box 490, Monticello, UT 84535; (435) 587-3235 or (800) 574-4386; or fax (435) 587-2425; jrbryan@state.ut.us.

1 Willow Flat: Canyonlands National Park

Location: About 9 miles southwest of the Island in the Sky Entrance Station
Facilities: Picnic tables, fire grates, and vault toilets
Sites: 12
Fee: $
Elevation: 6,200 feet
Road conditions: Gravel
Management: Canyonlands National Park, 2282 South West Resource Boulevard, Moab, UT 84532-3298; (435) 719-2313; canyoninfo@nps.gov
Reservations: None
Activities: Hiking, mountain biking, off-highway driving, photography, and picnicking
Season: Year-round
Finding the campground: From Moab, drive northwest on U.S. Highway 191 for about 10 miles, then make a left (southwest) onto Utah Highway 313. A sign points the way to the national park, as well as Dead Horse Point State Park. Continue southwest on the paved road for 20.4 miles to the fee station.

About the campground: Juniper and pinyon pine decorate this small campground, a good place from which to explore the Island in the Sky section of Canyonlands. A number of trails leads to striking vistas, delicate arches, and an assortment of geologic wonders. There's also a great mountain bike loop that travels through a section of the park. Check out Jughandle Loop in Gregg Bromka's book *Mountain Biking Utah*. Please note that there is no water in this section of the park.

Island in the Sky is the best place to go for overwhelming vistas. On this broad, level mesa wedged between the Green and Colorado Rivers, you'll see not only what's close by but also the distant horizon about 100 miles away. Three jagged mountain ranges loom in the distance; to the east you'll see the LaSals, to the south, the Abajos, and to the southwest, the Henrys.

2 Dead Horse Point State Park

Location: About 31 miles southwest of Moab
Facilities: Covered picnic tables, electric hookups, fire grates, drinking water, flush toilets, and a sewage disposal station
Sites: 22
Fee: $$
Elevation: 6,000 feet
Road conditions: Paved

Management: Dead Horse Point State Park, P.O. Box 609, Moab, UT 84532-0609; (435) 259-2614

Reservations: In the Salt Lake area, call (801) 322-3770; elsewhere, (800) 322-3770; fee

Activities: Hiking, photography, and picnicking

Season: Year-round

Finding the campground: From Moab, drive northwest on U.S. Highway 191 for about 10 miles, then make a left (southwest) onto Utah Highway 313. A sign points the way to the state park, as well as to Canyonlands National Park. After 14.7 miles, there's a junction to the state park. Go left (east) for 6.5 miles on paved UT 313 to the fee station. The campground is 0.25 mile beyond. There's also a group site (reservations required) about 1.5 miles prior to the fee station.

About the campground: Juniper and pinyon pine grace this lovely campground, with its nice views and footpath leading 2.5 miles to Dead Horse Point. The view from the point, 2,000 feet above the Colorado River, is breathtaking. Many of Canyonlands' sculptured pinnacles and buttes are visible from this peninsula of rock set atop sandstone. When taking in the view, you'll probably notice the unnaturally blue waters to the east; those are mine tailings.

The folks at the state park say water is at a premium here. It must be trucked in from Moab, so please use it sparingly. In addition to twenty-one single sites, there's a group site with a maximum of thirty-two people. There is also one wheelchair-accessible site, available by reservation only. From May through September, don't miss the nightly interpretive programs in the visitor center amphitheater.

3 Devils Garden: Arches National Park

Location: About 18 miles north of the entrance station and visitor center

Facilities: Picnic tables, fire grates, drinking water, and flush toilets

Sites: 56

Fee: $$

Elevation: 5,000 feet

Road conditions: Paved

Management: Arches National Park, P.O. Box 907, Moab, UT 84532-0907; (435) 719-2299 or TTD (435) 719-2319; archinfo@nps.gov

Reservations: For group reservations mail request to National Park Service, Reservation Office, 2282 South West Resource Boulevard, Moab, UT 84532; fax (435) 259-4285

Activities: Hiking, rock climbing, mountain biking, photography, and picnicking.

Season: Year-round

Finding the campground: From the visitor center, about 5 miles northeast of Moab, travel north through the park for about 18 miles

About the campground: Two group and fifty-four single sites usually fill by early morning here at Arches National Park, a wonderful place for hiking,

Visitors at the Double O Arch in Arches National Park.

mountain biking, rock climbing, and scenic driving. More than 2,000 cataloged arches vary in size; some have a mere 3-foot opening, the minimum considered an arch, while the longest, Landscape Arch, measures 306 feet from base to base.

Flush toilets and water are available from mid-March through mid-October. In winter fees are reduced, chemical toilets are the norm, and you'll have to get water at the visitor center. Campfire programs are offered in season at the amphitheater.

4 Dewey Bridge

Location: About 31 miles northeast of Moab
Facilities: Picnic tables, fire grates, vault toilets, and a boat launch
Sites: 7
Fee: $
Elevation: 4,000 feet

Road conditions: Gravel
Management: Bureau of Land Management, Moab Field Office, 82 East Dogwood, Moab, UT 84532; (435) 259–6111; UT-Moab@blm.gov
Reservations: None
Activities: Hiking, mountain biking, boating, off-highway driving, and picnicking
Season: Year-round
Finding the campground: From the junction of U.S. Highway 191 and Utah Highway 128, about 2 miles north of Moab, drive northeast on UT 128 for about 29 miles.

About the campground: Though you won't find much, there is some shade at this campground, with a mammoth cottonwood for those lucky enough to select the site close to it. The Colorado River flows nearby, with a boat ramp providing access for kayakers, rafters, and canoeists.

Mountain bikers, horseback riders, ATVers, and motorcyclists will be interested in the Kokopelli Trail, which passes through here. About 140 miles long, it crosses the old Dewey Bridge seen from the campground. Built in 1916, the bridge is just a small part of the trail (a series of old roads and some singletrack), which extends from Moab to Loma, Colorado.

5 Hittle Bottom

Location: About 25 miles northeast of Moab
Facilities: Picnic tables, fire grates, vault toilets, and a boat launch
Sites: 12
Fee: $
Elevation: 4,000 feet
Road conditions: Gravel
Management: Bureau of Land Management, Moab Field Office, 82 East Dogwood, Moab, UT 84532; (435) 259–6111; UT-Moab@blm.gov
Reservations: None
Activities: Boating, mountain biking, off-highway driving, and picnicking
Season: Year-round
Finding the campground: From the junction of U.S. Highway 191 and Utah Highway 128, about 2 miles north of Moab, drive northeast on UT 128 for about 23 miles.

About the campground: Cottonwoods and tamarisk shade this campground, while the muddy Colorado River flows nearby. A boat ramp provides access for kayakers, rafters, and canoeists who wish to travel down this wonderful water-carved canyon.

6 Big Bend Recreation Site

Location: About 9 miles northeast of Moab
Facilities: Picnic tables, fire grates, and vault toilets
Sites: 22

Fee: $
Elevation: 4,000 feet
Road conditions: Gravel
Management: Bureau of Land Management, Moab Field Office, 82 East Dogwood, Moab, UT 84532; (435) 259–6111; UT-Moab@blm.gov
Reservations: None except for the group site; call (435) 259–6111 for reservations
Activities: Hiking, mountain biking, off-highway driving, and picnicking
Season: Year-round
Finding the campground: From the junction of U.S. Highway 191 and Utah Highway 128, about 2 miles northwest of Moab, drive northeast on UT 128 for an additional 7.4 miles.

About the campground: Located along the Colorado Riverway, a colorful medley of towering sandstone spires, water-carved canyons, and striking cliffs, this campground has both single sites and a group site (the latter is available by reservation only).

Cottonwoods and oaks offer a limited amount of shade, with the Colorado River, a popular place for canoeing, kayaking, and rafting from late spring through fall, close by.

The Porcupine Rim Bike Trail starts here (or ends, depending on which direction you choose to bicycle), and there's a beach with a cement ramp for wheelchair access, too.

7 Hal Canyon/Oak Grove

Location: About 9 miles northeast of Moab
Facilities: Picnic tables, fire grates, and vault toilets
Sites: 18
Fee: $
Elevation: 4,000 feet
Road conditions: Gravel
Management: Bureau of Land Management, Moab Field Office, 82 East Dogwood, Moab, UT 84532; (435) 259–6111; UT-Moab@blm.gov
Reservations: None
Activities: Hiking, mountain biking, off-highway driving, and picnicking
Season: Year-round
Finding the campground: From the junction of U.S. Highway 191 and Utah Highway 128, about 2 miles northwest of Moab, drive northeast on UT 128 for about 7 more miles.

About the campground: Because Hal Canyon and Oak Grove are similar in appearance and a mere 0.3 mile apart, I've listed the two campgrounds together. Hal Canyon offers eleven sites and some shade among oaks and tamarisk. Oak Grove offers seven sites in the same kind of setting. RVers beware: There is no trailer turnaround space at Oak Grove.

Both campgrounds are located along the Colorado Riverway, a potpourri of picturesque cliffs, river-carved canyons, and towering sandstone spires. The river is a popular place for rafting, kayaking, and canoeing from late spring through early fall.

8 Goose Island

Location: About 3 miles north of Moab
Facilities: Picnic tables, fire grates, and vault toilets
Sites: 18
Fee: $
Elevation: 4,000 feet
Road conditions: Gravel
Management: Bureau of Land Management, Moab Field Office, 82 East Dogwood, Moab, UT 84532; (435) 259-6111; UT-Moab@blm.gov
Reservations: None
Activities: Hiking, mountain biking, off-highway driving, and picnicking
Season: Year-round
Finding the campground: From the junction of U.S. Highway 191 and Utah Highway 128, about 2 miles north of Moab, drive northeast on UT 128 for an additional 1.4 miles.

About the campground: There's a group site and room for RVs at this Colorado River camp, with tamarisk and cottonwood trees providing some shade. Located along the Colorado Riverway, a scenic blend of lofty spires, river-carved canyons, and colorful cliffs, this is a favorite place for kayakers, rafters, and canoeists. Look for water enthusiasts in the spring through early fall.

9 Jay Cee Park

Location: About 6 miles southwest of Moab
Facilities: Picnic tables, fire grates, and vault toilets
Sites: 6
Fee: $
Elevation: 4,000 feet
Road conditions: Paved to the campground, then gravel
Management: Bureau of Land Management, Moab Field Office, 82 East Dogwood, Moab, UT 84532; (435) 259-6111; UT-Moab@blm.gov
Reservations: None
Activities: Hiking, rock climbing, mountain biking, and picnicking
Season: Year-round
Finding the campground: From the junction of U.S. Highway 191 and Utah Highway 279 (Potash Road), about 2 miles north of Moab, drive southwest on UT 279 for about 4 miles to the campground.

About the campground: Six walk-in sites are offered here, along with the Portal Trail. It climbs 1,000 feet and offers great views of the surrounding area, with distant views to the LaSal Mountains.

If you're looking for a wonderful place to climb, head southwest from the campground. There are more than a hundred routes along Wall Street, where climbers can work routes ranging from easy to difficult. It's also a grand place from which spectators can watch climbers scaling the vertical wall. While traveling along the highway, be sure to look for prehistoric rock art and dinosaur tracks. You can see both along the way.

10 | Sands Flats Recreation Area

Location: About 3 miles east of Moab
Facilities: Picnic tables, fire grates, and pit toilets
Sites: 147
Fee: $
Elevation: 4,500 feet
Road conditions: Gravel
Management: Bureau of Land Management, Moab Field Office, 82 East Dogwood, Moab, UT 84532; (435) 259–6111; UT-Moab@blm.gov
Reservations: None
Activities: Hiking, rock climbing, mountain biking, off-highway driving, and picnicking
Season: Year-round
Finding the campground: From the junction of Main and Center in Moab, go east on Center for 0.5 mile, then turn right (south) onto 400 East. After another 0.4 mile, turn left (east) onto Millcreek Drive. You'll reach a fork in 0.6 mile; keep left (east) on unsigned Sand Flats Road. A sign reading SLICKROCK BIKE TRAIL points the way. Reach the entrance station after an additional 1.6 miles.

About the campground: Sand Flats Recreation Area is comprised of several clusters of campsites, as well as individual sites, spread out along several miles of slickrock, sage, and wonderful views. Because Clusters A and E are gravel and the others can be quite sandy, I recommend that RVs head to A and E.

The Moab Slickrock Bike Trail is a challenging test for mountain bikers. Porcupine Pine Rim is also a must-do. Both rides are listed in *Mountain Biking Utah,* by Gregg Bromka.

11 | Kane Creek

Location: From 3 to 8 miles southwest of Moab
Facilities: Fire rings and vault toilets
Sites: 37
Fee: $
Elevation: 4,000 feet
Road conditions: Gravel
Management: Bureau of Land Management, Moab Field Office, 82 East Dogwood, Moab, UT 84532; (435) 259–6111; UT-Moab@blm.gov
Reservations: None
Activities: Hiking, rock climbing, mountain biking, and picnicking
Season: Year-round

Finding the campground: From the junction of Main (U.S. Highway 191) and Kane Creek Boulevard in Moab, head west on Kane Creek Boulevard. Five small campgrounds are found from 2.9 miles to 8.1 miles up the road.

About the campground: Five campgrounds—Kings Bottom, Moonflower Canyon, Spring Site, Hunter Canyon, and Echo Canyon—exist in the Kane Creek area. The road parallels the Colorado River and is paved for the first 4.7 miles; then it turns to gravel.

Kings Bottom offers seven sites, Moonflower Canyon has eight walk-in sites, while Spring Site has four walk-in sites, but no toilet. The nearest toilet is 1 mile away at Hunters Canyon, where there are nine sites and a trailhead to Hunters Canyon. The last campground up the canyon is Echo Canyon, which offers nine sites.

The area is a wonderful place for outdoor enthusiasts, with some nice climbs, hikes, and mountain bike rides just waiting for those who enjoy the great out-of-doors. Hunters Canyon offers a nice hike up the canyon, with an arch and other rock formations visible along the way. Continue at least 3 miles up the canyon and you'll see a wonderful hanging garden complete with maidenhair fern.

12 Warner Lake

Location: In the Manti—La Sal National Forest, about 28 miles southeast of Moab
Facilities: Picnic tables, fire grates, drinking water, pit toilets, and a cabin that must be reserved
Sites: 20
Fee: $
Elevation: 9,400 feet
Road conditions: Gravel
Management: Moab Ranger District, 2290 South West Resource Boulevard, Moab, UT 84532; (435) 259–7155
Reservations: Call (435) 259–7155 to reserve the cabin
Activities: Fishing, hiking, mountain biking, horseback riding, and picnicking
Season: June through October
Finding the campground: From the junction of Main and Center in Moab, go east on Center for 0.5 mile, then turn right (south) onto 400 East. After another 0.4 mile, head left (east) onto Millcreek Drive, staying on it as it curves and heads southeast to a four-way stop in 3.7 miles. (Please note that en route the road will change to Spanish Valley Road.) Stay straight (southeast) on the paved road, known as the La Sal Mountain Loop Road, which winds around to the northeast and eventually turns to gravel after an additional 16.3 miles. Proceed another 0.7 mile on gravel, then 1.3 miles on pavement to the campground turnoff, which is on the right (east). Drive an additional 5.1 miles on a gravel road to the campground.

About the campground: Huge aspens grace this lovely campground, with its wonderful view of Warner Lake and Haystack Mountain in the background.

There are a couple of trails in the area: Miners Basin Foot Trail and the Trans Mountain Trail. A cute cabin is available by reservation only. Three Lakes and Burro Pass are mountain bike rides that you can enjoy from Warner Lake. For more information, read *Mountain Biking Utah,* by Gregg Bromka.

13 Hatch Point: Canyon Rims Recreation Area

Location: About 45 miles northwest of Monticello
Facilities: Picnic tables, fire grates, drinking water (though none is available in winter), and vault toilets
Sites: 10
Fee: $$
Elevation: 5,900 feet
Road conditions: Maintained gravel
Management: Bureau of Land Management, Moab Field Office, 82 East Dogwood, Moab, UT 84532; (435) 259–6111; UT-Moab@blm.gov
Reservations: None
Activities: Wildlife-watching, picnicking, hiking, mountain biking
Restrictions: ATVs are not allowed
Season: Year-round
Finding the campground: From Monticello, drive north on paved U.S. Highway 191 for 20.5 miles to a turnoff on the left (west) for both the Needles and Anticline Overlooks and the Canyon Rims Recreation Area. Take the paved road for 15.1 miles to a Y. The left (west) fork leads to Needles Overlook; you should keep right (north) on a maintained gravel road for another 8.4 miles to a road heading right (east). Take this 1mile to the campground.

About the campground: Juniper and pinyon pine decorate this scenic campground set on a high mesa with wonderful views of the LaSal Mountains to the east and a broad mesa below and to the north. If you're looking for wildlife, you might see pronghorn antelope, mule deer, peregrine falcons, and collared lizards. This is an excellent base for hikers and mountain bikers, who will find plenty to do in the area. The campground fee is reduced from November through March when the water is shut off.

14 Wind Whistle: Canyon Rims Recreation Area

Location: About 26 miles northwest of Monticello
Facilities: Picnic tables, fire grates, drinking water (though none is available in winter), and vault toilets
Sites: 18
Fee: $$
Elevation: 6,000 feet
Road conditions: Paved, then gravel in the campground
Management: Bureau of Land Management, Moab Field Office, 82 East Dogwood, Moab, UT 84532; (435) 259–6111; UT-Moab@blm.gov
Reservations: For group sites only, call (435) 259–6111; fee
Activities: Hiking, wildlife watching, and picnicking

Restrictions: ATVs are not allowed
Season: Year-round
Finding the campground: From Monticello, drive north on paved U.S. Highway 191 for 20.5 miles to a turnoff on the left (west) for both the Needles and Anticline Overlooks and the Canyon Rims Recreation Area. Drive west on this paved road for 5.8 miles to the campground.

About the campground: Juniper and pinyon pine decorate this scenic campground, tucked up near the mouth of a canyon on a high mesa with nice views. There's also a group site, though it's available by reservation only. A nature trail begins at the group site. Wildlife-watchers should look for mule deer, which are plentiful, as well as pronghorn antelope, peregrine falcons, collared lizards, and a whole lot more. This is an excellent base for hikers and mountain bikers, who will find plenty to do in the area. From November through March the fee is reduced, because the water is shut off.

15 Squaw Flat: Canyonlands National Park

Location: 3.5 miles west of Needles Entrance Station
Facilities: Picnic tables, fire grates, drinking water (though none is available in winter), and flush and vault toilets
Sites: 29
Fee: $$
Elevation: 5,100 feet
Road conditions: Paved
Management: Canyonlands National Park, 2282 South West Resource Boulevard, Moab, UT 84532-3298; (435) 719–2313; canyoninfo@nps.gov
Reservations: For group sites only, fax (435) 259–4285; fee. Or you can write to Reservations Office, 2282 South West Resource Boulevard, Moab, UT 84532.
Activities: Rock climbing, mountain biking, off-highway driving, hiking, photography, and picnicking
Season: Year-round; water is shut off in winter
Finding the campground: From the Needles Entrance Station, drive past the visitor center, located 0.4 mile from the entrance station, for a total of 3.5 miles to Campground A. Campground B is another 0.3 mile down the road.

About the campground: A few trees provide some shade, as do the various rock formations, at both of these campgrounds. Larger RVs should try for a space at Campground A, which will hold longer rigs (maximum length about 30 feet). In addition to the twenty-six single sites, there are three group sites. Split Top, Wooden Shoe, and Squaw Flat need to be reserved in advance; call for group fees.

Activities abound in the area. Though mountain bikes are not permitted on any of the trails, there are roads for bicycling. Four-wheel-drive vehicles can take advantage of the jeep trails. There are also multitudes of trails to hike, with one of the most popular leading to the green realms and magnificent Needle formations in and around Chesler Park. Though the Cedar Mesa sandstone in the Needles is soft and unsuitable for rock climbing, there are places to climb on the way into the park.

16 Hamburger Rock

Location: About 43 miles northwest of Monticello
Facilities: Picnic tables, fire grates, and pit toilets
Sites: 7
Fee: None
Elevation: 4,900 feet
Road conditions: Dirt
Management: Bureau of Land Management, Monticello Field Office, 435 North Main, P.O. Box 7, Monticello, UT 84535; (435) 587–1500; UT-Monticello@blm.gov

Campsite at Hamburger Rock.

Reservations: None
Activities: Rock climbing, mountain biking, hiking, and picnicking
Season: Year-round
Finding the campground: From Monticello, drive north on paved U.S. Highway 191 for 13.7 miles; at this point, head west on Utah Highway 211, a paved Scenic Byway. Continue another 29 miles to a dirt road on your right. A sign points the way to Lockhart Basin and Hurrah Pass. Proceed another 1.2 miles to the campground.

About the campground: Located 4 miles from Canyonlands National Park, sites at this campground sit around a huge rock appropriately named Hamburger. It really does resemble a hamburger, as do many other rocks found in the area.

If you don't mind the dirt and dust, this is a good place from which to make a base camp and then mountain bike or hike to your heart's content. There are also many rock climbing routes, ranging from 5.7 to 5.12, in the region.

17 Newspaper Rock Recreation Site

Location: About 26 miles northwest of Monticello
Facilities: Some picnic tables; vault toilet across the street
Sites: Dispersed
Fee: None
Elevation: 5,400 feet
Road conditions: Paved, then dirt in the campground
Management: Bureau of Land Management, Monticello Field Office, 435 North Main, P.O. Box 7, Monticello, UT 84535; (435) 587–1500; UT-Monticello@blm.gov
Reservations: None
Activities: Wildlife-watching, rock climbing, picnicking, the chance to see Indian ruins and petroglyphs, and photography. There are also hiking trails in the area.
Season: Year-round
Finding the campground: From Monticello, drive north on paved U.S. Highway 191 for 13.7 miles; at this point, head west on Utah Highway 211, a paved Scenic Byway. Continue another 12.3 miles to the Newspaper Rock Recreation Site. Famous petroglyphs grace the rock wall to the right (northeast), while dispersed sites rest in the trees to the left (southwest).

About the campground: These dispersed sites are small and not recommended for large RVs. Those with small rigs and tents will find a number of places to park along Indian Creek. You'll also find dense shade in the form of cottonwoods, oaks, junipers, box elders, and pinyon pines. Across the street you'll find petroglyphs that may be as old as 1,500 years. Amenities include a few picnic tables and a vault toilet.

Rock climbing is popular from this point to the end of UT 211 just past the Squaw Flat Campground. Climbs range from 5.7 to 5.12.

Visitors can see petroglyphs at Newspaper Rock.

18 Dalton Springs

Location: In the Manti–La Sal National Forest, about 5 miles west of Monticello

Facilities: Fire grates, picnic tables, drinking water, and vault toilets

Sites: 17

Fee: $

Elevation: 8,300 feet

Road conditions: Paved, then dirt in the campground

Management: Monticello Ranger District, 496 East Central, P.O. Box 820, Monticello, UT 84535; (435) 587-2041

Reservations: None

Activities: Wildlife-watching, fishing, picnicking, and photography. There are also hiking trails in the area.

Season: Memorial Day through Labor Day

Finding the campground: From Monticello, drive west on paved Blue Mountain/Harts Loop Draw Road. A sign points the way. Continue 4.9 miles to the campground, which is on the left (south) side of the road.

About the campground: The campsites here are shaded by a number of oak trees and may be open early in the season, when the water is off and the fee is reduced. It's a nice place to sit and watch the wildlife, if you're one of the lucky ones. There are plenty of deer in the area, as well as turkeys and other critters. The campground makes a nice base from which to hike one of the nearby trails or fish in a nearby stream. Check with the forest service for more information.

19 Buckboard

Location: In the Manti–La Sal National Forest, approximately 6.5 miles west of Monticello

Facilities: Fire grates, picnic tables, drinking water, and vault toilets

Sites: 12

Fee: $

Elevation: 8,600 feet

Road conditions: Paved, then dirt in the campground

Management: Monticello Ranger District, 496 East Central, P.O. Box 820, Monticello, UT 84535; (435) 587-2041

Reservations: Reservations for group sites are accepted and recommended. Call (877) 444-6777 or TDD (877) 833-6777; fee

Activities: Wildlife-watching, fishing, picnicking, and photography. There are also hiking trails in the area.

Season: Memorial Day through Labor Day

Finding the campground: From Monticello, drive west on paved Blue Mountain/Harts Loop Draw Road. A sign points the way. Continue 6.4 miles to the campground, which is on the left (south) side of the road.

About the campground: The campsites here are shaded by a number of oak, aspen, spruce, and willow trees. You may be able to camp early or late in the season, when the water is off and the fee is reduced. It's a great place to relax and enjoy the scenery, and a wonderful area to watch wildlife, if you're so lucky. There's an abundance of deer in the area, as well as turkeys and other critters. The campground makes a nice base from which to hike one of the nearby trails or fish in a nearby stream. There's a group site; contact the forest service for fees and more information.

20 Devil's Canyon

Location: In the Manti–La Sal National Forest, about 10 miles northeast of Blanding
Facilities: Fire grates, picnic tables, drinking water, and vault toilets
Sites: 33
Fee: $$
Elevation: 7,400 feet
Road conditions: Paved, except for a 0.2-mile section of gravel
Management: Monticello Ranger District, 496 East Central, P.O. Box 820, Monticello, UT 84535; (435) 587-2041
Reservations: For the group site only, call (877) 444-6777 or TDD (877) 833-6777; fee
Activities: Hiking and picnicking
Season: Memorial Day through Labor Day
Finding the campground: From Blanding, drive northeast on U.S. Highway 191 for about 9 miles. Now make a left (west) onto the paved road where a sign points the way to Devil's Canyon. Continue another 0.6 mile to the campground turnoff, which is on the right (east). Please note that you'll encounter a 0.2-mile stretch of gravel en route.

About the campground: Campsites are set amid a forest of juniper, pinyon pine, and stately ponderosa pine. An interpretive trail that starts near site 33 tells the story of humankind's life in the forest. You'll see some ruins along the 1,400-foot trail, too. A group site is available; call the forest service for fees and additional information. Campground fees are reduced when water is not available.

21 Nizhoni

Location: In the Manti–La Sal National Forest, about 13 miles northwest of Blanding
Facilities: Fire grates, picnic tables, drinking water, and vault toilets
Sites: 23
Fee: $
Elevation: 7,600 feet
Road conditions: Gravel
Management: Monticello Ranger District, 496 East Central, P.O. Box 820, Monticello, UT 84535; (435) 587-2041
Reservations: For the group site only, call (877) 444-6777 or TDD (877) 833-6777; fee

Activities: Hiking, fishing, and picnicking.
Season: Memorial Day through Labor Day
Finding the campground: From the junction of U.S. Highway 191 and 100 East in Blanding, drive northwest on 100 East (also County Road 285) for 12.6 miles. The road is paved except for the last 4.4 miles, which is gravel. You'll pass Dry Wash Reservoir 1.4 miles prior to the campground.

About the campground: Ponderosa pines and oak trees provide a nice setting for this campground, with its close access to Dry Wash Reservoir. There's a dock there, but powerboats are not permitted. If you're interested in the group site, call the forest service for fee information.

22 Hovenweep National Monument

Location: About 45 miles southeast of Blanding
Facilities: Fire grates, picnic tables (some covered), drinking water, and flush toilets
Sites: 31
Fee: $$
Elevation: 5,300 feet
Road conditions: Paved
Management: Hovenweep National Monument, McElmo Route, Cortez, CO 81321; (970) 562–4282; hoveinfo@nps.gov
Reservations: None
Activities: Hiking, mountain biking, photography, wildlife watching, and picnicking
Season: Year-round
Finding the campground: From Blanding, drive south on U.S. Highway 191 for about 14 miles, then turn left (east) onto Utah Highway 262. Continue 8.4 miles to County Road 414; head left and follow the signs to Hovenweep. Along the way you'll travel on County Roads 401, 414, and 413 for another 22.1 miles to the Hovenweep National Monument and Campground. The campground is located about 0.9 mile from the visitor center.

About the campground: Utah junipers decorate this delightful campground, with easy access to an array of ancient ruins. Ancestral Puebloans (formerly called Anasazi) built their homes here about 700 years ago; some of the homes are still standing and available for observation.

Several trails allow access to the ruins. A trail to the Holly Ruins, one of six villages protected by the monument, begins near campsite 10. Gnats can be a nuisance in May and June; bring insect repellent.

23 Sand Island

Location: Along the San Juan River, approximately 4 miles west of Bluff
Facilities: Fire grates, picnic tables, vault toilets, and boat launch
Sites: 23
Fee: $
Elevation: 4,300 feet

Road conditions: Gravel
Management: Bureau of Land Management, Monticello Field Office, 435 North Main, P.O. Box 7, Monticello, UT 84535; (435) 587–1500; UT-Monticello@blm.gov
Reservations: None
Activities: Hiking, fishing, boating, wildlife watching, petroglyphs, and picnicking
Season: Year-round
Finding the campground: From the junction of U.S. Highways 191 and 163 in Bluff, drive west then south on U.S. 191 for 4 miles. Turn left (east) and continue 0.3 mile to the campground.

About the campground: Stately cottonwoods provide some shade at this campground set along the San Juan River. The campground, which is a popular place for rafters and kayakers to put in, is set up in two sections, Area A and Area B. Area A is a place for vans or tents; RVs are not allowed, because the maximum length is 22 feet. Big rigs will find plenty of space at Area B, where length isn't a problem.

Near Area B be sure to look for the famous Petroglyph Panel. Though Sand Island is a fine place for fishing and boating, it's probably most noted for its numerous Kokopelli figures. Kokopelli was the humpbacked flute player of ancient mythology.

24 Goosenecks State Reserve

Location: About 7 miles northwest of Mexican Hat
Facilities: Picnic tables and vault toilet
Sites: 4
Fee: None
Elevation: 4,971 feet
Road conditions: Paved to the dirt parking area
Management: Goosenecks State Park, P.O. Box 788, Blanding, UT 84511-0788; (435) 678–2238
Reservations: None
Activities: Photography and picnicking
Season: Year-round
Finding the campground: From Mexican Hat, drive north on U.S. Highway 163 for 3.1 miles, then make a left (west) onto Utah Highway 261 for 0.9 mile; now continue left (west) on Utah Highway 316. A sign points the way to the paved road that ends at the reserve after another 3.4 miles.

About the campground: Primitive sites and a vault toilet are all that you'll find atop this lofty mesa, where the wind often blows and tent camping is not recommended. If you do camp here, you'll have a wonderful view into a 1,000-foot-deep chasm shaped through the Pennsylvanian Hermosa Formation compliments of the silt-laden San Juan River. The river zigs and zags, meandering more than 5 miles while advancing only 1 linear mile toward the Colorado River and Lake Powell.

25 Natural Bridges National Monument

Location: 0.3 mile west of the visitor center
Facilities: Fire grates, picnic tables, and vault toilets. There's drinking water and a telephone at the visitor center.
Sites: 13
Fee: $$
Elevation: 6,500 feet
Road conditions: Paved
Management: Natural Bridges National Monument, Box 1, Lake Powell, UT 84533-0001; (435) 692–1234; nabrinfo@nps.gov
Reservations: None
Activities: Hiking, picnicking, and photography
Season: Year-round
Finding the campground: From Blanding, drive about 2 miles south on U.S. Highway 191, then turn west onto Utah Highway 95 for 29.9 miles. Upon reaching the junction with Utah Highway 275, turn right (north) where a sign points the way to the national monument. Continue 4.5 miles to the visitor center.

About the campground: If there's one thing that needs to be stressed here, it's that there is a strict adherence to the park's 26-foot vehicle limit. There just isn't space for longer units. And note that this limit means a total of 26 feet—not 26 feet for a travel trailer or fifth-wheel trailer plus the tow vehicle, but a total of 26 feet. Still, if you're longer than 26 feet, don't fret. There's a BLM-managed overflow area 6.2 miles from the visitor center. To reach this area, head south on Utah Highway 261 for about a mile, then drive east 0.5 mile.

There's plenty to do from the pinyon- and juniper-blessed park campground. Bridge View Drive, paved and 9 miles long, leads to overlooks and trailheads for the park's three famous natural bridges—Sipapu, Kachina, and Owachomo. Trailers and towed vehicles should be left in the visitor center parking lot. There's also a wonderful loop trail that's nearly 9 miles long and passes under the three bridges. If you enjoy ancient ruins, you'll want to look for them here.

26 Hite: Glen Canyon National Recreation Area

Location: In the Glen Canyon National Recreation Area, about 49 miles southeast of Hanksville
Facilities: None in the campground, but a central building a few hundred yards away offers a public telephone, drinking water, sewage disposal station, fish cleaning station, boat ramp, and flush toilets.
Sites: Dispersed
Fee: $
Elevation: 3,900 feet
Road conditions: Paved

Management: Glen Canyon National Recreation Area, P.O. Box 1507, Page, AZ 86040-1507; (520) 608–6404; GLCA_CHVC@nps.gov
Reservations: None
Activities: Fishing, boating, water sports, swimming, picnicking, and photography
Season: Year-round
Finding the campground: From Hanksville, drive south then southeast on Utah Highway 95 for 49.1 miles, then turn right (west) at the sign for Hite Marina. Continue a couple of miles to the primitive site.

About the campground: There's a nice view of Lake Powell from this location, which is best suited for those with their own toilets—the nearest rest rooms can be a hike from some of the campsites. If you need a boat ramp or boat rental, you'll find it at the marina. Visitors can enjoy a variety of activities, including water sports, boating, fishing, and photography.

27 Farley Canyon: Glen Canyon National Recreation Area

Location: About 56 miles southeast of Hanksville
Facilities: Chemical and vault toilets
Sites: Dispersed
Fee: $
Elevation: 3,900 feet
Road conditions: Maintained dirt
Management: Glen Canyon National Recreation Area, P.O. Box 1507, Page, AZ 86040-1507; (520) 608–6404; GLCA_CHVC@nps.gov
Reservations: None
Activities: Fishing, boating, water sports, swimming, picnicking, and photography
Season: Year-round
Finding the campground: From Hanksville, drive south then southeast on Utah Highway 95 for 53.5 miles, then turn right (west) at the sign for Farley Canyon. Continue 2.2 miles down a maintained dirt road to the primitive site.

About the campground: The vegetation may be sparse, but the views from this primitive site are abundant. Lake Powell visitors can enjoy water sports, boating, fishing, photography, and a whole lot more.

28 Halls Crossing: Glen Canyon National Recreation Area

Location: A few miles west of the east entrance fee station
Facilities: Fire grates, picnic tables, flush toilets, sewage disposal station, soda pop machine, and drinking water; there's also a boat ramp nearby.
Sites: 65
Fee: $$$
Elevation: 3,900 feet
Road conditions: Paved

Management: Glen Canyon National Recreation Area, P.O. Box 1507, Page, AZ 86040-1507; (520) 608–6404; GLCA_CHVC@nps.gov
Reservations: None
Activities: Fishing, boating, water sports, swimming, picnicking, and photography
Season: Year-round
Finding the campground: From the east entrance fee station, east of Halls Crossing and about 95 miles southwest of Blanding, travel west a few miles to the campground, which is off Utah Highway 276 on the left (south).

About the campground: An assortment of deciduous trees provides some shade in the campground, which overlooks lovely Lake Powell. The campground is near a small store, where you'll also find hot showers and a self-service laundry. Just down the hill, at the marina, you'll find a boat ramp and boat rentals. There's also a ferry: The *John Atlantic Burr* travels between Halls Crossing and Bullfrog and saves 145 road miles. Lake Powell visitors have plenty to do—water sports, boating, fishing, and photography are perhaps the most popular activities.

29 Halls Crossing RV: Glen Canyon National Recreation Area

Location: A few miles west of the east entrance fee station
Facilities: Fire grates, picnic tables, water, electric, and sewer hookups, flush toilets, showers, sewage disposal station, drinking water, public telephone, store, and self-service laundry; there's a nearby boat ramp.
Sites: 32
Fee: $$$$
Elevation: 3,900 feet
Road conditions: Paved
Management: Glen Canyon National Recreation Area, P.O. Box 1507, Page, AZ 86040-1507; (520)–608–6404; GLCA_CHVC@nps.gov
Reservations: None
Activities: Fishing, boating, water sports, swimming picnicking, and photography
Season: Year-round
Finding the campground: From the east entrance fee station, east of Halls Crossing and about 95 miles southwest of Blanding, travel west a few miles to the campground, which is just off Utah Highway 276 on the right (north).

About campground: A few trees provide some shade in this full-amenity campground. If you need a boat ramp or boat rental, just head down the hill to the lake and marina. There's also a ferry: The *John Atlantic Burr* travels between Halls Crossing and Bullfrog and saves 145 road miles. Lake Powell visitors have plenty to do—water sports, boating, fishing, and photography are perhaps the most popular activities.

Appendix

Hunting and Fishing Information

Division of Wildlife Resources
1596 West North Temple
Salt Lake City, UT 84116
(801) 538–4700
Division of Wildlife Resources Fishing Hot Line: (800) ASK–FISH.
www.nr.state.ut.us/dwr/dwr.htm
nrdwr.sfowlks@state.ut.us

Recreation

Bicycle Utah (a statewide organization promoting on- and off-road cycling)
P.O. Box 738
Park City, UT 84060
(435) 649–5806
info@bicycleutah.com
www.bicycleutah.com

Raft Utah/Utah Guides and Outfitters
452 North Main
Moab, UT 84532
(435) 259–8946
www.raft.utah.com
www.utahguidesandoutfitters.com

Ski Utah (ski industry trade association)
150 West 500 South
Salt Lake City, UT 84101
(801) 534–1779
Snow report: (801) 521-8102
www.skiutah.com

Roads, Weather, and Public Safety

Department of Transportation (UDOT)
4501 South 2700 West
Salt Lake City, UT 84119
(801) 965–4000
www.dot.state.ut.us
Road report: (801) 964–6000 (Salt Lake area)
Road Report: (800) 492–2400 (toll-free within Utah)

I-15 road information: (888) INFO-I-15 (888) 463-6415
I-15 Web site: www.il5.state.ut.us
Other state highway construction: (800) 492-2400

Emergency: 911

National Weather Service (8:00 A.M.-4:00 P.M. live; after hours, recorded information):
(801) 524-5133

Public Safety (Utah Highway Patrol)
4501 South 2700 West
Salt Lake City, UT 84119
(801) 965-4461 (administration)
(801) 965-4505

Travel Information

Utah Travel Council
P.O. Box 147420
Council Hall/Capitol Hill
Salt Lake City, UT 84114
(801) 538-1030 or (800) 882-4386
Fax (801) 538-1399
www.utah.com
travel@utah.com

Web Sites

Bureau of Land Management
www.blm.gov

National Park Service
www.nps.gov

National Weather Service
www.nws.noaa.gov

Recreation Site (where federal agencies pool their information)
www.recreation.gov

U.S. Fish and Wildlife Service
www.fws.gov

U.S. Forest Service
www.fs.fed.us

U.S. Forest Service Campground Reservations
reserveusa.com

Utah State Parks and Recreation
www.nr.state.ut.us/parks/utahstpk.htm

Reading Material

Bromka, Gregg. *Mountain Biking Utah* (Guilford, Conn: Falcon/Globe Pequot Press, 1999).

Green, Stewart. *Rock Climbing Utah* (Guilford, Conn: Falcon/Globe Pequot Press, 1998).

Hall, David. *Hiking Utah* (Guilford, Conn: Falcon/Globe Pequot Press, 1991).

Harmon, Will. *Wild Country Companion,* (Guilford, Conn: Falcon/Globe Pequot Press, 1994).

Mike Vining and Donna Ikenberry at Bryce Canyon National Park.

About the Author

Donna Ikenberry is a full-time freelance writer, photographer, and book author who lives in South Fork, Colorado. A year-round traveler from 1983 to 1999, Donna married Mike Vining on January 6, 1999, and the two of them settled in Colorado later that year.

Donna and Mike travel about six months of the year, engaging in a variety of activities for Donna to write about and illustrate. Besides photography, favorite activities include rock climbing, mountaineering, hiking, skiing, and biking.

Donna is the author of twelve books, with all of them except for *Camping Utah* related to hiking and biking. Titles include *Hiking Oregon, Hiking Colorado's Weminuche Wilderness, Bicycling the Atlantic Coast,* and *Bicycling Coast to Coast.* She has also had more than 500 magazine and newspaper articles published as well as nearly 3,000 photographs.